In Appreciation

This ambitious project required the generous support of many people to make it a reality. We are grateful to all those who enabled us to do so. We especially recognize and pay tribute to **Morry and Judy Weiss**, who launched this project with love, awe and conviction. Their mission to hold dear the memory of the victims of the Holocaust, to create an everlasting memorial, so that future generations will reflect with pride upon their ancestors, inspired them as they inspired us. They follow in the noble tradition of the Patriarch of their family, **Mr. Irving Stone**, who together with his wife, **Helen**, have become legends in the field of Torah education and philanthropy. No project is too great, no endeavor too small, if it will promote and enhance the study of Torah and if it will effect a stronger and more vibrant *Am Yisrael*, they are at the forefront. Lovingly called "*Mr. Hebrew Academy*," Irving Stone has always been there from the very beginning, as a caring and loving father nurturing his child to maturity, sharing in the joy of its success.

We are deeply indebted to **Mr. Leonard Stern** and the **Stern Family Foundation** for graciously investing our vision, to develop and publish this curriculum. Mr. Stern came forward during the project's inception providing support and encouragement. His confidence in our work has meant a great deal to us. In addition, we are especially grateful to **Richard & Amelia Bernstein; Max Fisher; George Klein; and Sam & Arie Halpern** for sponsoring The Living Memorial's educational programs. Their friendship and support has been vital to our success.

With the publication of our third volume on Hungary/Romania we gratefully acknowledge these benefactors: **Dr. Joseph** and **Fay Geliebter**, previous sponsors of the Poland volume, are totally committed to preserving the memory of all *Kedoshim*. **Andrew Farkas** has focused his philanthropy efforts on the all important area of Holocaust education. **Sidney** and **Phyllis Reisman**, sponsors of this volume have demonstrated unparalleled and genuine commitment to the furtherance of Jewish education and specifically to commemorating the memory of the 6 million *Kedoshim*. They demonstrate abiding friendship and support with no expectation of reward or recognition. **Mr. Hershel Ostreicher and his wife Helly** also sponsored this book. Holocaust survivors, they triumphed over great adversity and transformed the challenges they encountered into a springboard for opportunity to rebuild Torah in America.

To all those who have given assistance and offered counsel; to the thousands of students, teachers and principals throughout the country who have implemented our programs; to the parents and grandparents who encouraged us, we say — Thank You. May the Almighty guide and inspire us that this volume be the forerunner of a curriculum that will illuminate and pay tribute to an era that was lost but never forgotten.

Unit I: The World That Was
Section IIIa:
Hungary/Romania

A Study of the Life and Torah Consciousness of Jews
in the cities and villages of Transylvania,
The Carpathian Mountains and Budapest

by Rabbi Yitzchak Kasnett

THE LIVING MEMORIAL

A Curriculum developed by the Hebrew Academy of Cleveland

The Living Memorial
Unit I: The World That Was
Section IIIa: Hungary/Romania
First Printing...June 1999

ISBN: 0-9635120-9-9

Published by:
The Living Memorial
c/o Hebrew Academy of Cleveland
1860 South Taylor Road
Cleveland Heights, Ohio 44118
216-321-5838 ext. 165
Fax: 216-321-0588

Distributed by:
Mesorah Publications, Ltd.
4401 Second Avenue
Brooklyn, New York 11232
718-921-9000
800-MESORAH
Fax: 718-680-1875

Designed and produced by:
Kenneth Fixler/KF Graphics
Cleveland, Ohio
216.421.8520

Printed in the United States of America

The cover picture of Reb Menachem Ostreicher *z"l*, is dedicated in his memory by his son, Mr. Hershel Ostreicher

Photo Credits:
We would like to thank Mr. Hershel Fischer and Mr. Erno Friedman for their gracious donation of personal photographs for use in this book. Their efforts on our behalf are deeply appreciated, and we thank them for enriching this volume. Additionally, we would like to acknowledge and thank the following publishers for graciously allowing us to use their material in this volume: William Morrow and Co., New York; The Beth Hatefutsoth - The Nahum Goldmann Museum of the Jewish Diaspora: The Museum of the Federation of Jewish Communities in Romania, Tel Aviv, Israel; Farrar, Straus and Giroux Publishing Co., New York City; Macmillian Publishing Co., New York City; Simon and Schuster Publishing Co., New York City; and Weidenfeld and Nicolson Publishing Co., New York City; Barry A. Cik, Cleveland, Ohio.

The publisher has made every effort to determine and locate the owners of the additional photos used in this publication. Please notify The Living Memorial in case of accidental omission.

This volume is dedicated by

Sidney and Phyllis Reisman

in loving memory of his parents

Avrohom and Rochel Reisman ז"ל

*who arrived in American imbued with the spirit and consciousness of the Jewish heritage of their motherland *- Hungary. With love and pride they raised their children in the traditional manner of their own upbringing. They imparted their rich culture, commitment to Torah and love for one's fellowman - the cornerstones which characterized the homes of their youth.*
and in tribute to their sons and daughters,
six of whom served with distinction in the United States military during World War II.

Joseph Reisman ז"ל	*U.S. Air Force*
Max Reisman ז"ל	*U.S. Air Force*
Daniel Reisman ז"ל	*U.S. Army*
Israel Morris Reisman	*U.S. Air Force*
Milton Reisman ז"ל	*U.S. Army*
Esther Reisman Davis	*U.S. Navy*
Miriam Reisman Sheinberg	
Pearl Reisman Skolnick	

The faith and conviction that was fostered in their parents' home sustained them through the crises of battle. They returned to these shores exemplifying the Jewish ideal. Their own children and grandchildren continue to support Torah life and culture in the proud tradition of their parents and grandparents.

With deep appreciation and love,

Sidney and Phyllis Reisman
Pepper Pike, OH
Jupiter, FL

**Avrohom Reisman - born Puspokladany*
Rochel Sonnenfeld Reisman - born Boldogkovaralja

In Honor of Our Parents

Asher Moshe and Malka (nee Sprei) Grosz,

ר׳ אשר משה ומלכה גרוס, עמו״ש

Survivors of the Holocaust who kept their faith,
and instilled in their children the true love
of בטחון בהקב״ה *and* תורה מצוות

May they be זוכה עד מאה ועשרים שנה *to continue to see*
Yiddishe נחת *from their children, grandchildren*
and great-grandchildren who are עוסקים בתורה.

With deep appreciation and love,

Abe and Gita Wagschal

Dedicated In Loving Memory of

Our Family and Friends
who perished in my native Hungary
על קידוש השם

הנאהבים והנעימים בחייהם ובמותם לא נפרדו

יהי זכרם ברוך

Mrs. Rose Estreicher

Mr. and Mrs. Leo Feigenbaum and Family, *Chicago Illinois*

Mr. and Mrs. Zvi Feigenbaum and Family

In Memory of

Harry and Gizi Weiss

צבי בן יואל ע"ה

גיטל בת ישראל ע"ה

Their faith in the Almighty sustained them
through the fires of the Holocaust.
They came to America and rebuilt a life
committed to their heritage.
They valued a Jewish education
and this legacy lives on.
Their devotion to each other and to their family
will always serve as an inspiration
to their children and grandchildren,
in whose hearts their memory will live on forever.

from their loving children

Morry and Judy Weiss
Erwin and Myra Weiss

FOREWORD

זכור את אשר עשה עמלק

"Remember what Amalek did to you!"

(Devarim 25:17)

t happened on Simchas Torah, in the Auschwitz concentration camp. Fifty *bochurim*, were taken to the crematorium to be executed. As they entered the crematorium the Nazi guard told them the usual ruse, "Take off your clothes, so that you may shower and cleanse yourselves." One young man, knowing full well what awaited them in the "showers," overcame fear and apathy and, in a voice full of determination and resolve, proclaimed to his friends: "My friends, tonight is Simchas Torah! True, we have no Torah in our possession, but the *Ribbono Shel Olam* is with us, here and now. Let us dance with Him before we perish!" Immediately, they gathered in a circle and began to sing and dance with a fervor and ecstasy never before experienced. They sang **אשרנו מה טוב חלקנו ומה נעים גורלנו**, "We are fortunate - how good is our portion, how pleasant is our lot." They concluded with **וטהר לבנו לעבדך באמת**, "Purify our hearts to serve You in truth." The sounds of their singing reverberated within the walls of the crematorium and throughout the camp as they reached a frenzy of devotion in expressing their apparent joy in being Jewish!

The sounds of their singing reverberated within the walls of the crematorium and throughout the camp expressing their apparent joy in being Jewish!

The Nazis, seeing their display of unparalleled martyrdom, ran into the room in an attempt to put an end to this "foolishness" and also to question their motivation. "What are you so happy about?" questioned the commandant angrily. The young men responded, "We are doomed to die momentarily. This specifically is our source of joy, for we will be able to leave a world where such vile miscreants as you make decisions regarding the lives of others. To be relieved of such accursed degenerates as you is enough of a reason to sing and dance. But, we have another more profound reason for singing. Soon we will meet our parents and other members of our family who you mercilessly slaughtered in the most heinous ways. Yes, we have reason to be joyous!"

The sadistic beast, the Nazi commandant, screamed back in fury, "No, I will not permit you to die quickly. I will cast you all into solitary confinement where I will subject you to the most agonizing tortures. I will slice pieces from your bodies until the souls that you care about so much will leave you very slowly and painfully."

The young men ignored him and returned to their singing and dancing until he broke up the circle and carried them off to a solitary block. The very next day a transport taking Jews to labor camps in Germany was leaving. It so happened that miraculously the majority of these fifty men were selected to be on that transport. The remainder of them were integrated into other work forces in Auschwitz so that no one recognized them. In the end, all fifty young men were miraculously saved.

This moving and powerful story was related to me by my *rebbe*, Horav Tzvi Hirsch Meisels, *zt"l*. The *zchus* of joyful expression, the merit of *mesiras nefesh* with ecstasy, the ability to transcend physical pain and deprivation out of love for Hashem, stood by these young men on that fateful day. To paraphrase one of the survivors of Auschwitz, "They can take my body, but not my soul!"

The Holocaust, indeed, exposed the best and worst qualities of which man is capable. The unspeakable atrocities of the Nazis have been well documented. however, the indomitable Jewish spirit and heroic acts of *mesiras nefesh* (self-sacrifice), performed without fanfare, need to be recorded as well. It is incumbent upon us to teach our children and bequeath our future generations with this legacy.

The zchus of joyful expression, the merit of mesiras nefesh... out of love for Hashem, stood by these young men on that fateful day.

The countless acts of *mesiras nefesh* demonstrated during the Holocaust years are unparalleled. These manifestations of selflessness are far more noble and courageous than any physical demonstration of power and strength.

Each of our interviewees have exemplified this quality of being *moser nefesh* for their families and other Jews at critical times in their lives. They are indeed shining lights in one of the darkest periods of our history and certainly in the history of mankind. We extend our heartfelt gratitude to them for baring their souls and transcending their personal pain to share their experiences with us. More than most, they realize the critical importance of revealing what happened to them so we and our children will learn and be inspired. May Hashem bless them with good health and *nachas* from their families.

It is our hope that by studying the life and times of the past generation, our children/students, many of whom unfortunately did not have the opportunity to meet and develop a relationship with grandparents, will realize their spiritual roots. This realization will instill a sense of pride, heighten awareness and inspire them to continue to build upon the foundation which was tempered by their ancestors. Come join with us as we delve into this "world that was" so that we may learn to appreciate our heritage.

Several diverse approaches to a Torah way of life were reflected in the Hungarian and Romanian *shtetlachs* and cities of pre-World War II Europe. Nevertheless, there was a sense of *Achdus*, unity, that permeated each Jewish community. There was commitment to a life of Torah Judaism and learning, as well as profound faith and courage demonstrated in the face of adversity. The pure hearts and warm spirits that characterized the *Chassidic* segment of this region was a source of inspiration that continues to serve as a noble example for us to emulate. Unfortunately, vicious anti-Semitism was rampant and the Jews were always the scapegoats and suffered terribly. Despite this, the light of Torah continued to burn brightly in Hungary and Romania. Presented herein is a Torah oriented appreciation of The World That Was: Hungary/Romania.

The countless acts of mesiras nefesh demonstrated during the Holocaust years are unparalleled.

Acknowledgments

We are truly gratified by the wonderful response we have received for our previous volumes on Lithuania and Poland. With the publication of volume III in our series, we are inspired anew and deeply moved by the *mesiras nefesh*, special spirit and benevolence demonstrated by our interviewees. To be involved in the production of a curriculum of such depth and meaning brings a sense of satisfaction that can only find fulfillment in our expressions of appreciation to *Hashem Yisborach* for the opportunity He has given us. It is our most heartfelt prayer that these volumes serve as a tribute to the spiritual greatness of the Orthodox Jews of Eastern Europe, while inspiring our children and ourselves to strive to replicate such levels of spiritual purity.

It is our most heartfelt prayer that these volumes serve as a tribute to the spiritual greatness of the Orthodox Jews of Eastern Europe, while inspiring our children and ourselves to strive to replicate such levels of spiritual purity.

The success of this project can be attributed to many reasons. First, we are grateful to **Morry Weiss** whose brainchild it was to provide a Holocaust-oriented curriculum for the Yeshiva Day School student so that the "world that was"– the world into which he was born – would never be forgotten. He gave up much of his personal time and attention, despite his heavy schedule. He has been both parent and friend to this project throughout its tenure.

Harry M. Brown, president of the Living Memorial has been a pillar of strength and encouragement. His belief in the project's success, and his sense of obligation to the Holocaust victims spurred us on, while it helped us overcome the challenges in our path.

Rabbi Yitzchak Kasnett began as the curriculum writer and became so intensely involved in every aspect of this project that he has become a driving force in its success. His ability to relate to the interviewees and put them at ease as they recall the most glorious, yet tragic, periods of their lives is remarkable. He will have eternal merit for his exceptional interpretation of the world that was.

Rabbi Nochum Zev Dessler, *Shlita*, Dean, Hebrew Academy of Cleveland, was our spiritual mentor. A scion of the Lithuanian *Mussar* dynasty, he "lives" the "world that was".

Arlene Jaffe, our Director of Development, has toiled throughout the entire project, keeping us on schedule, seeing to it that we never lost sight of where we were going and never gave up hope.

Kenny Fixler of KF Graphics, himself the child of Holocaust survivors, was personally inspired by the experiences and feelings of that era. His creative talents are evident on each page. The compelling logo of the Living Memorial was magnificently designed by him and is a true manifestation of our mission.

The dedication, hard work and talent of many people are all factors in the success of this project. Indeed, we are grateful to each of them for their unique contribution.

Yitzchak Saftlas for his beautiful and creative graphic design and layout of volumes I and II and for his assistance in the present volume.

Ethel Gottlieb is the editor par-excellence and a part of herself has gone into this project. She has given life to the words as she helped produce a book that will be accepted by laymen and students throughout the panorama of Judaism.

The Hebrew Academy of Cleveland spearheaded this project and has set the standard of Torah-oriented curricula. We are grateful to **Rabbi Sholom Strajcher**, its Educational Director, during whose tenure this project saw fruition. His expertise in Jewish education has been of great assistance to us. **Ivan Soclof**, President of the Hebrew Academy, has been a guiding force in the realization of this curriculum. His propensity for detail maintained our perspective in achieving our goal. He has always been a firm believer that the Hebrew Academy's mandate extends beyond Cleveland. It is because of his vision, and that of his predecessors, that the Hebrew Academy has become a world-class Torah institution.

We are honored that **Dr. Leatrice B. Rabinsky**, noted Holocaust historian and author, who has devoted her life to teaching the Holocaust to thousands of students, has joined us to co-author part of the curriculum.

We pray to Hashem that our work will truly serve as a "Living Memorial" to the victims of the Holocaust.

We gratefully acknowledge and appreciate the contribution and support of **The Conference on Jewish Material Claims Against Germany**.

We would like to express our sincere appreciation to **Rabbis Meir Zlotowitz** and **Nosson Scherman** of Mesorah Publications for their efforts on our behalf in disseminating these volumes to Jewish communities throughout the world.

Last but not least, we are grateful to Torah Umesorah, the National Society for Hebrew Day Schools, and its Director, **Rabbi Joshua Fishman**, for their advice, support and encouragement throughout this endeavor.

We pray to Hashem that our work will truly serve as a "*Living Memorial*" to the victims of the Holocaust.

Rabbi A. Leib Scheinbaum
National Director, The Living Memorial
Iyar 5759 / May 1999

AUTHOR'S PREFACE

With this, the third volume of THE WORLD THAT WAS, I want – indeed need – to express my gratitude and sense of complete indebtedness to *Hashem Yisborach* for my involvement in this project. After the publication of the first two volumes (Lithuania and Poland) it was impossible to imagine that I could be further moved and affected by the spiritual greatness and countenance of humility that defines our interviewees. The number three, however, defines the dimensions through which we experience our world. With the completion of this third volume, I find that I have been blessed even more to experience– with heightened awareness – the multi-dimensional grandeur of *the world that was* through the greatness of spirit, self-sacrifice and compassion demonstrated by our interviewees under the worst and most trying of circumstances in the history of *Klal Yisrael* since the חורבן בית המקדש.

To share even the smallest portion of their world is to realize the endless dimensions inherent within the Jewish soul.

How utterly tragic it is to live less than a full and meaningful life. Yet, how much of each day do we squander in pursuit of the petty attractions of our very materialistic world? To share even the smallest portion of *their* world is to realize the endless dimensions inherent within the Jewish soul. To such an extent is this true, that life is experienced and appreciated differently – in kind, and not just by degree. It is impossible to truly understand our unique stature as the *Am HaNivchar*, the Chosen Nation, until one of these special *neshamos* holds you, eye-to-eye, captured in his or her evanescent expression of quietude– disarming and eloquent – that reflects with complete faith and love their acceptance, their partnership, in Hashem's awesome judgment.

I thank each and every one of them for bestowing upon me, my family and the reader their personal chapter in the eternity of *Klal Yisrael*; a chronicle that is transcribed by each generation from Avraham *Avinu* until the arrival of the גואל הצדק במהרה ובימינו אמן.

The student should actively project him or herself into their mind's eye view of life as it once was... you will be rewarded with the ability to transcend the decades of time.

It is essential for the student to approach the reading of these interviews from the unique perspective of life presented by each of our interviewees. Therefore, the student should actively project him or herself into their thoughts and emotions, their mind's eye view of life as it once was. For this you will be rewarded with the ability to transcend the decades of time and the barriers of social change that have ensued to capture and experience, at least in some small measure, their clear, unobstructed view of a Jew's purpose in life, a life of striving for spiritual purity and closeness to Torah.

This project is sponsored by The Living Memorial and the Hebrew Academy of Cleveland. In truth, this project is a "living memorial," for it will be the rare individual who will read these pages, share these lives, and not be changed by doing so—reflecting upon the values and beliefs lived and expressed by our interviewees.

The interviews presented in this volume expose us to the harshest realities of *Galus* (Exile). Rabbi Yaakov Emden, in the introduction to his *siddur*, writes that even greater than the miracles Hashem performed for *Klal Yisrael* in *Mitzrayim* is the fact that *Klal Yisrael* has survived over 2,000 years in this present *Galus*–since the time of the destruction of the second *Beis Hamikdash*. It does not take much imagination to realize the truth of his words after the events of fifty years ago. As Rabbi Avigdor Miller, שליט"א, stated in his interview in *The World That Was: Lithuania:* "...that just as Hashem will never change, the Jewish nation will remain a holy people forever. There may be ups and downs, but the Jewish nation will reassert itself at some point. There is no question, *Am Yisrael*, the Jewish people, are a holy nation. That is the Jewish spirit...*Am Yisrael* is an Eternal nation, that is why we are called *Am Olam*, a nation that is forever. Therefore, we have to know that just as Hashem is eternal, we also are eternal because He took us to Him as it says, "*Shema Yisrael, Hashem Elokainu...*" The awareness that we belong to the Eternal Nation is enough to support the confidence and idealism of the Jewish people...the awareness that we are forever."

Our interviewees are the manifestation of these visions. They represent the eternity of *Klal Yisrael*, that Hashem will never forsake us in this final *Galus*–not completely and not ever.

Our interviewees represent the eternity of Klal Yisrael, that Hashem will never forsake us in this final Galus–not completely and not ever.

There are many people who make a project of this magnitude come to fruition. I list them here and thank all of them for their involvement and support:

Rabbi N. Z. Dessler, *Dean and Founder, The Hebrew Academy of Cleveland*
Morry Weiss, *Chairman and Founder of The Living Memorial*
Harry M. Brown, *President of The Living Memorial*
Rabbi A. Leib Scheinbaum, *National Director of The Living Memorial*
Arlene Jaffe, *Director of Development for The Living Memorial*
Ethel Gottlieb, *Editor, Project Coordinator*
Kenny Fixler and Rick Shaffer, *graphic design & layout / KF Graphics*
Rabbi Moshe Kolodny, *Archivist / Agudath Israel of America*

In particular, I would like to express my special thanks and הכרת הטוב to Leibel Scheinbaum, Ethel Gottlieb and Kenny Fixler the day-to-day "team" involved in publishing *The World that Was*. *The World that Was* is a very special publication, and I would like to express that the "team" behind it is comprised of very special individuals as well. Finally, I would like to thank my wife, Shulamis, and my family, for their support, interest and counsel during my involvement in *The World That Was*.

Together we have tried, with G-d's blessing, to produce a curriculum that does, in more than small measure, capture the essence of a time in our history that was literally wiped off the face of the earth. Our interviewees are our bridges to a past that is slowly coming to its end. We thank them for bequeathing to us their living memorial in their lifetimes, and in the merit of their great deeds may they be granted long life, and serve as bridges to the future redemption as well.

Rabbi Yitzchak Kasnett
Shevat 5959 / January 1999

TABLE OF CONTENTS

The National Society for Hebrew Day Schools

COMMITTING GENERATIONS TO TORAH

June 17, 1999

Rabbi N. W. Dessler
Dean
Hebrew Academy of Cleveland
1860 South Taylor Road
Cleveland Heights, Ohio 44118

Dear Rabbi Dessler,

Klal Yisroel will be ever grateful to you and your staff for developing "The World That Was" a study of the Torah consciousness of Eastern European Jewry before World War II.

While the series is designated as a curriculum for Yeshiva students, it will surely become a classic and will find its place on the bookshelves and in the hearts and minds of the families of more than 200,000 students in yeshiva Day Schools in the entire English speaking world.

This new volume of y*ahadus* Hungary/ Romania is particularly inspiring. Munkacz, Satmar, Sighet and Budapest will be imprinted even more deeply in the hearts of those who, until the coming of Moshiach will live their lives in accordance with those magnificent and sacred traditions.

Yasher Koach to you and your staff.

Sincerely,

Joshua Fishman

Rabbi Joshua Fishman
Executive Vice President

160 BROADWAY, 4th Fl.
NEW YORK, NY 10038
TEL: (212) 227-1000
FAX: (212) 406-6934
E-mail: umesorah@aol.com

Committee Members

Morry Weiss, *Chairman*
Harry M. Brown, *President*

Rabbi Eli Dessler
Joseph Geliebter, Ph.D.
Rabbi Yitzchak Kasnett, M.S.
Rabbi A. Leib Scheinbaum
Ivan Soclof
Rabbi Sholom Strajcher
Arlene Jaffe, MSSA, LISW.
Leatrice B. Rabinsky, Ph.D.

TEACHER'S GUIDE INTRODUCTORY STUDENT EXERCISES

...for enhancing the study of the history of Orthodox Jewish life in Pre-World War II Hungary/Romania

LESSON 1:

- ❏ Teacher directed lesson
- ❏ Consider concepts of size and importance from a spiritual perspective

Materials

- ❏ 2 copies of Work Sheet #1 per student

A. Exercise One

1. Draw a circle approximately 1/8th of an inch in diameter in the middle of the box on Work Sheet # 1 Consider the relative size and importance of the circle in relation to the rest of the area of the paper. Does the circle assume a position of dominance on the paper?
2. Repeat this exercise using the second copy of Work Sheet #1, only draw the circle in the lower left hand corner of the box.
3. Place the two Work Sheets next to each other and compare the two papers. On which Work Sheet does the circle assume the greatest importance? Why? Most students will respond that it is the *position* and not the *size* of the circle on the first Work Sheet that makes it important, because if it were a bigger circle it would be prominent even in the corner of the Work Sheet.

B. Exercise Two

1. As Jews, what principle do we often find in life that is expressed through this exercise? You may discuss this question together with your classmates. After you have composed your answer, write it on a sheet of paper. (Henceforth, we will refer to this principle as the *Shtetle Principle* since we have derived it from our study of everyday Jewish life in Hungary and Romania).
2. Have several students read their statements of principle to the class. Then write a statement that expresses the majority sentiment of the class. Each individual may still retain his/her unedited statement of principle.

Student Exercises

Sample answers:

1. Often it is not the size or strength of something that bestows upon it its sense of importance, it is the position it holds in the life of a person or in the history of a nation. Not always are our largest or most expensive possessions the ones most important to us.
2. Importance is not judged by external characteristics such as size, beauty, strength or wealth, etc., but by the vital role that the object (person, place or thing) plays in the quality of life and well-being of the person or people it affects.

C. Homework Assignment:

1. Geography, demographics and map skills of present day Hungary and Romania:
   a. In square miles, how large is each country?
   b. To which of the states in the U.S. can each country be compared to in size?
   c. What is the capital city of Hungary? Romania?
   d. Which are the three largest cities in each of these countries?
   e. List the major geographical features of each country.
   f. If it is 12:00 noon in your city, what time is it in the capital city of Hungary? Romania?
   g. How many miles is it from your location to Munkacs? Klausenberg?
   h. Which countries and geographical features surround each country?
   i. What is the population of each country today and before WWII?
   j. How many Jews lived in Hungary before WWII? In Romania? How many live in each country today?
   k. What percent of the population did the Jews comprise in each country before WWII?
   l. What currency is used in each country?
2. What are the Hungarian, Romanian and Yiddish words for the following:
   a. mountain
   b. village
   c. river
   d. farm
   e. well
   f. vegetables
   g. shoes
   h. country
   i. town
   j. street
3. Research Assignment
   Using the map on page 10, how do the pre-World War II boundaries of Czechoslovakia, Hungary, Poland, Germany, Romania and Russia differ from their boundaries today?

D. Homework Assignments:

1. Review answers to questions from the beginning exercises.
2. Carefully review the maps so that you will have a greater understanding of the shifting political boundaries when they are mentioned in the interviews.
3. Each student should choose one of the towns or cities mentioned and write a short history of Jewish life in that place, or interview someone who lived there (or in that area).
4. If possible, gather together pictures of Jewish life in Eastern Europe before WWII to be placed in an Album of Remembrance. Short histories of the towns and villages should be written to accompany the pictures. When possible, use pictures from families, relatives or friends and compose a short biographical portrait of the family or individual.
5. Little models of the towns / villages can be built by small groups. Students with greater artistic ability should be encouraged to create other renderings depicting life at that time, using various artistic mediums, including: murals, picture montages, paintings, drawings and live taped interviews with accompanying visual organizers and graphics materials.

Student Exercises

WORK SHEET #1

Student: ______________________ **Date:** ______________________

Class: ______________________ **Instructor:** ______________________

Follow your instructor's directions for using the box below. Use separate sheets of paper if necessary

Student Exercises

LESSON 2:

- ❑ Teacher directed lesson
- ❑ Review *Shtetle Principle* and homework from Lesson 1
- ❑ Focus on map skills

Materials

- ❑ One or more copies of each blank map. It is important that the students spend the next few periods (and at home) reviewing the completed maps and filling in the blank maps. In order to fully appreciate the precarious living situation of the Jews at that time, the student must be familiar with the political maneuvers (and changing boundaries) that transferred control of Transylvania between Hungary, Romania and Czechoslovakia during this period.

A. Exercise One

1. Review *Shtetle Principle* and homework from Lesson 1

B. Exercise Two

Extend discussion of *Shtetle Principle* in Lesson 1 by leading the students to appreciate that while the Jewish towns and villages in Hungary and Romania (Munkacs, Klausenburg, Satmar, Debrecen, Ungvar) were geographically small and insignificant in size, no match for the cultural and social centers of European life at that time, such as Paris, Vienna, Berlin, Milan, Rome, Prague or Budapest, nonetheless, they stand out as major cities of the world on the Heavenly map of earth. As Jews we measure greatness by a different standard, one which is almost completely foreign to the rest of the world. Though great museums, palaces, hotels, plazas and opera houses may determine the importance of a city by world standards, Jews measure the greatness of a city or town by the spiritual giants who, together with their *chassidim* and townspeople, built structures of spiritual purity that is the lifeblood of existence for the Jewish people and the whole of creation.

C. Exercise Three

1. Study the completed maps and fill in the blank maps that accompany them.

D. Homework Assignments:

1. The students should study the maps in preparation of being tested on their ability to properly fill in the blank maps from memory.

Student Exercises

Student: ______________________ Date: ______________________

Class: ______________________ Instructor: ______________________

EUROPE AND THE AUSTRIAN-HUNGARIAN EMPIRE BEFORE WORLD WAR I (1914)

Student Exercises

Student: ______________________ **Date:** ______________________

Class: ______________________ **Instructor:** ______________________

Identify the unlabeled countries

EUROPE AND THE AUSTRIAN-HUNGARIAN EMPIRE BEFORE WORLD WAR I (1914)

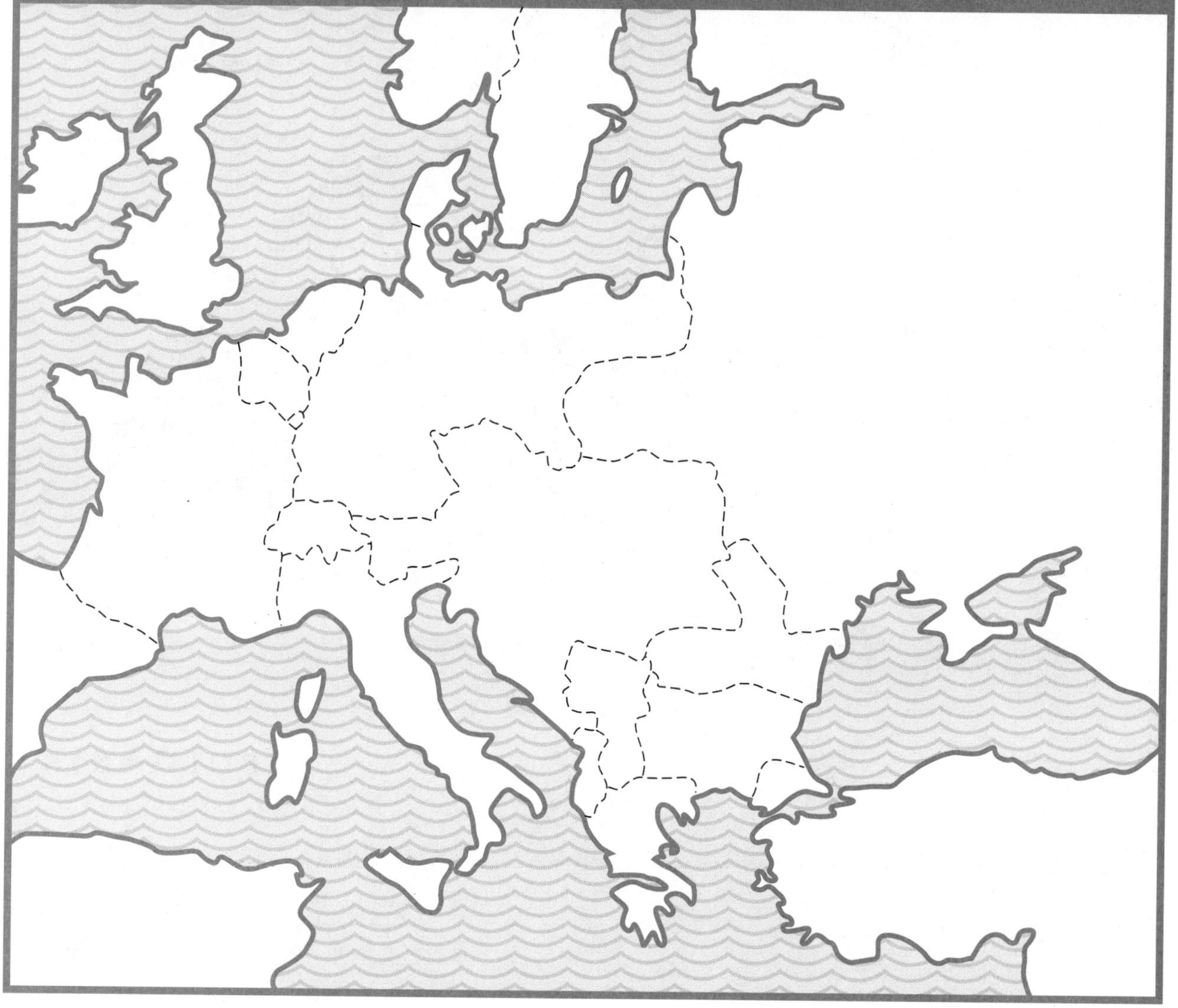

Student Exercises

Student: ______________________ Date: ______________________

Class: ______________________ Instructor: ______________________

HUNGARY 1867-1945

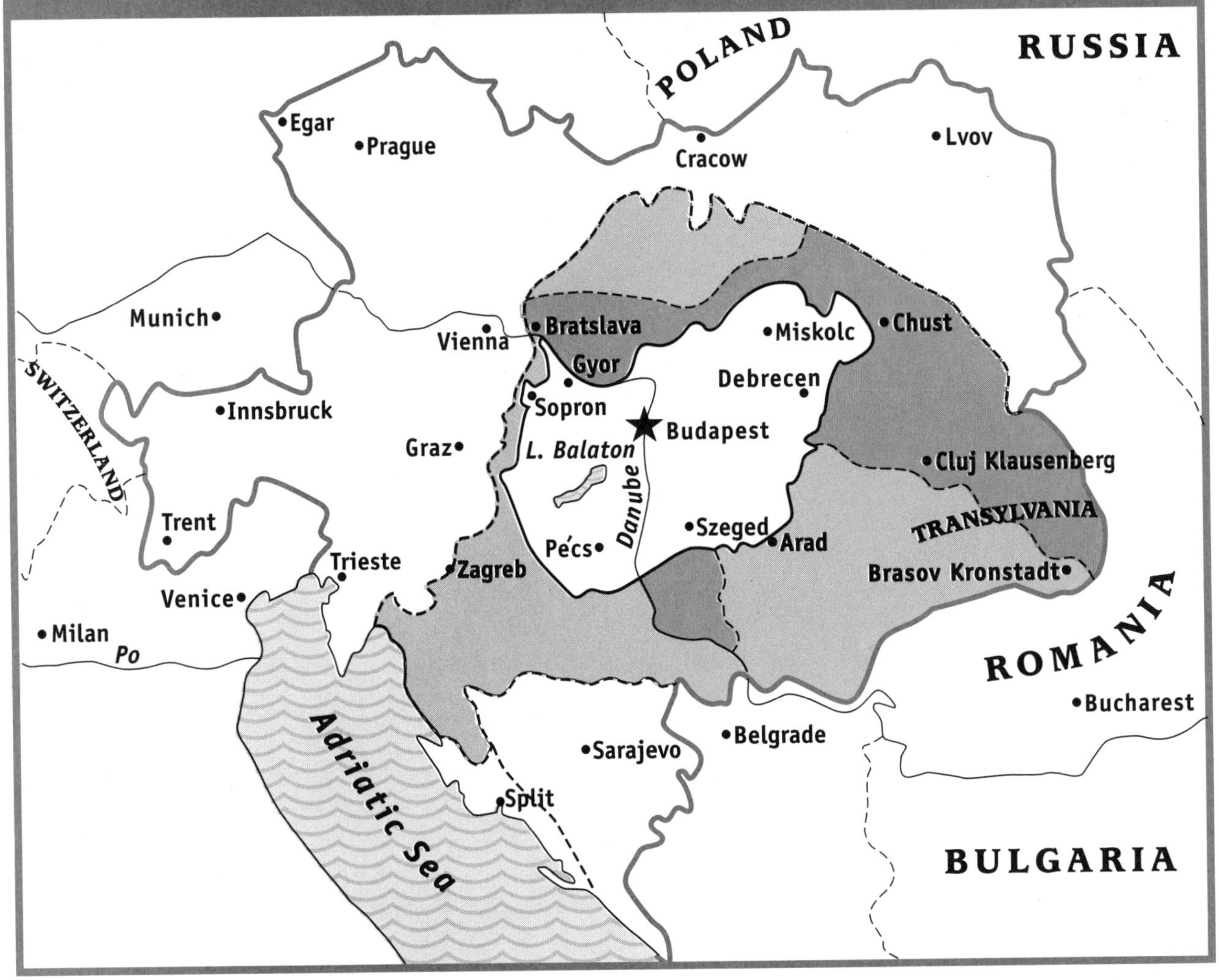

POLAND
RUSSIA
Egar
Prague
Cracow
Lvov
Munich
Vienna
Bratslava
Miskolc
Chust
Gyor
Debrecen
SWITZERLAND
Innsbruck
Sopron
Budapest
Graz
L. Balaton
Cluj Klausenberg
Danube
TRANSYLVANIA
Trent
Szeged
Arad
Trieste
Pećs
Zagreb
Brasov Kronstadt
Venice
Milan
Po
ROMANIA
Bucharest
Sarajevo
Belgrade
Adriatic Sea
Split
BULGARIA

1967-1918
Austria-Hungarian Empire
Kingdom of Hungary

1919
Territory Lost

1920
Hungary as laid down by Treaty of Trianon

1938-1941
Territory regained but lost in 1945

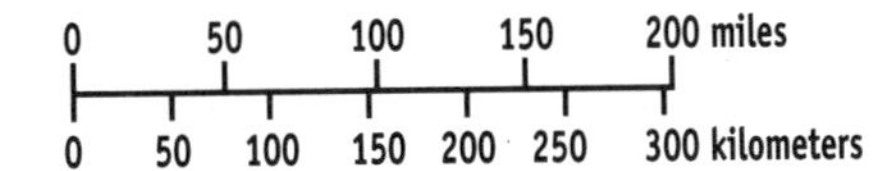

Student Exercises

Student: ______________________ **Date:** ______________________

Class: ______________________ **Instructor:** ______________________

Identify the unlabeled countries, cities and towns, and indicate (color or shade) the land areas that were taken away and re-annexed by Hungary and the date when these events occurred.

HUNGARY 1867-1945

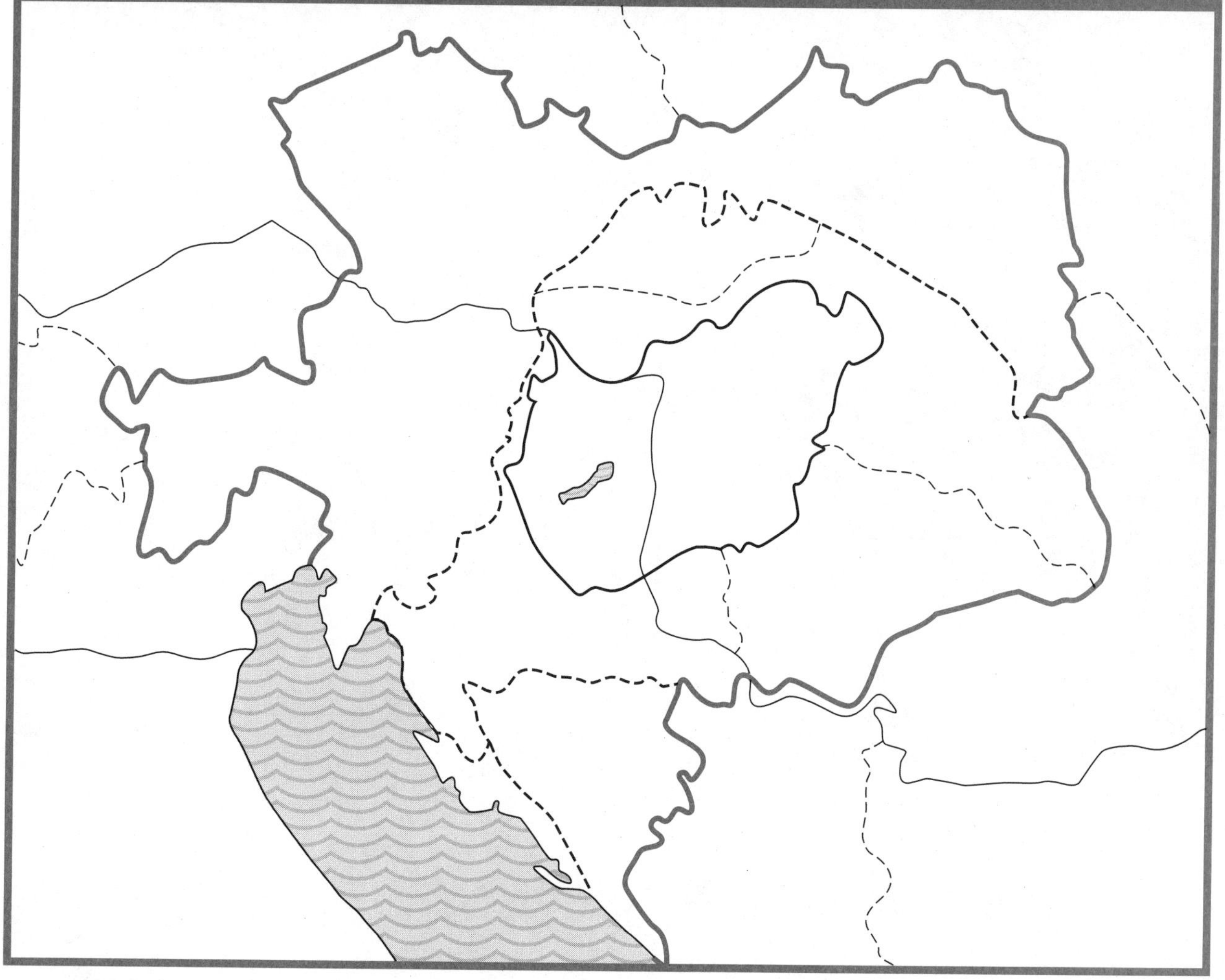

1967-1918

Austria-Hungarian Empire 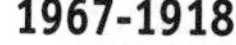

Kingdom of Hungary - - - -

1919

Territory Lost

1920

Hungary as laid down by Treaty of Trianon

1938-1941

Territory regained but lost in 1945

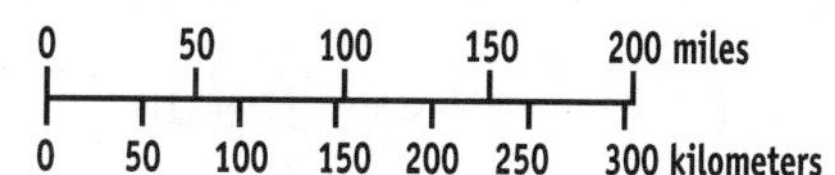

Student Exercises

Student: ______________________ Date: ______________________

Class: ______________________ Instructor: ______________________

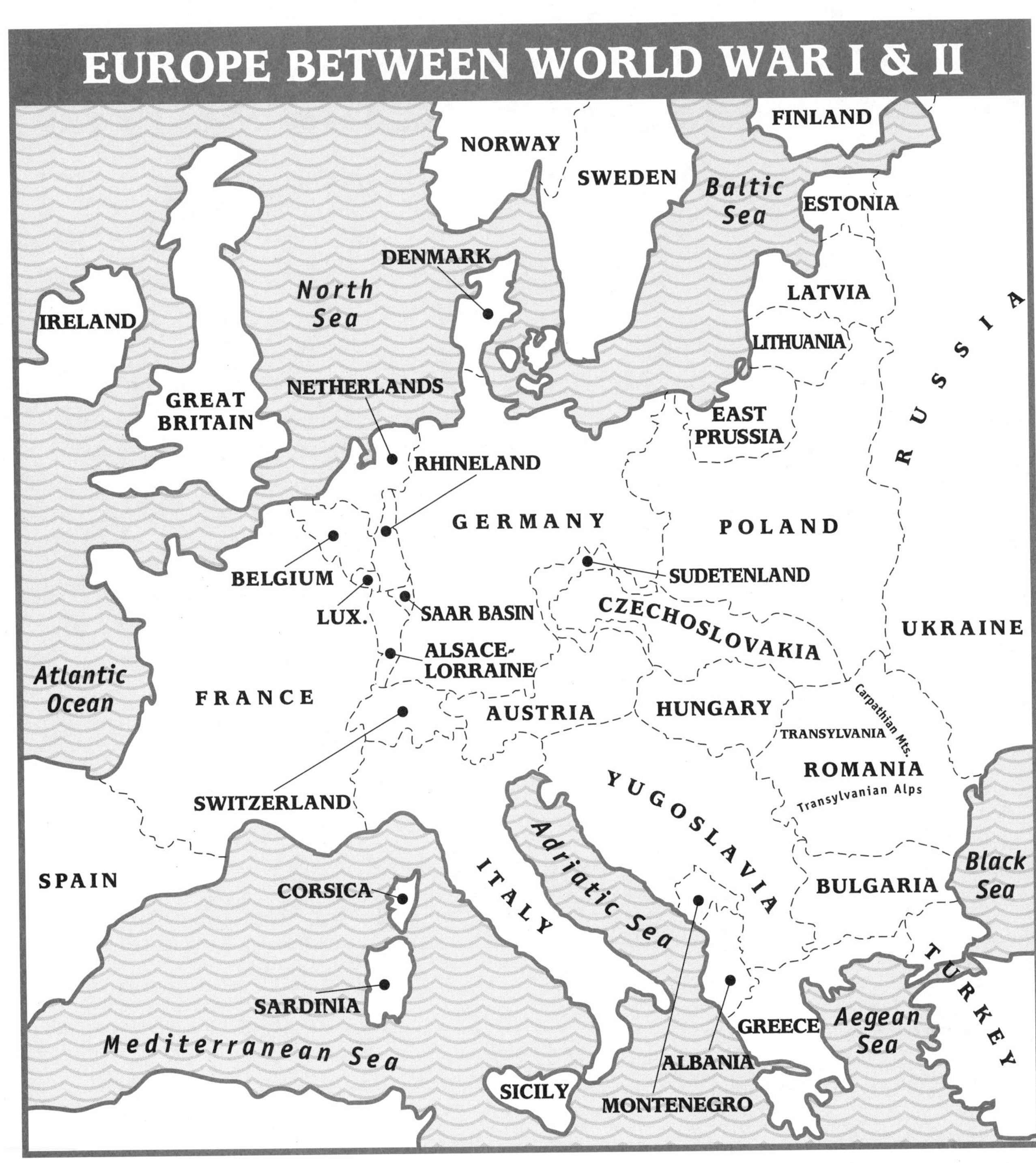

Student Exercises

Student: ______________________ **Date:** ______________________

Class: ______________________ **Instructor:** ______________________

Identify the unlabeled countries

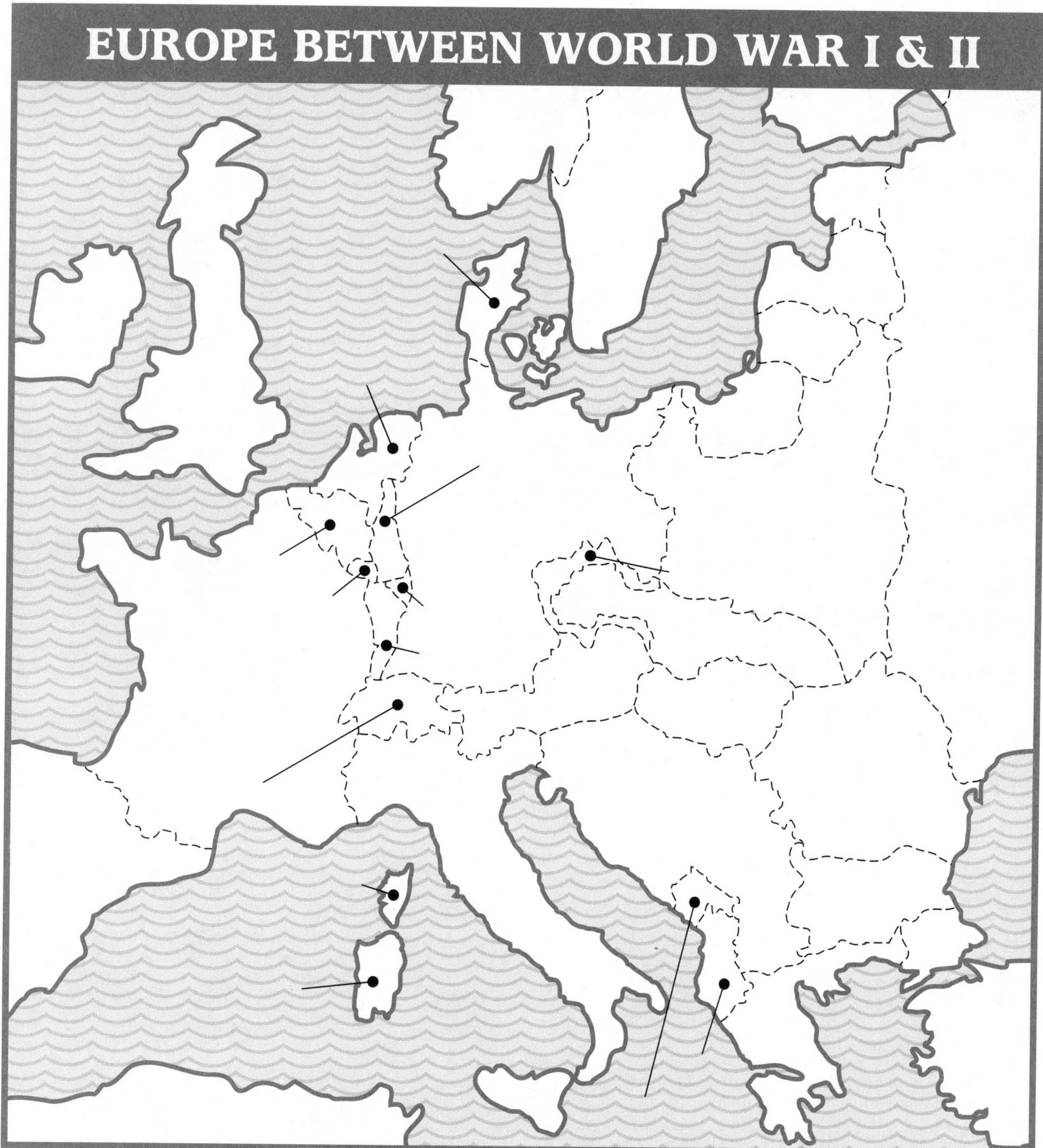

Student Exercises

Student: ______________________ **Date:** ______________________

Class: ______________________ **Instructor:** ______________________

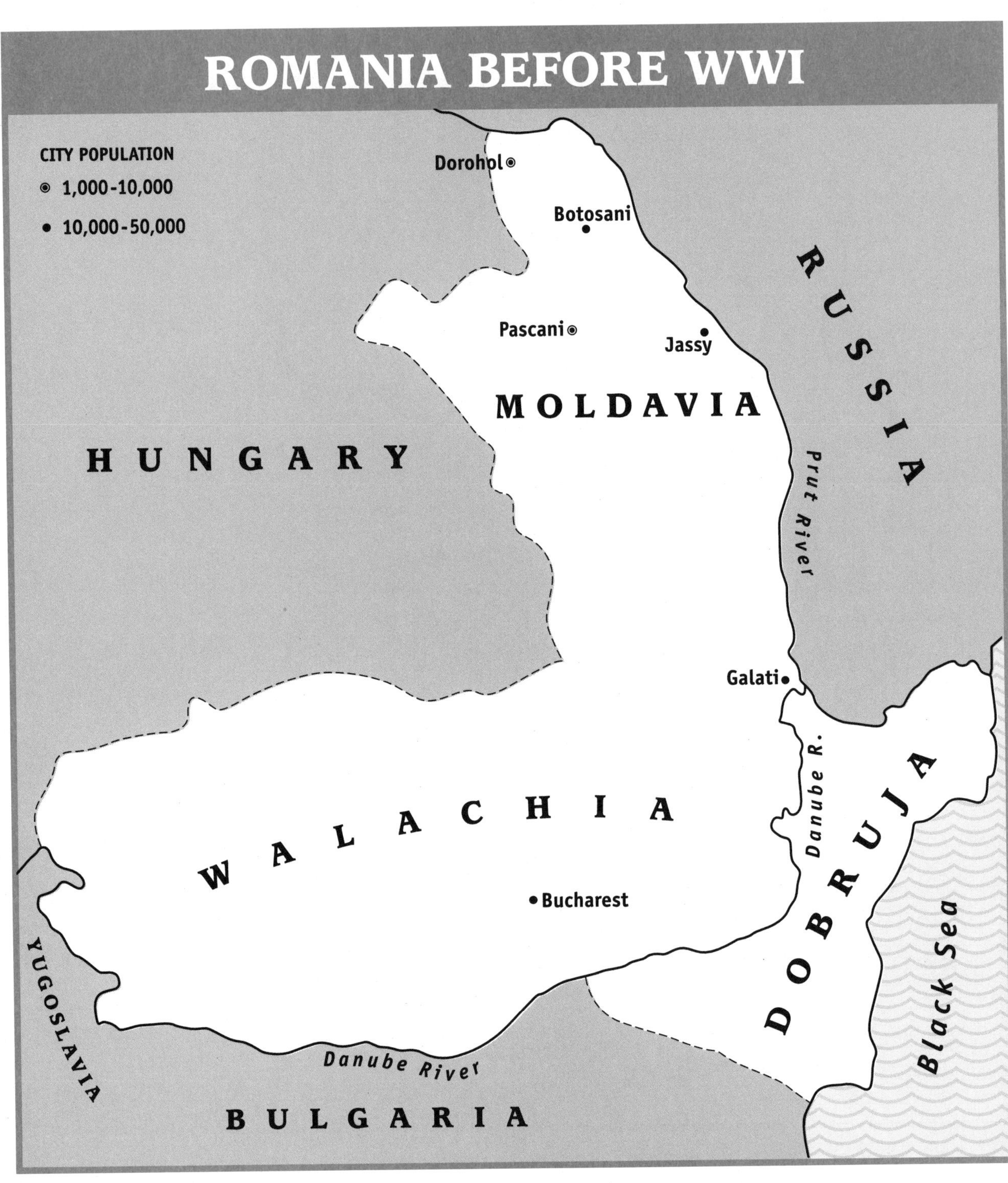

Student Exercises

Student: ______________________ **Date:** ______________________

Class: ______________________ **Instructor:** ______________________

Identify the unlabeled countries, cities and towns

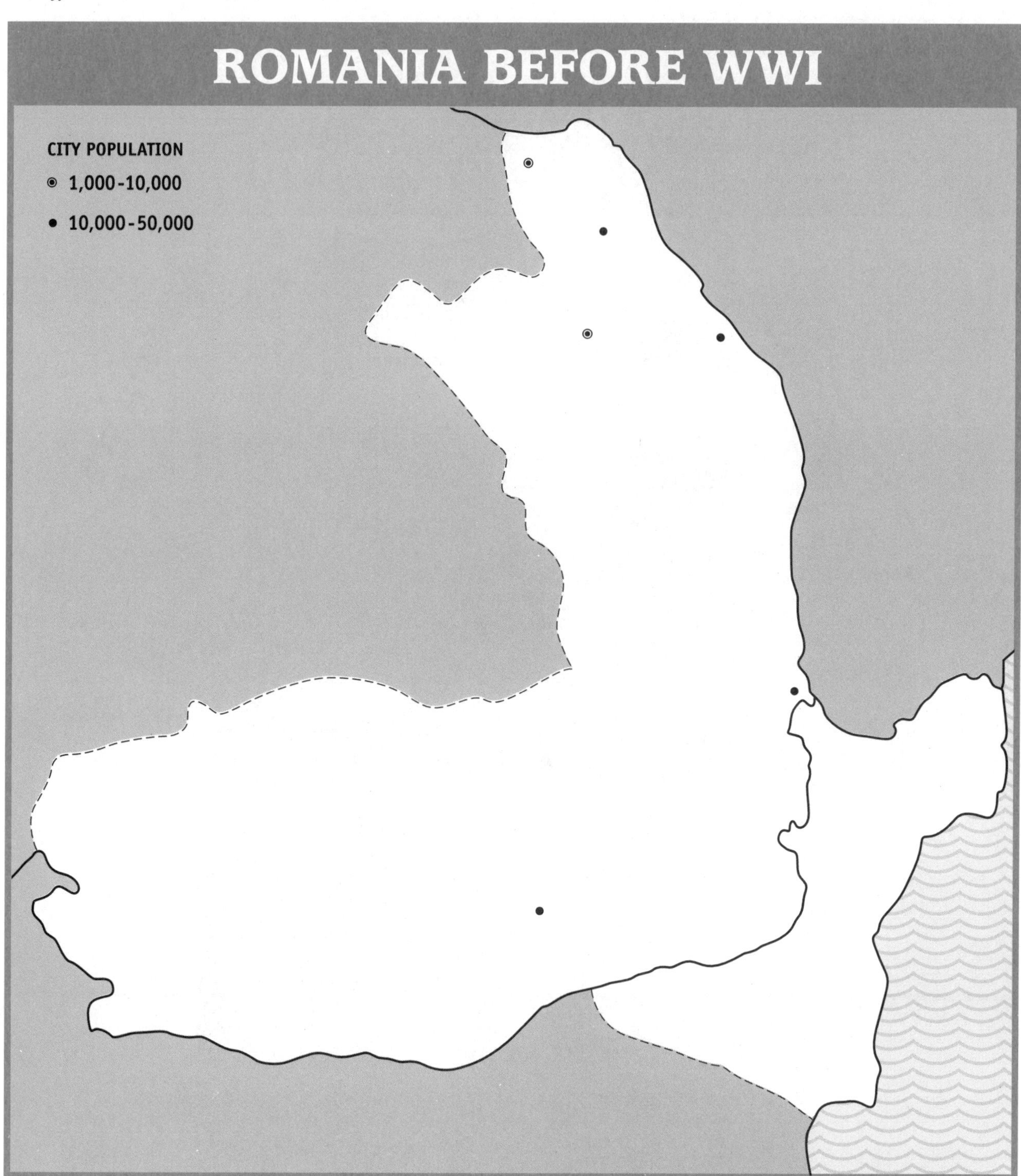

Student Exercises

Student: ______________________ Date: ______________________

Class: ______________________ Instructor: ______________________

Student Exercises

Student: ______________________ **Date:** ______________________

Class: ______________________ **Instructor:** ______________________

Identify the unlabeled countries, cities and towns, and indicate (color or shade) the areas taken away from Romania after the beginning of WWII.

ROMANIA BETWEEN WWI & WWII SHADED AREAS TAKEN AWAY AFTER BEGINNING OF WWII

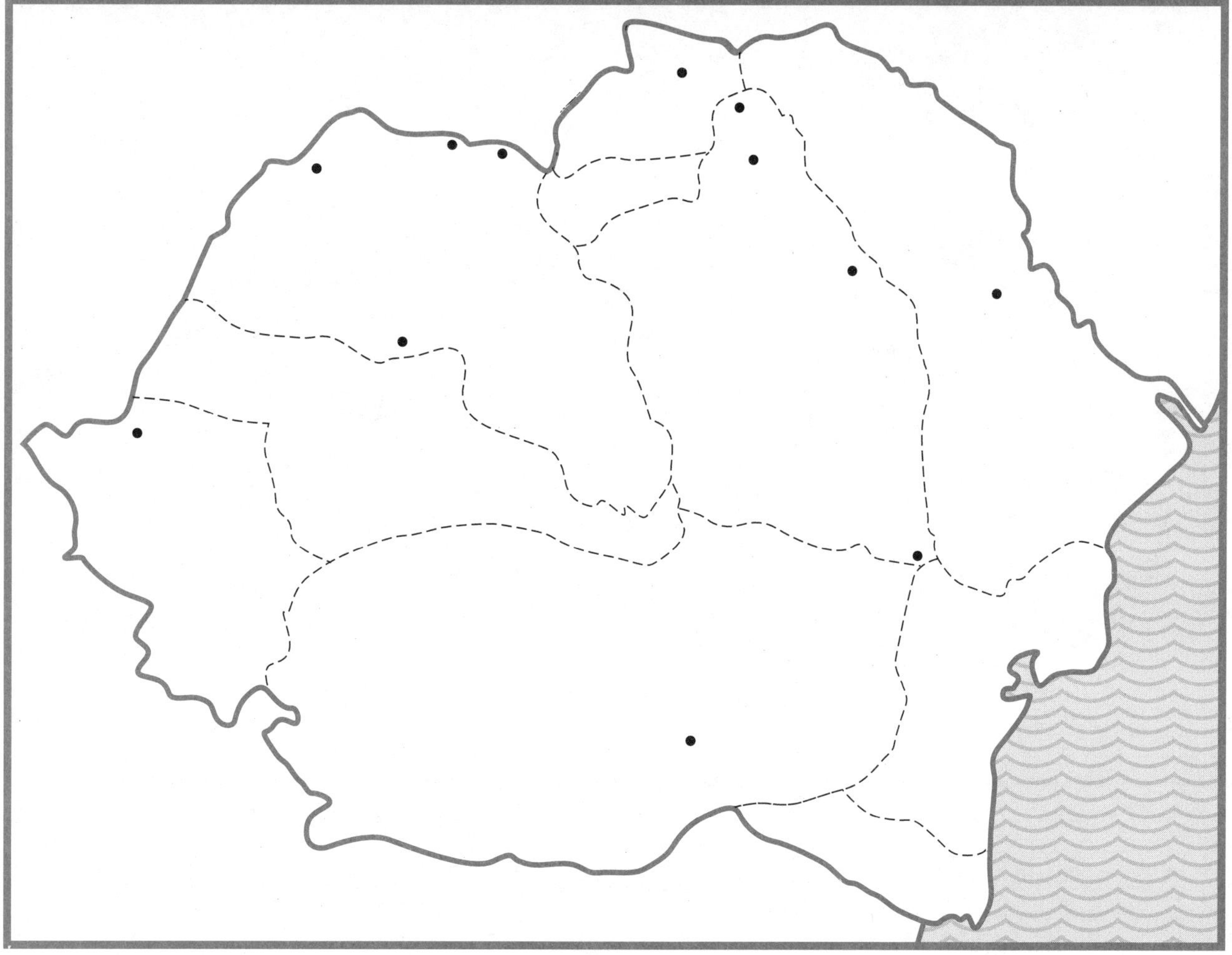

Student Exercises

Student: ____________________ Date: ____________________

Class: ____________________ Instructor: ____________________

Student Exercises

Student: ______________________ **Date:** ______________________

Class: ______________________ **Instructor:** ______________________

Identify the unlabeled cities and towns

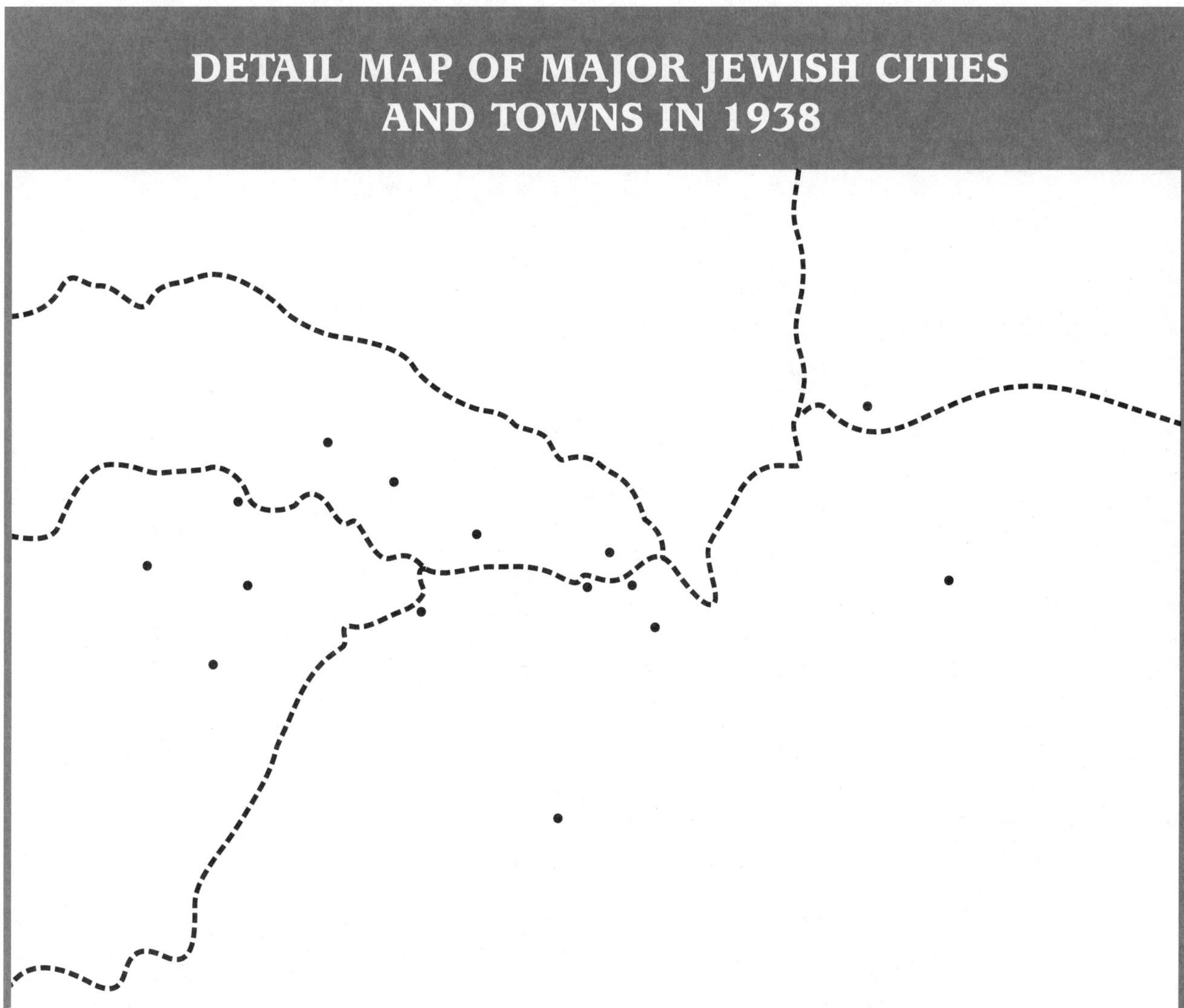

Student Exercises

Student: ______________________ Date: ______________________

Class: ______________________ Instructor: ______________________

Student Exercises

Student: ______________________ **Date:** ______________________

Class: ______________________ **Instructor:** ______________________

Identify the unlabeled countries

Legend:

1. A deal between a Jew and a Huzul in Carpatho-Russia, a region which formed part of Czechoslovakia after World War I. **2.** *Cheder* out for a stroll, Marmaros-Sighet, Romania. **3.** A rebbe and his pupils **4.** Two members of the Jewish Central Milk Co-operative in Bilka, 1925. **5.** Choir of Great Synagogue, Berehovo-Beregszaz **6.** A Jew in Munkacs (Mukachevo) in Carpatho-Russia. **7.** Jewish villagers going to town. **8.** A *chassid* and a young Jewish farmer in Carpatho-Russia 1930.

AN OVERVIEW: THE HISTORY OF JEWISH LIFE IN HUNGARY

Middle Ages in the Ottoman Conquest

• Archaeological evidence indicates that Jews were present in Pannonia and Dacia at the time of the Roman occupation of that area. This could mean that a Jewish presence in Hungary can be traced to the time of the destruction of the second *Beis HaMikdash*. Jewish settlements at that time were established as far west as the Rhineland area in Germany. Jewish historical tradition, however, cites the presence of Jews in Hungary from the second half of the 11th century, when Jews from Germany, Bohemia and Moravia settled there.

• In 1092, at the Council of Szaboles, the Church prohibited marriages between Jews and Christians, work on Christian festivals and the purchase of slaves.

• King Koloman protected the Jews in his territory at the end of the 11th century, when the remnants of the crusader armies attempted to attack them.

The area of Hungary[1] is 35,921 square miles (93,036 square kilometers). It is bounded on the north by the Czech Republic and Slovakia; on the northeast by Ukraine; on the east by Romania; on the south by Slovenia, Croatia, and Yugoslavia; and on the west by Austria. It is 328 miles (528 kilometers) from east to west and 167 miles (269 kilometers) from north to south. The major river is the Danube, which flows for 255 miles (410 kilometers) in Hungarian territory.

Ancient Hungarian Castle in Diosgyor

IMPORTANT EARLY JEWISH SETTLEMENTS IN HUNGARIAN TERRITORY	
Buda	**12th Century**
Pressburg (present day Bratslavia)	**Mentioned in 1251**
Tyrnau Mid	**11th Century**
Esztergom	**Mid 11th Century**

1. Material for this section was adapted from, **Encyclopedia Judaica**, Keter Publishing House, Jerusalem, 1976, Vol. 8, pages 1087-1110.

• During the 12th century, Jews occupied important positions in economic life – a pattern that is repeated throughout the exile.[2] Nobles curb this trend in 1222 and prohibit Jews from holding certain offices and receiving titles of nobility.

Cemetery in Liska

• King Bela IV (1251) grants lenient privileges to Jews because they are educated and capable of managing their estates and business affairs.

• Jews constitute important middle class in Hungarian economy. Church remains repressive in their attitude toward the Jews.

• Church Council of Buda (1279), forbade Jews to lease land and compelled them to wear the Jew's badge. These edicts are not upheld because the king objects. This Church- versus-royalty struggle regarding the attitude displayed toward the Jews and the way they were treated was an on-going source of confrontation throughout Europe for centuries.

The Church-versus-royalty struggle regarding the attitude displayed toward the Jews was an on-going source of con-frontation throughout Europe for centuries.

• Louis the Great (1342-82) is hostile towards the Jewish population. He is influenced by the Church.

• Black Death Plague leads to first expulsion of the Jews from Hungary in 1349.

• A general expulsion of the Jews from Hungary was decreed in 1360. Authorized resettlement was approved in 1364, though Jews were subjected to severe restrictions governing their rights and freedom.

• In 1365, the office of "Judge of the Jews" to supervise Jewish internal affairs and taxation was instituted.

• King Matthias Corvinus (1458-90) brought a change in favor of the Jews. Despite his support, Germanic inhabitants of the towns and villages were belligerent to the Jews whom they viewed as dangerous rivals.

• Blood libel in Tyrnau in 1494 – 16 Jews are burned at the stake and anti-Jewish riots broke out in the town.

• Anti-Jewish violence breaks out in Pressburg, Buda and other towns at the beginning of the 16th century

• King Ladislas VI (1490-1516) canceled all debts owed to the Jews.

• In 1515, Jews are placed under the direct protection of Emperor Maximilian I.

Ancient Castle in Csesznek Vara

2. The student is referred to the interview with Rebbetzin Zlota Ginsburg in **The World That Was: Lithuania.**

Farm house and well

• A degrading form of an oath for Jews is introduced into the courts system, and remains for 300 years.

• During the reign of Louis II (1516-26) hatred of the Jews intensified. This was a result of the activities of Isaac of Kashau, the director of the Royal Mint, and the apostate Imre Szereneses, the royal treasurer, who devalued the national currency and raised the taxes in order to provide funds for the war against the Turks.

• In middle of the 14th century Szekesfehervar is the most important Hungarian community, with a limited form of self-government under supervision of the crown (this was common in many European countries).

• During the 15th century the community of Buda gained in prominence as Jews expelled from other countries began settling there.

• Spiritual life of Hungarian Jewry during the Middle Ages is less developed in comparison to neighboring countries because of the dispersion of the communities and their small numbers. The first rabbi of renown was Rabbi Isaac Tyrnau (late 14th-early 15th century). In the introduction to his *Sefer HaMinhagim* ("Book of Customs") he describes the poor condition of Torah study in Hungary.

Spiritual life of Hungarian Jewry during the Middle Ages is less developed because of the dispersion of the communities and their small numbers.

Period of the Ottoman Conquest

• The first (but temporary) Ottoman conquest of Buda occurs in 1526 and many Jewish inhabitants join the retreating Turks establishing important Jewish communities in the Balkans.[3]

• After central Hungary is incorporated into the Ottoman Empire in 1541, the Jews lived a relatively stabile economic and social life. Settlements in Buda are renewed, and Sephardim from Asia Minor and the Balkans settled there.

Ancient Hungarian Fortress in Visegrad

3. Presently the Balkans (meaning mountains in Turkish) is comprised of Albania, Bulgaria, Greece, Turkey, Yugoslovia and part of Romania. This area is comprised of mainly mountainous terrain.

- During the 17th century Buda is one of the most important communities in the Ottoman Empire due to the authority of its rabbi, Ephraim ben Yaakov HaKohen, author of the *sefer Sha'ar Ephraim* (1688).
- Hatred toward the Jews increased in the Hapsburg ruled area of Hungary at the end of the 17th century.
- Blood libel in Bazin (1529) with 30 Jews burned at the stake and others expelled from Pressburg, Oedenburg (Sopron), and Tyrnau. Nobles in western Hungary provide protection to Jews expelled from these towns.
- The Jews expelled from Vienna found refuge on the estate of Count Esterhazy in Eisenstadt and six small neighboring towns in 1670. Eisenstadt is the oldest of the "Seven Communities" of Burgenland.
- In Transylvania, under the rule of Gabriel Bethlen (1613-29), the status of the Jews was stabilized by a privilege granted in 1623. The favorable attitude toward the Jews there stemmed from Reformation influences in Transylvania.

At beginning of the 18th century few Jewish settlements still existed. However, Jewish migration began the formation of Hungarian Jewry of the modern era.

18th to 19th Centuries (Until 1867)

- At the beginning of the 18th century Hungary was under Hapsburg rule. Few ancient Jewish settlements still existed. However, Jewish migration began the formation of Hungarian Jewry of the modern era. The census of 1735 enumerated 11,600 Jews (greatly underestimated). Few were born in Hungary, with the majority coming from Moravia and the minority from Poland. Most Jews were peddlers and small tradesmen. The atmosphere of hostility that existed in towns throughout Hungary caused most of the Jews to live in villages.
- During the reign of the rabidly anti-Semitic Austrian empress, Maria Theresa (1740-80), conditions for the Hungarians improved, but the situation of the Jews deteriorated.
- In 1744, an annual "tolerance tax" of 20,000 guilders was levied. This tax was increased until it reached an annual sum of 160,000 guilders at the beginning of the 19th century.
- The reign of Joseph II brought some improvements. In 1783, Jews were

City of Miskolc

Sheep grazing in the Jewish Cemetery in Miskolc

In the 1830s and 40s, there was a tendency in favor of civic rights for Jews, however, there was a reserved attitude toward them.

authorized to settle in the royal cities. There were 81,000 Jews in Hungary in 1787.

- In the 1830s and 40s, a period of governmental and social reform in Hungary, the Jewish question was discussed in legislative forums, in literature and in the periodicals and press. In general, there was a tendency in favor of civic rights for Jews, on the whole, however, there was a reserved attitude toward them. This period of relative peace enabled Hungarian culture to flourish.
- In 1848, Hungarian patriot Lajos Kossuth declared an independent Hungarian state in the Austrian territories. In 1849, the Russian army sent troops to aid Austrian Emperor Franz Joseph, defeating the Hungarians and reestablishing Austrian control. In 1867, realizing that the Hapsburg Empire could not exist without Hungarian support, the Austrians arrived at a compromise whereby Hungary was given control of its internal affairs and the emperor was crowned as king of Hungary. The dual monarchy of Austria-Hungary lasted until 1918. The suppression of the revolution of 1848-49 affected the Jews since many of them were active in the revolution. The Austrian government imposed a fine of 2,300,000 guilders on the Jewish communities. It was later reduced to 1,000,000 guilders and in 1856 the sum was reimbursed in the form of a fund for educational and relief institutions.

Lajos (Louis) Kossuth

- During the 1850s the Jews were still subjected to judicial and economic restrictions (the Jewish oath, the need for a permit to marry, prohibition on acquiring real estate, etc.). Most of the restrictions were abolished in 1859-60 when the Jews were allowed to participate in all professions and settle in all localities.

• The first political leaders of the new Hungary (Count Gyula Andrassy, Ferencz Deak and Kalman Tisza) expressed their approval in the granting of civic and political equality to the Jews. The bill on Jewish emancipation was passed in Parliament without considerable opposition on December 20, 1867.

• During this period the Jewish population of Hungary rapidly grew, due to natural increase and immigration from neighboring regions, especially Galicia (southern Poland). The number of Jews rose to 340,000 by 1850, and in the first population census held in modern Hungary in 1869, the population rose to 542,000.

• Jews are prominent in marketing and export and the establishment of banks and other financial enterprises. Jewish capital contributed significantly to the financing of heavy industry at the close of the 19th century. The role of the Jews in agriculture was also considerable.

• The Jewish population numbered 910,000 in 1910. The identification of the Jews with the Magyar[4] element in the Hungarian kingdom was an important factor in determining the general political attitude toward them.

• In 1895, Judaism is officially recognized by the state and accorded rights enjoyed by the Catholic and Protestant religions. This law is enacted despite vigorous objection from the Catholic Church who succeeded in delaying passage on three occasions.

In 1895, Judaism is officially recognized by the state and accorded rights enjoyed by the Catholic and Protestant religions.

The Emancipation Period, 1867-1914

• Hungarian Jewry consolidated their political, economic and cultural position, establishing a strong presence in the daily life of the country. Jews played a considerable role in the development of a capitalistic-based national economy, with large numbers of Jews entering the liberal literary professions, particularly in journalism, in the 1880s.

OCCUPATION	PERCENTAGE OF JEWS PRIOR TO WORLD WAR I
Merchants	**55-60%**
Craftsman	**13%**
Landowners (medium to large estates)	**13%**
Contractors	**45%**
Literature and the Arts	**26%**
Journalism	**42%**
Medicine	**49%**
Law	**45%**
Public Administration	**Few**
Total population in 1910: 910,00	

4. The Hungarians are descended from the ancient Magyars, who came from an area near the Ural Mountains more than a thousand years ago. The Hungarian language belongs to the Finno-Ugric group and is distantly related to Finnish. Presently, the population of the country approaches 11 million, of whom about 97 percent are Hungarians. There are small numbers of Germans, Slovaks, Croats, Romanians, and Gypsies.

Anti-Semitism

- From the mid-1870s, anti-Semitism emerges as an ideological trend, soon to become a political platform under the leadership of Gyozo Istoezy, a member of Parliament.
- Following the usual pattern of anti-Semitism, political and economic change led to disenfranchised segments of the populace who sought a convenient target to vent their frustration. The gentry were the main bearers of anti-Semitism in Hungary at this time.
- The German model of anti-Semitism also played some part in its Hungarian counterpart. Anti-Jewish propaganda intensified in 1880 and reached a climax with the blood libel of Tiszaeszla in 1882, with severe anti-Jewish disturbances in several towns. The acquittal of the accused and the condemnation of the libel by many gentile leaders did not calm the negative feelings.
- In 1884, an anti-Semitic faction of 17 members of Parliament organized, but without much power. Jewish defense against anti-Semitism took the form of apologetic and polemic literature. On the whole, the government and main political parties were strongly against anti-Semitism.
- In 1890, the Catholic People's Party became the main bearer of anti-Semitism. It regarded anti-Semitism as its main weapon to combat anti-Christian and socially destructive trends such as Liberalism and Socialism, which, according to Church doctrine, was closely associated with the Jews. Jewish intellectuals and their alleged harmful influence were targets for such unrestricted attacks. Jewish reaction to clerical anti-Semitism was stronger, more pronounced and more courageous than the response to the anti-Semitism of the 1880s, which seemed to be less menacing. Many of the tenets of anti-Semitism in this era became cornerstones of the anti-Jewish ideology in the inter-war period. Anti-Semitism was also widespread among the national minorities, especially the Slovaks, because Jews tended to identify themselves with the nationalist policy of the Magyars.
- As with Jews throughout Europe during World War I, the Jews of Hungary suffered. Approximately 10,000 Jews were killed in battle. Anti-Jewish feeling increased because of the many Jewish refugees from Galicia (previously under Russian control) and because the gentiles thought the Jews were profiting from their suffering, a typical canard leveled at the Jews in many countries. In reality, the Jews usually suffered at the hands of the armies of both their own country and that of the enemy.

During World War I, the Jews of Hungary suffered. Approximately 10,000 Jews were killed in battle. Anti-Jewish feeling increased.

A Hungarian Village

Internal Life During the 19th Century

• The language and cultural tradition of Hungarian Jewry was divided into three sections: Jews of the northwestern districts (Oberland) of Austrian and Moravian origin spoke German or a western dialect of Yiddish; the Jews of the northeastern districts (Unterland) mostly of Galician origin, spoke an eastern dialect of Yiddish; and the Jews of central Hungary, the overwhelming majority of whom spoke Hungarian.

• The Jews were party to the struggle between the ruling Magyars and the other minorities of Hungary striving for national recognition.

• Internal Jewish life during the 19th century was marked by a struggle between the Orthodox, Torah observant Jews and those enlightened Jews advancing the dogma of modern culture, integration and assimilation with the gentiles. A strict Orthodox spirit was established in Hungary under the influence and leadership of Rabbi Moshe Sofer, the *Chasam Sofer*, whose yeshiva was located in Pressburg. The *Chasam Sofer* was one of the towering Torah leaders of his time, a personality who transcended the generations. He was an unwaivering fighter against the Enlightenment–fearless in his dedication to insure total observance of Torah and *mitzvos*. He was a leader who was completely dedicated to Hungarian Jewry. Rabbi Sofer's influence was felt throughout the length and breadth of Hungary long after his *petirah*. His teachings were carried on by his eldest son, known as the *Kisav Sofer*, and his son, known as the *Michtav Sofer*. Pressberg (now known as Bratslavia) became a spiritual center for the Orthodox Jews of Hungary and its yeshiva the most important in central Europe.

Internal Jewish life during the 19th century was marked by a struggle between Torah observant Jews and those enlightened Jews advancing the dogma of modern culture.

Rabbi Moshe Schreiber-Sofer The Chasam Sofer, זצ"ל (1762-1839)

Rabbi Avraham Shmuel Binyomin Sofer, known as the Kisav Sofer, eldest son of the Chasam Sofer. Became Rosh Hayeshiva after his father. (1815-1871)

Rabbi Shimon Sofer 2nd son of the Chasam Sofer known as the Michtav Sofer who was Rav in Mattersdorf and Crakow. (1820-1883)

Photos Credit: Encyclopedia Judaica

• The Enlightenment movement made its appearance in Hungary in the 1830s. Though this Reform ideology spread to several communities, the movement was unable to take root in Hungary, due to the resolute opposition of the Orthodox communitiy. The debate between the Orthodox and the reformers (who were referred to as Neologists in Hungary) gained in intensity, becoming a central issue at the General Jewish Congress convened by the government in 1868.

The Congress was assembled in order to define the basis for the autonomous organization of the Jewish community.

• The Congress was attended by 220 delegates (126 Neologists and 94 Orthodox). The conflict between the factions was aggravated when the majority refused to accept the demands of the Orthodox to recognize the validity of the laws of the *Shulchan Oruch* in the regulation of community life. The Orthodox did not accept an overall ruling favoring the Reform movement and appealed to Parliament to exempt them from the authority of these regulations. Parliament consented in 1870 and the Orthodox organized themselves within separate communities.

• The *Chasam Sofer* decisively influenced the development of Orthodox Jewry in western and central Hungary. Torah study was widespread among large sections of Orthodox Jewry, with vibrant yeshivos established in every large community. The most renowned of these, besides that of Pressburg, were in Galanta, Eisenstadt, Papa, Huszi (Khut) and Szatmar (Satu-Mare).

• During the 19th century the Hungarian rabbinate was composed of scholars of exceptional levels of learning and piety including: Rabbis Abraham Samuel Benjamin Sofer, Simhah Bunim Sofer, Moshe Schick, and Judah Aszod (1794-1866) in Szerdahely (Mercurea), Aharon David Deutsh (1812-78) in Balassagyarmat and Shlomo Ganzfried (author of the *Kitzur Shulchan Oruch*) among others. Torah literature was produced that would affect future generations of Jews for generations to come.

• *Chassidic* courts spread in the north-eastern region of Hungary. Communities were founded by Rabbi Moshe Teitelbaum in Satoraljaujhely. His *chassidic*-rabbinical dynasty was also active in Maramarossziget (Sighet) and its surroundings. Another center of *Chassidim* was located in Munkacs[5] (Mukachevo) in Carpathian Russia, where Rabbi Tzvi Elimelech Shapiro (known as the *Bnei Yisoschor*) settled in 1825. In addition, the dynasties of the *tzaddikim* of Belz, Sanz and Vishnitz had considerable influence in Hungary. From Pressberg in the west to the Carpathian villages in the east, Hungary was rich with a pure and vibrant Torah way of life.

• With the close of the 19th century, however, assimilation became widespread within great portions of Hungarian Jewry and there was an increase in apostasy, especially among the upper classes. Mixed marriage became a common occurrence, particularly in the capital of Budapest.

With the close of the 19th century, assimilation became widespread within great portions of Hungarian Jewry and there was an increase in apostasy.

• Attachment to *Eretz Yisrael* was ingrained within Hungarian Jewry from the time of the *Chasam Sofer*, with some of his most distinguished disciples emigrating to *Eretz Yisrael* where they ranked among the leaders of the *Ashkenazi yishuv* during the middle of the 19th century.

• At the close of the 19th century the nationalist ideal of secular, political Zionism, only attracted a limited circle of academic youth and intellectuals. Assimilationists and the overwhelming majority of the Orthodox were sharply and firmly opposed to this new movement. The *Kolel Ungarn* (Hungarian Community) in Jerusalem was a center of extremist opposition to Zionism in *Eretz Yisrael* and the *Neturei Karta* faction later developed from it.

5. See Ostreicher interview.

1919 to 1939

• The Communist regime which came to power in Hungary after its defeat in World War I included a considerable number of Jews in the upper ranks of the government led by Bela Kun. After the Communist revolution had been suppressed, the establishment of the new regime was accompanied by riots and acts of violence against the Jews – "The White Terror" – with an estimated 3,000 killed.

• The political situation stabilized and acts of violence decreased, but the policy of the government remained anti-Semitic. In 1920, a bill was passed restricting the number of Jews in the higher institutions of learning to 5%. The situation improved while Stephen Bethlen was prime minister (1921-31). In 1928, an amendment was introduced to this bill, but the restrictions were not entirely abolished.

In 1928, Jews received the right of representation in the Upper House of Parliament as all other religious communities.

House of the Karistierer Rov, Rabbi Shaya Steiner

• In 1928, Jews received the right of representation in the Upper House of Parliament as all other religious communities. During the first few years after World War I, political Zionist activity was brought to a halt by the government, but was eventually reinstated.

• The relative tranquilization in the situation of the Jews in Hungary also continued after the resignation of Bethlen and the rise to power of the political right. A sharp anti-Jewish turn took place during the late 1930s as a result of the strengthening of Rightist circles and growing German-Nazi influence.

• In 1938, the "First Jewish Law" was presented in Parliament to restrict the number of Jews in the liberal professions, in governemnt administration, and in commercial and industrial enterprises to 20%. The term "Jew" included not only members of the Jewish religion, but also those who became apostates after 1919 or who had been born of Jewish parents after that date. The bill aroused objections from the opposition parties but it was ratified by both Houses of Parliament.

• In 1939, the "Second Jewish Law" was passed; it extended the application of the term "Jew" on a racial basis (including some 100,000 Christians, apostates or their children) and also reduced the number of Jews in economic activity to 5%. Political rights of Jews were also restricted. As a result of these actions 250,000 Hungarian Jews lost their livelihood.

• Jewish reaction to the anti-Jewish legislation was expressed by greater emphasis on their patriotic attachment to Hungary. The Jews believed that the anti-Jewish current was a fleeting phenomenon. Jewish communal organizations, led by the community of Budapest, initiated social aid activities to assist those who lost their jobs. Within certain factions of the community, conversions increased, with up to 5,000 apostates, after the enactment of the First Jewish Law. However, wide segments of the Jewish public reacted with a return to Judaism, through a fostering of Jewish values, literature and religious education. Zionism was strengthened and *aliyah* to Israel increased.

Gendarmerie restoring order on Budapest street (1942)

• Hungarian Jewry in the interwar period underwent great changes. Following the dismemberment of the country after World War I, the number of Jews was reduced by about a half to 473,000 in 1920. Their number further declined during the 1920s and 30s. Over half of Hungary's Jewish population lived in greater Budapest after WWI.

Hungarian troops at the battle-front (1942)

The Holocaust Period

• In 1930, 445,567 Jews lived in Hungary and an additional 78,000 Jews came under Hungarian rule when southern Slovakia was annexed by Hungary on November 2, 1938. The 72,000 Jews who lived in the Czechoslovak province of Sub-Carpathian Ruthenia came under Hungarian jurisdiction when Hungary moved in on March 15-16, 1939. The Jewish population of former Romanian Northern Transylvania (awarded to

Sorting through Jews' personal belongings at Auschwitz

The decimation of the Jewish population began in the fall of 1940, shortly after the incorporation of northern Transylvania.

Hungary on August 30, 1940) numbered 149,000. According to the January 31, 1941 census, of a total Hungarian population of 14,683,323, Jews number 725,007 (184,453 of them in Budapest alone). In April 1941, there were about 20,000 Jews in the former Yugoslav territory (Bacska), occupied in the course of time by joint German-Hungarian military operations.

• In conformity with the "Third Jewish Law" (1941), which defined the term "Jew" on purely racial principles, 58,320 persons not belonging to the Jewish faith were considered Jewish. Thus, the total number of persons officially registered as Jews in mid-1941 was over 803,000.

• The Third Jewish Law, based on the Nuremberg Laws, prohibited intermarriage. By mid-1941, anti-Jewish measures placed Hungarian Jewry in a most disadvantageous position in every sphere of political, economic and social life. The government party, *Magyar Elet Partja* (M.E.P., "Party of Hungarian Life"), pursued a pro-Nazi (anti-Semitic) policy, while various national-socialist groups and the Arrow-Cross Party exerted increasing pressure upon the government to radicalize its anti-Jewish policy.

• The decimation of the Jewish population began in the fall of 1940, shortly after the incorporation of northern Transylvania, from where thousands of Jews whose citizenship was in question were forcibly expelled, mainly to Romania. The first large-scale loss of life among Hungarian Jews occurred in July 1941, when the Office of Aliens' Control expelled to German-held Galicia about 20,000 Jews from annexed areas of Czechoslovakia whose Hungarian citizenship was in doubt. They were taken to Kamenetz-Podolsk and murdered in the autumn of 1941 by S.S. men, assisted by Hungarian troops.

• The second great loss of life occurred in January 1942, when 1,000 Jews were massacred by *Gendarmeries* and soldiers in Backsa, mainly in Novi-Sad.

• In May 1940, special forced labor units were already set up for enlisting Jews excluded from army services. When Hungary joined the war against the Soviet Union, the labor units were sent with the troops. At that time there were 10 to 12 labor battalions comprising about 14,000 men, but the number of Jews on the eastern front later reached 50,000. After the breakthrough of the advancing Soviet army near the River Don (January 1943), the Second Hungarian Army disintegrated and fled in panic. It is estimated that of the 50,000 Jews, 40,000-43,000 died during the retreat.

• The position of the labor units remaining in Hungary was much better, particularly after March 10, 1942, when the anti-Semitic prime minister, Laszlo Bardossy, was succeeded by the moderate, conservative Miklos Kallay. Nevertheless, that month Kallay announced the draft law for expropriation of Jewish property and envisaged clearing the rural areas of Jews. He announced successive measures to eliminate Jews from economic and cultural life.

• In April 1942, Kallay pledged the "resettlement" of 800,000 Jews as a "final solution of the Jewish question" pointing out, however, that this could be implemented only after the War. Presumably, these extreme anti-Jewish plans were meant to curry favor with the Germans while, in fact, Kallay, in an agreement with Regent Nicolas Horthy, refrained from drastic steps and resisted pressure from the German government. Dissatisfied with Kallay's halfhearted measures, Germany exerted greater pressure upon Hungary from October 1942, for legislation to completely eliminate Jews from economic and cultural life, mandatory wearing of the yellow badge, and evacuation to the east. The Kallay government rejected the German requests for deportation mainly on economic grounds, arguing that deportation would ruin Hungary's economy and would harm Germany as well.

• In April 1943, Hitler conferred with Horthy and condemned Hungary's handling of the "Jewish question" as irresolute and ineffective. Again, the Hungarians rejected German demands for the deportations. By 1943, the Kallay government completed the program of eliminating the Jews from public and cultural life, while action was taken in economic life to restrict Jews according to their percentage in the total population (about 6%). Jewish agricultural holdings were almost entirely liquidated, while "race-protective" legislation segregated Jews from Hungarian society.

• At the end of 1943, the Kallay government secretly conferred with the Allies in preparation for Hungary's extrication from the War. Under these circumstances, the Nazi-style handling of the "Jewish question" hardly suited the country's interests. In December 1943, a military court procedure was initiated against the criminals involved in the anti-Serbian and anti-Jewish massacres in Bacska (January 1942). The Germans

Hungarian Castle destroyed by Allied bombings

The Kallay government rejected the German requests for deportation mainly on economic grounds.

The Arrow-Cross ruler, Ferenc Szalasi (L) with two henchmen in the yard of Buda Castle (1944)

Laszlo Baky, State Secretary for the Minister of the Interior standing trial for War Crimes. He worked together with Laszlo Endre.

regarded the prosecution of the murderers of Jews as an attempt to gain favorable footing with the Jews and the Allies, and the incident exacerbated the tension between Berlin and Budapest.

At the time of the German occupation, approximately 63,000 Jews (8% of the Jewish population) had been killed.

German Occupation

• In March 1944, the Germans decided to occupy Hungary. This was prompted by Hungarian foot-dragging regarding the "final solution of the Jewish question." Kallay's rejection of the German demands for deportation was considered as evidence of Hungary's determination to join forces with the Western Allies. "Operation Margaret," as the occupation of Hungary was known, took place on March 19, 1944.

• At the time of the German occupation, approximately 63,000 Jews (8% of the Jewish population) had been killed. Prior to the occupation, on March 13, 1944, Adolf Eichmann, head of the R.S.H.A. (Reich Security Main Office) began preparations in Mauthausen, Austria, for setting up the *Sondereinsatz-kommando* (Special Task Force) destined to direct the liquidation of Hungarian Jewry. Most of the Sonderkommando members, among them Hermann Krumey and Dieter Wisliceny, arrived in Budapest on the day of the occupation, while Eichmann arrived on March 21. On the German side, special responsibility for Jewish affairs was assigned to Edmund Veesenmayer, the newly appointed minister and Reich plenipotentiary, and to Otto Winkelmann, S.S. and police leader and Himmler's representative in Hungary.

• On March 22, a new government was set up under the premiership of the former Hungarian minister in Berlin, Dome Sztojay. The government consisted of extreme pro-Nazi elements, willing collaborators with Germany in the accomplishment of the "Final Solution." The new regime's Minister of the Interior, Andor Jaross, was in charge of Jewish affairs; however, actual execution of the anti-Jewish measures was directed by Laszlo Endre and Laszlo Baky, state secretaries of the Ministry of the Interior. Immediately after the entry of German troops into Hungary, hundreds of prominent Jews were arrested in Budapest and other cities. Over 3,000 were detained by the end of March, increasing to 8,000 by mid-April. A great number of provincial Jews were rounded up, mainly at the Budapest railway stations, on the very evening of the occupation. They were interned at Kistarcsa and other concentration camps.

• Jewish organizations were dissolved throughout the country, and on March 20, a Jewish council (*Zsido Tanacs*) with eight members was set up in Budapest by the Germans to act as the head of the Jewish communities. The Germans would manipulate this Council to execute their measures without resistance and avoid an atmosphere of panic. By the end of March, similar Jewish councils were constituted in several larger provincial towns. However, unlike the Budapest Jewish Council, their activity was minimal and their existence short-lived. From the first days of the occupation, Eichmann and his collaborators endeavored to persuade the members of the central Jewish council that deportations were not intended and that Hungary Jewry would not undergo brutal treatment. They assured them that no harm would befall the Jews, but only on condition that they obediently carry out the directives regarding their segregation and their new economic status.

Laszlo Endre, State Secretary for the Minister of the Interior, who carried out anti-Jewish measures. Seen here being taken to trial for war crimes.

• The "Provisional Executive Committee of the Jewish Federation of Hungary," appointed by the Hungarian government on May 6, aimed to ensure complete observance of the anti-Jewish directives. By the time this committee was set up, the Jews of the provinces had already been concentrated in ghettos and Jewish community life had ceased to exist. The "Executive Committee" was a fiction devised with the additional goal of lending a semblance of legality to the government's measures.

• Another task imposed on the Jewish organizations established after occupation was to assure the complete and unhindered transfer of Jewish assets and valuables. Simulytaneous with the German actions, the Sztojay government enacted intensive anti-Jewish legislation, and numerous anti-Jewish decrees aimed at the total exclusion of Jews from economic, cultural and public life were also instituted. Jews were dismissed from all public service and the professions, their businesses were closed down and assets over 3,000 pengo (about $300) were confiscated, as well as their cars, bicycles, radios and telephones.

• On March 31, 1944, Jews were ordered to wear the yellow badge. Actually, in a few places (e.g, Munkacs), the local authorities issued this order earlier.

• On April 7, the decision was taken to concentrate the Jews in ghettos and afterwards to deport them. The ghettoization process was entrusted to the Hungarian *Gendarmerie* in collaboration with local administrations.

Eichmann and his collaborators endeavored to persuade the members of the central Jewish council that Hungary Jewry would not undergo brutal treatment.

The ghettoization process was started in the provinces. The rest of the country, except for the capital, was completed simultaneously.

• By mid-April, an agreement was reached between the Hungarian government and the Germans stipulating the delivery of 100,000 able-bodied Jews to German factories in April and May.

• By the end of April, the Germans modified this plan by dismissing any criteria on ability to work and demanded the deportation of the entire Jewish population to concentration camps in the eastern territories. However, at the end of April, several groups of able-bodied Jews were transported from the outskirts of Budapest to Germany (1,800 persons on April 28 and a small group from the Topolya Concentration Camp on April 30).

Ghettoization and Deportation

• The ghettoization process was started in the provinces. The Jews of Sub-Carpathian Ruthenia were evacuated to ghettos on April 16-19. By April 23, about 150,000 Jews were concentrated in the northeastern areas of Hungary pending their deportation to Auschwitz, which started on May 15 with daily transports of 2,000-3,000 Jews. At the same time as the Carpatho-Ruthenian action, some ghettos were set up sporadically in different parts of the country, arbitrarily initiated by local authorities (the Nagykanizsa Jews were forced into a ghetto on April 19 and a number of the Jews of Veszprem county were crammed into improvised concentration camps as early as the last day of March).

• North Transylvania Jewry was evacuated to ghettos in the first days of May, when the process of ghettoization had already been concluded in northeastern Hungary. The ghettoization in the rest of the country, except for the capital, was completed simultaneously. The Jews were driven out of their homes in the night, allowed to pack only a minimal supply of food and some strictly necessary personal belongings, and then assembled at temporary collection points. The provisional ghettos were set up in school buildings, synagogues or factories outside the towns. In the large Jewish population centers, ghettos

Taking personal belongings from deportation trains

AREA	NUMBER OF GHETTOS	NUMBER OF PERSONS
Northeastern Hungary	**17**	**144,000**
Transdanubia	**7**	**36,000**
Tisza Region	**4**	**65,000**
Northern District	**5**	**69,000**
Transylvania (except Maramaros Satmar counties)	**7**	**97,000**
Totals	**40**	**411,000**

were established in the vicinity of the towns, mainly in brickyards, barracks or out in the open.

• Ghettoization was immediately followed by an inventory of the movable property and the sealing of the houses belonging to the Jews. Jews were permitted to add a few items of food and clothing to their scanty baggage during the inventory, which in most cases was accompanied by *Gendarmerie* brutality and looting by the civilian auxiliary personnel. In this first phase of the ghettoization, the Jews in the villages were evacuated to temporary ghettos (collection points) set up exclusively in or outside towns (with two to four collection ghettos per county).

• The second phase consisted of the evacuation from the collection ghettos to the larger, central ghettos. The concentration of Jews in the central ghettos is presented in the above chart.

• The living conditions of over 400,000 Jews forced into makeshift ghettos were characterized by overcrowding and lack of elementary hygiene facilities. Some of the inmates had no roof over their heads, and some ghettos were erected entirely outdoors. During the short period that ghettos existed in the provinces, inhuman conditions and torture claimed a number of victims and there were also numerous cases of suicide. When the next phase of the deportation began, the majority of the Jewish population was already in a state of physical and mental exhaustion.

• The deportations that began on May 14, were jointly organized by Hungarian and German authorities, but the Hungarian government was solely in charge of the Jews' transportation to the northern border. Between May 14-15 and June 7, about 290,000 persons were evacuated from Zone 1 (Sub-Carpathian Ruthenia) and Zone II (northern Translyvania). More than 50,000 Jews of northwestern Hungary and those

When the next phase of the deportation began, the majority of the Jews were already in a state of physical and mental exhaustion.

Children in the ghetto

north of Budapest, constituting Zone III, were deported by June 30. Zone IV (southern Hungary, east of the Danube) with about 41,000 persons, was also evacuated by the end of June. The last phase was concluded by July 9 with the deportation of more than 55,000 Jews from Zone V, comprised of Transdanubia and the outskirts of Budapest. According to Veesenmayer's reports, a total of 437,402 Jews were deported from the five zones. (There appears a slight difference, within a few thousand, between Vessenmayer's figures and other sources.)

• The bulk of the transports reached Auschwitz via central Slovakia by freight train. Each freight car was to carry about 45 persons but actually, in most cases, 80-100 persons were crammed in under hardly bearable conditions. Thousands of sick people, the elderly and babies died on the trains during the three to five days of the journey due to lack of water and ventilation.

• The ghettoization and deportation were not condemned by Hungarian public opinion, and instances of overt sympathy and willingness to help and rescue were an exception to the rule. Noteworthy among the few protests was the outspoken plea of Aron Marton, the Catholic Bishop of Alba-Iulia. Hungarian authorities expelled him from Kolozsvar (now Cluj) in May, 1944 for preaching in defense of the Jews. Attempts were made throughout the country to evade deportations, but most of them were only successful in northern Transylvania due to its common border with Romania. The number of Jews who managed to cross the southern Transylvanian border and escape to Romania in April-June is estimated at 2,000-2,500. In addition, a few hundred Jews went into hiding in the countryside, especially in northern Transylvania. Likewise, some hundreds of Jews were spared deportation when exempted by the authorities on grounds of military or other merit. A few thousand provincial Jews managed to evade deportation by either hiding in Budapest or living in the Budapest ghettos alongside the bulk of the capital's Jewish population.

The ghettoization and deportation were not condemned by Hungarian public opinion... willingness to help and rescue were an exception to the rule.

• 95% of the deportees were directed to Auschwitz where, under camp commander Rudolf Hess, large-scale preparations had been made for their mass murder. The able-bodied were dispersed to 386 camps throughout the German-held Eastern territories and in the Reich. A small percentage of provincial Jews managed to evade deportation to Auschwitz. In the framework of a deal made by Rudolph Kastner with Eichmann (see below), some transports totaling several thousand (mostly from Debrecen, Szeged and Szolnok) were directed to Austria. This group was spared selections, families remained united and the majority survived.

• In January 1943, a Zionist relief and rescue committee was formed in Budapest to help Jews in the neighboring countries. Otto Komoly was president of the committee, Kastner its vice-president, with Joel Brand responsible for underground rescue from Poland. Shortly after the German occupation, Kastner and Brand established contact with Eichmann. Their names, especially that of Kastner became linked with the transaction known as *Blut fuer Ware* ("Blood for Goods"). Brand was sent to Istanbul to mediate between the Allies and Germans for war materials, particularly trucks, in exchange for Hungarian Jewish lives, a mission doomed to failure. Kastner went to Switzerland several times to meet with representatives of the American Jewish Joint Distribution Committee, the Jewish Agency and the War Refugee Board in order to work out a rescue plan and arrange for its financing by Jewish organizations. Kastner succeeded in concluding a deal with Eichmann resulting in the transport on June 30, 1944, of 1,658 Jews from Hungary to Switzerland at the fixed price of $1,000 per head. Two other transports on August 18 and December 6, consisted of 318 and 1,368 Jews respectively, most of whom were of Hungarian and Transylvanian origin.

The first group was first detained at Bergen-Belsen but, as a result of Himmler's intervention, finally reached Switzerland by the end of December.

• After deportations from the provinces were completed, preparations began for the deportation of Budapest's Jews. The timing of the Budapest deportations was to follow the completion of the "*Entjudung*" ("ridding of Jews") of the provinces and was set for technical, economic and tactical reasons. On June 15, 1944, the Ministry of the Interior ordered the concentration of the Budapest Jews in some 2,000 houses marked with a yellow star and was designated to enclose about 200,000 Jews.

• On June 25, a curfew was ordered for the capital's Jews, who from this date led the life of prisoners, in utter destitution. A series of foreign interventions on behalf of the Jews that began in May increased in June, taking on a more organized form and exerting a favorable influence upon the fate of Budapest Jewry.

• In June, the Swiss press, and subsequently the press in other neutral states and in the Allied countries, published details about the fate of Hungarian Jewry. The press campaign and the activity of Jewish leaders in Switzerland brought about a series of interventions with Horthy. Among others, the king of Sweden, the Vatican and the International Red Cross intervened. (Neither the Vatican nor the Red Cross exerted any real effort to save Jewish lives during the War, as recent revelations regarding the Red Cross

Neither the Vatican nor the Red Cross exerted any real effort to save Jewish lives during the War.

Awaiting the gas chambers

have borne out.) Among the Hungarian personalities who interceded with Horthy for the cessation of the deportations were Protestant bishops and Prince-Primate Justinianus Seredi. These interventions, along with the concealed intention of the Hungarian government to create favorable conditions in case of a separate armistice treaty with the Allies, brought a halt to further deportations on July 8. At the same time, Baky and Endre, the chief Hungarian organizers of the "*Entjudung*," were dismissed.

Arrow-Cross leader, Ferenc Szalasi, surrounded by American soldiers during his arrest for war crimes (1946)

- At the end of July, Himmler also gave his approval to the suspension of the deportations. Meanwhile, as many Jews as possible were successfully placed under the protection of some neutral countries such as Sweden, Switzerland and Portugal.
- In August a turning point was reached when Horthy and his supporters dismissed the Sztojay government. A new government less servile to the Germans was formed under General Geza Lakatos with the aim of preparing the armistice with the Allies. Throughout July and August, the situation of the Budapest Jews and of the labor conscripts appeared more hopeful. However, on September 4, the Lakatos government declared war against Romania, which had joined the Allies on August 23. Hungarian units crossed the southern Transylvanian border and perpetrated acts of savagery against the Jewish residents in the strip they occupied up to the beginning of October. They massacred the whole Jewish population of Sarmas and Sarmasel (126 persons), committed murders at Ludus and Arad and made preparations for the introduction of anti-Jewish measures in the temporarily occupied territories.

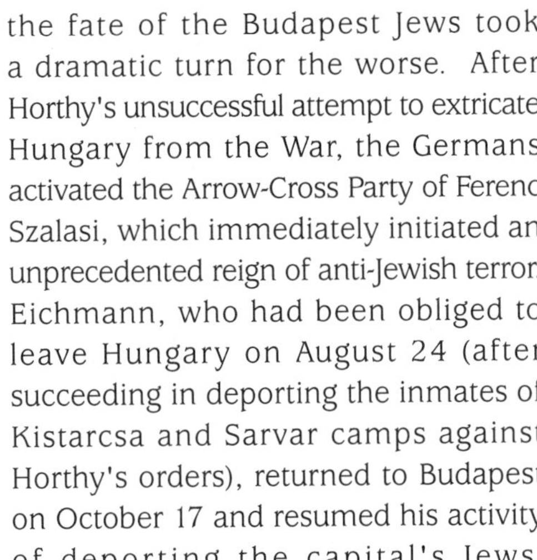

- On October 15, the fate of the Budapest Jews took a dramatic turn for the worse. After Horthy's unsuccessful attempt to extricate Hungary from the War, the Germans activated the Arrow-Cross Party of Ferenc Szalasi, which immediately initiated an unprecedented reign of anti-Jewish terror. Eichmann, who had been obliged to leave Hungary on August 24 (after succeeding in deporting the inmates of Kistarcsa and Sarvar camps against Horthy's orders), returned to Budapest on October 17 and resumed his activity of deporting the capital's Jews.

After October 15, the Budapest Jews were divided into two groups: the majority were enclosed in a central ghetto, while the smaller segment lived in the quarters "protected" by the neutral states. As a preliminary step in the deportations, the Jewish male population aged 16 to 60 was ordered out to work in fortifications. In accordance with the deportation plans, transports of about 50,000 Jews were to leave in November for Austria and the Reich. However, these plans were thwarted by the military situation on the Eastern front.

• On November 2, Soviet troops reached the outskirts of Budapest. Under these circumstances, the labor battalions were driven toward western Hungary and on November 8, a group of about 25,000 Budapest Jews were directed on foot toward Hegyrshalom at the Austrian border. They were later followed by other contingents of up to 60,000 Jews. A high percentage of persons on this "death march" perished on the way.

• From the Arrow-Cross seizure of power until the Soviet occupation of Budapest (January 18, 1945), about 98,000 of the capital's Jews lost their lives in forced marches and train transports, as well as through Arrow-Cross extermination squads, starvation, diseases and cases of suicide. Some of the victims were shot and thrown into the Danube.

Resistance and Rescue

• Organized resistance among Budapest Jews made itself felt only in the autumn months, but failed to develop on a large scale. A few small, armed groups were active in Budapest, attacking Arrow-Cross men and performing rescue operations. In several cases, armed Jewish youths, disguised as Arrow-Cross men or as soldiers, prevented executions and killed Szalasi's men. One form of resistance was the Zionist Halutz Movement rescue activities, which consisted of forging identity cards, supplying money, food and clothing, and facilitating escape or safe hiding places. An attempt by the *Haganah* to activate the rescue work by aiding Hungarian-born Jews from Palestine failed in the summer of 1944. A few members of the *Haganah* were parachuted by the British into Yugoslav territory, from where they crossed into Hungary, but were captured. Two of them, Perez Goldstein and Hannah Szenes, were executed.

Budapest under attack

Organized resistance among Budapest Jews made itself felt only in the autumn months, but failed to develop on a large scale.

The Soviet occupation of Hungary brought freedom to the Jews of the Budapest ghettos and to those labor conscripts who were within the borders.

- The rescue operation by some neutral states proved to be efficient. Up to the end of October 1944, more than 1,600 Jews in Budapest were provided with San Salvador documents. By the end of the year, the number of Jews receiving protection of neutral states and of the International Red Cross in the "protected houses" rose to 33,000.
- The Arrow-Cross authorities recognized, among others, 7,800 Swiss and 4,500 Swedish safe-conduct passes. Prominent figures in this rescue work were Charles Lutz, a Swiss diplomat, and Raoul Wallenberg, secretary of the Swedish Legation in Budapest.
- By September-October 1944, northern Transylvania was occupied by Soviet armies, followed by Hungary's eastern, southern and northeastern strip. The Soviet forces occupied Budapest on January 18, 1945, and by early April all "Trianon" Hungary.[6] The Soviet occupation of Hungary brought freedom to the Jews of the Budapest ghettos and to those labor conscripts who were within the borders.

Demographic Total

- Statistical data on the destruction of Hungarian Jewry show that about 69,000 Jews were saved in Budapest's Central Ghetto and 25,000 in the "Protected Ghetto." In addition to these two categories, which also include persons safeguarded in the buildings of some neutral diplomatic missions, about 25,000 Jews came out of hiding in Budapest. A few thousand survived in Red Cross children's homes.
- An exact assessment of the number of Jews who returned to Hungary is difficult to calculate since northern Transylvania, Sub-Carpathian Ruthenia, Felvidek and Baeska were once again detached from Hungary. Throughout the first post war months there was a large-scale fluctuation of population between "Trianon" Hungary and the so-called "succession states" (territories given to Romania, Czechoslovakia and Russia).
- The number of Jewish forced laborers who returned to Hungary or were liberated there, including those who later returned from Soviet captivity, may be estimated at 20,000. By the end of 1945, some 70,000 deportees had returned. The number of Jews saved in all these categories in postwar Hungary totaled 200,000. The losses of Hungarian Jewry from the Trianon territories was 300,000. A relatively high proportion of the survivors were non-Jews who were, however, considered Jews according to the racial laws.
- A total number of about 25,000-40,000 Jews who were saved returned to northern Transylvania, some 15,000 to Sub-Carpathian Ruthenia and about

The fallen German Eagle

6. Hungary and the Allies signed the Treaty of Trianon in 1920, which was part of the WWI peace settlements. Hungary was stripped of more than two-thirds of its territory. Parts of Hungary went to Czechoslovakia, Romania, Austria, and the kingdom of the Serbs, Croats and Slovens (later known as Yugoslavia). Hungary's present boundaries are about the same as those set by this treaty.

10,000 to Felvidek, which was reapportioned to Czechoslovakia. The number of Jews who returned to Baeska is estimated at a few thousand.

- The relatively small number of survivors outside Hungary, who failed to return in 1945 to their former homes, cannot be assessed.
- Of the 825,000 persons considered Jews in the 1941-45 period in greater Hungary, about 565,000 perished and about 260,000 survived the Holocaust.

Contemporary Period

- As a result of the Holocaust, the demographic composition and geographical distribution of Hungarian Jewry had radically changed after the War. When the survivors of the death camps and forced labor returned to Hungary, a few took up residence in their previous homes and 266 communities were reestablished (out of 473). In the following years, however, most left the provincial towns and the Jewish communities there ceased to exist. When possible over the subsequent decades, Jews emigrated to Israel.
- The postwar Hungarian regime abolished the anti-Jewish legislation enacted by its predecessor. The men who had governed during the War and many who had been directly responsible for the deportation and destruction of Jews were brought to trial and sentenced to death, and thousands of other war criminals were imprisoned. On the other hand, no comprehensive law was passed for the restitution of Jewish property that had been confiscated or forcibly sold, and the existing regulations and ordinances did not provide a solution for this vital problem. Although anti-Semitism was officially banned, there were strong anti-Jewish sentiments among the population, which blamed the Jews for the country's postwar economic plight. This was felt particularly in the provincial towns, whose inhabitants resented the return of the surviving Jewish deportees.
- In May 1946, there was a pogrom in Kunmadaras, and in July, another took place in Miskolc in which five Jews were killed and many injured. Anti-Semitic feelings were also voiced in the political literature of this period in which the Jews were warned "not to try to capitalize on their sufferings during the War." The pogroms ceased by the end of 1946 when the economy stabilized, but popular anti-Semitism continued to exist and found expression in such acts as the desecration of cemeteries. Recurrent anti-Semitism strengthened the desire of the Jews to emigrate in the subsequent decades.
- The Jewish community in Hungary continued to exist throughout the Communist years. There was an exodus of Jews after the failed Hungarian revolution of 1956, but Jewish communal institutions remained even under those difficult conditions including a Rabbinical Seminary in Budapest, the only one permitted by the Communists. With the collapse of the Communist regime attempts have been made to revive Jewish life in Hungary, including the opening of the large Chabad-Lauder School in Budapest, the restoration of several synagogues and the opening of a Jewish camp for young people from across Eastern Europe. These signs of renewed life flourish in a community that is but a remnant of a remnant of a world that once was.

Recurrent anti-Semitism strengthened the desire of the Jews to emigrate in the subsequent decades.

HUNGARIAN SYNAGOGUES THROUGH THE CENTURIES

Photos Credit: World Federation of Hungarian Jews: The Synagogues of Hungary, 1968

Legend:

1. Nagyvarad Orthodox Synagogue on Zarda Street **2.** Chust **3.** 18th Century Shul in Naznanfalva. First synagogue built from wood in Hungary. **4.** Debrecen **5.** Kazinczy Street Orthodox Synagogue, Budapest. View from women's balcony. **6.** Sopron Synagogue from the 14th Century. Notice fortress-like windows and small *Aron Kodesh* recessed into the wall.

AN OVERVIEW: THE HISTORY OF JEWISH LIFE IN ROMANIA

Once part of the Roman Empire, as its name and language indicate, Romania[7] has had a long and varied history. At various times its territory has been occupied by Hungarians, Turks, and Russians, but after World War I Romania emerged as a united country. The area of Romania is 91,699 square miles (237,500 square kilometers). It is bounded on the north and east by Ukraine and Moldova, on the northwest by Hungary, on the southwest by Yugoslavia, on the south by Bulgaria, and on the southeast by the Black Sea. About 30 percent of the country is covered by mountains. The main ranges are the Eastern and Southern Carpathians. Some peaks in the Eastern Carpathians reach more than 7,500 feet (2,280 meters) in height, while the Southern Carpathians reach 8,346 feet (2,544 meters) at the peak of Moldoveanul, the highest point in Romania. In the west there is a smaller area of mountains known as the Western Carpathians. They reach more than 5,900 feet (1,800 meters) in height. Bordering the Carpathian ranges are zones of hills and tablelands. The longest river is the Danube, which flows for 668 miles (1,075 kilometers) through Romanian territory to the Black Sea.

The Jewish Presence in Romania

• The territory of present-day Romania was known as Dacia in antiquity. Jews may have come as merchants (and in other capacities) with the Roman legions who occupied the country from 101 C.E. Another wave of Jewish immigrants spread through Walachia (a Romanian principality founded circa 1290) after expulsion from Hungary in 1367. In the 16th century some of the refugees from Spain came to Walachia from their places of refuge on the Balkan Peninsula.

• Some Jews served as physicians and diplomats at the court of the sovereigns of Walachia. Since this was on the trade routes between Poland-Lithuania and the Ottoman Empire, many Jewish merchants traveled through Moldavia, the second Romanian principality (in the northeast) founded in the middle of the 14th century. A number of Jews settled there and were favorably received by the rulers of this underpopulated principality.

• At the beginning of the 16th century there were Jewish communities in such Moldavian towns as Jassy, Botosani, Suceava and Siret. More intensive waves of Jewish immigration resulted from the Chmielnicki massacres in 1648-49.

The territory of present-day Romania was known as Dacia in antiquity. Jews may have come as merchants with the Roman legions.

7. Material for this section was adapted from the, **Encyclopedia Judaica**, Keter Publishing House, Jerusalem, 1976, Vol. 14, pages 386-416.

Shul of Mareh Yechezkel in Alba Iulia

From the beginning of the 18th century, the Moldavian rulers granted special charters to attract Jews from Poland, including:

1. Exemption from taxes.
2. Land for prayer houses and *mikvaos*.
3. Land for cemeteries.
4. The right of representation in local town councils.

• Jews were invited to reestablish war-ravaged towns (1761, Succeava) and to enlarge others (1796, Focsani). The newcomers were encouraged by the landowners to found commercial centers called burgs. In some cases these newcomers undertook the task of attracting Jews from other countries.

The Jews brought their scholarship, business acumen and disciplined organized community life with them.

• When two counties of Moldavia were annexed (Bukovina by Austria in 1775 and Bessarabia by Russia in 1812), the Jews from these counties relocated in Romanian Moldavia where they lived peacefully and had both family and business connections. Jewish merchants exported leather, cattle and corn. Many of the Jews were craftsmen including: furriers, tailors, bookmakers, tin-smiths and watchmakers.

• As has happened so often in the diaspora, Jews were encouraged to settle in sparsely populated and underdeveloped towns, cities and provinces by the local governmental officials or royalty. The Jews brought their scholarship, business acumen and disciplined organized community life with them. They developed the political and economic viability of the area and then became victims of their success, suffering from the jealousy of the local population and eventually the many anti-Semitic measures of violence and expulsion. Most often these measures were fomented by the Church, and Romania was no exception.

• From an early date one of the main components of anti-Jewish hatred in Romania was commercial competition. In 1579 the sovereign of Moldavia, Petru Schiopul (Peter the Lance) ordered the banishment of the Jews on the grounds that they were ruining the native merchants. In the Danube harbors it was the Greek and Bulgarian merchants who incited riots against the Jews,

The Carpathian Mountains

Rural Romanian town

especially during Easter. Anti-Jewish excesses which occurred in the neighboring countries often extended to Romania.

• In 1652 and 1653 Cossacks invaded Romania, murdering a great number of Jews in Jassy (later the site of Nazi and Romanian atrocities against the Jews of that region during WW II).

• The Greek Orthodox Church preached intolerance toward Jews and shaped the first codes of law: the Church Laws of Moldavia and Walachia in 1640. These laws proclaimed Jews as heretics and forbade all relations with them, and with the exception of physicians Jews were not accepted as witnesses in trials. In Romanian civil law codes of 1746 and 1780 the Jews are scarcely mentioned. The first books of anti-Semitic propaganda of a religious nature, the "Golden Order" (Jassy, 1771) and "A Challenge for Jews" (Jassy, 1803), appeared at this time as well.

Emerging Romania

• Modern day trouble for the Jews of Romania began in 1821, with the first awakening of Romanian independence and unity. In the course of the rebellion against the Turks and the Ottoman Empire, Greek military volunteers crossed Moldavia on their way to the Danube, plundering and slaying Jews in Jassy, Herta [now Gertsa], Odobesti, Vaslui and Roman.

• Between 1819 and 1834 Moldavia and Walachia were occupied by Russia and were granted a unifying constitution. From 1835 to 1856 these two principalities were protectorates of Russia, under whose influence anti-Semitism increased. From then on the prevailing attitude was that the Jews exploited the Christian population in order to enrich themselves, and, therefore, all Jewish immigration must be stopped. Fashioned after the Russian model (Pale of Settlement), Jews were forbidden to settle in villages, to lease lands and to establish factories in towns. Citizenship was denied to Jews and corrupt Romanian administrators used this legislation to add to their income by persecuting the Jews.

• Legislation enacted in 1839 and 1843 included special measures directed against Jews, allowing local authorities to determine which Jews were useful to the country, while all others were declared vagrants and expelled.

Communal Institutions

• In 1719, a *Chacham Bashi*, Bezalel Cohen, was appointed for Walachia and Moldavia by the Suzerain, the Sultan. The *Chacham Bashi* resided in Jassy and had a representative for Walachia in Bucharest. His status was hereditary and included the right of collecting

Modern day trouble for the Jews of Romania began in 1821, with the first awakening of Romanian independence and unity.

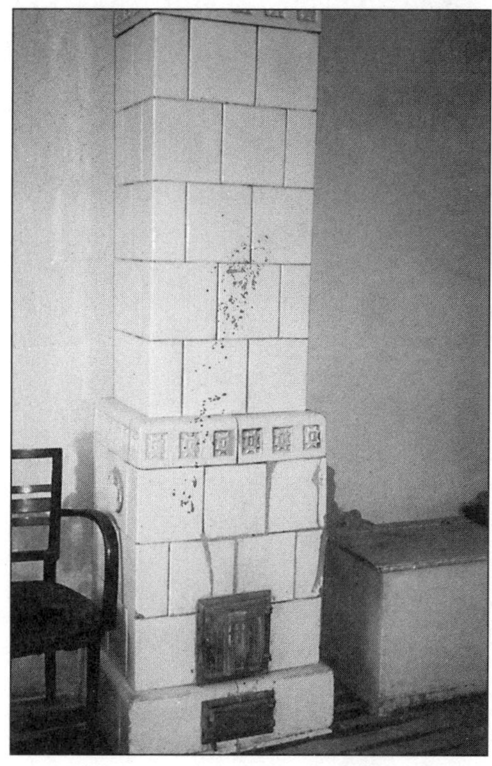

The stove from the Mareh Yechezkel Shul in Alba Iulia

taxes on religious ceremonies, collection of taxes from each family (30,000 taxpayers in the two principalities in 1803), as well as granting exemption from taxes and tolls as appropriate. Yet, his prestige was limited and the true Torah scholars were considered the real spiritual leaders.

• The growing Russian and Galician element in the Jewish population at the beginning of the 19th century opposed the *Chacham Bashi*, since such an institution was unknown to them and many of them were followers of *chassidic* leaders. Being foreign subjects, the Russian and Galician Jews asked the political consuls of their respective native countries to intercede on their behalf. In 1819, the Prince of Moldavia decided that the *Chacham Bashi* should have jurisdiction only over "native" Jews. Ultimately, because of permanent strife among the diverse groups of Jews and their complaints to the authorities, the Prince abolished the office of the *Chacham Bashi* in 1834.

Along with the office of the Chacham Bashi, a Jews' Guild also existed. It acted as the legal body of the community.

• Along with the office of the *Chacham Bashi*, a Jews' Guild also existed. It was one of 32 guilds organized according to nationality (Armenians, Greeks, etc.) or profession. The guild was responsible for tax collection from its members. The Jews' Guild acted as the legal body of the community. The collective tax was paid from the tax on kosher meat, while the expenses of the institutions (Talmud Torah, synagogue, cemetery) were covered with the remainder.

• When the office of the *Chacham Bashi* was abolished, the Jews' Guild ceased as well. With no internal organization to conduct communal affairs, communal structures weakened considerably. The collective tax, formerly fixed by the guild, was now imposed by the government and the functions of the community fell upon the various synagogues, artisans' guilds, and, in several cases, on the *Chevrah Kadisha* or the Jewish Hospital (in Jassy).

Independent Romania

• Both in the 1821 revolt against the Ottoman-appointed rulers, as well as in the 1848 revolt against Russia, the revolutionary parties appealed for the participation of the Jews, proclaiming their civic equality. Some Jews took part in the 1848 revolt, which was quelled by the Russians.

• The Peace Treaty of Paris (1856) that concluded the Crimean War and granted the principalities a certain autonomy under the Ottoman Sultan, proclaimed, interalia, that in the two Danubian principalities all the inhabitants, irrespective of religion, are granted religious and civil liberties (including the right to own property and to trade) and to occupy political positions. This did not apply to foreign nationals. Leaders of Moldavian and Walachian Jewry addressed themselves to both the Romanian authorities and the great international powers asking for the abolition of discriminatory laws against Jews. This initiative was blocked by the opposition of Russia and the Romanian political leaders.

• In 1859, these two principalities united under Alexandru Ioan Cuza, a member of the 1848 Revolutionary Group. Cuza was not an anti-Semite. The Jewish population at that time was 130,000 or 3% of the total Romanian population.

• In 1864, native Jews were granted suffrage in their local councils. However, Jews who were foreign nationals could not own land. Political rights were granted to non-Christians at this time, but only Parliament could vote on the naturalization of individual Jews. Not a single Jew was naturalized.

Gypsy wagons in the town of Bisritz, near the marketplace

• In 1866, Cuza was ousted by anti-liberal forces. A new sovereign, Carol of Hohoenzollern-Sigmaringen, was elected and a new constitution adopted. Under pressure from demonstrations organized by the police (during which the Choir Temple in Bucharest was demolished and the Jewish quarter plundered), the seventh article of the constitution restricting citizenship solely to the Christian population was adopted.

• In the spring of 1867, the Minister of the Interior, Ion Bratianu, expelled Jews from a number of villages and banished non-citizens from the country. In the summer of the same year, Sir Moses Montefiore arrived in Bucharest and demanded that Prince Carol put a stop to these persecutions – they continued despite the assurances he was given. Hundreds of Jewish families, harassed by humiliating regulations (*succos* were prohibited, etc.), were forced to leave their villages. Local officials regarded such regulations as an effective method of extorting bribes (a repressive act against Jews that took place in more than one European country). Neither the repeated interventions of Great Britain and France, nor the condemnatory resolutions in the Parliaments of Holland and Germany had any effect in reversing this situation. The Romanian government reiterated that the Jewish problem was an internal one and the great powers limited themselves to protests.

• At the Congress of Berlin (1878), which finalized Romanian independence, the great powers made Jewish civil rights a condition for independence in spite of opposition by the Romanian and Russian delegates. Romanian representatives threatened delegates of international Jewish organizations, as well as the representatives of Romanian Jewry, by hinting at a worsening of their situation. Indeed, after the Congress of Berlin other anti-Semitic measures were introduced, and there was a general incitement against the Jewish population in the press and public demonstrations organized by the authorities following the Russian model of an organized governmental anti-Semitic policy. This was done to prove to the great powers that the Romanian people were against Jewish emancipation.

At the Congress of Berlin (1878), which finalized Romanian independence, the great powers made Jewish civil rights a condition for independence in spite of opposition by the Romanian and Russian delegates.

A farmer with scythe in hand–Sharmosh, Romania

• Additionally, their aim was to create an anti-Semitic hysteria on the eve of the parliamentary session that would decide on modification of the constitutional article limiting Jewish naturalization. Prince Carol, upon opening Parliament, declared that the Jews were a harmful influence on economic life, especially regarding the peasants. After several stormy debates, Parliament did modify the article making citizenship conditional on Christianity (sort of a quasi-apostate status), and enacting that naturalization would be carried out individually and by vote of both chambers of Parliament. During the following 38 years only 2,000 Jews were naturalized by this oppressive procedure; 883 being voted in as one group for having taken part in the 1877 war against Turkey.

Prince Carol, upon opening Parliament, declared that the Jews were a harmful influence on economic life, especially regarding the peasants.

• This legislative action caused the great powers to withhold, for a time, recognition of an independent Romania. Eventually, however, they followed the example of Germany and granted Romania the recognition she sought. Meanwhile, the situation of the Jews continued to deteriorate. Up to this point, they had been considered Romanian subjects, but now they were declared to be foreigners. The Romanian government persuaded Austria and Germany to withdraw their citizenship from Jews living in Romania, and Jews were forbidden to be lawyers, teachers, chemists, stockbrokers, or to sell commodities which were a government monopoly (tobacco, salt, alcohol). They were not accepted as railway officials, as workers in state hospitals, or as law officers.

• In 1893, Jewish pupils were expelled from public schools.

• Both liberal and conservative political parties were highly anti-Semitic, with only slight degrees of difference between them politically. In 1910, the first specifically anti-Semitic party, the National Democratic Party, was founded under the leadership of university professors, A.C. Cuza and Nicolae Iorga.

Social Structure

• The Jewish population of Romania was for the most part an urban one. According to the 1899 census, 79.73%

1899: % OF JEWISH POPULATION: A SAMPLING OF TOWNS IN MOLDAVIA	
Falaticeni	**57%**
Dorohoi	**53.6%**
Botosani	**51.8%**
Jassy	**50.8%**
Gertsa	**66.2%**
Mihaileni	**65.6%**
Harlau	**59.6%**
Panciu	**52.4%**

Bread store in rural Romanian town. No electricity, just bread.

of the Jews lived in cities, forming 32.10% of the entire urban population of the country. Only 20.27% lived in villages, forming 1.1% of the entire rural population. This phenomenon was a result of the ban on Jews dwelling in rural areas. In the Maldovian province, where the Jews were most heavily concentrated, they formed the majority ethnic group in several towns.

• The Romanian population was 84.06% agrarian, with the Jews constituting the middle class. According to 1904 statistics, 21.1% of the total number of merchants were Jews, but in some cities of Moldavia they were a definite majority including: Jassy, 75.3%; Botosani, 75.2%; Dorohoi, 72.9%; and Tecuci, 65.9%. Jews represented 20.07% of all artisans, and in several branches they were the majority.

• Industry was not advanced in Romania before World War I. Of the 625 industrial firms, 122 (19.5%) of them were owned by Jews. Jews comprised 5.3% of the officials and workers in these industrial enterprises. In several branches of industry, Jews represented a significant percent of factory ownership.

• In the arts and science professions only medicine was permitted to Jews, and they constituted 38% of the total number of doctors.

• The provinces of Bessarabia, Transylvania and Bukovina were annexed to Old Romania after the fall of the Austro-Hungarian Empire in World War I. This caused a threefold increase in the Jewish population. In every province their occupational structure differed according to the historical development of that area. In the two annexed provinces of Transylvania and Bukovina, Jews enjoyed civil rights from the days of the Austro-Hungarian Empire and were also represented in the liberal professions. On the other hand, their situation in Bessarabia in czarist times was worse than in Old Romania, a fact which also influenced their occupational structure.

• The only census taken in Bessarabia was in 1930 and, according to those

1904: % OF JEWISH ARTISANS IN SELECTED TRADES IN MOLDAVIA	
Engraving	**81.3%**
Tinsmith	**76%**
Watchmakers	**75.9%**
Bookbinders	**74.6%**
Hatters	**64.9%**
Upholsterers	**64.3%**

In every province the Jews' occupational structure differed according to the historical development of that area.

PERCENT OF FACTORY OWNERSHIP BY JEWS	
Glass	52.8%
Wood/Furniture	32.4%
Clothing	32.4%
Textile	26.4%

ROMANIA: DISTRIBUTION OF JEWS BY OCCUPATION	
Agriculture	2.5%
Industry & Crafts	42.5%
Trade & Banking	37.9%
Liberal Professions	3.2%
Various Other	13.7%

figures, the occupational distribution of the Jewish population was as follows: industry and crafts, 24.8%; trade and banking, 51.5%; liberal professions, 2.9%; miscellaneous, 8.2%. It should be noted that Jewish bankers (such as the bank of "Maramaros-Blank") invested money in the developing industry of Greater Romania. Some industrial enterprises, comprising several factories such as the sugar, metal and textile workers, etc., were owned by Jews. In the late 1930s, under the influence of the Nazi movement in Romania, the whole occupational structure of the Jews collapsed because of economic persecution. These economic actions preceded the eventual political persecutions, atrocities and murder.

Since most Romanian Jews were of Polish or Russian extraction, their religious and cultural traditions were similar to the Jews of Eastern Europe.

Cultural Life

• Since most Romanian Jews were of Polish or Russian extraction, their religious and cultural traditions were similar to those of the Jews of Eastern Europe. *Chassidism* was particularly widespread in the Moldavia province which borders on Galicia (southern Poland) and Russia. *Chassidic* centers were established at the "courts" of the *Tzaddikim* of the Ruzhin dynasty in the towns of Stefanesti, Buhusi, Adjud and Focsani.

Holocaust Period

• German penetration into the Romanian economy increased as the Nazis moved eastward with the *Anschluss* of Austria in 1938, and was followed with the annexation of Czechoslovakia in 1939 and the occupation of western Poland at the outbreak of World War II. A considerable number of Romanian politicians agreed to serve German interests in exchange for directorships in German-Romanian enterprises. German trade agreements with Romania always demanded the removal of Jews in the branch involved. In this way, Jews were stripped of economic viability.

Main Shul in Sighet
(see Weisshaus Interview)

• In the summer of 1940, Romania succumbed to German pressure and transferred Bessarabia and part of Bukovina to the Soviet Union, northern Transylvania to Hungary and southern Dobrudja to Bulgaria (the territory that remained was called Old Romania). When the Romanian army retreated from these areas, its soldiers murdered many Jews, particularly in northern Bukovina and Moldavia; they also threw Jewish travelers from moving trains.

• On June 30, 1940, 52 Jews were murdered in Dorohoi by a retreating Romanian regiment. Hoping to ensure its borders after the concessions, Romania, which had not been invaded by the German army, became a satellite of Nazi Germany. The first consequence of this move was the cancellation of Romanian citizenship for Jews, a measure taken by the government, (including members of the fascist Iron Guard) under direct German pressure in August of 1940.

• On September 6, when King Carol abdicated, Ion Antonescu, former Minister of Defense in the Goga government, came to power. His government included ministers from the ranks of the Iron Guard, and Romania was declared a Nationalist-Legionary State (the members of the Iron Guard styled themselves as "legionnaires"). The Legionary Police were organized along Nazi lines with the help of the Nazi S.S. A five-month period of anti-Semitic terrorism followed. It began with the confiscation of some Jewish owned shops, posting signs identifying other businesses as Jewish owned and picketing by the green-shirted Legionary Police. The reign of terror reached its height when Jewish industrial and commercial enterprises were handed over to the members of the Legion under pressure from the Iron Guard. The owners of the enterprises were arrested and tortured by the Legionary Police until they agreed to sign certificates of transfer. Bands of legionnaires entered Jewish homes confiscating any sums of money they found. This resulted in a mortal blow to the Romanian economy. The ensuing chaos frightened even the German diplomats. On several occasions Antonescu tried to stop the waves of terrorism, during which a number of Romanian statesmen opposed to the Iron Guard were killed.

• On January 21, 1941, the Iron Guard revolted against Antonescu and attempted to seize power and carry out its total anti-Semitic program. While part of the Legion was fighting the Romanian army for control of government offices and strategic points in the city, the rest carried out a pogrom against Bucharest's Jews, aided by local hooligans. Jewish homes were looted, shops burned and many synagogues desecrated, including two that were razed to the ground: the Great Sephardi Synagogue and the old *Beis Hamedrash*. Some of the leaders of the Bucharest community were imprisoned in the community council building and worshipers were ejected from synagogues.

• The Palestine Office of the Zionist Organization was attacked and its director murdered. Wealthy Bucharest

Hoping to ensure its borders after the concessions, Romania, which had not been invaded by the German army, became a satellite of Nazi Germany.

Frasin–a small farm town

Jews were arrested and taken to detention centers of the Iron Guard. This pogrom claimed 120 Jewish lives.

Names of towns where Jews once lived

Jews were arrested, based on a previously prepared list. They were taken to detention centers of the Iron Guard movement. Some were brought into the forests near Bucharest and shot, while others were murdered and their bodies hung on meat hooks in the municipal slaughter-house bearing placards stating "kosher meat." This pogrom claimed 120 Jewish lives.[8] There were no acts of violence in the provinces because the army, loyal to Antonescu, was in firm control. This was also Hitler's reason for supporting Antonescu, since Romania held an important role in the anticipated war against the Soviet Union, not only as a supply and military jumping-off point, but as an active partner in the invasion of Russia itself. Therefore, a radicalized and destabilized population would not serve Hitler's purpose.

A period of relative calm followed the Bucharest pogrom, permitting Romanian Jews to gather strength after such a violent attack.

- A period of relative calm followed the Bucharest pogrom, permitting Romanian Jews to gather strength after such a violent attack. Thereafter, however, Antonescu, was under constant German pressure because after their failed revolt, members of the Iron Guard sought refuge in Germany where they constituted a permanent threat to Antonescu's government. Unfortunately he lacked the full support of his own party to serve as a counterbalance.
- In January 1941, Manfred von Illinger, a veteran Nazi known for his anti-Semitic activities, was appointed German

8. A subsequent pogrom in Jassy on the eve of the German invasion of Russia resulted in 14,000 deaths. An eyewitness reports that "Where the slaughter had been the heaviest the feet slipped in blood; everywhere the hysterical and ferocious toil of the pogrom filled the houses and streets with shots, with weeping, with terrible screams and with cruel laughter." (Levin, Nora, **The Holocaust**, Crowell Publishers, New York, 1968, pages 568-569)

ambassador to Romania. In April he was joined by Gustav Richter, an adviser on Jewish affairs attached to Adolf Eichmann's department. Richter's special task was to bring Romanian anti-Jewish legislation into line with that of Germany.

During the War

• On June 22, 1941, when Germany invaded Russia, the Romanian and German armies were scattered along the banks of the Prut River in order to penetrate into Bukovina and Bessarabia. This front line was activated on July 3 and even though a war for national survival was taking place, Romanian and German soldiers occupied themselves with slaughtering the Jewish population of Jassy on June 29, 1941. When the Romanian soldiers finally went into action, they were joined by units of *Einstatzgruppe D*, under the command of Otto Ohlendorf (may his name be obliterated). Their combined advance through Bessarabia, Bukovina and the Dorohoi district was accompanied by massacres of the local Jewish population.

• At the beginning of August, 1941, the Romanians ended their deportations of Jews from Bukovina and Bessarabia over the Dniester River into a German-occupied area of the U.S.S.R. (later to be known as Transnistria). The Germans refused to accept the deportees, shooting some and returning the rest. Many Jews drowned in the river, while others were shot by the Romanian *Gendarmerie* on the western bank. Approximately 25,000 Jews crossed the Dniester near Sampol, but only 16,500 were returned by the Germans. Some of these survivors were killed by the Romanians and some died of weakness and starvation on the way to camps in Bukovina and Bessarabia. Half of the 320,000 Jews living in Bessarabia, Bukovina and the Dorohoi district (which was in Old Romania) were murdered during the first few months of Romania's involvement in the War from July 3 until September 1, 1941.

Jewish orphans in Romania

• After this period the Jews were concentrated in ghettos if they lived in cities, and in special camps if they lived in the countryside or in townlets such as Secureni, Yedintsky and Vertyuzhani. German killing squads and Romanian *Gendarmerie*, fashioning themselves after the Germans, habitually entered the ghettos and camps, removing Jews and murdering them.

• Jews living in villages and townlets in Old Romania (Moldavia, Walachia and southern Transylvania) were resettled in the nearest large town. The Jews of

Even though a war for national survival was taking place, Romanian and German soldiers occupied themselves with slaughtering the Jews of Jassy.

The prohibition against Jews working in certain professions and the "Rumaniazation of the economy" exacerbated the already intolerable economic situation of the Jewish population.

northern Moldavia, which bordered on the battle area, were sent to western Romania, with men under 60 sent to the Targui-Jiu camp and the women, children and aged sent to towns where the local Jewish population was ordered to care for the deportees (who owned nothing more than the clothing on their backs). The homes and property of these deportees were looted by the local population immediately after deportation.

• On September 16, 1941, 118,847 Jews in camps in Bessarabia, Bukovina and the Dorohoi district began to be deported to the region between the Dniester and the Bug rivers called Transnistria, from which the Germans had withdrawn, handing control over to the Romanians under the Tighina Agreement of August 30, 1941.

• At the intervention of the Union of Jewish Communities in Romania, an order was given to stop the deportations on October 14, nevertheless they continued until November 15, leaving all the Jews of Bessarabia and Bukovina (with the exception of 20,000 from Chernovtsky) and 2,316 of the 14,847 Jews from the Dorohoi district concentrated in Transnistria. In two months of deportations 22,000 Jews died, either because they could walk no further or from disease. The majority, however, were murdered by the *Gendarmerie* who accompanied them on their journey. All monies and other valuables were confiscated by representative of the Romanian National Bank. The Jews remaining in Old Romania and in southern Transylvania were compelled into forced labor and were subjected to various special taxes.

• The prohibition against Jews working in certain professions and the "Rumaniazation of the economy" continued, exacerbating the already intolerable economic situation of the Jewish population.

• According to the statistical table of potential victims of the "Final Solution" introduced at the Wannsee Conference, 342,000 Romanian Jews were destined for extermination. The German Embassy in Bucharest conducted an intensive propaganda campaign through its journal, *Bukarester Tageblatt*, which announced "an overall European solution to the Jewish problem" and the deportation of Jews from Romania.

• On July 22, 1942, Richter obtained Vice-Premier Mihai Antonescu's agreement to begin the deportation of Jews to Poland the following September. However, as a result of the efforts of the clandestine Jewish leadership and the pressure exerted by diplomats from neutral countries, as well as by the Papal Nuncio, A. Cassulo, Antonescu canceled the agreement. He could afford a measure of independence since Hitler was then seeking the mobilization of additional divisions of the Romanian army against the Soviet Union. Nevertheless, Eichmann's

Small Romanian town. This is the view the Jews saw when they were deported.

Bucharest office, scheming with local authorities, succeeded in deporting 7,000 Jews from Chernovtsy, Dorohoi, as well as groups from other parts of Romania to Transnistria by claiming they were "suspected of Communism" (being of Bessarabian origin and having asked to be repatriated with the Soviet Union in 1940), and had "broken forced-labor laws" and other such trumped up charges.

• At the beginning of December 1942, the Romanian government informed the Jewish leadership of a change in policy toward the Jews. Henceforth, Jews would be deported to Transnistria to emigrate to Palestine. The defeat at Stalingrad, where the Romanians had lost 18 divisions, was already anticipated and they needed to inprove their image with the international community.

• In 1942-43, the Romanian government began tentatively to consider signing a separate peace treaty with the Allies. Although the plan for large-scale Jewish emigration failed because of German opposition and lack of facilities, both small and large boats left Romania carrying "illegal" immigrants to Palestine, some of whom were refugees from Bukovina, Poland, Hungary and Slovakia.

• By August, 1944 (when Romania withdrew from the War) a total of 13 boats left Romania carrying 13,000 refugees. Yet, even this limited activity was about to cease as a result of German pressure exerted through its diplomatic missions in Romania, Bulgaria and Turkey. Two of the boats sank: the *Struma* on February 23, 1944, with 769 passengers and the *Mefkure* on August 5, 1944 with 394 passengers. Despite German efforts, the Romanian government refused the wholesale deportation of its Jews to the east.

• At the beginning of 1943, however, there was a return to the traditional economic pressures against the Jews in order to reduce the Jewish population. This was achieved by forbidding Jews to work in the civilian economy and through the most severe measure of all, forced labor (from which the wealthy managed to obtain an exemption by paying a considerable sum). In addition, various taxes were imposed on the Jewish population payable in the form of cash, clothing, shoes or hospital equipment. These measures, particularly the taxes to be remitted in cash–the largest of which was a levy of 4 billion *lei* (about $27,000,000) imposed in March 1943 – severely pressed Romanian Jewry. W. Filderman, chairman of the Council of the Union of Jewish Communities, who opposed the tax and proved that it could never be paid was deported to Transnistria for two months.

• At the end of 1943, as the Red Army drew nearer to Romania, the local Jewish leadership succeeded in obtaining the gradual return of those deported to Transnistria. Several times the Germans tried to stop this process, and even succeeded in bringing about the arrest of the leadership of a clandestine Zionist pioneering movement in January and February of 1944. However, these leaders were released through the intervention of the International Red Cross and the Swiss ambassador in Bucharest who contended that they were indispensable for organizing the emigration of those returning from Transnistria and for the supervision of Jewish refugees who had found temporary shelter in Romania.

• In March 1944, contacts were made in Ankara between Ira Hirschmann, representative of the U.S. War Refugee Board, and the Romanian ambassador,

Although the plan for large-scale Jewish emigration failed because of German opposition and lack of facilities, boats carrying "illegal" immigrants sailed to Palestine.

A. Cretzianu, at which time Hirschmann demanded the return of all those deported to Transnistria and the cessation of the persecution of Jews. At the same time the Red Army was defeating the Germans in Transnistria and there was a danger that the retreating Germans might slaughter the remaining Jews. Salvation came at the last moment, when Antonescu warned the Germans to avoid killing Jews while retreating.

• Concurrently, negotiations over Romania's withdrawal from the War were being held in Cairo and Stockholm, and thus Antonescu was eager to show goodwill toward the Jews for the sake of his own future. That spring Soviet forces conquered part of the Old Romania (Moldavia), and on August 20 an all-out attack was launched.

Following the War, successive governments did not acknowledge their obligation to restore property or possessions to the Jews.

• On August 23, King Michael arrested Antonescu and his chief ministers and declared a cease-fire. The Germans could no longer control Romania for they were dependent on the support of the Romanian army, which had been withdrawn. Eichmann, who had been sent to western Romania to organize the liquidation of Jews in this region, did not succeed.

• Fifty-seven percent of the Jewish population under Romanian rule during the War (including the Jews of Bessarabia and northern Bukovina) survived the Holocaust. Out of a pre-War Jewish population of 607,790, 43 % or 361,615 Jews were murdered. Of this number, 166,597 perished from atrocities committed during the first period of the War. 151,513 were from Bessarabia and Bukovina, with 43,505 from other parts of Old Romania. The rest died during the deportations to Transnistria or in the camps and ghettos of this region. Others were murdered while still others died in epidemics, or from famine or exposure.

• In areas from which Jews were not deported, 78.2 % of the Jewish population were left without a livelihood as a result of the discriminatory measures implemented up to 1942, the date at which statistics were last calculated. The demographic effect was that the ratio of births to deaths felt to 34.1 % births for every one-hundred deaths in 1942 from 116.5 births for every one-hundred deaths in 1934.

The End of the War[9]

• Anti-Semitic legislation was abolished on December 19, 1944, however, properties were not returned nor was indemnification paid to the Jews. The state also took its time restoring civil rights to the Jews.

• The period between the liberation of Romania and final victory over the Nazis was at least a time of accomplishment for the Jewish organizations. Under Dr. Wilhelm Filderman's leadership Jewish youth were deferred from being drafted into the anti-Semitic Romanian army.

• Anti-Semitism again reared its head because of the problems facing Romanian Soviet occupation, pillage and confiscation of property by the Soviet army, the fierce rivalry between the Soviet Communist party and the more traditional political forces, and attempts to obtain reparations from the Romanian government.

9. The remaining information in this history has been adapted from the **Encyclopedia of the Holocaust**, Macmillian Publishers, New York, 1990, Vol. 3, pages 1298-1300

Post-War Romania

• Strained economic circumstances in Romania created a strong desire among the surviving Jews to emigrate to Palestine. However, this could not be realized because of the British White Paper restricting Jewish emigration. Illegal immigration was launched by way of Yugoslavia and Hungary.

• Following the War, successive governments did not acknowledge their obligation to restore property or possessions to the Jews. The job of Jewish rehabilitation of the Jewish community fell upon the existing Jewish organizations. The solutions presented were not commensurate with the magnitude of the problem. These organizations continued working until the monarchy was abolished and the Communists seized control in 1948. At this point active Jewish organizational life came to an end.

• By war's end, more than 350,000 Romanian Jews were dead. Two-thirds of them had been killed, not by the Germans, but by Romanians and Hungarians. 300,000 more remained alive, waiting to be ransomed.

• The idea of ransoming Jews for money had a long history in Romania. During the Holocaust, as the fate of German forces in the East took a turn for the worst, Marshal Antonescu became suddenly sensitive to the prospect of Allied victory and changed his tactics. He refused to deport the Jews from "Old Romania", regions that included Walachaia, Romanian Moldova and the city of Bucharest. He decided to use Romania's surviving Jews as hostages, to be traded to the Allies for cash at the asking price of $1,336 per head. Even orphans from Transnistria were repatriated to increase his bargaining chips. Whatever his motivation, these Jews remained alive. Under Communism the Jews of Romania were also ransomed. As one eyewitness privy to the asking price described it, "Jews were traded for the price of the most valuable animal in Romania, a horse." By these means, under the leadership of Chief Rabbi Moshe Rosen, who was both the chief Rabbi and a member of the Romanian Parliament, all but some 15,000-25,000 of Romania's Jews made their way to freedom in Israel. For those who remained, mainly the elderly and those with strong ties to Romania, the institutions of the Jewish community remained – synagogues and old age homes, community centers and schools – even as the community diminished from year to year.

• By the end of 1980 only a small number of Jews remained in Romania.

The vast majority of Romanian Jews moved to Israel after the state was established. By the end of 1980 only a small number of Jews remained in Romania.

The Exodus 1947

GIANTS OF THE SPIRIT:
RABBONIM OF TRANSYLVANIA AND THE CARPATHIANS

Rabbi Yosef Panet זצ"ל
Rav of Daishe

Rabbi Moshe Teitelbaum זצ"ל
"Yismach Moshe"
Rav of Ujhely

Rabbi Eliezer Zushe
Portugal זצ"ל
Rav of Skulen

Rabbi Yosef Tzvi Duschinsky זצ"ל
Rav of Galant/Chust
Yerusholayim

Rabbi Avrohom Yehoshua
Freund זצ"ל
Rav of Nasad

Rabbi Yehuda Greenwald זצ"ל
Rav of Satmar

Rabbi Moshe Schick זצ"ל
"Maharam Schick"
Rav of Chust

Rabbi Yonoson Shteif זצ"ל
Rav of Budapest

Rabbi Yisrael Hager זצ"ל
Rav of Vishnitz

Rabbi Shmuel Dovid Halevi
Ungar זצ"ל
Rav of Nitre

Rabbi Yitzchok
Valitchker-Ashkenazi זצ"ל
Rav of Stanislav

Rabbi Yehoshua
Greenwald זצ"ל
Rav of Chust

Meeting With History: Jewish Life in Hungary/Romania

The spiritual and material life of Torah Jewry
from early 1900 through the dark years of the Holocaust,
as retold through the life experiences of:

Rabbi Gershon Weiss—
Survival in Budapest

Mr. Hershel Ostreicher—
Remembering Munkacs: A Mother City of Israel

Mr. Eliezer Feig—
Ruscova: Remembering Life in the Carpathian Mountains

Mrs. Gizella Weisshaus—
Sighet: Remembrance of Life in Hungary

BUDAPEST: WAR AND SURVIVAL

An Interview with Rabbi Gershon Weiss

“As a young boy, I lived in Prague, Czechoslovakia. When the Germans occupied Czechoslovakia in 1939, we escaped to the city of Munkacs in Hungary. My family then consisted of my father, ז"ל, and mother, ז"ל, my brother, Dovid, and my sister, Tova (my brother Marcus was born in America). Hitler contended that WW II was really a continuation of the First World War that began in 1914 on *Tishah B'Av*, the eternal day of Jewish suffering and tragedy. Although World War I was not a war against the Jews specifically, the Jews suffered horribly nonetheless. World War II, of course, was a war of annihilation against *Klal Yisrael*. One of the *gedolim* from Europe, the Skoloya Rebbe, cried at the end of WWI that real peace had not yet arrived. He pleaded that *Klal Yisrael* should do *teshuvah* so that no further suffering would ensue. He perceived that this period of time was like the spacing that Yaakov *Avinu* placed between the various portions of the *matanah*, the gift, that he sent to Eisav. This *gadol* prayed that there should now be a period of calm for *Klal Yisrael*, so they may repent and be spared further destruction.

Although World War I was not a war against the Jews specifically, the Jews suffered horribly nonetheless.

It is important to convey how Hashem prepared miracle after miracle for us with each step we took during the War years. The *yom tov* of Pesach is associated with the current exile that we are in today. There is an interesting Ramban in *Parshas Vayechi* explaining that Yaakov *Avinu's* descent into Egypt parallels our present exile, the exile of Edom-Rome. Ramban states that the Egyptian exile was a portrayal of our present exile, and that the redemption from Egypt parallels what our redemption will be like in the time of *Moshiach*. We saw during the War that the Germans and Hungarians used almost the same tactics as did Pharaoh. Accordingly, we have to use the same strategies as our forefathers did to earn our redemption.

I was born in Liberec, about two hours drive from Prague, the capital city of Czechoslovakia, which was composed of two separate states: Czech and Slovakia. With the recent break-up of the Soviet Union these two states peacefully separated from each other and established separate sovereign states. However, in contrast to the tranquility of this political realignment of states between the Czechs and the Slovakians, I recently heard that of all the Jewish children who lived in Czechoslovakia before the War, only 500 survived. In 1938, Hitler demanded that the western most territory of Czechoslovakia, the Sudentenland,[10] be given to Germany.[11]

The Czech part of the country where we lived was called the "little America of Europe" as it was a very prosperous area economically. My parents had a very good business – we were very comfortable – and had absolutely no notion of leaving Prague until Hitler came. Even with the political situation that existed in the previous few years, we never believed that anything bad was going to happen until that morning when the Germans came marching into the city. We were completely unprepared for this emotionally, and even if we thought we were strong psychologically, almost nothing can prepare you for something like this. We were trapped.

The Czech part of the country where we lived was called the "little America of Europe" as it was a very prosperous area economically.

The German invasion

Early Life

In 1939, when I was only six-years-old, I awoke one morning to the sound of German troops marching through the streets of Prague. Imagine that only a few blocks from your house German soldiers were marching through the streets! This is exactly what took place. The president of Czechoslovakia at that time was named Eduard Benes. The first president of Czechoslovakia was Tomas G. Masaryk, a true friend of the Jews.[12]

10. Sudentenland is a territory of about 9,000 square miles Germany took from Czechoslovakia in 1938 and was restored to Czechoslovakia in 1945. The 1930 population consisted of approximately 3,000,000 ethnic Germans and 800,000 Czechs.

11. Germany is referred to in *Germora Megillah* as גרממיא, *"Germamya."* Rabbi Yitzchak teaches in this *Gemora* that if *Germamya* were allowed to break loose from its restraining forces it would destroy the entire world. Later, Germany was referred to as *"Ashkenaz"* and this term is still in use today.

12. The nation of Czechoslovakia was created after the Austria-Hungarian Empire collapsed in defeat following World War I. Masaryk served as president from the country's birth until 1935, when he was succeeded by Benes. After the Sudentenland was given to Germany in 1938, Hungary and Poland made territorial claims as well. Later, in 1939, the Czech government surrendered to Hitler's demands for control over the entire country and the German occupation began.

The Carpathian Mountains

My father went to the Gestapo office to register us as Hungarians in order to receive visas to go to Hungary.

We had a neighbor who had two sons: one was a Communist and the other a Fascist. These two boys would fight with each other because of their differing ideologies, and once I saw one of them split open the mouth of the other with a soda bottle, that's how intensely they believed in their political positions. The boy who was the Communist sympathizer was just standing with his mouth open as the Germans marched in, he was sure that the Communists would take over the Czech area and supply everyone with food and work, true to the Communist ideology. Some of the important community leaders were immediately removed to Germany where they were killed, while others were murdered locally. The Germans spread terror wherever they went. Someone in one of the villages assasinated a German officer soon after the invasion and in retaliation the Germans murdered everyone who lived in the village and burned it to ashes, wiping the village out of existence. That is how they conducted themselves.

Originally, my parents came from the Carpatio-Russian area of the Carpathian Mountains. Before 1938 that area belonged to Czechoslovakia, but once the Germans invaded they gave this territory to Hungary, their ally. Now that this area was considered Hungarian territory, my parents decided to become Hungarian citizens. So my father went to the Gestapo office to register us as Hungarians in order to receive visas to go to Hungary. This probably saved our lives since the Hungarians were allied with the Germans

German Waffen-SS and Hungarian Nazis in Budapest

more closely than the Czechs. It was an act of total *mesiras nefesh* since it was practically unthinkable to voluntarily enter Gestapo headquarters. My father wasn't sure that he would come out again alive, nonetheless, he went to try to save his family.

There was a *Yid* working in the Gestapo office. Jews were often used to provide such services for the Germans, even in the concentration camps. This *Yid* knew that if my mother would not be present we wouldn't receive the visas and, somehow, was able to leave the office long enough to phone a neighbor to tell my mother to go to the Gestapo office immediately. She left right away and took the tram directly there. The Gestapo occupied a very large mansion, almost like a castle, and the people watching her go in were stunned that anyone would enter this building on their own accord since very few who entered ever came out alive. As she entered the building one of the officers asked her to explain her action. She replied that she was told to come, realizing that if she revealed the name of the man who called it would mean his death. The Germans tried to figure out who called her, and by process of elimination realized that it must have been the Jew. For performing this act of kindness, one of the Germans went over to the man and punched him in the mouth so brutally that he knocked out many of his teeth.

The German then turned to my mother and asked if she is the wife of the Weiss brothers who had come for visas (my father's brother also came with him to apply for visas for his family). My mother had her wits about her and quickly replied, "No, Sir. You're mistaken. I'm only the wife of one of them!" With this, the German exploded in laughter, only to quickly catch himself realizing that it was inappropriate for him to respond in this manner. He immediately clicked his heels, and thrust out his arm shouting , "Heil, Hitler!" Just like that, like a robot, he reverted to his Nazi persona.

With obvious *siyata d'Shemaya* we received the visas and caught the last civilian transport leaving Prague for Hungary. Eventually we approached the Hungarian border where the *Gendarmerie*, the Hungarian National Guard, boarded the train to see that

People watching her go in were stunned that anyone would enter this building voluntarily since very few who entered ever came out alive.

The hated and feared Hungarian Gendarmerie

It was almost unheard of for a family to remain united under such conditions.

everyone's papers were in order. When they reached us they began teasing us by calling us "late birds" for coming back so late after the invasion. Our papers were not completely in order and they threatened to throw us off the train right there at the border. Sitting next to us was a Jewish man who quickly took out a pad and wrote down his address for us so that we could use it as our place of residence. Meanwhile, my mother was begging these wicked gendarmeries to allow us to remain on the train. Eventually they relented and permitted us to continue on our journey. With each step we saw Hashem's guiding hand leading us: the call from the Gestapo office, the Jewish man on the train...all of this was Divine assistance protecting us along the way. Very few Jews from Czechoslovakia remained alive, and even less remained together as families, yet here we were, my mother and father, sister and brother and my uncle and his family, all of us had escaped and survived. It was almost unheard of for a family to remain united under such conditions.

After crossing the border we went to my *Zaidy's* town, Munkacs. Munkacs was a very *Yiddishe* town. I don't know how legal we were in terms of our papers, but this is where we remained for a year and a half. Soon after arriving, my father, like many others, went to Budapest in search of a livelihood. I went to *cheder* in Munkacs. I remember that I looked like a real European *cheder* boy with my hair cut very short and with little *payos*. We didn't receive report cards, but every Thursday the *rebbe* would give a *faher*, a test, to see how well you learned that week. If you didn't do well the *rebbe* put your head between his knees and, using a freshly cut twig, gave you a bit of a thrashing on the behind. I wasn't used to such treatment and when I received my *me'sheberach*[13] because I was fresh to the *rebbe*, for yelling something at him, I quickly ran home to my *Zaidy*. I complained to *Zaidy* about the *rebbe* and told him I wanted to learn with a different *rebbe*. You didn't necessarily go to a school in Eastern Europe in those days. Each town had *rebbaim* who came to teach a class of boys, and there were several *rebbaim* teaching at the same or different levels. However, because of the competition the *rebbe* had to produce or he wouldn't make a living.[14] My *Zaidy* would test me and so did my uncle, and I had to know the material we studied or they would take me to another *rebbe*. The *rebbaim* knew they had to produce positive results to retain their *talmidim* and *parnasah*. Anyway, I complained to my *Zaidy* that the *rebbe* was not good and that I didn't want to continue learning with him.

Years later, my aunt reminded me that *Zaidy* gave me a *pengo* (a Hungarian dollar) to induce me to return to the *cheder*. I took the money and started back, only to return home and give the *pengo* to *Zaidy* telling him that he should go to the *cheder* instead. When *Zaidy* saw that this didn't work, he took out his cane and gave me a spanking worse than the one I received from the *rebbe*. At that point, I figured it was better to return to *cheder*. There was no such thing

13. *Me'sheberach* means "He who blessed...", but is used here, humorously, to refer to the punishment received for not doing well.

14. The reader is referred to the interview with Rabbi Landau in THE WOLRD THAT WAS: POLAND, for further explanation of this type of educational system and its effectiveness.

as the parent disagreeing with the *rebbe*. We were disciplined to behave properly. After one year I was ready to begin learning *Gemora*. We learned in a very intense atmosphere with our *rebbe*, accomplishing much more in the course of a year than is accomplished in *yeshivos* in America today.

Main Street in Budapest

In the meantime, a local gentile boy started up with my younger brother calling him a filthy Jew. My brother, not considering how precarious our situation was, responded by calling the boy a filthy *goy*. That was all we needed! Since our papers were not perfectly in order, we were advised to quietly disappear.

Life in Budapest

My father was still in Budapest, working for an engineering firm, but he never told my mother exactly what he was doing. Before the War we owned two cars, and now he didn't want to upset my mother by letting on that he was involved in less than glamorous work, so he was always very vague regarding exactly what he was doing. In reality, he was digging ditches for a construction company that was building apartment houses on the outskirts of the city. When we had to leave Munkacs he wrote us that he had managed to secure an apartment in Budapest. Remember that we were used to living in a very nice house, and in comfort. When we arrived in Budapest we found that our apartment was really only a room and a half in a large wooden tool shed located in the pit of the foundation that had been dug out for an apartment building. These foundations were several stories deep. You can imagine our reaction. The shed was not well constructed, you could see out between the boards, and it was in the middle of the winter. Nonetheless, we referred to this shed as our *Gan Eden*. This move saved our lives since eventually almost all of the Jews in Munkacs were deported to Concentration Camps where the majority perished.[15] We, on the other hand, were able to escape those transports in Budapest at that time. This took place at the end of 1942.

This move saved our lives since eventually almost all of the Jews in Munkacs were deported to Concentration Camps where the majority perished.

15. The reader is referred to the interview with Mr. Hershel Ostreicher in this volume.

I used the star selectively, passing myself off as a gentile to secure supplies for the family.

The troubles for the Jews of Hungary began slowly, just like the enslavement of our forefathers in Egypt.[16] At first the Jews were told to join the army like everyone else. Then, slowly, their military uniforms were taken away and they had to wear a special badge. Along with this, the men were removed from active military duty, not being trusted to carry weapons, and were placed in labor brigades to dig trenches and foxholes. This placed the Jews on the front line of the battles where they were exposed to the enemy from one side and the Hungarian anti-Semites from the other. Many, many Jews were murdered as a result.[17] The rest of the Jews were ordered to wear a yellow star that was three to four inches in size, and had to be sewn onto the garment in a permanent manner. I was ten-years-old at this time and decided that I didn't want my star sewn on in such a permanent manner. My mother, sensing that there was wisdom in this decision, placed six snaps on the underside of each of the six points of the star with the base of each snap placed in position on my outer garment. Consequently I was able to use the star selectively, passing myself off as a gentile when it was to my advantage in order to secure food and other available supplies for the family. In any case, whether I wore the star or not, the local gentile boys ran after me to fight with me, throw stones or shoot objects from their slingshots.

The next decree the Hungarians imposed was to relocate all of the Jews to special buildings for Jews only. My family ended up being placed in an old school building with a gigantic star painted on the facade of the building. My father had already been taken into a labor brigade, so my mother, sister, brother and I shared a classroom with an elderly couple. The man was over 90 and his wife was in her 80s. My mother took very good care of them, and I believe that it was in the merit of this kindness, and the other deeds of kindness that my parents performed during the War, that we were saved and survived the Holocaust. We placed two clothes closets in the middle of the room as a divider to provide privacy. The Nazis would come to check on us from time to time.

Hungarian troops at the battle front. The Labor Battalions were sent ahead of the troops.

16. The student is referred to the following volumes, **The Holocaust and Jewish Destiny: Jewish Heroism, Human Faith and Divine Providence**, and **The Holocaust Haggadah**, soon to be published by Rabbi Weiss for a complete treatment of this theme.

17. The reader is referred to the interview with Mr. Heshel Ostreicher in this volume for a more complete treatment of the infamous *Munka Tabor*, the Hungarian Labor Brigades.

Miklos Kallay, Hungarian Prime Minister eventually arrested by Hitler. He was friendly to the Jews.

The Allies, particularly the Americans, were bombing Hungary at this point in the War (1943). They had huge bombers, B-52 Flying Fortresses, that could fly extremely high and drop their bomb loads with frightening accuracy. They bombed many strategic positions such as bridges and factories. The gentile neighbors complained to the authorities that we were signaling the Allied pilots where to drop their bombs. Once a large contingency of Hungarian police raided our building to look for the "spies." They were particularly interested in the roof. Had it been painted in several different colors we would have been arrested as spies since particular color schemes painted on the roofs of building were often codes to reveal information to the enemy.

A lady who was mentally unstable was housed in the same building with us. From time to time, she opened up the windows facing the hospital across the street to shout curses at the Germans and taunt them by screaming how wonderful it was to see maimed and mutilated German soldiers without hands and feet. Her actions placed us in very great danger.

Once, about a mile away from us, the British dropped a type of bomb that explodes in the air above its target. We were sure that our building had been hit because of the shock waves set off by the explosion. The air raid siren went off and we all went down to the bomb shelters. My *Zaidy* gave me a small *Sefer* Torah and one of the girls in the building made a little *mantel* (cover) for it. I took it to the shelter and we placed it on a shelf on one of the walls. Meanwhile, the bombs kept raining down on us without end. We all recited *Shema Yisroel* in such a manner that I can only compare it to the *Shema* recited on *Yom Kippur* in the yeshiva. There were people in the shelter who weren't religious, who ate *triefa* food, but the *Kabbolos Ohl Malchus Shamayim* they made with that *Shema* was unbelievable.

Soon we heard knocking and four German officers, guns drawn, entered the shelter. They were very drunk, *ad d'lo yada*.[18] Since Hungary

We were sure that our building had been hit because of the shock waves set off by the explosion.

Bridge across the Danube River destroyed by Allied bombing raids

Women cleaning rubble after American bombing raid

18. A play on words (from Purim) meaning unable to distinguish between well known facts, just as one is supposed to drink on Purim until he cannot distinguish between, "Blessed is Mordechai and cursed is Haman."

Munka Tabor, Jewish Labor Brigade, group photo, 1940

Horthy bestowing honors upon WWI veterans. Note guard in ceremonial uniform.

was an ally of Germany, the Germans, unlike in other countries, were not at liberty to take care of the Jewish Problem on their own initiative. We belonged to the Hungarian government, and the Germans didn't act against us unilaterally. The Hungarian Prime Minister during the War years was Miklos Horthy – an anti-Semite, but he was not willing to follow German policy completely. He played along with the Germans, but did not let them murder the Jews. Later on it became worse for the Hungarian Jews, but at this point in the War the Hungarians did not give us over for complete destruction. In any case, these drunk Germans entered the shelter. My mother spoke a few languages, including German. She stood up and began speaking to them very boldly in German, and they were surprised and quite taken aback. She scolded them for their behavior, remarking that they are supposed to be a cultured nation and how could they display such behavior! She told them that there were only women and children in the room because the men were in the labor brigades. Then she demanded to know why they thought they could enter in such a manner. She gave them a whole *mussar shmues*. Stunned, they just turned and left.

Another time a German entered our school building through a window on the first floor, causing one of the women to begin screaming hysterically. My mother heard what was going on and, opening our window, began yelling for a guard to come. A guard in front of the hospital came running over and she gave him the same *shmues* that she gave the four Germans in the shelter. She asked what kind of a nation they were and have they no shame? The guard, who was very young, took the drunken soldier away. He came back and began talking with my mother. This took place in the middle of the night. It was such a strange scene that I remember it very vividly. The guard was telling my mother that he has Jewish cousins in Germany and that not all Germans were so bad. He told my mother that he doesn't sympathize

German Bomber flying over Budapest. Parliament building is in the background.

with the government. He offered her chocolate, cigarettes and blankets, but, for whatever reason, she refused his offers whereupon he apologized for the disturbance and went away. The German army, you see, was composed of regular German soldiers and the infamous SS. The Germans existed on varying levels of evil. Some of the plain soldiers were on a much lower level of evil than the SS, who were completely evil just for the sake of being evil. In other words, they were evil incarnate.

Because of our financial position before the War, my father owned two cars. When the men were taken to the labor brigades, my father claimed he was a mechanic. The same way one person would claim he was a cook, my father said he was a mechanic. Because of this he was stationed at a Hungarian army compound in Budapest where the repair facilities were located. This saved him from being sent to the battle front. The compound was surrounded by a very tall security fence, but every once in a while my father would climb the fence, remove his yellow badge, and pretending to be a *goy* bring us food that he stole from the Hungarians. I remember after one of these visits how my parents were crying as they said goodbye to each other, fearing that they may never see each other again. My father was *moser nefesh* to bring us potatoes! Once he stayed overnight with another man who also escaped from his camp. In the early morning hours some Hungarian Nazis came to search our building. As soon as they entered the building my father jumped out of the window. Our building was located

The Germans existed on varying levels of evil. The SS were evil incarnate.

Hungarian Nazi officers

on the corner, so even if the Nazis had guards waiting by the door they entered, you could still exit from another side. The other man ran down to the cellar and climbed into a little potbelly stove. After the Hungarians searched the upper floors, they went to check the cellar. When they saw the stove, they stuck their bayonets inside just in case someone was hiding there. This man barely fit into the stove in the first place, and he related afterwards that the bayonets missed him by a hairbreadth, *k'chut ha'sa'arah*! He would have been killed instantly had they found him.

At that time the Church spread the rumor that any Jews who came to the Church to become Christians would be protected by the Church and they would not be killed. The *Yidden* made a big joke out of this offer. "What do they do there?" the people joked, "they spray you with some perfume and all of a sudden you're a *goy*?" People wrote songs making fun of this offer. Very few people went. This is one of the sins of *yaiharaig v'al ya'avor*, when one must give up his life rather than transgress.

We all had rucksacks packed with clothing, some sugar, and, interestingly, spare soles for our shoes.

There was a Hungarian soldier, a drunkard, who came to our house quite frequently because he wanted to marry a Jewish woman. On one of his visits he told us that all of the Jews from Buda, which was the very fancy section of the city, were going to be taken away to Germany. This was the part of Budapest that geographically was closest to Germany, and it was there that the Germans were settling in. There were a lot of private villas located in the area and the mountains were nearby, it was a very beautiful section. In any event, we all laughed at him because he was a drunk, a *shicker*. My mother, as you have already seen, was a very sharp and insightful person, and her response was, "*Shicker* or not, Hashem sent him here to tell us this information and we have to take this ominous warning seriously."

We all had rucksacks packed with clothing, some sugar, and, interestingly, spare soles for our shoes. Soles were a very precious item then, worth even more than gold. They could be sold for bread, and certainly used to repair one's shoes in case we were led on forced marches. We each took our rucksack, left the school building and went to Pest to live with my aunt who had settled there years earlier. It was not easy because my brother, sister and I were a very active crew, and my aunt's apartment was small. After a little while the scare died down and things seemed to be quiet in Buda so we wanted to return. My aunt was an incredible hostess, her *hachnosas orchim* (hospitality) under such conditions was truly exemplary. When we suggested that we would return my aunt replied, "No! I am not letting you go back there. It is dangerous and I will not let you return." Eventually my mother acquiesced and we remained with my aunt and uncle in Pest.

At one point my mother left my sister and brother with my aunt and took me with her to go back to the school building to see what was happening. We had hidden money there, and still had other possessions there as well. We arrived at the building wearing our stars and found a policeman standing by the front gate guarding the main entranceway. As soon as we saw this, we went around to the other side of the building and knocked on the window of an elderly woman we knew. When she saw it was my mother she became very excited, "Mrs. Weiss! Mrs. Weiss! Come in! Come in!" My mother was one of the youngest women in the building and the other women liked her very much – she was considered their *Rebbetzin*. On Purim she read *Megillas* Esther for them and *Megillah Eichah* on *Tishah B'Av*, telling them stories of the *churban Beis Hamikdash*. When we asked about the policeman stationed at the front of the building, the woman assured us that he was only there to protect us. The Germans, you know, always tried to mislead the Jews. On the transports they made the Jews write postcards to their relatives back home stating they were being resettled and that everything was very good for them. They did this in the concentration camps as well.[19] Also, they tricked the people into thinking that they were taking a bath when they entered the gas chambers. All of this subterfuge was to keep the Jews from revolting and to insure their orderly and efficient extermination. My mother didn't accept what the woman was trying to tell us. Her instincts told her that something was wrong. We took the money we had hidden in one of the mattresses and the remaining shoe soles and left, returning to my aunt. After the War we asked some of the survivors who had been in the building what finally happened, and were told that not long after we fled the occupants were rounded up and deported to Auschwitz and other camps in Germany. Many of them were murdered. If we would have listened to that lady and returned to the building it could have been our end. I want you to know that my mother exhibited this same intuitive understanding in one life threatening situation after another throughout the War.

People thought that the *Yidden* were *lemilach*, that they were passive – sheepishly going to their demise, but nothing could be further from the truth. Jews infiltrated the Nazi Party, set up underground cells, fought as partisans, and gave aid and performed acts of kindness under the most horrid situations that can be imagined. These are the acts that will forever define the true manifestation of courage and strength. We should not allow ourselves to measure courage and strength of character in gentile terms. Never!

A Jew who had infiltrated the Nazi Party found out that the Germans were going to search the residential buildings to find additional young people for the labor brigades. Sometimes the safest place to hide is in the lion's den, and this is what my father did to hide my mother at this time. He had her smuggled into the army compound where he was stationed and hid her there, right under the nose of the Nazis. There was a small crawl space underneath one of the barracks – my mother said it was big enough only for a cat – and that is where she hid. Not long after I received a message that I had to go there to help her return home. It was impossible for her to stay any longer. I was 11-years-old at this time, and it was one of the only times during the War that I was *m'challel Shabbos*. It was *pikuach nefesh*, a matter of life and death, and thus a *mitzvah*, but it was one of the only times I performed any forbidden actions on *Shabbos* by taking the tram to the army compound to take my mother home.

People thought that the Yidden were passive – sheepishly going to their demise, but nothing could be further from the truth.

Another time the Hungarian Nazis announced that all the Jews had to assemble at a local raceway. "All the Jews" meant the women and children since the men had already been taken into the labor brigades. Upon hearing

19. The reader is referred to the interview with Mr. Hershel Ostreicher in this volume.

Hungarian cattle cars used to deport Jews to Auschwitz. Picture taken in 1945.

This was my father's chachmah, wisdom, that we should tarry at the end of the line, and in this way we were saved.

of this decree, from the underground, my father sent a message to us that we should try to be one of the last ones in the line. Usually the nature of a person is to be at the front of a line, but he warned us to be at the end. And this is what we did. We stood at the end of the line all day long; there were hundreds and thousands of *Yidden* gathered in that place. Cattle cars were lined up at a railroad siding that was adjacent to the raceway, and those who were found acceptable (for slave labor) were loaded into the cars to be sent to Auschwitz. I remember it was a very hot day and that we just stood at the back of the line all day long. Finally we reached the check point at the front of the line, but by then the cattle cars were jammed full and we were sent home. This was my father's *chachmah*, wisdom, that we should tarry at the end of the line, and in this way we were saved.

This is how life proceeded, with one decree of annihilation after another. It was unimaginable. Sometimes I walked through the streets without my star. Once I met my mother with my brother and sister. All I needed was for my brother to call out, "Hey, Gershon!" Fortunately, he didn't recognize me, and as we passed I told them to ignore me. They got on one tram car and I got on another, and that's how we went home. You always had to be careful, very careful.

Raoul Wallenberg, the famous Swedish diplomat, along with another Swiss official, *zichronom l'tov*, made a deal with the Nazis (for money, of course) to purchase buildings that would belong to the Swedish Embassy (1944-1945). In one of the great paradoxes of the war, the Germans, mass murders of millions of innocents, were very law abiding. Thus, if these buildings belonged to the Swedish government, they wouldn't be able to enter. The plan was that these newly acquired buildings would be an extension of the existing Swedish embassy and safe from German control. Thousands of Jews were saved in this manner, residing, as it were, under Swedish jurisdiction.[20] However,

Raoul Wallenberg

20. Nevertheless, life in Budapest was not easy for the Jews by any means – especially since the Hungarian Nazi Arrow-Cross would frequently shoot Jews on sight, regardless of papers or the protective houses set up by the Swiss, the Spanish and the Swedish under Raoul Wallenberg (Kranzler, David, **Thy Brother's Blood: The Orthodox Jewish Response During the HOLOCAUST**, Mesorah Publications, New York, 1987, page 215).

the Nazis did break their promise unofficially and would, at times, enter these buildings at night, taking Jews to the bank of the Danube River and shooting them.

In order to receive the necessary documents to enter the Swedish buildings you had to apply for them. However, my father was in a labor brigade and it was gravely hazardous for my mother to go out into the streets. The only one who could go was me, I was the *b'chor*, the oldest. I went early one morning to the Swedish Embassy to receive the *shutzpatsa*, protection papers. I figured that I would be early, but people had been waiting in line most of the night and the line was blocks and blocks long. I felt we had no chance, and I started to cry from despair. We lived with constant fear . . . I remember I just started to cry. A young man, who some said fit the description of Wallenberg, came by and saw me crying. He lifted me up on his shoulders and carried me into the building. I still had to wait until late in the afternoon for my name to be called, but it was a tremendous *tovah* to be attended to in such a manner and to be inside the building. *Zichrono ish l'tov*...it was a very kind deed that he performed on my behalf. Meanwhile, the entire day passed and no one knew who would receive the protection papers. Finally, about five o'clock in the afternoon, some of the embassy employees came outside calling out the names of those who had received the *shutzpatsa*: "Steinberg. . .Gross . . . Weiss" . . . our name was called out! Can you imagine the *simchah rabah*, the great joy, at such news? Think about it for a second. We thought that this was our ticket to *Gan Eden*.

I went early one morning to the Swedish Embassy to receive the shutzpatsa, *protection papers.*

The embassy was located in one of the most fashionable sections of Budapest. While waiting for the tram to return home by way of one of the bridges that cross the Danube River, I saw a group of gentile youths called *rugginturs*, meaning soldiers in training. They didn't have uniforms, but they had badges, army hats and guns. I saw them grab an

Photo Credit: Weis Wiesenthal

Lines outside Swiss Consulate, Budapest, waiting for safe passes

elderly Jewish woman off the sidewalk and shlep her into their headquarters building. I sensed that one of them was walking towards me and I bolted. I must have set world speed records running through the streets and around blocks until I was finally able to leap onto a moving tram. I was terrified and, although I was in good condition because I used to play soccer and other sports, fear motivated me far beyond mere physical conditioning. When I arrived at the end of our block – which was a very long block – I saw German soldiers all around and that the large, heavy blocks of stone used to pave the street had been torn up and placed as barricades around the block. I was confused. What were they afraid of? An attack? I didn't know why they had done this. In order to get to the apartment I had to walk between these German soldiers with their machine guns. I don't know if you ever saw a machine gun . . . I was terrified. These were the German Nazis, not the Hungarians. I remember the hand grenades hanging from their belts, and I had to walk between them to get home wearing my yellow star. I had no other choice, but this was a horrifying experience. I finally reached the door of my aunt's building and knocked, and knocked and knocked and no one answered the door. I was ready to fall apart – I mean really have a nervous breakdown – when, finally, the next-door neighbor, a Jewish doctor, opened his front door and peered outside. He told me that my father had obtained Swiss protection papers (no one knew how), slipped out of the army compound with the assistance of a Hungarian solider who he bribed and took the family to a building at a safer address. When I heard this, I gave the doctor the papers I received from the Swedish embassy so that he should benefit from the protection they offered. I later found out that my parents greatly despaired, thinking they would never see me again, and that I would never get the message they left with the doctor and thus find them!

I must have set world speed records running through the streets and around blocks... fear motivated me far beyond mere physical conditioning.

When I arrived at the new building, the joy of our reunion was beyond description. To be reunited was overwhelming. The buildings that the Swedish embassy obtained were some of the nicest buildings directly across from the Danube River. The Nazis, however, did not completely keep their promise to respect Swedish diplomatic jurisdiction and did round up some of the Jews occupying these buildings. They made them take off their clothing, tied them together with ropes, and in the freezing cold winter weather marched them around the city to torture them and then shot them to death at the bank of the Danube. One of the Jews who was tied together with a boy was saved by swimming across the Danube to the other side. The gentiles joked that the fish will be big and healthy for a long time because there will be plenty of Jews for them to eat.

My father, using the Swiss papers, managed to find an apartment in a small, dingy three floor apartment house in a slum area bordering the railroad tracks on one side. This was a *hatzalah* for us since many of the Jews with the papers I received were killed by the Nazis. We lived in this house for a few months. One morning we were awakened by gunfire and a group of Hungarian Nazis – anti-Semitic animals no better than the Germans – entered our building. One of these Hungarians was yelling and cursing. He seemed to be the meanest in the group. There were 300-400 *Yidden* living in the neighboring building they had surrounded. This building was used by the underground for forging diplomatic papers. In our apartment building official government ink stamps, representing the different police districts where the forged papers were valid, were printed. Every document had to have proper stamps. How were these stamps made? A potato was cut in half and placed on top of a legal government stamp. The image on the stamp became absorbed into the potato and was then transferred onto the paper to be used as stamps. Many *Yidden* were very ingenious in how they responded to the horrible situations they were in during the War, both in practical physical terms and in the fulfillment of their religious obligations as well. Unfortunately, people were caught– some were imprisoned, but all were beaten, their blood flowing in the street.

Across from our apartment house was a school building that had been converted into a hospital. We could see the hospital from our windows. It was now at the end of 1943, or the beginning of 1944, and the Russians were advancing westward in their fight against the Germans, who were suffering a high rate of casualties. Many of the wounded were brought to this hospital.

Divine Hashgachah

At this point I wish to interject the following historical details to help you understand how so many incidents in the War hung on subtle – almost imperceptible – dictates of Divine *Hashgachah*. Poland was crushed by Germany in approximately six weeks. The Poles, so capable of killing defenseless Jews, and despite their entire army, couldn't muster the courage to combat the Germans for a longer period of time. However, a handful of Jews held off the Germans for weeks in the Warsaw Ghetto Uprising. The Jewish underground received money from *Yidden* in Western Countries through clandestine means. This money was given to the Polish underground to supply the Jews in the Ghetto with ammunition and guns. The Poles, however, were rabid anti-Semites (killing Jews even after the War was over) and they double-crossed the Jews in the ghetto by withholding their support and the much needed weapons, effectively leaving the Jews trapped in the ghetto. *Hashgachah* saw to it that the Polish underground was repaid, measure for measure, for their treachery against the Jews in the ghetto. After the Russians drove the Germans out of Soviet territory, they continued westward pushing the Germans back in the face of their advance. The Germans retreated to Warsaw and the Russians surrounded the city. The Polish underground made a secret agreement with the Russians that with the beginning of their assault on the city, the underground would revolt against the Germans from

Wounded German soldiers in front of a hospital in Budapest

Many Yidden were very ingenious in how they responded to the horrible situations they were in during the War.

within the city and together they would destroy the Nazi army. At the appointed time the underground began their offensive against the Germans, but the Russians stayed in their encampments. The result was that the Germans and the Poles began destroying each other while the Russians just sat outside the city, biding their time while the Polish slaughter took place. Afterwards, with the Germans in a much weaker position, the Russians finally entered the city. This was an open display of retribution against the Polish underground for the duplicitous manner with which they dealt with the Jews in the Warsaw Ghetto.

The Germans and the Poles began destroying each other while the Russians just sat outside the city, biding their time.

In any case, the Germans initially planned their attack of Poland in such a manner as to facilitate a future invasion of Russia before the start of winter. On August 23, 1939, the German-Soviet Non-aggression Pact divided Eastern Europe between the Nazis and the Soviets, clearing the way for the invasion of Poland. The pact provided the assurance that neither nation would attack the other, and that all disputes would be resolved through negotiations. Hitler had no intention of keeping this pact, but pursued it because he and other German leaders maintained that Germany lost World War I because it had to fight a war on two fronts. To prevent this, Hitler sought the non-aggression agreement with Stalin. On September 1, 1939, Germany annexed the free city of Danzig and invaded Poland. On September 17, Russia invaded Poland from the east. On September 28, 1939, Germany and the Soviet Union signed a treaty in Moscow partitioning Poland between them.

The Germans knew their history very well, using Napoleon as a prime example. Hitler realized that he could not attack

Hungarian troops at the battle-front, winter 1943

Russia in the winter. Russian winters are brutally cold, so cold in fact, that the machinery of war (tanks, large guns, troop-carriers, etc.) can literally freeze and not function properly. This is even more true for the soldiers who have to fight in such freezing temperatures and in deep snow and ice. Additionally, the all-important supply lines to furnish the soldiers at the battlefront often become impassable in such weather. There was a young partisan, Tito (later to become the dictator of Yugoslavia) who somehow publically embarrassed Hitler, infuriating him to the point that he redirected several of his armies south to invade Yugoslavia, instead of marching eastward to begin the invasion of Russia well before the onset of winter. Hitler finally began the invasion of the Soviet Union on June 22 (1941), giving himself very little time to successfully establish his armies in Russian territory before winter began. The Russians knew that the winter weather would benefit any initiatives they took against the invaders. As the German army was closing in on Stalingrad, the severity of the winter interrupted their supply lines and the Russians were able to counterattack and turn the tide of an invasion that had been successful until this point. Their slogan was "From Stalingrad to Budapest and onto Berlin."

Ghetto Life

They marched us out into the street where Jewish blood was flowing freely from the savage beatings that the Hungarian Fascists were delivering left and right. We were marched into the ghetto that had been set aside for the *Yidden*. My father was with us that morning, having smuggled himself out of the army compound the previous day and spending the night with us. He was dressed like a *goy*. He knew he had to escape before the Nazis entered our apartment. He would climb up to the roof and jump from one roof top to another until he reached the gentile neighborhood and then with great stealth re-enter at street level and make his way back to the army compound. This is what he usually did when he managed to visit us, and he was preparing to do so again. I remember thinking that this was the end, that we would never see each other again. Then, suddenly, my mother broke down. Crying she said, "You're leaving us here alone?!" I recall that my father stood there, rooted to the floor, thinking about my mother's plea when he stamped his foot firmly and said, "I'm staying!" The finality of his decision was resounding. That was it, we would all share the same fate, and if we perished, we would perish together.

We were marched to the ghetto, each with a rucksack and blankets on our backs. My mother had punctured her arm with a fish bone and the wound

They marched us out into the street where Jewish blood was flowing freely from the savage beatings of the Hungarian Fascists.

Deportation to the ghetto

was horribly infected. She was sick as a result of the infection and, lacking strength, strayed from the line we were marching in. A 14-year-old Hungarian girl ran up to her screaming, "Get back into line you filthy Jew!", over and over again. Hearing the commotion, a Hungarian guard came running over and chased the girl away. We felt a certain sense of satisfaction when the soldier did this. This was our revenge. We were constantly subjected to this kind of systematic humiliation.

There were gigantic crates located in this park and we were told to place all our valuables in these crates.

Eventually we reached a park. There were gigantic crates located in this park and we were told to place all of our money and valuables in these crates. My father was so loaded down with the provisions he was carrying for us that he could no longer stand, so he sat down on a park bench. Meanwhile, we were standing in the line leading to the guards by the crates. When we reached the guards my mother, who had valuable items hidden on her, told one of the Hungarians that her wedding ring was very tight and she could not remove it from her swollen finger. He replied, "No, problem. We'll cut off the finger." My mother quickly managed to remove

Arrow-Cross leader Ferenc Szalasi and his party members

Arrow-Cross henchman Beregfy Karoly addressing a member of his troops

the ring. Meanwhile, her ploy worked, because the guard was satisfied with the ring and let us pass. One of the items she had hidden was an expensive American pen, a Waterman Pen, and some money. The pen doesn't sound like much in America, but it was rare in Hungary and considered very precious. Now we were worried about my father who, sitting on the bench, still had to get through the checkpoint. My father was about 40-years-old and someone that age was supposed to be in the labor brigades. If so, why was he here with the women and children? If even suspected of being a deserter, he would be shot right away. Meanwhile, our group was on other side of the checkpoint and we were being guarded by a policeman. There were different levels in the Hungarian system: the regular policeman, the Hungarian army soldier, the Hungarian Nazis and the ultra-nationalistic Arrow-Cross fascist murderers. In addition, of course, were the German soldiers and the infamous SS. The policeman guarding us was an older man not fit for front-line duty. Hashem blessed my mother with intelligence and an uncanny sense of insight, which she employed to our benefit during the War in ways that seemed completely contrary to commonsense. In this case, she approached the policeman guarding us and told him that she has a very expensive American pen and that it was his, but he would have to bring her husband to her without going past the inspectors. This was completely illogical, because for just having the pen he could have shot her and simply taken it. But he didn't, and he only wanted to know how she was going to give it to him. My mother told him to pretend he is helping my younger sister with her rucksack and while he is doing that she will slip the pen to him. Then, he went over to the bench where my father was sitting and started screaming, "You filthy Jew, get over to that line right away!", and he escorted my father to the line, right past the inspectors! The Divine guidance we had at that time was unimaginable, because this policeman escorted us all the way to the ghetto – to the apartment building where we were to stay – pushed us inside and told us not to step out all night (just like on *Pesach* night) and then he said goodbye.

In the *Tochachah* / Admonition *(Devarim 28:25, 32)* it states: "*Hashem will cause you to be struck down before your enemies; on one road you will go out against him, but on seven roads you will flee before him. Your sons and daughters will be given to another people – and your eyes will see and pine in vain for them all day long, but your hand will be powerless.*"[21]

The Divine guidance we had at that time was unimaginable, because this policeman escorted us all the way to the ghetto.

Here we were, 250 people, being guarded by just four men. The Hungarian cursing and bossing everyone around during the initial roundup was the head of the group. Throughout the War we saw the prophecy of the *Tochachah* come true before our eyes. There was a Hungarian song made up in the camps mocking our ability to escape the net of hatred that surrounded us on all sides. Where could we run? If you tried to escape you could get, maybe, a few blocks away before the *goyim* handed you over to the Germans. Where was

21. Translation from **The Stone Edition: The Chumash**, Mesorah Publications, Brooklyn, New York, 1993, page 1079

there to go? Nowhere! Some people who had money were able to secure forged papers stating they were gentiles, while others paid gentiles to let them hide in their attic or cellar. These options weren't foolproof, but they gave *some Yidden* a chance to survive. As it turned out, this Hungarian Nazi who was the head guard taking us from our building was actually a Jew who had infiltrated the Hungarian Nazi Party and gained rank and power. He took up a position at the rear and, as subtly as possible, saw to it that the Jews at the back of the line were able to disappear. This is an example of the amazing *mesiras nefesh* displayed by Jews during the War. In order to help other Jews, this *Yid* risked his life to infiltrate the Hungarian Nazis.

Outside death haunted the streets, and inside there was fear and trepidation.

The ghetto was no picnic, even though we weren't exposed to open public abuse. We were with about 80 other people, all placed in a six-room apartment. We chose the maid's room for our quarters. There were two couches in the room with a couple of feet between them, just enough to open the drawer of one of the couches. There were five people in my family plus my elderly grandmother, and another elderly couple who were placed in the room with us. This couple had one couch and my grandmother slept on the other one with my brother and sister. I put two chairs together and slept on the chairs. I woke up with a terrible backache, but this was *Gan Eden* compared to what could have been and what others were suffering at the time . . . *Gan Eden*! We were eight people in a very small room, while the larger rooms had many more.

It says in the *Tochachah* (*Vayikra* 26:26)[22] that many women will have to cook using one oven, and here we had many, many women cooking whatever food they had at the one little stove located in our apartment. Unfortunately, not everyone ate kosher, and we were desperately trying to eat only kosher. You can imagine the scene at the stove. You put your food on the stove and it starts to boil. The good lady at the stove wants to make sure that the food doesn't burn and takes her *treife* utensil from her pot to stir yours, and she only means good. To secure food was hard enough, to try to watch over what was cooking caused tremendous *agmas nefesh*, distress.

If you had money, you could buy food. Somehow my father was able to buy a pound of bacon. You just couldn't go out and order kosher meat, and we resolved not to eat it unless we were in a state of *pikuach nefesh*. During the winter we kept it between the two outside windows so that it would stay frozen. I want you to know that many people were starving and complained that we were hoarding food, yet no one ever touched the package of bacon. Can you imagine? People from another nation would have smashed the windows open to take the food, maybe even kill to get to it, and here no one even touched it. This show of restraint and gentility constituted a tremendous tribute to *Klal Yisrael*.

Outside death haunted the streets, and inside there was fear and trepidation.[23] The Russians were raining bombs down on the German positions throughout Budapest. The Americans flew huge

22. Ibid., page 713. "When I break for you the staff of bread, ten women will bake your bread in one oven, and they will bring back your bread by weight; you will eat and not be sated."

23. Ibid., page 715. "You will become lost among the nations: the land of your foes will devour you(26:38)."

B-52 bombers that were capable of dropping large bombs with great accuracy from high altitudes. The Russians, not having this capability, flew very low dropping clusters of small bombs. One American bomb could devastate four floors of a cement and brick building, but the Russian bombs weren't capable of this. They had to drop many bombs at one time to make sure that they hit the target and caused maximum destruction. Near us was a German anti-aircraft installation that tried to shoot down the Russian planes. The total fire power surrounding us was unbelievable, and here we were, hated by everyone, sitting in the middle. Nearby was a bombed-out building. My father carefully made his way there and brought back a stove from one of the abandoned apartments. Somehow he brought it to our room and installed it within the chimney of the heating system. Now my mother could cook without worrying that the food would not remain kosher. Every such little improvement in our living condition was a *ye'shuah gedolah*, a great salvation, for us. This was a real luxury: a stove for cooking.

Meanwhile, we still had some flour we bought before the ghetto was sealed. I was elected to remove my star and, pretending to be a gentile sneak out of the ghetto to have it baked into bread by a non-Jewish baker.[24] I didn't have to wait in line to buy bread because I wanted to bake bread, so I went right in. I also wasn't in a hurry to leave, because once the commercial bread was baked I would buy a loaf of that bread, as well as bake my own. For whatever reason, the baker didn't mind doing this for me. To get out of the ghetto wasn't easy because it was completely sealed off. I'm sure you have seen pictures of the various ghettos, *rachmana litzlan*. At first there were policemen guarding the ghetto and you had to sneak past them; later the streets were sealed off with walls and fences that were usually topped with barbed wire. If you tried to climb over these barricades you could be easily seen and reported to the Germans by the *goyim*. The main street, however, ran through the ghetto and was open at both ends (like Zgierska Street that ran through the Lodz Ghetto and was used only by Germans and Poles). In Budapest the guards checked your papers at each exit, and if you were a Jew you were not allowed to go out. To avoid this I used to jump onto the rear axle area between the two back wheels of the horse drawn coach of a city (or army) official. When the soldiers were checking the papers of those inside the coach, I would sneak around the opposite side of the coach and escape into the crowds on the sidewalk outside the ghetto walls.

The total fire power surrounding us was unbelievable, and here we were, hated by everyone, sitting in the middle.

I remember standing in line on the block just across from the ghetto, where there were piles of Jewish bodies lying in the open courtyard of the *Beis Hakanesses* (synagogue) waiting to be identified by relatives. I once met my mother there searching for someone who had disappeared. Can you imagine, a young child sifting through piles of dead bodies looking for a relative? Another time as I was waiting to return to the ghetto a young *sheigetz* turns to me and said, "Oh! It stinks from those

24. This was permissible because of *Pikuach Nefesh*, the *mitzvah* to preserve life.

Jews." "Yeah, yeah . . .", I replied. I had to say something, but I was seething inside.

I happened to discover that between a certain house and apartment building at one end of the ghetto you could sneak through a breach in the wall, enter into the basement of a gentile house on the other side and escape to the street. It took a few weeks until the Hungarians figured out what was going on, but in the meantime we had a fairly safe escape route out of the ghetto. Once, after removing my star and exiting in this manner, I saw a group of *Yidden* who had been caught by the Hungarian Nazis. I was frightened beyond description. I was shaking violently inside, but I had to keep on going so that I wouldn't call attention to myself. I don't know how I did this, but I did. I can't tell you the pure fear that I experienced at that moment. Anyway, after this particular excursion I returned – badly shaken but safe – to the ghetto.

What should we do? Do we take a chance with the bombs, or with the Nazis?

For a few years after the War when I learned in Yeshivas Ner Israel of Baltimore, I used to lie down for a few minutes after supper. At first my *chavrusah* was shocked that I was so frenzied when he would awaken me, but then he understood. You see, after so many nights (night after night) of waiting for the Nazis to come barging in and take us away, I became conditioned to fear any intrusion or disturbance, especially at night, no matter how innocent it may have been. Many Holocaust survivors suffered (and continue to suffer) endless nights with dreams that tormented them and deprived them of both sleep and the ability to forget, or at least suppress, what they went through. Many of those who function successfully are very brave and strong willed, suppressing myriad memories that are prompted by normal sights, smells, sounds and textures that they experience during their daily routine – normal, at least, to most people. It took a few years for this particular response pattern to fade, and I was fortunate that it did, because many times such behaviors last a lifetime.

Besides the lack of food, we now had two problems to face on a daily basis: the incessant bombing by the Russians and the fear that the Germans could hold a *selektion* at any time and deport us to the camps. If you lived on an upper story, you faced the possibility of death with each bombing raid. The ground floor or cellar was much safer since the smaller Russian bombs could only penetrate a couple of stories down from the roof. However, while the location of the cellar provided protection from the bombs, you remained vulnerable to a raid by the Nazis who merely machine gunned to death everyone they found. The question confronting us was: What should we do? Do we take a chance with the bombs, or with the Nazis? My mother told my father that whatever happens is Hashem's will and that we should remain upstairs. My father, however, felt that it was wiser to be closer to the cellar. To convince her, he took my mother across the street to show her what an apartment looked like after it was hit by a bomb. One of the people killed in that apartment was cut in half by the explosion. After this, my mother agreed to move closer to the cellar. However, every time we heard a knock on the door we said *Viduy*, fearing that our end was imminent.

One day the Germans did come to our building looking for young people to work. In the beginning they were more discriminating in who they took. Now, however, they were in desperate need of laborers. My mother was lying in bed with her infected arm, and there was another woman in the room who was hiding inside the other couch! But what could my father do? He had no excuse! The Nazis came to make their search. There were two staircases in this apartment building and on the landing between each floor there was a bathroom – just a closet, really – with no lock. We were signaling the Nazis' movements to my father, but in the end the only choice he had was to step into the bathroom on the landing, just eight steps down the staircase from our floor. Soon after, the soldiers came up the stairs to the landing, walked right past the bathroom, and turned and went up to the next floor. *Siyata D'Shemaya*! This was an open miracle, there is no other way to explain it. They just walked right past the door! Finally, they reached my mother's room, saw her lying in bed and one of them said, "We don't need a bunch of fakers like you! What's wrong with you?!" My mother told him about her wound, but, of course, he didn't believe her. She began unwinding the bandage. As she was unwrapping it a horrible and foul odor was emitted and pieces of skin fell off. This soldier took one look at her arm and said, "You're going to drop dead soon anyway. . . ." Then they turned and left the room. Both my mother and the lady hiding in the couch were saved. It took a great deal of sacrifice for my mother to hide this lady in our room, for if they would have been discovered she would have been doomed together with the lady.

Just a few weeks before the Germans sealed off the ghetto, my father was able to obtain a large sack of beans and an equally large sack of peas. Each sack must have weighed at least 50 kilograms. My mother asked him what he was going to do with these "...*bumblach mit arbis*... (beans and peas)"? My father told her to be patient and see what the future will bring. In the end, the beans and peas saved our lives because this is what we ate for months, when there was no more food available. After the War I couldn't look at beans or peas. They were completely unpalatable to me.

I remember in the last few weeks before the War ended, when we were liberated by the Russians, people would come to our apartment to eat our leftovers. Former millionaires would wipe off the remains from our plates. We were living the teaching of the *Gemora* that explains when two people are walking in the desert and there is only enough food for one to survive, the person with the food is not obligated to share what he has. This is the rule of "*Chayecha v'chayei acheirim, chayecha kodem*" (when life is endangered, your life takes precedence over the life of your companion). This is how we were living then, there was barely enough food for a single individual to exist, to share only meant that both people would die and no one would survive. It is extremely important for the present generation to realize how great the anti-Semitism was in Eastern Europe – their cruelty was without a limit: this is the *halachah* of "Eisav *sonai es* Yaakov," that Eisav hates Yaakov as the *Medrash* explains.

In any event, the starvation was so great that my sister broke out in boils from lack of vitamins and minerals. We took her to a doctor who prescribed a certain medicine for her, but we could only get it from a gentile pharmacy outside the ghetto. Obviously, I had to be the one to get the medicine for her. The Jewish Hospital was just outside the wall of the ghetto, and the doctor gave me a pass to go to the hospital. Once there, I took off my star and went

Siyata D'Shemaya! *This was an open miracle, there is no other way to explain it. They just walked right past the door!*

to the pharmacy. I was standing outside the pharmacy when there was a Russian air raid over the city. They pilots were dropping bombs and strafing the streets with machine gunfire. It was total chaos, a nightmare, only I was awake and it was really happening. I always wondered how is it possible to describe such a situation to someone? How can you ever convey the feeling of terror that becomes rooted in every cell of your body? It's really impossible.

Photo Credit: Captain S.M. Kasnett

House-to-house combat

It was total chaos, a nightmare, only I was awake and it was really happening.

Eventually I was able to go back to the hospital after I got the medicine. My hands were so frozen from the cold that I couldn't manipulate the star to put it back on when I was ready to leave. My feet were frostbitten and this was a condition that recurred for years after the War–it just came back automatically. Having no choice, I asked a person standing in the hallway of the hospital – I don't know if he was a *Yid* or *goy* – to snap on my star. Being a child it was easier to ask someone to do this, an adult would have been in grave danger, but as a child I was able to get away with it. I successfully returned to the ghetto and brought the medicine to my sister.

Until the last day of the War we ate our beans and peas. I remember, as we were listening to the machine guns of the Russian soldiers advancing through the streets of the city, my sister was asking my mother to give her a little more beans and peas. My mother refused, telling her that she had to ration the amount everyone received so that there would be food for tomorrow. The next day, on January 15th, 1945, we were liberated from the Budapest Ghetto. The fighting, however, was not over as ongoing house-to-house fighting continued for the control of some sectors of the city between the Russian and German armies. This included heavy machine gun fire, as well as bombs and howitzer shells landing in the city. Just before liberation the Russians surrounded Budapest cutting off all supply lines to the city. This meant that the Germans could no longer get any supplies as well. This took place on December 31, during their holiday season. In order to build up the morale of the troops, the German military executed an airlift of supplies and ammunition to the German troops in the city. At first, as we watched the parachutes floating down from the sky, we thought that Russian soldiers were making their final assault on the city and we were full of joy. This feeling soon turned to trepidation as we realized that secured to the ends of the parachutes were supplies for the German forces.

Hungarian Arrow-Cross Party and Nazi officers in Budapest, 4 months before the city was liberated by the Russians.

My father was walking in the street at this time looking for food and was caught by German soldiers who wanted him to climb into a bombed-out building to carry out a load of supplies that landed in this dangerous place. He figured that this was the end for him. He went with some other men to bring down one of the large containers from the building and then tried to leave. The Germans refused to let him go and told him that he was to remain with them. He soon found out that the container contained cigarettes, chocolate, and many other types of treats to boost the spirits of the Nazis. Soon, another company of Germans arrived at the scene, and while they were talking together and going through the treats in the container, my father quietly slipped away and made his way back to the apartment. If they had seen him leaving they would have shot him.

Liberation

Finally, on January 12th, the Russians came into the ghetto and we were liberated from the Germans. Budapest is made up of two municipalities– Buda and Pest – which are divided by the Danube River that flows between them. The Germans were beaten back across the river from Pest to Buda, but the end of the fighting wasn't until May or June. Now we had trouble with the Russians, so our ordeal was still not over. My mother knew how to speak Russian, so she taught us some elementary words. We called the Russian soldiers, Father. "Father, please give us a piece of bread . . ." "Father this and Father that...," that's how it was.

Now we had trouble with the Russians, so our ordeal was still not over.

Vicious anti-Semitic thugs from the Arrow-Cross Party

Meanwhile, my mother wanted to leave the apartment and speak with the Russians face to face, to tell them that we are Czechoslovakians (who were allied with the Russians) and not Hungarians. My father, however, told her not to show off by speaking in Russian with the soldiers. My mother felt that this would establish a rapport with them, but my father was adamant that she should only speak Czech.

Soon after, my mother was walking through the street when she heard someone calling, "Mrs. Weiss! Mrs. Weiss!" You see, there were many Jews who were living with false papers as *goyim*, and this man was one of them. In the Russian army there were many Ukrainians, and the Ukrainians were as bad to the Jews–maybe even worse–than the Germans. Having caught this man, they didn't want to let him go. Many Jews were taken as prisoners by the Russians after the War, sent to Siberia and never seen again. Similarly, Jews traveling back to their hometowns after the War were captured and sent away. After everything they went through during the War, it was after the War that they were killed.

I vividly remember that after the War we were starving... People were starving and there was chaos.

Anyway, my mother started to explain to these Russians that this man is a Jew and that he was hiding in disguise from the Germans. One Russian started screaming, asking her why didn't the man fight against the Germans? He was ranting on and on, and my mother was begging and pleading with him not to kill the Jew – to let him go. Finally, the soldier relented and let the *Yid* go, but he told my mother that she must go with him because they need an interpreter. Now my mother perceived the wisdom of my father's insistence that she shouldn't speak Russian. They took my mother, however, when these soldiers met up with some others and began talking they ignored my mother for a few minutes and she used the opportunity to slip away.

I vividly remember that after the War we were starving. There was no food to be found. In *Pirkei Avos* (3:2) the *Mishnah* teaches that one should always pray for the welfare of the government, for if not for the fear of [governmental] law one human being could swallow another alive (because of the lack of fear of punishment for wrongdoing). We had such a time, for a day or two, when there was no government. The Russians had control of the city, but they were only soldiers with no governmental authority. They walked down the street with the soldiers on one side covering the windows on the other side of the street, looking for snipers. We would hear a burst of gunfire and then find someone bleeding to death, or dead, in the street. Seeing that there was no order, people broke into the stores to find whatever they could to eat or provide for their needs. We broke into a chocolate factory where the Germans had stored mountains of large, heavy chocolate squares. Each block weighed over twenty pounds. There were also sugar-covered orange and lemon peels. People were starving and there was chaos. After a day or two, a military government was put in place and the looting stopped.

Eventually we were given an apartment by the military government. I remember that my parents went through great personal sacrifices to supply us with kosher food for Pesach that year since there was practically no food to be found in the city. They found a *shochet* who lived in a village a hundred or so miles outside the city. My parents took several geese to be slaughtered. We bought eggs, and through some American organization we were able

Photo Credit: Weis Wiesenthal

Entering the ghetto, Budapest, 1944

obtain matzohs. I remember seeing people standing over a dead horse cutting the meat from the carcass. *Baruch Hashem*, we never ate any *treife* meat during the War, but what could you do? People were starving to death. Anyway, how did my parents get back from the village? My mother stood beside the train tracks and when a Russian army transport train came by she begged for a ride, saying that she had to return to her children. The soldiers did her a favor and literally hoisted her on top of the train, not inside, but on top of the car. Once on top, she pointed to my father and said that he was her brother and they put him on top as well. You should know that the train passed through several tunnels, and the top of the tunnels was not elevated very much above the height of the train. My parents had to press themselves into the roof of the train to pass through the tunnels. They were let off near Budapest and continued to the city on foot, arriving *erev* Pesach in the afternoon. I remember my grandmother preparing the apartment for us.

We finally were able to leave and board a train going west from Hungary to Prague, Czechoslovakia. We stopped at a train station when a train heading east to Russia carrying German prisoners of war pulled up alongside our train on the next track. We could hear screaming, horrible screaming coming from our train. Eventually we found out what it was about. The train stopped at different cities on the way back to Russia and the guards, who loved vodka, would go into the town or city to get something to drink. (In fact, vodka was used during some of the toughest battles as a motivating force to move the Russian troops forward.) While they were in town at one stop some of the German POWs escaped. Each car held approximately 120 prisoners, and each guard was responsible for his group of 120. What were the guards going to do, show up in Russia without their full complement of prisoners? They could be shot for this! So the guards with missing prisoners went over to our civilian train and grabbed the first men they saw to ensure the full count.

We finally were able to leave and board a train going west from Hungary to Prague, Czechoslovakia.

They simply took them off the train heading west, to freedom, and put them on the POW train heading east, to Siberia. No one in Siberia cared where the men came from, just as long as the appropriate number showed up. *Yidden* also ended up in Siberia like this.

Eventually we made our way back to Prague, but it was a very difficult journey. Slowly, people began finding out who had perished and who had survived. Often survivors found each other in sudden and shocking encounters. Once we were on a street car and my mother found one of her sisters! My aunt was on a tram when she saw her brother. She quickly got off. He had escaped to Russia and joined a unit of the Czech army that was organized by the Russians. He served as a paratrooper, and here he was walking down a street in Prague!

Photo Credit: M.D. Yarmish and Torah Personalities, Inc.

Rabbi Moshe Feinstein, זצ"ל

Rabbi Y.Y. Ruderman זצ"ל

Photo Credit: Gedolim Photos, Baltimore

Rabbi Dovid Kronglass זצ"ל

Photo Credit: Yated Neeman

Rabbi Reuven Feinstein שליט"א

Jewish Heroism

I told my children that Jews performed untold acts of heroism during the War – they didn't just go like sheep to their deaths. If a Jew killed a German, the Germans would wipe out an entire village in retribution. Jewish children were placed on German tanks and used for protection, and babies were tortured to death in front of their parents. There were only so many avenues of resistence open to the Jews, but their acts of kindness and their exalted behavior, even under the most inhuman conditions, defined them as the Chosen Nation, and the Germans knew this.

Early in the War, when the *tzores* was in Poland, my *Zaidy* was part of an Underground that helped smuggle Polish Jews out of Poland. Once he was helping to smuggle his sister and her two daughters when they were caught by the Germans. The gentile women guiding them across the border took one of the girls with her and escaped. This girl survived the War, grew up and a Jewish boy wanted to marry her. The boy's father said that if he married a gentile he would kill him, especially after everything the *goyim* did to the Jews during the War. The boy apologized and told her that he had to break off the relationship. She responded that she thinks she is Jewish. She related how she vaguely remembered past events which led her to believe that she is a Jewess, and that he should speak to the woman who raised her. The young man went to speak with the woman and she related the events to him truthfully. Soon after, the couple were married. A year later the Polish government allowed Jewish emigration to *Eretz Yisrael*, and they went. Meanwhile, a cousin of this girl, who after the War was smuggled out of Hungary by the *Breicha* (an organization that helped smuggle Jews out of Europe) also went to *Eretz Yisrael*. She heard that a Jewish boy and his Polish *shiktza* (as they referred to her) came from her hometown to settle in Israel. No one believed that she was Jewish. This cousin assumed that everyone left behind had perished, so she didn't go to speak to them. In time, she again heard the story and something drew her to go and speak with them. She went to the town and asked where the *Polishe shiktza* lives. She went to the house, knocked on the door and, because of their strong family resemblance, they immediately recognized each other and an emotional reunion followed.

America

We arrived in New York in 1946, after having been sponsored by an aunt who came to America before the War. My parents immediately enrolled me in Mesivta Tifereth Jerusalem, located in the Lower Eastside of Manhattan, where I finished my elementary school education. Though I had no direct relationship with him at the time, Rabbi Moshe Feinstein, זצ"ל, had already assumed the position of *Rosh HaYeshiva* of MTJ. In 1948, I went to Yeshiva Ner Israel in Baltimore for my high school studies. I remained there for the next 18 years, eventually becoming a rebbe and *menahal* of the High School program. At one point,

We arrived in New York in 1946, sponsored by an aunt who came to America before the War.

The 26th American Army Division meets the 297th Russian Red Banner Rifle Division in Czechoslovakia, 1945

Photo credit: Capt. S.M. Kasnett

after I was in Baltimore for close to nine years, the *Rosh HaYeshiva*, Rabbi Yaakov Yitzchak Ruderman, זצ"ל, sent me to Toronto for a short period of time to help start the Ner Israel Mesivta and Yeshiva in Canada. I benefitted greatly from my close relationship with Rabbi Ruderman, and with Rabbi Dovid Kronglas, the *Mashgiach*, during my years in Baltimore. These giants of Torah and *Mussar* had a great influence on my development in Torah and *Yiddishkeit*. This is true of my relationship with the administration and *rebbaim* of the yeshiva as well. In 1965, I went to the Yeshiva of Staten Island where I have been *zocheh* to be *marbitz* Torah for the last 34 years. I enjoyed a warm and meaningful relationship with Rabbi Moshe Feinstein, זצ"ל, until his *petirah* in 1986, and I continue to share a wonderful relationship with his son, Rabbi Reuven Feinstein, the *Rosh HaYeshiva*. I am eternally indebted to Hashem for saving my family from the Nazi inferno, and to my parents for guiding me on my path in *Yiddishkeit*, allowing me to spend my life within the *daled amos* of Torah.

The story of each survivor is replete with endless miraculous events, and we need to study these lives.

This is what we lived through, and by witnessing all of these events we saw the *Hashgachah* of the *Ribono shel Olam* with every step we took. The story of each survivor is replete with endless miraculous events, and we need to study these lives, appreciating the greatness of those who survived and of those who perished. The Holocaust is part of our present exile, and just as we were redeemed from Mitzrayim through unparalleled miracles, so will we be redeemed from this exile, בע"ה. It is up to us to merit this salvation by remaining Torah-true Jews, loyal to the greatness of our historical role as G-d's Holy Nation and Chosen People.

While this interview was being completed during the summer of 1998, Rabbi Weiss lost both of his parents, Reb Menachem Mendel ben Meir, z'l, and Rochel bas Mordechai Shmuel, a'h, within a few weeks of each other. In death, as well as in life, they were united – "Beloved and pleasant in their lives and in their death not parted" (Shmuel II, 1:23). May they serve as מליצי יושר *in our behalf.*

We hope that the inspiration derived by the reader from the interviews in this series will serve as a tribute, not only to them, but to all of those survivors who were moser nefesh and revived the true spirit of Yiddishkeit throughout the world.

ת.נ.צ.ב.ה

REMEMBERING MUNKACS: "A MOTHER CITY OF ISRAEL"

An Interview with Mr. Hershel Ostreicher

Munkacs was known as an *Ir v'aim b'Yisrael* (a mother city of the Jewish people). It was a city that was saturated with a deep *chassidic* spirit. No Jewish shops were open on Shabbos, and, thus lacking business, even the gentiles closed their stores. Without the Jews, with whom were they going to do business? *Erev* Shabbos a shofar was blown (like the siren today in Jerusalem) to let everyone know when it was time to light the Shabbos candles. Ten minutes before this there was a blast of the shofar reminding the bakers to put the *cholents* into the ovens, and warning the storekeepers to close their stores.

*The spirit in Munkacs was that **here** Torah reigns supreme and that **this** is the way to live.*

One *erev* Shabbos a *chassid* came to the Minchas Elozer (Rabbi Chaim Elozer Shapiro), the *rov* of Munkacs and one of the Torah giants of the generation, to tell him that one of the *yiddishe* stores was open after the shofar blast. The Rebbe responded with disbelief, "What? One of the *yiddishe mentchen* has his store open on Shabbos?!" He sent the *gabbai* to close it up. *Bochurim* from the yeshiva came and *chasidim* in *streimels* and *bekishehs*, and began dancing in front of the store. The storekeeper called the police, who came right away. The *bochurim* took hold of the policeman and brought him into their circle, dancing all around him. They put a *streimel* on his head and kept him trapped in the circle. The officer was yelling, "Let me go! Let me go! I just want to get out of here." After the policeman left, the *bochurim* pulled down the shutters in front of the store and locked the storekeeper in until Shabbos was over. This was Munkacs! The spirit in Munkacs was that **here** Torah reigns supreme and that **this** is the way to live.

The *rabbonim* and lay people would not let a few individuals create a breach in the *halachah*. This was Munkacs!

Before the War, 30,000 Jews lived in Munkacs, including the surrounding small towns and villages. It was a city with 35 *Battei Medrashim*. The Minchas Elozer had his own *Beis Medrash* and

Chassidim passing in front of Munkacs City Hall

court. In addition, he administered the *kollel* in *Eretz Yisrael*. Everyone had a *pushke* in their home and this money supported the *kollel*. One of the *chassidim*, Reb Shmuel Chaim Deutsch, went around before *yom tov* to collect the *pushke* funds for the *kollel* families. He would also collect money from the surrounding towns, where many of the men belonged to the local Munkacser Kollel, *Teferes Tzvi*, even though they weren't Munkacser *Chassidim*. The *kollel* still exists today.

The *Kehillah* had its own *shul* and *Beis Medrash Hagadol* which belonged to the entire community. There were also a number of *shtiblach* that belonged to different *chassidic* groups or sects. Besides the Munkacser *Chassidim*, there were also Vizhnitzer, Belzer and Spinker *Chassidim*. Both the Belzer Rebbe and the Spinker Rebbe lived in Munkacs at one time. The two Zidtchover Rebbes, Reb Menashele and Reb Moshele, both *mekubalim*, had their courts in Munkacs. The dominant figure in the city, however, was the Minchas Elozer.

The Kehillah had its own shul and Beis Medrash Hagadol which belonged to the entire community.

The Minchas Elozer had his own special matzah bakery at home. He often made surprise visits to the local bakeries to see that the *matzohs* were baked properly. Once I announced that the Rebbe was coming to the bakery. We always did this when the Rebbe came to *shul*. As we saw him approach

Students honoring a visiting Rebbe to Munkacs, Reb Chaninah Halbershtam, the Kalashitzer Rebbe.

The Spinka Rebbe (circled) at the Levaya of the Minchas Elozer

we would run inside to tell everyone. He gave me a little slap, smiled and told me that I'm not supposed to tell anyone when he comes to check the matzoh bakery. He also made surprise visits to the butcher shops. He diligently monitored the ritual functioning of the city. He was a *kanoi*, a zealous and independent spirit, who upheld the Torah without compromise.

The Minchas Elozer was a kanoi, a zealous and independent spirit, who upheld the Torah without compromise.

Geography and Politics

After WWI Czechoslovakia assumed political control over the Carpathian Mountains and the Jewish people lived, more or less, בשלום ובשלוה, in peace and tranquility, with their neighbors. It was a time of prosperity, and the Jews shared in this prosperity with everyone else. Czechoslovakia was a republic with laws that protected her citizens. In this respect, our experience was very different from that of the Polish Jews who suffered from poverty, pogroms and anti-Jewish economic legislation resulting from the newly acquired Polish independence and spirit of nationalism after WWI. In Czechoslovakia there was very little outward anti-Semitism, and many Jews succeeded in living very comfortably.

There were instances involving tax collection policies where Czechoslovakian government officials entered Jewish homes and appropriated personal possessions in lieu of taxes that were owed. Since most Jews were in retail or wholesale businesses, this happened quite often. As a young *bochur*, I remember a tailor who suffered this fate. People brought him material to make suits of clothing for themselves and their children before Pesach. Shortly before *yom tov*, when all the suits were ready

Merchant selling kosher ice cream

(R-L) The Minchas Elozer, Rabbi Meir Shapiro and their Gabboim in Marienbad, Czech.

Mr. Ostreicher as a 17 year old yeshiva bochur

to be delivered, the government officials came and took everything away. The tailor was heartbroken, not only because the people wouldn't have their suits for Pesach, but because he wouldn't have the money he needed for his *yom tov* expenses as well. This took place in 1936. This kind of activity was not just directed against the Jews, but it affected a great many non-Jews as well.

In addition to property, sometimes the tax people took away household goods.

Another instance of this nature involved the Minchas Elozer. It was a Friday afternoon when the tax agents came to his house. They wanted to take away his *seforim* as payment for the taxes. He explained to them that as a Rabbi his *seforim* are his most important possessions since he requires these books to decide Jewish law. As the argument between them continued, one of the agents spied the Rebbe Meir Baal Hanais *pushke* that was built into the wall. Noticing this, the Rebbe went to the wall and stood in front of the *pushke*. The tax collectors tried to push him away, but, firmly standing his ground, he solemnly announced, "The only way you'll reach this *pushke* is to come through my heart." At that point many of the yeshiva *bochurim* entered the room and created chaos by yelling and pushing the tax collectors. It reached the point that the Rebbe wanted the police to come and help. Although he was very influential in the city they refused to assist him because they themselves were afraid of the government officials. In this case the situation was resolved satisfactorily.

In addition to property, sometimes the tax people took away household goods as well. In fact, this course of

Top Right: The Darkei Teshuva, Top Left: The Minchas Elozer, Center: Rabbi Boruch Rabinowitz, Bottom: Rabbi Nota S. Shlissel with Talmidim

action was one of the main issues that the Minchas Elozer protested to the government. In one sense you can see how good the Jews really had it at that time if this was the most difficult outstanding issue between them and the government. The Czechoslovakian government didn't legislate against the Jews economically the way the Poles did, they only wanted to collect the taxes they felt were owed to them. The political atmosphere in the two countries was notably different. In any case, when Dr. Edward Benes, the Czechoslovakian president, once visited Munkacs the Rebbe was invited to greet him. During their meeting the Rebbe strongly protested the treatment of the people by the tax collectors and the overall government policy in this area. The Rebbe assured the President that if people could not pay the entire tax at once, over time they surely would, and that the government does not have the right to confiscate personal property for delinquency in paying taxes. Benes only smiled and said, "I understand your feeling concerning this issue, Rabbi, however, we are running a country."

Mr. Ostreicher's father, Reb Menachem, leaving the Munkacs Beis Hamedrash with a friend's child.

Some say that the Minchas Elozer did not particularly like the Czechs because he felt they were not meticulous in their religious observances. By and large they were not a very religious people.[25] The Russians and the Hungarians went to church to observe their holidays, but the Czechs were lazy about attending. This he opposed. The Rebbe felt that the Hungarians were a more religious nation, and therefore he had greater respect for them. Unfortunately, we were to find out later that, in great measure, the strong Hungarian adherence to religion generated a rabid hatred for the Jews.

My father was the Minchas Elozer's right-hand-man, the Secretary of State as it were. He executed the political policies of the Rebbe. The Rebbe had no time to enter into these affairs, but he directed my father regarding which actions to take on behalf of the Carpathian-Russian Jewish political organization. The Carpathian Russian community was a very big and beautiful one. Some of the communities that

25. This stands in stark contrast to the very strong influence of the Catholic religion that existed in Poland at that time. The Church in Poland was so powerful that its clergy were easily able to incite the masses against the Jews. **See The World That Was Poland**, History Section.

Carpathian Mountain villagers: a child taking his first ride

comprised this area were: Chust, Munkacs, Brezna, Ungvar, Svaliva, Szolos, Michalovce, Bergszaz, Kiraly-haz, Kiraly-Helmec, Slotfino and Irsava.

The Orthodox Council would speak out on social and political issues as they affected Orthodox Jewry living in Hungary, Slovakia and the Carpathians.

The Minchas Elozer was the head of the Orthodox Council Office of the Carpathian Russian area. Hungary's office was in Budapest, the Czechoslovakian office was in Pressberg, and the Carpathian office was in Ungvar. The Orthodox Council would speak out on social and political issues as they affected Orthodox Jewry living in Hungary, Slovakia and the Carpathians. I remember when I was very young that my father ran for the office of Council Deputy (similar to the level of a state assemblyman in the U.S.) in the Carpathian Russian Provincial government. I remember him traveling from community to community speaking on the issues confronting the Jewish population. He came from a small town called Strobicsi, and when he returned there during the campaign he was greeted with a tumultuous reception. People were calling out "Menachem is here!" I'll never forget that and how he stepped up to the platform and took off his *streimel* (it was Saturday night) to greet the crowd, revealing his *yarmulke* underneath–he was a proud Jew and the gentiles appreciated his earnestness. I was so proud of him. In the elections at that time each candidate ran by name and number. My father ran as candidate number 21. I asked him why

DETAIL MAP OF MAJOR JEWISH CITIES AND TOWNS IN 1938

GALICIA
U.S.S.R. (UKRAINE)
Carpathian Mountains
SLOVAKIA
Kamenets Podolsk
Uzhorod
Mukacevo (Munkacs)
Satoroljoujhely
BESSARABIA
BUCOVINA
Miskolc
Chust
Rachoy
Nyiregyhaza
Sighet
Ruscova
Botosani
Satu-Mare (Satmar)
Viseul-de-sus
HUNGARY
Debrecen
MOLDAVIA
TRANSYLVANIA
Cluj (Klausenburg)
ROMANIA

Some of the more well known Jewish towns in the Carpathian Russian area

he chose that number and he responded that twenty-one numerically equals the Hebrew word אך, as in אך טוב. The word אך means *only*, so אך טוב means *only good*. I asked him how the election turned out, and laughingly he replied, "Not so good."

Munkacs was not a farm town, it was a city that greatly valued formal education, consequently you had many intellectual gentiles living there as well. This was one of the few larger cities in the entire Carpathian area. From Chust and eastward (further to the east toward the Romanian part of Transylvania and the Carpathian mountains area was the Carpathian Maramaros area). Sighet was also Maramaros, but it was a larger city as was Teitch. These were predominately poor communities. Sighet and Slotfino, where I learned in yeshiva, were near the border between Hungary and Romania. Many Jews from this area made a living by transporting goods over the borders from one country to the other.

Early Life

As in most of Eastern Europe, there was no indoor plumbing in Munkacs (we used outhouses) and we often had to melt water kept in the house overnight during the winter. Many of the houses were built from brick, but the poorer people lived in little houses, really nothing more than glorified shacks. Some of the poor would go around town on Friday asking for a piece of *challah* for their children. Others would go out to try to find wood to make a little fire to keep their children warm. Many poor from the Maramaros area came asking for *nedavos*, or a piece of bread. A sizable number remained in Munkacs from one *yom tov* until the next because in Munkacs at least they were able to survive.

As I mentioned, our relationships with the gentiles seemed tolerable (we didn't suffer from pogroms), however, no one I know was saved by gentiles during the War. My father repeatedly asked one of the gentiles who worked for us in the *mikveh* to hide us when the persecutions began and he replied, "If you ask me once more then I will report you!" In general, for the Jews of Eastern Europe it was far from simple living in such a precarious situation with such neighbors.

I was born in a house on Zrinyi Street, in 1921. I was named after the *Darkei Teshuvah*, Rabbi Tzvi Hirsh Shapiro. I am the oldest of six brothers. Three of us survived the War. My parents and three brothers perished in the concentration

Munkacs was not a farm town, it was a city that greatly valued formal education.

Courtyard of Reb Yosef Zorach's shul. Chassid has removed his streimel and placed it under his bekisheh to protect it from the rain.

camps. We always lived in heart of Munkacs because my father was already leasing the *mikveh* when I was born.

My father leased the *mikveh* from the *Kehillah*, paying a fixed amount for the managerial rights. There were four *mikvoas*: one for the *maisim*, the dead,

Present day picture of Mikveh building

for their *teharah*; then there was the first class *mikveh*; the second class *mikveh*; and the *mikveh* for the women. The first class *mikveh* was very fancy, with private changing rooms, bathtubs, a steam room and swimming pool. It cost two and a half *kronen*. Those who couldn't afford to pay that much went to the second class *mikveh*, but it wasn't as fancy. The womens' *mikveh* was very beautiful. If someone couldn't afford the cost of the *mikveh* they received a coupon from the *Kehillah* that my father would later redeem for payment. We made a very nice living from this.

My father leased the mikveh from the Kehillah, paying a fixed amount for the managerial rights.

Soon after I was born we moved to Masaryk Street. A little *Beis Hamedrash* founded by a great, great uncle of ours, Reb Yosef Zorach Horowitz, a decendent of the *Sh'lah HaKadosh* was located there. Reb Yosef Zorach supported *asarah batlanim* to learn in his *Beis Hamedrash* 24 hours a day, in three shifts. I remember, once a great *Chassidishe* Rebbe came to the *Beis Hamedrash* to visit. As he walked in the door, he lifted his hand to kiss the *mezuzah*. Suddenly he exclaimed, "How awesome is this place–" the same words Yaakov *Avinu* said when he reached *Har HaMoriah*! It was a holy place. Reb Yosef Zorach was a man who dedicated himself to *Avodas Hashem*.

He was a Sanzer *Chassid*. He once went to the Sanzer Rebbe, the famous Divrei Chaim, to receive a blessing for children. The Rebbe promised him that he would have children, but stipulated that he must not stop on his way home for any reason. Unfortunately, he forgot, and on the way he stopped for a business transaction. When no children were forthcoming he asked the Sanzer Rov why, and the Rov reminded him that he was told to go directly home.

He paid for all of his Torah and *chesed* activities from his own monies. He was very wealthy. His *Beis Hamedrash* was always full. Even those who *davened*

Reb Yosef Zorach's small Beis Hamedresh. Mr. Ostreicher is pointing out the porch to his son, grandchildren and the Rabbi of the Carpathians.

with the Minchas Elozer on Shabbos, would *daven* in Reb Yosef Zorach's *shul* during the week. There was one *minyan* after another throughout the morning. Most of the *bochurim* who received *smichah* came from that *shul*. There was a young man, later known as the Ulemer Rov (he passed away last year), who came from this *Beis Hamedrash*. He married the Spinka Rebbe's sister after the War. His father was a *melamed* in Munkacs. They were very poor. This young man used to come to Reb Yosef Zorach's *Beis Hamedrash* everyday to learn. He ate a piece of bread and a little piece of onion for his meal. He learned until 1:00 am and was in *shul* again at 5:00 am. There were many *bochurim* like him. Once I asked him how he was able to dress so nicely if he barely had money for food. He said, "My mother told me that no one will ever look into my stomach to see what's there, but people will always see how I present myself. My mother is concerned that I should always look neat and presentable." There was always tea available in the *shul*, so he had tea with his meal. About this *bochur* my father quoted *Chazal*, that one should be careful with the children of the poor, because from them will come the future Torah leaders. If you want to know what a *tzaddik* is, he was a true *tzaddik*. After the War he came to America. He learned night and day without a stop.

Reb Yosef Zorach and his wife had no children, so he supported some of the poor *kallahs* and orphans in Munkacs. He was a one man *chesed* organization. When Reb Yosef Zorach died, he left a substantial fund to marry off some orphans and poor of the city. Realizing that someone was needed to oversee these funds, my great-grandfather became the *apotropus*, the guardian, of the orphans. He was a brother-in-law of Reb Yosef Zorach. After my great-grandfather died we moved into Reb Yosef Zorach's house, and eventually my father became the *apotropus*. To live in an apartment on the first floor was wonderful. It was a beautiful house. There was a porch facing the street with the following insignia carved into the wrought iron fencing surrounding the porch: *Yosef Zorach Segal*– תרל"ט. When I was living there I was unaware of this inscription.

Chazal say, One should be careful with the children of the poor, because from them will come the future Torah leaders.

On one of my recent trips to Munkacs I went back to see the house. After the Communists took control at the end of World War II, the house was subdivided into two apartments. Originally it had the shape of an "L" and the apartments were formed at the juncture of the "L". One of the

Reb Yosef Zorach's porch with wrought iron inscription

Back of Reb Yosef Zorach's house where the Ostreichers lived.

occupants let us in to her side to see the apartment, but the other tenant would not let us come in. I wanted to see all of the rooms, but she wouldn't allow. She set her dog on us. We went back a second time and the same Russian woman let us in to her apartment again. We brought cigarettes with us and other things to give her as a present. My wife said that we brought the wrong items, since they had practically nothing to eat we should have brought food. The woman began talking to us in Hungarian. She told us to go away, because the other Russian woman told her that we are here to take away the house. She was begging us to go away. I told her, "Lady, if you were to give me the whole house filled with gold and silver I wouldn't want it. I don't want to come back here."

The buildings remain, but the deep roots of Yiddishkeit that once flourished were long ago violently uprooted and have withered.

I have returned to Munkacs three times with my children and grandchildren since the end of the War. The buildings remain, but the deep roots of *Yiddishkeit* that once flourished were long ago violently uprooted and have withered. As with so many destroyed *Yiddishe* cities and towns in Eastern Europe, the cemetery in Munkacs was destroyed and left in disarray. On one of my first visits my son Yossi and grandsons Menachem and David were sickened to see cows grazing in the cemetery. There were bones and skulls strewn all about. The cows just kicked them out of their way as they grazed. It was horrible. Recently the mayor from Munkacs visited America and the Rebbe met with him. A large parking garage had been built over part of the cemetery. Altogether the cemetery is four or five square blocks in size. The Rebbe appealed to the mayor's sense of decency and respect for the dead and upon returning to Munkacs he was instrumental in having the parking garage torn down. The cemetery

Memorial Plaque for the Martyrs of Munkacs on the side of the former shul, which is presently three stores.

Goats grazing in the old Munkacs Cemetery

he had passed away. This *Rov* was instrumental in having the man's body exhumed and buried in the smaller Jewish cemetery. He uses the old Spinker Rebbe's *shul* for his base of operations, and serves meals there for the local Jews. He has a "*minyan*" comprised of a few old people sitting around who can't *daven*. After all, who remained in Hungary after the revolution in 1956? Only those Jews who didn't know or care about *Yiddishkeit*. He feels that he is accomplishing something and that is what keeps him going. He travels from one community to another during the year to help the Jews in whatever way he can.

We visited the house of the Minchas Elozor during that trip. It became the office of the NKVD, the feared Russian police force. The two *succos* were turned into offices. The *Beis Hamedrash* was completely torn down. This is what is left of a city that was once a fortress of *Yiddishkeit* as I will now describe to you.

Mr. Ostriecher standing in the Ohel of the Minchas Elozer

has since been restored and is now surrounded with a strong fence and proper gates. At least our ancestors once again rest in dignity, but their original tombstones were used by the Germans and Hungarians to pave the streets. There is a newer Jewish cemetery, only a few steps away from the gentile cemetery, that was given to the remaining Jews of Munkacs by the Communists after the War.

Presently there is a young man from Israel who calls himself the "*Rov* of the Carpathians." He performs many deeds of kindness for the few remaining Jews of that area. When I met him there several years ago he told me that there would be a burial that day. A Jew who was mentally ill had been brought to an institution in Munkacs many years ago. Eventually he died and they buried him in the gentile cemetery. He had a niece who visited him from time to time. Recently she came and discovered that

Gravestones dumped in corner of parking garage construction site

Minchas Elozer's courtyard. (L-R) Minchas Elozer's Mother's house, Center: Minchas Elozer's house, Right: The two Succahs (converted into offices).

Education

The Munkacs Talmud Torah schools only taught *Lemudei Kodesh* studies, for secular subjects we went to public school.

Boys coming out of Talmud Torah building. Mr.Ostreicher's brothers Shmuel Zanvil and Dovid. (circled)

There were two schedules for the public school classes. One shift went from 8:00 am until 1:00 pm, the second shift was from 1:00 pm until 6:00 pm. The Jewish children went separately from the gentiles. We had the same teachers as the non-Jewish children. One of the teachers once pulled my *payos* when I did something wrong, but I don't remember them acting overtly anti-Semitic. In any case, I was afraid to tell my father that I had done something wrong. The Jewish *Kehillah* had tremendous power in Munkacs–*no one* wanted to start up with them or the Minchas Elozer. He was a very fiery spirit possessed of an iron will. In general, the non-Jews were hesitant to start up with the *Kehillah* politically, or otherwise.

There were three Talmud Torahs in Munkacs. Each one had close to 1,000 children in attendance. The scope and sequence of the different levels of learning was as follows:

Level 1.	Kindergarten to Aleph-Beis
Level 2.	Tefillah (learning to Daven)
Level 3.	Chumash
Level 4.	Rashi Instruction
Level 5.	Mishnayos
Level 6.	Gemora

As you progressed in *Gemora* you were expected to know two or two and a half *blatt*, of *Gemora* each week. At the end of each *zeman* there was a week of review. One *zeman* ended right before Rosh Hashanah. Unlike in America where the *bochurim* remain in the yeshiva for the *Yomim Noraim*, we returned home to be with our parents and Rebbe. Wherever we learned, we always returned to Munkacs for *yom tov*. We learned 50 to 60 *blatt* during the winter or summer *zeman*, so before returning home we had a two week *Chazarah*, review period. We had to know these *blatt* by heart. During this review period we studied the *Gemora* over and over again, testing each other on all 60 *blatt*, including *Rashi* and *Tosafos*. It was like this throughout almost all of the Yeshivos in Hungary.

Board of Directors of Munkacser Yeshiva. Mr. Ostreicher's father is seated to the right. Standing are the officers of the various Yeshiva services: Chevra Bochurim, Tzedakah, Kinyon Seforim, Kinyon Mezonos and Maskil L'Dalim.

The Talmud Torahs in Munkacs were structured very formally, and run under the direction of the *Kehillah*. Everyone attended *cheder* from 6-8am. First session public school children returned to *cheder* at 2, while noon session children returned from 6-8pm. Every Shabbos afternoon the children from the age of *Chumash* Level and above gathered in their Talmud Torah to review their week's lessons. The Board of the Talmud Torahs would visit each of the schools to test the children. Some of the members would bring candy to give to the children if they knew their lessons well. Sunday the *rebbe* would admonish those students who didn't do well, having been informed by the Board which *talmidim* needed to improve.

Yeshiva "Machene Chaim" in Slotfino

The Board was comprised of *ba'alei battim* who volunteered to serve for a specific period of time.

When you finished learning in the Talmud Torah (usually at 14 or 15 years of age) you went on to learn in a yeshiva. I learned in four different yeshivos. At the first, Sinina, the Rosh Yeshiva had no children, so he picked out 25 to 30 *bochurim* to learn with him. We slept in his house and were treated like his own children. I remained in Sinina for a short period of time and then went to Slotfino. The Slotfino Rosh Yeshiva (and *Morah D'asra*) was a brother-in-law to the present Satmar Rebbe (Rabbi Moshe Teitelbaum, *shlit'a*). He was an unbelievable *dayan* (rabbinical judge), one of the greatest *bororim* (one who clarifies legal circumstances) in the Carpathian Russian province.

When you finished learning in the Talmud Torah (usually at 14 or 15 years of age) you went on to learn in a yeshiva.

In Slotfino I had to know 2½ to 3 *blatt* by heart each week. I didn't really have a problem understanding the *Gemora*, but committing it to memory was not so easy for me. The test on *Gemora*, *Rashi* and *Tosafos* was on Thursday, on Friday we were tested on *Chumash* and *Rashi*, and *on motzei* Shabbos we were tested on *Shulchan Orach-Orach Chaim*. This was done so that we would be busy learning all of Shabbos. The *gabbai* of the yeshiva called out the names of the boys who were to be tested each week. You weren't necessarily called on each week, but since you didn't know when you would be tested you always had to be ready. When the *rebbe* called me I took my *Gemora* with me. He asked me why I needed the *Gemora* and I told him that, "My memory is a bit *shvach*, a bit weak, it doesn't serve me right." He responded very cutely, "Really! Where do you come from? What is the address of your house? What is your father's name? What is your mother's name?" I answered each question in turn. So he responded, "If you can remember this, you can remember the *Gemora* as well." Do you understand what he was teaching me? If the *Gemora* will mean to me what my home means to me... what my father and mother mean to me... then I will certainly be able to remember the *Gemora* by heart!

If you didn't remember the *Gemora* there was a *k'nas*, a fine. We ate in a *menzo*, something like a restaurant. The poorer *bochurim* had *teig gegessin*, which means they took their meals with different families throughout the week. My father was able to afford the *menzo*, so that's where I ate. The money was sent directly to the restaurant, not to me. When I didn't do well on the *Gemora* test the *rebbe* instructed the people at the *menzo* not to serve me that week, so I had to ask my parents for money and got into even more trouble. I assure you that I knew the *Gemora* by heart the next time.

I was 14 at the time. My father was not happy with my progress so he sent me to Galanta. Galanta was a yeshiva with 300 *bochurim*. It was in the Oberland area of Hungary. Actually, it was located in Slovakia at that time. The Carpathains and part of Slovakia were under the control of the Czech Republic before World War II, thus the President of the Czech Republic also governed over these areas as well. Oberland means to the west–the western part of the country. Munkacs was located in what would be called the Unterland, or eastern part of the country. The very good yeshivos were located in the Oberland area. Some of the cities and towns located there are: Pressburg (where the *Chasam Sofer* had his yeshiva), Galanta, Szerdohely, Nyitra and Piestan.

Spiritual Life
Yomim Noraim

When the days of *Slichos* arrived my father woke us at 3:30 in the morning. He told us, "Even the fish in the water are trembling! How can you sleep?!" We immediately got up and went to the *mikveh*. My father was paid extra for *davening* during the days of *Slichos*, Rosh Hashanah and Yom Kippur. He didn't need the money, but he took it for a special reason. After Yom Kippur, he doubled the amount of the money he was paid from his own personal funds. He distributed this money to the poor so they would be able to buy potatoes and other food stuffs to store away for the winter. My brothers and I were all *meshorerim* during this time of the year and we were also paid. We used to put down a little plate for people to leave tips for us figuring that Father wouldn't find out. This way we could make a little extra money. After Yom Kippur, when Father prepared the monies for distribution to the poor, he told us to give him the money we received, and then he added, "...and the tips as well." This was in addition to four weeks of allowance. He called it *kaporah gelt*, atonement money. After *Slichos* we went around the town collecting *tzedakah* to distribute to the poor for Rosh Hashanah and Succos.

The Munkacser Shul's Choir

My father distributed this money to the poor so they would be able to buy food stuffs to store away for the winter.

Erev Rosh Hashanah we went to the Rebbe to give him our *kivitalach* and to receive a blessing. Each year my father told the Minchas Elozer that he would like to *daven* in the Rebbe's *Beis Medrash*, rather than be the *ba'al tefillah* in another *shul*. However, the members of that *shul* insisted that since they couldn't *daven* with the Rebbe because there was absolutely no room to squeeze in another body, my father should *daven* in their *shul* so they could hear the *nusach* and the *niggunim* of the Rebbe. My father knew the *nusach*

Reb Chaim Yosef(in front) was chazen of the Great Beis Hamedrash in Munkacs. Reb Yossel Rupp (in back) was the leader of the Rebbe's Kapalia.

by heart–forwards and backwards. The Rebbe told my father, "If my *chassidim* want to *daven* with me, with my *nusach* and *niggunim*, but they can't because there is no room, then it is your job to *daven* with them. After you finish *davening* you will come to me." When the Minchas Elozer finished *davening* on Rosh Hashanah day the *gabbaim* would announce that *Kiddush Hayom* could no longer be made that day. That's how long the prayers lasted. Many of the *chassidim* would quickly *daven Minchah*, and then go to another *shul* to *daven Maariv* because the Rebbe would not be *davening Maariv* until much later, around 11:00 pm. People had not eaten the whole day and it was now 6:30 in the evening!

It was my father's minhag to remain awake the entire night on Yom Kippur... Every year he introduced new niggunim into the service.

The day after Rosh Hashanah it was impossible to approach the Rebbe because on this day the *chassidim* from out of town were given preference to see him and receive a blessing. They had to travel back to their homes and businesses, so the Rebbe saw them first. Eventually, we were able to get into the Rebbe, *kivital* in hand, and he would *bentch* us.

It was my father's *minhag* to remain awake the entire night on Yom Kippur. He would say *Tehillim* and then learn from the *Zohar*. The next day he *davened Musaf* and *Neilah*. Every year he introduced new *niggunim* into the service. *Motzei* Yom Kippur the air became electrified with the preparations for Succos.

Reb Hersh Freidis, who gave malkos to the Minchas Elozer every Erev Yom Kippur. He died at the age of 108. Left: Mr. Ostreicher's uncle, Avraham Hersh Broyde, Second Chazon of the main Shul.

As a side business, my father sold *esrogim*. Right after Rosh Hashanah he went to Trieste, Italy, to purchase the *esrogim*. The dealer had them all prepared for him, so it didn't take him much time to conclude his business dealings and return home immediately. One year the dealer showed him five exceptional *esrogim*. Father figured that one would be for the Minchas Elozer, another for the Spinka Rebbe, and the other three for whoever would pay such a high price. The *esrog* dealer told my father that the five *esrogim* cost 500 *kronen*. Father responded that he would only pay 400 *kronen*. The man, a *goy*, took one of the *esrogim* and bit off the *pitim*. Then he said, "Now I have four *esrogim*. Will you give me 500 *kronen*?" My father quickly took out the 500 *kronen* and paid him. The man was so evil. He received more pleasure from ruining the *esrogim* than he did from the profit he made! After Father returned home he quickly unpacked the *esrogim* because the people were anxious to buy.

Succos was *Zeman Simchasainu*, a time of real rejoicing. We already needed a light coat at that time, but it wasn't very cold. Anyone who had the same name as one of the *Ushpizen* served cake and wine in his *succah* to any visitors who came by. We had two *Ushpizen* in our family, Moishe and Yosef Dovid.

The Rebbe had two *succos*. One was very large where he held his *tish*, while the other was smaller for his snacks and sleeping. On each night of *Chol Hamoed* we went to the Rebbe for a *Simchas Beis Hashoaivah*. A band played and everyone danced and sang, it was very uplifting. The Rebbe read aloud the *Mishnah* describing the *simchah* of the *Simchas Beis Hashoaivah* in the *Beis HaMikdash*. This infused the *chassidim* with a tremendous spiritual fervor, and when the band actually started playing this tremendous *ruach* would burst forth. Every year the Rebbe composed a new *niggun* for *Simchas Torah*. In order that everyone should know this tune for the dancing on *Simchas Torah* the band played it over and over again during *Chol Hamoed*. To see two to three thousand people dancing around and around to this melody on *yom tov* was a beautiful, beautiful spectacle to behold.

On *Hoshanah Rabbah* the Rebbe finished *davening* about 4:00 in the afternoon. After every *hakafah* circuit he delivered a *drashah* on the meaning of the *Hoshanah* that was read preceding the *hakafah*. The present Rebbe finishes at 3:30 in the afternoon on *Hoshanah Rabbah* because, like the Minchas

Title page of the Minchas Elozer's drashos, Divrei Kodesh, on Yomim Noraim, compiled by his students.

ב"ה

דברי קודש

דרושים ורשמי התעוררות אמרות ה' אמרות טהורות
שנאמר בבית מדרש רבנו בסדר אמירת ההושענות

ביום הושענה רבה תרצ"ג

מפי קודש אדמו"ר רב האי גאון שר התורה והיראה
צדיק יסוד עולם רעיא מהימנא קדישא עילאה.

רבינו חיים אלעזר שפירא שליט"א
הגאבדק"ק מונקאטש והגלילות יע"א
ונשיא כולל מונקאטש ועשרה גלילות באה"ק תובב"א.

והוספנו עוד מחאה ·מהיראים· מירושלים נגד התועים.

הודפס ע"י היראים דפה

פעיה"ק ירושלים תובב"א
שנת טובים דברי קודש לפ"ק

דפוס "המערב" ירושלים.

Elozer, his custom is that after each *hakafah* the shofar is also blown. The pattern of our *hakafos* differs from that of everyone else. They originated with the *Bnei Yisuschar*, the Minchas Elozer's great-grandfather. Special *tefillos* are added with beautiful melodies. It is a completely different *nusach*. The Rebbe danced, running back and forth between the *chassidim* who were lined up on each side. Because it was so crowded, people were literally hanging on to the windows to look inside. You just couldn't get in. It was so crowded that the walls were sweating. For the sixth *hakafah* the Rebbe danced in one spot. A chair was brought for him to sit on, only he never sat down. He would jump up and down, on and off the chair that entire *hakafah*, holding the Baal Shem Tov's *Sefer* Torah. Today, the Rebbe dances with this *Sefer* Torah on *Simchas Torah* night and *leins* from it for *Minchah* on Yom Kippur. On *Shemini Atzeres* night the Minchas Elozer used Reb Moishe Leib Sassover's *Sefer* Torah. For each *hakafah* on *Shemini Atzeres* and *Simchas Torah* he danced with a different *Sefer* Torah, some were from *dorei doros*, handed down from many, many previous generations.

The joy that we experienced on Chanukah in Europe was much different from that in America.

Some time ago my brother and I bought the Baal Shem Tov's *Sefer* Torah from the owner in *Eretz Yisrael* as a gift for the present Rebbe. I didn't realize that my father was one of the men who brought this *Sefer* Torah to the Minchas Elozer in Munkacs many years before. The Minchas Elozer sent my father and some others to buy this *Sefer* Torah at a cost of 100,000 *kronen*. The Rebbe told my father to go to the bank and tell them that he needs 100,000 *kronen*. My father responded that he was wearing his *streimel* and *kapoteh*, meaning that it was *Chol Hamoed*, and that he does not write on *Chol Hamoed*. The Minchas Elozer replied, "You're a *batlan* (lazy)! You go to the bank and tell them that Rabbi Chaim Shapiro sent you and they will give you the money." This is exactly what happened.

This Torah scroll is very small, only four or five inches in length. It is now in the Munkacser Rebbe's *Beis Hamedrash* in Boro Park. It has it's own silver *Aron Hakodesh*. It was saved from the fires of Europe by the Rebbe's father when he escaped from Munkacs and went into hiding in Budapest. On Simchas Torah the Minchas Elozer used to dance back and forth holding this *sefer* Torah. The Torah had its own little *keser*, its own little crown, and while dancing with the Torah one year the *keser* fell off. The Minchas Elozer gasped and turned white. He remarked that this was not good– "*Es is nisht goot.*" He was *nifter* that year in Munkacs. Rabbi Shapiro was the undisputed leader of Carpatio-Ruthenian Jewry in his time.

Chanukah

The joy that we experienced on Chanukah in Europe was much different from that in America. There we did not give gifts, this is an American custom that has nothing to do with Chanukah, and everything to do with America. Our enjoyment was more spiritual in nature. However, there was one aspect of Chanukah that we really did enjoy. Usually we didn't leave *cheder* until 8:00 o'clock every evening, but during Chanukah we were dismissed at 4:00. This change, and the evening we spent at home with our families lighting the *menorah* and singing together, was just wonderful.

We received Chanukah *gelt* from our parents and grandparents, aunts and uncles. In the evenings we didn't have potato *latkes* fried in oil. This we had on Pesach. For Chanukah we had *greevin* (fried onions) on baked potatoes. On Chanukah the women would clean the kitchen, take out some Pesach pots and prepare *schmaltz* (fat) from chickens and geese. There was no prepared oil, so we made our own. Some of this fat was used on Chanukah (this is what we put on top of our potatoes), and the rest was stored until Pesach.

The children didn't light their own Chanukah *menorah*, only the head of the household did this. After lighting and singing together, we all went to see the Rebbe light his *menorah*. The *chazonim* and the Rebbe's *kopelia* sang *Haneiros Halalu* and *Moaz Tzur*. After singing, the Rebbe gave a *Dvar Torah* about the meaning of Chanukah, followed by the distribution of *shirayim*–cookies, cake and schnapps.

Purim

During each of the *Megillah* readings we all broke out in song when it was read that Haman and his sons were hung. To see a whole *Beis Medrash* respond like that is very uplifting.

After the *Megillah* reading in the morning the children dressed in costumes corresponding to the theme of the Purim *spiel*. The whole day we went from house to house entertaining and collecting money for *tzedakah*. Many of the adults also went collecting for the poor. These funds were used for poor families for Pesach. The streets were crowded with children delivering *mishloach manos*[26] throughout the city. The *chassidim* streamed to the house of the Minchas Elozer to bring him *mishloach manos*. Jewish musicians walked through the streets playing Purim music, and, interestingly, so did the gypsies who passed through the town. When a group of them came to the house of the Minchas Elozer, he invited them in, listened to them play, gave them money and then sent them on their way. He said that they were the *Sa'ir Hamishtalaiach*, the goat that was sent into the desert to atone for the sins of *Klal Yisrael*. The connection the Rebbe made between Purim and *Yom HaKippurim* was as follows: On Purim one gives *tzedakah* without question when someone extends his hand to you. This same idea applies to Yom Kippur, as we recite in the *Musaf* prayer that Hashem, as it were, extends His hand to us, to receive us in *teshuvah*. In the merit of our giving to the poor who extend their hands to us on Purim, Hashem extends His hand to receive us, though we are poor in deeds, on Yom Kippur.

The streets were crowded with children delivering mishloach manos throughout the city

I vividly recall Purim 1937, when dressed as a *Chassidic* Rebbe with *streimel* and *bekishe*, white socks, slippers and a special white beard and *payos*, I held court in the *kleine Beis Hamedrash* where I ate and gave out *sherayim* to "my *chassidim*."[27] Around midnight I was accompanied by my *chassidim* to the house of the Rebbe where our two "courts" joined into one mass celebration. We sang and danced in the streets all the way to the Rebbe's house. When I entered, the Rebbe stood up and I was seated next to him. I had prepared special Purim Torah that I delivered at the *tish*. Then the Purim *spielers* (entertainers)– acrobats, dancers, musicians, etc.– came to perform before the Rebbe. They were rewarded for their efforts with Purim *gelt* from the Rebbe.

26. A gift of at least two prepared foods that are sent to at least one friend on Purim.

27. This took place in 1937 when Mr. Ostreicher was 16-years-old.

Mr. Ostreicher as the "Purim Spiel Rebbe."

We gathered at the Rebbe's tish where the bochurim performed plays and other acts of entertainment for those assembled.

On *Shushan Purim* we had a *seudah* in the afternoon. After *Minchah* we gathered at the Rebbe's *tish* where the *bochurim* performed plays and other acts of entertainment for those assembled. And who wasn't there? The whole community was there! That evening the famous *badchon*, Reb Usher Zelig, ascended to a table top and began his *spiel*, making fun of everyone and everything in Munkacs with his usual wit and good taste. All year he made his living performing at *simchos* and *chasunos*. Another *badchon*, Reb Kalman, then had his turn to entertain on the table top. Spontaneously, Reb Usher Zelig jumped up to join Reb Kalman, and the two of them put on a Purim show that took everyone by surprise and was spoken about long afterwards. Reb Kalman composed the well known *niggunim*, "*Adir Hu V'lo Yonum*" and "*Vhen Ich Bin Alt Gevoren 13 Yohr.*" This last *niggun* he introduced on the second night of Succos while singing before the Minchas Elozer on the *yahrtzeit* of the Darkei Teshuva. To this day it is sung on the second night of Succos by the Rebbe in Boro Park.

Pesach

Pesach was a busy time for us because most people didn't have new dishes for *yom tov*, they *kashered* what they had. Since we provided the process of *hagalah* at the *mikveh* we were very busy. The oven we used to heat the *mikveh* was also used to burn the *chametz*. People came *erev* Pesach to throw their *chametz* into the fire. Besides all of this activity, the *mikveh* itself was very, very busy.

My father was very tired the night of the first *Seder*, but we still didn't finish until 2:00 in the morning. Then we went to the Minchas Elozer's *Seder*. When we arrived the Rebbe wasn't even up to washing for the matzoh yet. Once the Minchas Elozer told his father, the Darkei Teshuva, that the *afikomen* should be eaten by *chatzos*, by midnight. The Darkei Teshuva quipped in return, "What! You're a *Yekki*, too!" People received *kimcha d' Pischa*–matzos and special funds–for Pesach. My mother gave away the clothes we had outgrown so that the poorer people could take them to be altered for Pesach. This way they also had something new. It was a very big treat if you could afford something brand new for Pesach. Poverty was very prevalent at that time, particularly in the Marmorish region.

For the first day of *yom tov* we *davened Minchah* as usual, and then went to *daven Ma'ariv* at the big *shul* of the *Kehillah* so that we could hear the *chazon* sing the *tefillos* with his *meshorerim*.[28] This *chazon* composed new *niggunim* for every *yom tov*.

Present day Rov of Munkacs preparing Charoses for Pesach Seder

We were all eager to hear him *daven* ...it was extremely uplifting. I never again heard such a *ba'al tefillah*. Those who wore a *streimel* and *kapoteh* on *Yom Tov* did so on *Chol Hamoed* too.

It was a very big treat if you could afford something brand new for Pesach.

Shavous in Munkacs

Very early in the morning on *erev* Shavuos we arose to the smell of Mother's baking. Her specialty was cheese *krepelach* and *deltalach* (cheescake and chocolate filled horns). First she finished the dairy baking, then she turned over the kitchen for the *fleishig* (meat) dishes to be prepared. It was my father's custom

28. The meshorerim differ from a choir in that they sang along with the tune of the chazon, including the refrains, while a choir actually sang the words of the refrain themselves.

The Munkacs Dynasty

REBBE	PLACE	WRITTEN WORKS	DATES
Bnei Yisoschor Rabbi Tzvi Elimelech Shapiro	Dinov Munkacs	*Bnei Yisoschor* *Derech Pikudechah* *Agro D'pirku* *Agro D'kalo* (11 other works published including one on *Zohar* and one on *Tanach*)	Came to Munkacs in 1825 Born 1786 Died 1841
Shem Shlomo Rabbi Shlomo Shapiro	Strizov Munkacs	*Shem Shlomo* (requested in his will that his works not be printed)	Became Rebbe after his grandfather in 1882[a]- Died in 1893 Born 1831
Darkei Teshuva Rabbi Tzvi Hirsh Shapiro	Munkacs	*Darkei Teshuva*-6 Vols. *Tiferes Bonim* *Tikunei Zohar*	Became Rebbe after his father in 1893- Died in 1914 Born 1849
Minchas Elozer Rabbi Chaim Elozer Shapiro	Munkacs	*Minchas Elozer*-6 Vols. *Divrei Torah*-9 Vols. *Shaar Yisoschor* *Os Chaim V'sholom* *Chaim V'sholom*	Became Rebbe after his father in 1914- Died in 1936 Born 1871
Rabbi Boruch Y.Y. Rabinowitz (son-in-law of Minchas Elozer)	Munkacs Brazil Chief Rabbi of Holon, Israel Currently in Petach Tikva, Israel	*Sefer Ateres Zahav Al HaTorah-2 Vols.*	Became Rebbe after his father-in-Law in 1936 (only served as Rebbe through the War years)
Rabbi Moshe Leib Rabinowitz (son of Rabbi Boruch Rabinowitz and grandson of the Minchas Elozer)	Brooklyn, New York	*Olas Shabbos*-3Vols. *Chodesh b'Chodsho*-3 Vols. *R'shimos Shiurim*-8 Vols.	Born 1940 Became Rebbe in 1960[b]

a. Reb Elozer Lanceter, the son of the Bnei Yisoschor and father of Shem Shlomo was Rov in Lancet. Bnei Yisoschor *chassidim* were his followers.

b. No Rebbe was appointed from after the War until Rabbi Moshe Leib Rabinowitz became Rebbe in 1960.

Divrei Torah of Munkacser Rebbes

The Bnei Yisoschar: Rabbi Tzvi Elimelech Shapiro

One who renders *halachah* according to the true intent of the Torah, and for no other purpose than to fulfill the Will of Hashem, can be relied upon more assuredly than one who receives Eliyahu *HaNavi*. The proof for this contention is found in the *Gemora* (*Gittin* 6b) where the Sages ask, "Who said that Rabbi Avisar is really bar Samcha?" The *Gemora* continues, "We find that Rabbi Avisar met with Eliyahu *HaNavi* and asked him what the Creator was doing at that time. Eliyahu responded that "Hashem was reciting a *halachic* ruling in your name, 'Avisar, My son, says thus...'" This the *Gemora* says, proves that Rabbi Avisar is bar Samcha. However, why doesn't the Gemora learn that Avisar is bar Samcha from the very fact that Eliyahu *HaNavi* spoke with him?! Can there be a greater *bar samcha* (man of virtue) than this? We learn from this that only one who understands the *halachah* as the Torah intended it to be rendered, can be considered a *bar samcha*. One who reaches this level – that his Torah is *emes* – is even greater than one who has experienced the revelation of Eliyahu *HaNavi*.

The Shem Shlomo: Rabbi Shlomo Shapiro

"*Zos HaTorah* . . . This is the Torah (law) of the *korbon olah, mincha, chatas and asham* . . . (*Vayikra* 7:37). " This posuk can be expounded to mean: This is the Torah – it is one – for the *olah*, the person who elevates his spiritual level, and his deeds are considered as a *Mincha* Offering to Hashem. Correspondingly, This is the Torah . . . for the sinner and guilt ridden as well, for should he choose to grasp the Torah and repent, it will prevent him from stumbling further and will bring him back to the proper spiritual path.

The Darkei Teshuvah: Rabbi Chaim Eliezer Shapiro

בראשית, the Holy Torah begins with a "ב" רבתי (a large *bais*) since the ב alludes to the future *Beis HaMikdosh* that is crowned with the title of בית (*Pesachim* 88a). Regarding this the prophet Chaggai states, "Great is the glory of this last House"(2:9). The giving of the Torah and the fulfillment of the *mitzvos* is for the singular purpose of perfecting the world and building the third and final *Beis HaMikdosh* – and this is hinted to in the very beginning of the Torah with the "ב" רבתי. From the following two teachings – *sof maaseh b'machshavah techilah* (last in deed, but first in thought), and that the first letter of the Torah contains the entire Torah itself – we understand that the reason a neshama (soul) descends into this world is a *yeridah l't-zorech aliya* (a descent in order to rise). With the exaltation of the soul, through Torah and *mitzvos*, one raises *Klal Yisrael* from the depths of *galus* which, in turn, will lead to the building of the *Beis HaMikdosh*, speedily in our days. Amen.

The Minchas Elozer: Rabbi Chaim Elozer Shapiro

The juxtaposition of the phrases "Plucked of cheek" . . . and . . . "given over to the whippers . . ." in the *Hoshana*, אום אני חומה (Nation That Declares) can be explained through the perspective of Hitler (*yemach sh'mo*) and the German nation. Some of the Jews who went to their deaths at Hitler's hands were not religious Jews, they were not Torah observant (i.e., shaving with a razor which is a Biblical prohibition), and some actually denied the Jewish faith completely. There are those who might say, since these Jews did not live like Jews, clinging openly and actively to the Jewish faith, how can they be saved? A Jew has a distinctive look, and since these Jews are distinctively not Jewish looking, how can they be saved with *Am Yisrael*? Forbid the thought! We saw, however, that these Jews were hunted down with every available resource because Hitler knew what many of them tried to deny – that the soul of a Jew is eternally Jewish whether or not he or she practices their faith as is expected. This is what is meant by " Plucked of cheek . . .", that even those who tried to hide their Jewishness and look like their gentile neighbors were taught by their tormenters that they, indeed, are Jewish (". . . given over to the whippers . . .") and that their Jewishness is forever. Thus, as the *Hoshana* continues, ". . . she [Israel- even those who deny their faith] shoulders Your burden. . ." as do all other Jews, and thus it is our enemies who remind us that we are Jews when we forget. If the German murderers recognize that a Jew is a Jew whether or not he or she fulfills the obligations of their faith, certainly the *Av Harachamon*, their Merciful Father, the One Who loves them and looks for their repentance, will surely embrace their martyred souls. This is what we ask for on this day of the *Hoshana*, that Hashem should save *Klal Yisrael* from every situation of distress and bring us back to Him.

The Present Munkacser Rebbe: Rabbi Moshe Leib Rabinowitz

Chazal state (*Shabbos* 153a), "Rebbe Eliezer teaches, 'Repent one day before your death.' Hearing this, the Rebbe's *talmidim* responded, 'Does a person know on which day he will die?' Rebbe Eliezer answered, 'Therefore, repent today for tomorrow you might die, and then all of your days will be spent in repentance.'" From this *Gemora* we learn that a Jew should repent each day as if this is his last day. Then he will view each hour as the only one left for him to instruct his wife and children to continue to conduct their affairs as loyal Jews, and praise Hashem for all of the good He has bestowed upon them until this time. We must bless Hashem with deep and sincere thought and emotion. ". . . Who has kept us alive, sustained us and brought us to this time" for perhaps we have only been given life to *this time*, and if we do not praise Hashem and instruct our family in the proper path of life, who knows if we will ever have the opportunity again– "And if not now, when?" (*Avos* 1:14).

to make a *milchig* (dairy) *kiddush*, wait one half hour, and then wash for the *flesihig seudah* Shavuos at noon.

As children, we were sent out to find nut trees from which we took green leaves to decorate the house.

As children, we were sent out to find nut trees from which we took green leaves to decorate the house. Flowers were not yet in season, so we used leaves instead. Later in the day members of the community went out into the streets to greet the many *chassidim* who came from far and wide across Europe to spend the *yom tov* with the Rebbe. The *mikveh* was very busy *erev yom tov*.

The Rebbe's courtyard was filled with *chassidim* waiting in line to greet him with "*Shalom Aleichem Rebbe*." When candle lighting time came the streets were mobbed with men and boys rushing to *shul* to *daven Minchah*. In such confusion it was important for the little children to hold on tight to their fathers or older brothers so they would not get lost.

I was very busy *erev yom tov*. It was my responsibility to find places for the *yeshiva bochurim* who had nowhere to eat over *yom tov*. This involved a two day placement–a bit more complicated than placing the *bochurim* only for Shabbos. Also, there were many, many guests present who had come to be with the Rebbe. I had orders from my mother that any *bochur* who was not placed with a family was to be brought to our house for his meals. Shabbos and *yom tov* we always had a full house.

After the *seudah* the streets were again full of men and boys going back to *shul* to recite *Tikun Lail Shavuos* and then to learn for the rest of the night. For the youngsters there was a fixed schedule in our house. Before Bar Mitzvah we were only allowed to stay up until *chatzos*, midnight, but after Bar Mitzvah we could stay up the whole night.

After *Tikun*, the *chassidim* celebrated with the Rebbe at the *tish*. He danced up and down on his chair, tears streaming down his face, accompanied by the whole

Motzei Shabbos "faheir" (test) of students by the Munkacser Rebbe and the Mashgiach

congregation singing *Ahava Rabah* to a special Munkacser *niggun*.

Just before daybreak the streets were again filled with the men and boys, this time running to the *mikveh* before *Shacharis* began. Most of the local *chassidim davened* in their usual *shuls*, but then came to the Rebbe's *Beis Hamedrash* to hear his *drashah*, and see him dance before reading the *Akdamos Milim* prayer. We were *zocheh* to *daven* together with the Rebbe. We were able to hear him *daven* and then ascend the *bimah* to dance and sing the Munkacser *niggun* to *Boruch Elokainu Sh'brawnu Lichvodo*. During the *Akdamos Milim* he would, at times, stop and sing a *niggun* of great *hisorirus* to further inspire us to appreciate and love the Torah that we were receiving that *yom tov*. The Rebbe *davened Shacharis* and *Musaf* from the *amud*. The *kopelia*, of which I was a member, accompanied the Rebbe.

We finished *davening* close to 2:00 pm. When the Rebbe's mother was alive, we escorted the Rebbe to her house where he made *kiddush*, delivered a very intricate *D'var Torah* in honor of the *yom tov*, and then handed out *sherayim*–cheese *kreplach* prepared by his mother. After his mother's passing, he made *kiddush* in his son-in-law's house. Reb Boruch said the *drashah* and the Rebbe's daughter made the cheese *kreplach*.

After the *seudah* everyone went to the Rebbe's *tish*, which ended in the late afternoon. At the *tish* the Rebbe sang *Brich Shemay* with a beautiful and inspiring *niggun*. After this he delivered a very deep and uplifting *D'var Torah*. This was his custom at every *tish* on Shabbos and *yom tov*. The second day of *Shavuos* was very much like the first–very, very uplifting. On each day the Rebbe finished the special *yotzros* prayers with a traditional Munkacser *niggun*.

At the *tish* of *Ne'ilas HaChag* (conclusion of the *yom tov*), which started late in the afternoon on the second day, the Rebbe danced together with the *chassidim* in a very large circle while singing *Na'aseh V'nishma* over and over again. After the general crowd completed their dance, the yeshiva *bochurim* began their own circle, singing *Na'aseh V'nishma* and dancing with the Rebbe. This dance went on for a very long time. Before *bentching*, the Rebbe said a long *D'var Torah*. After *Maariv* the Rebbe began to walk home, only to be stopped in the courtyard and surrounded by his *chassidim* and the dancing began once again. This lasted until late in the night. When the Rebbe finally reached home he went out on the balcony of his house and blessed the entire congregation standing outside. Those guests who were leaving that night, or early the next morning, began converging on the Rebbe's house. He received them in his study, consulted with them and gave his blessing.

On the Eve of War

Basically, life proceeded peacefully until 1938. At that time the Hungarians assumed control of the area of Transylvania encompassing eastern Hungary and western Romania, including areas of southwestern Czechoslovakia. These territorial areas were given back to Hungary by Hitler. This area was apportioned to Romania and Czechoslovakia at the end of World War I after the defeat and collapse of the Austro-Hungarian Empire. As I previously stated, our experience during this period of time was much different from that of the Polish or Russian Jews. Until this time we lived at peace with our neighbors and we didn't suffer government approved pogroms.

Basically, life proceeded peacefully until 1938. At that time the Hungarians assumed control of this area of Transylvania.

Shaded area returned to Romania after defeat of the Austria - Hungarian Empire in World War I

I was 17-years-old when the Hungarians came into Munkacs in 1938. They entered with a big parade, with dancing and singing. It was very festive. Many of us thought that if the Rebbe thinks so highly of the Hungarians then perhaps it won't be so bad. It didn't take long for us to find out.

I arose at 5:00 am the next morning to go to the yeshiva. Our house was next to the big *shul* and *Beis Hamedrash*. At that time *shiurim* were already taking place in the *Beis Hamedrash*. As I walked down the sidewalk I passed by two Hungarian soldiers on the street. They suddenly attacked me, trying to cut off my *payos*. Screaming, I ran through the yard of the *shul* with the soldiers running after me, following me right up the stairs of the *shul* itself. The men learning inside quickly locked the doors after I dashed in, since they were afraid that the Hungarians would enter.

We realized that we had no choice but to learn to live with these Hungarians.

We realized that we had no choice but to learn to live with these Hungarians. Little by little we got used to their ways and mannerisms. In time, however, we also learned what their agenda was. Eventually they began revoking the government licenses needed by the Jews to continue operating their businesses. They also stopped selling bread on the open market, allowing only a very measured amount–two *decas* worth (approximately one thin slice)– for each member of a household. Germany wanted the wheat and the Hungarians gave it to them. Some of the youth

Beis Hamedrash Hagadol gate that Mr. Ostreicher ran through when escaping from the soldiers.

bought bread on the black market and sold it to whoever could afford it. Rice, potatoes and fish were available, but bread or *challah* was very difficult to get.

Where possible, Jews went into partnership with non-Jews they felt they could trust so that they would not lose their *parnasah* altogether. Since Jews could no longer obtain the licenses needed to run their businesses, their gentiles partners secured the licenses under their own names. Many times these forced unions worked out. Nonetheless, many Jews left for Budapest to engage in business there. My father lost his income because the *Kehillah* took back the lease of the *mikvaos*. There was not enough income generated anymore, so the *Kehillah* could no longer afford to lease the *mikvaos* to my father to operate and take his salary from the profits. Our family had very little money in reserve at this time. Because of these two factors, my parents acquiesced to my request that my brother, Yumi, and I leave for Budapest. This was in 1940 when I was 19 and Yumi was 18. I remember that we felt that we had an obligation to help the family. My parents had six children and my grandmother to support, so we knew that we needed the money.

Budapest

We knew no one in Budapest. We were told that on Dohany Street you could rent a room for a cheap price, but no one told us that there were ten men sharing each room. The mood in Budapest was intense to say the least. Many people came there to deal in different goods to make money for themselves and their families. My father gave us the little money he had to purchase whatever merchandise was available. After arriving and getting settled, we went to a kosher restaurant called Goldmans. There were people in the restaurant showing samples of materials for ladies' clothes to prospective buyers who were dining there. It was

Where possible, Jews went into partnership with non-Jews they felt they could trust.

The still unfinished Royal Castle, seen from the Pest

Mr. and Mrs. Ostreicher (with grandchildren) in front of the apartment building on Dohany Street, where he stayed while in Budapest.

Others got involved in the textile market and the price per meter went very high. So I decided to get out.

a little commodities market. People knew that this was one of the places where you could make good business contacts. I learned two new words there my first day: *flokon* (a cotton material) and *korton* (another type of material). Anyway, I approached one of the men showing these samples and asked him the basic two questions of a *greener* (a newcomer): 'Where do you purchase the material?' and 'What do you buy?' He told me that he would supply me with material. In this way he became the middleman, a much easier position than going around from table to table trying to sell the cloth yourself. I asked him (in a round-about way) how I knew I could trust him, and he responded very earnestly. 'I know why you're here. I'll help you out. I'm not going to cheat you. We're all sharing the same difficulties, we're all Jews.' He began supplying me with cloth. I made two *pengos* for each meter of cloth sold. I bought a meter of cloth for 5 *pengos* and I sold it for 7 or 8, and there were always customers. Eventually I learned that my suppliers were getting their material from a man named Stern. I went to him and told him that I'm a *Yid* from Munkacs, that I have to make a living for my family. He agreed to sell me the cloth directly. So now I became a wholesaler who supplied the middlemen. I moved up a notch on the business ladder, making five or six *pengos* per meter instead of two. This went on for about five or six months, from Rosh Hashanah of 1940, until after Pesach in the spring of 1941. At that time Mr. Stern told me that he could no longer supply me with the material I needed because he wanted to sell it directly to different *rabbonim* and *tzadikkim* who had come to Budapest to seek refuge from their local Nazi sympathizers and the gendarmerie. Now the *rabbonim* and *tzadikkim* became the middlemen and I bought from them. They sold the material from their apartments because they wouldn't go out and sell on the street. Soon, however, others got involved in the textile market and the price per meter went very high. At that point I could no longer make a profit, so I decided to get out. However, I made a very good living while dealing in textiles...*b'revach*. My brother and I had plenty of money for our needs in Budapest and money to take home to my parents each week as well. We went home every Thursday night and returned to Budapest again Sunday morning. I only paid 14 *pengos* per week to stay in the rooming house. What expenses did I have? There was plenty of food in Budapest, we even took *challah* home with us for Shabbos. *Boruch Hashem*, we did very well then.

After leaving the textile trade I looked around for something else to get involved in. I learned that trading in gold and foreign currencies was very lucrative, but also *very* dangerous. If caught dealing in gold you were immediately arrested and put in prison. Nevertheless, we decided to try. We dealt in American dollars and gold Napoleans (French minted gold coins), called *napshis* in Hungarian. People who lost their businesses (or who came into gold or American dollars in some other way) would come to Budapest to sell their jewelry or dollars for *pengos*. We bought the gold and U.S. dollars and soon built up a very good business. The profit margin was excellent in this business, but it had its drawbacks. For one thing, as I said, it was dangerous, and for another, it was a *tzorosdika* business, a business built on the anguish of others.

We never took advantage of anyone–we always offered the top exchange rate for the currency or gold. In turn, we sold the gold to the stores. Most of these transactions took place in the Jewish owned restaurants. Often, government officials would conduct a *razia*, a search, to find anyone who was staying in Budapest illegally by checking everyone's residence papers. If everything was in order, fine, and if not, you were arrested. When a *razia* occurred, I immediately headed for the bathroom to jump out of the window, with my brother literally following on my heels. First, however, we locked the bathroom door, and by the time the agents broke it down we were long gone. I remained in Budapest until I was 20, when I had to report home to the draft office for my army physical.

I learned that trading in gold and foreign currencies was very lucrative, but also very dangerous.

Expulsion

As time went on, the Hungarians issued a new decree. They wanted to evict all Polish and non-Hungarian Jews from the country. Without citizenship papers proving you were a Czech or Hungarian citizen you could not remain in Hungarian territory. People were careful now to see to it that they had proper papers. However, it was not easy to secure such papers. Eventually the government brought in the gendarmerie, the National Police Force, or National Guard. They terrified us, especially when they appeared in their uniforms with the feathers extending from their hats. In truth, they

Jews from Budapest were taken to the courtyard of this community building to dig their own graves after which they were shot to death.

were animals, low-life animals...wicked, wicked people. They were ordered to arrest all Jews who didn't have proper citizenship papers.

Rabbi Boruch Yehoshua Yerachmeil Rabinowitz was the Munkacser Rov at the time. He assumed the position of his father-in-law after the Minchas Elozer's *petirah*. In his will the Minchas Elozer quoted the words of one of the *brochos* we recite after the *Haftorah* on Shabbos, "*Al kiso lo yaishev zar...*' (On his [David's] throne a stranger should not sit...). From this it was understood that even though the Minchas Elozer had no son to assume his position of *Rov*, it should be filled by his son-in-law. Rabbi Rabinowitz was a Torah scholar of the first degree, a man who showed great concern and compassion for his fellow Jews during the War. Since he was a Polish national, he was forced to leave Munkacs for Budapest where there were people who promised to protect him. On the way he made a stop at Ujhely where he was caught by the authorities. To this day we don't know if someone reported him, or if he was recognized and caught by coincidence, as it were. He was put in chains and brought back to Munkacs on a Thursday night. They kept him in prison until Shabbos when he was sent together with his young son, Hirshele, and other Jews who had been arrested to the Kamenetz-Podolsk area of the Ukraine. Unfortunately, most of the Jews were shot and their bodies dumped into the Dnieper River.

Many people followed the group of deported Jews the Rebbe was with as they were being led to one of the cattle cars.

This took place in 1941, on the 10th of *Av*. Shabbos was the ninth of *Av*, so the fast was pushed off until Sunday. It was an especially sad fast that year. Many people followed the group of deported Jews the Rebbe was with as they were being led to one of the cattle cars. The Rebbe blessed them as he went...the people were hysterical. No one was allowed to approach the cattle car when the Rebbe was put inside, so people ran down the tracks to find a place where they could at least be near the Rebbe as his cattle car rolled by. Four train loads of Jews were taken away that day.

In Kamenetz-Podolsk two Hungarian soldiers wanted to shoot the Rebbe and his son. Before shooting them, however, the soldiers began arguing over which of them would become the new owner of the Rebbe's gold watch—each arguing that he took hold of the Rebbe first, and thus the watch belonged to him. One of the soldiers stated, "If you want me to shoot him, I get the watch." With that the other responded, "Then let's not shoot him at all." In the meantime, given the distraction taking place, the Rebbe and his son ran away and eventually found sanctuary in a Jewish home.

Rabbi Boruch Y.Y. Rabinowitz (to right), with Rabbi N.S. Shlissel, Chief Justice of the Munkacs Beis Din.

At this time (1941-42) the Hungarians also began the horrifying ritual of taking Jews to the cemetery, in Poland, ordering them to dig their own graves and then shooting them as they stood in the pits they had dug. This continued until the deportations to Auschwitz began in the spring of 1943. The Hungarians as much as the Germans, the Germans as much as the Poles...they all shared in this destruction.

Meanwhile, in Munkacs the search began to try to find the Rebbe. His mother-in-law, the Minchas Elozer's Rebbetzin, went to Budapest where she met Avrum Mann, a Munkacser *chassid*, who said that he would try to find the Rebbe. He was in the *Munka Tabor*, the forced labor brigades, who were sent to the front lines ahead of the troops so that if the fields were mined the Jews would be the first ones to be killed. He was presently in Budapest on a legal leave of absence, but Avrum risked his life to find the Rebbe by going to Kamenetz-Podolsk, which was on the Russian border with Poland. If he was caught he would be shot as a traitor. He discreetly began inquiring about the Rebbe's whereabouts and eventually found him. He helped hide the Rebbe in a secure place until he could return to Budapest and arrange for the Rebbe's return disguised as a soldier. His plan was to bribe an officer who was sympathetic to the Jews and secure his help. After returning to Budapest he indeed found a high ranking officer who came with him to retrieve the Rebbe in an army ambulance. They dressed the Rebbe up in bloody bandages to cover his beard and hid Hirshele under one of the seats. This trauma affected Hirshele greatly, and even as an adult he suffered from the effects of the abduction, attempted assassination and subsequent flight and hiding. The Rebbe returned to Munkacs on a Friday.

The first *Slichos* was said that Sunday morning. When the Rebbe began the *Slichos* there was not a dry eye in the entire congregation. People were crying their hearts out. He added to the *Yehe Ratzon* the following:

אוי לעינים שכך ראות
ואזנים שכך שמעות

Woe to the eyes that sees all of this; Woe to the ears that hear of this.

The Hungarians as much as the Germans, the Germans as much as the Poles...they all shared in this destruction.

This took place in 1941 and I remember it well. I was 20-years-old then, but I was crying uncontrollably. Rosh Hashanah was the same. The *davening*...the tears...it was just unbelievable. *Erev* Yom Kippur people came from all over to see the Rebbe and speak with him, give him their *kivitlach* and receive his blessing. On Yom Kippur itself the Rebbe's *kittel* was soaking wet with tears. I was singing in the *kopelia*, as usual, and I saw this with my own eyes... the Rebbe was soaked in his own tears.

Subsequent to his arrest and escape, the Rebbe was given assurances by the local government officials that he would be left alone, but those close to him advised him not to trust such assurances. In addition to the emotional impact of returning to Munkacs, *Slichos* and the *Yomim Nora'im*, the Rebbe found out that his mother had passed away in Warsaw. Now, along with the sense of bereavement he felt for his *chassidim* and the Jewish nation in general, he included his personal mourning for his own mother. The Rebbe's *Kaddish Yasom* tore at one's heart, it was totally infused with his mourning for *Klal Yisrael*.

I was 20-years-old then, but I was crying uncontrollably. Rosh Hashanah was the same.

During the days of Succos, *Zeman Simchasainu*, that year (1941) the Rebbe rejoiced, and through his rejoicing he lifted the spirits of his *chassidim*. On the second day of Succos, the *yahrtzeit* of the Darkei Teshuvah, the Rebbe went with his *chassidim* to the grave of the Darkei Teshuvah. *Tehillim* was said, followed by the Rebbe's *drashah*. Then the Rebbe addressed the *neshamah* of the Darkei Teshuvah, appointing it as a *shliach mitzvah* to go directly before Hashem's holy throne and plead for the well being of *Klal Yisrael* who were suffering destruction on all sides. Afterwards, the Rebbe and the *kopelia* sang "*Bar Yochoi*," the song about Rabbi Shimon bar Yochoi, because the Darkei Teshuvah had written a commentary explaining the *Zohar*, which was written by Rabbi Shimon bar Yochoi. In addition, there is a tradition among the *chassidim* that the soul of the Darkei Teshuvah is a spark from the soul of Rabbi Shimon bar Yochoi.

During the *Simchas Bais Hashoaivah* that took place on *Chol Hamoed* in the big *succah*, the *chassidim* all danced with the Rebbe, who between dances gave out little cookies and a small glass of schnapps to each *chassid*. *Hoshanah Rabbah* was another Yom Kippur. After every *hakafah* the Rebbe gave a *drashah* and then he blew the shofar. *Minchah* was *davened* late in the afternoon in the *succah*. Afterwards everyone danced to the *Beis Hamedrash* singing farewell to the *succah*. Then we *davened Maariv*. On *Shemini Atzeres* and *Simchas Torah* the pain and tears were forgotten as the Rebbe danced between the rows of his *Chassidim* holding the little Torah scroll of the Baal Shem Tov in his arms. After *Succos* the Rebbe took the advice of those close to him and left for Budapest.

Budapest was full of Polish Jews who managed to escape the round-ups and forced expulsions. However, they desperately needed legal identification papers because the gendarmerie stopped Jews in the street and demanded proper identification. Legal documents also had to be produced to use public transportation. Upon arriving in Budapest (winter of 1941-42) the Rebbe became very involved in this vital function of securing false papers to protect the Polish Jews. It was very dangerous to hide Polish Jews in one's house, for anyone found doing so was sent to Auschwitz. The Rebbe was instrumental in securing hiding places for many of these Jews who didn't, as yet, have papers. He worked day and night to make sure that these Jews had a place to lay down their heads at night. He was also busy with various community affairs on behalf of the Hungarian Jews.

The Army

In Munkacs itself at this time (1941-1942), men who had reached the age of twenty were ordered to take a medical examination for the army. This is when I returned from Budapest for my army physical. Many men fasted for days to lose weight, staying up all night, night-after-night, in the *Battei Medrash* to wear themselves down.

German soldiers during invasion of Russia, June, 1941.

Hopefully, in this manner, they would be rejected from the army. Those who could learn would learn throughout the night, and those who couldn't learn would find other things to do to stay awake. Many were successful and were rejected from military service.

After the Germans attacked Russia in 1941, they requested that Hungary join them in the war effort by providing soldiers for the eastern front. In the months that followed the Hungarians responded, sending out several army divisions in support. By the beginning of 1942, close to 200,000 Hungarian soldiers had arrived in the Ukraine to fight together with the Germans. On January 2, 1942, the Russians counterattacked by the River Dan. During the ensuing battle a great majority of the Hungarian troops were killed by the Russians.

Interestingly, at that time the repression of the Jews in Hungary was lessened a degree. Business picked up and travel restrictions were rescinded within the country, even use of the trains was permitted with proper identification. It was at this point I believe, that the Belzer Rebbe was able to escape to Budapest. Hundreds and hundreds of Belzer *Chassidim* came to Budapest for the High Holy days that year dressed in their *kapotehs* and *streimels*. This was something you rarely saw in Budapest at any time, much less during the War.

Many men fasted for days to lose weight, staying up all night to wear themselves down.

For Rosh Hashanah that year (1942), I went to Budapest to sing in Reb Boruch Yehoshua's *kopelia* and it was then that I saw the Belzer Rebbe. In fact, I remained in Budapest and this move saved me from being captured by the Nazis much earlier than I was, but more about this later.

Eventually, Reb Boruch Yehoshua and the Belzer Rebbe were warned to leave Budapest, which they did. Reb Boruch Yehoshua took along all of his *Sifrei* Torah and the Minchas Elozer's *seforim* and escaped to Turkey. From there he traveled to *Eretz Yisrael*. His daughter who came with us on one of our recent trips to Munkacs was born during this escape. The Rebbe arrived in *Eretz Yisrael* before Purim. The strain of the escape had a very deleterious effect on the Rebbetzin's health and soon after arriving she was hospitalized.

Not long afterwards she died. She was only 31. Reb Boruch Yehoshua was left with five little children. Soon after this he gave up his position of Rebbe. So for many years there wasn't a Rebbe until one of his sons, the present Rebbe, assumed the position of Rebbe.

Under Nicolas Horthy the Hungarian government secretly attempted to collaborate with the Allied governments, but did not realize the extent they were being spied upon by the Germans. Horthy was not exactly a lover of the Jewish people, but realizing who was winning the war, he tried to help the Jews as well as protect the Hungarian economy.[29] Despite great pressure, he refused to carry out Hitler's demand that the Jews either be exterminated or sent to concentration camps. He paid dearly for this when his only son was killed by the Germans as a warning for him to stop. He successfully escaped Hungary and an extremely anti-Semitic fascist regime under the leadership of Ferenc Szalasi took over control of the country. Szalasi instituted an extreme Nazi political agenda throughout Hungary. Any protection that the Jews had from the national government was now completely obliterated and they were left totally unprotected from Szalasi and his murderous gang.

None of the Allies bombed the railway tracks that led to the concentration camps, though they knew where the trains were going.

When the German high command realized what was taking place, they sent in German troops to occupy the country. On March 19, 1944, the Germans took over Hungary and immediately began to implement their plans to send the Jews to concentration camps. Eichmann came into Hungary with 200 people, and with this small task force, from May 15 until June 20, 1944, 289,000 Jews from the Carpatho-Russian region and another 138,000 from Hungary proper were sent to concentration camps. This means that 427,000 Jews were sent to their deaths in approximately 36 days.[30] Churchill once remarked that this act against the Jews during such a short period of time was the greatest crime of the Hungarians. Of course, none of the Allies bombed the railway tracks that led to the concentration camps, though they knew where the trains were going.[31]

Slave Labor

The Jews serving with the Hungarian Army between 1939 and 1941 were declared untrustworthy, removed from the active fighting units and placed in the slave labor battalions. They would go to the front of the battlefield to clear out mines and debris, and many were killed and maimed in this manner. In 1941, however, the situation became even worse, and, as mentioned, in order to demonstrate their loyalty to the Germans the Hungarians sent 200,000 more troops to the front. 60,000 slave laborers were sent with them. The commanders of the Jewish slave laborers were low ranking, rabid anti-Semites. These Jews had to lay anti-tank mines in the fields, and perform other such tasks at the front. Thousands were killed in the line of duty. On June 13, 1943, the Russians attacked Hungary. The Jewish slave-workers who were with the Hungarian troops fighting the Russians

29. For a more complete treatment of this political situation the reader is referred to Fuchs, Abraham, **The Unheeded Cry**, ArtScroll Publications, Brooklyn, New York, 1986.
30. Ibid., page 167.
31. In some of the industrial camps the Allies actually dropped leaflets describing which parts of the complex were being rebuilt after previous bombings and which parts would soon be bombed again. These bombings took place with great accuracy. Yet the railway tracks to the camps were left untouched. The reader is referred to the interview with Eliezer Feig.

Jews being assembled for forced labor

suffered horrible losses. As the Hungarians ran away from the advancing Russian troops, they left the Jews to perish on the battlefront with no food and little clothing.

These slave laborers were always treated cruelly. One example is what took place on the last day of Pesach in 1942, in the small town of Zitomer where 700 Jewish slave-workers were herded into a small building. The building was surrounded with a barbed wire fence and then set on fire. All 700 young men were burned alive. This was done, the Hungarians said, to control an outbreak of typhus. It is estimated that of the 60,000 Jewish slave laborers only 5,000 survived the ordeals of the War, the rest disappeared. Only one out of every 12 men survived. If each group of 12 represented one of the 12 Tribes of Israel, then only one tribe escaped the catastrophe.

Flight

Some Jews from Poland and Slovakia, for great sums of money, were smuggled across the border into Hungary and made their way to Budapest. The Munkacser Rebbe helped them to secure Aryan papers and found them places to stay. The Bobover Rebbe was also in Budapest with Aryan papers at that time. Towards the end of the War he left for Romania.

It is interesting to note that the Hungarian Jews knew very little of what was happening to the Polish Jews. In Budapest, we were told what was occurring, but we just couldn't believe such stories...who would ever think such a thing? Polish Jews who came to Munkacs cautioned us that something was going to happen to us, but no one would believe them.

The Hungarian Jews knew very little of what was happening to the Polish Jews.

Children on their way to Levente, where they trained for slave labor

The Polish Jews were welcome in Munkacs, but somehow, in a very strange manner someone reported their presence to the police. Those who were reported were immediately arrested and sent to Auschwitz. On one *motzei Shabbos*, when it was dark in the *Beis Hamedrash*, Shimeon Deutsch, who now lives here in America, took a poison powder that causes blindness when it comes into contact with the eyes, and, upon identifying the *moser*, the one reporting the Polish Jews to the Hungarians, threw the powder in his eyes blinding him. This act effectively brought his dirty business to an abrupt stop. This *moser* had a partner named Getzel, and when he asked who it was who blinded him, Shimeon responded that it was Getzel. You see, Shimeon could imitate anyone, so he disguised his voice and the *moser* thought that it was actually Getzel, his partner, who had blinded him. When he asked why he did it, Shimeon told him, "Because you didn't give me my half of the money for the Jews we turned in. I had no choice but to blind you. Now I can do the job myself." When the police came and asked who had attacked him, he responded that Getzel was responsible. The police apprehended Getzel, took him to the Police Station and shot him then and there–right on the spot.

There was another *moser* in Munkacs who wore a *streimel* and *kapoteh*. He didn't report the Polish Jews, but he reported the Munkacser Jews who didn't go into the army or the *Munka Tabor*. In my case he came to my father and told him, "Look, I know your son didn't go into the army or the *Munka Tabor* and I need money!" My father made a mistake and started giving him money, and the extortion never stopped. Over and over again he had to give him money until my Father finally refused. One morning at 3:00 am the police came and arrested me. They took me to a basement room in the Korner Kastely, the prison where army deserters and spies were brought. Many were shot there. They questioned me regarding how I had dodged induction into the army. I replied that I was partially blind. My father had paid a doctor to support this claim, but if discovered the consequences would have been horrible. The *gendarmerie* were beating me and screaming the entire time, but I insisted I was partially blind. I knew that I had to maintain a very clear mind no matter what they did to me, because if I changed my story they would shoot me.

Eventually they let me go, telling me that I would have to report for the *Munka Tabor*. This was just before Rosh Hashanah in 1942. I told my father that for Rosh Hashanah and Yom Kippur I had to sing in the Rebbe's choir and was leaving immediately to be with the Rebbe in Budapest. Additionally, I would work out a plan how to get out of the *Munka Tabor*.

When the members of the choir arrived in Budapest the community arranged places for us to stay. I was very, very depressed, wondering whether I had made the correct decision to leave and not report for the labor battalion. I spoke to the Munkacser Rov and he said, "Look, to report for the labor unit you always have time. In the meantime, you are safe here and we will see what to do after *yom tov*." We *davened* in the Polish Shul, and ate by a different family each day. Between Rosh Hashanah and Yom Kippur the *shul* paid for us to eat in a restaurant.

After the yomin tovim I initiated my plan to receive an exemption from the Munka Tabor.

Subterfuge

After the *yomin tovim* I initiated my plan to receive an exemption from the *Munka Tabor*. I arranged to see a doctor, complaining that I was suffering from terrible headaches. He advised me to see Dr. Yanosh, a psychiatrist, who was the head of the Yanosh Hospital. When I met the doctor I told him that I was experiencing severe headaches and had also became very depressed. He said that the only way he could help was for me to check into the hospital, to be exact, the psychiatric ward. I was afraid to go to the ward and since my brother, Yumi, and I look and sound the same, I asked him to go in my place. He had already received an exemption from a doctor my father paid. He agreed. I took him to the hospital, being very careful that I wouldn't run into the psychiatrist, Dr. Yanosh. Once I (that is, my brother) was admitted he would only be seen by Dr. Keranyi (a Jew) and a medical assistant of a Professor Shimoni. So on this account we were safe.

Obviously, there were other Jews who were looking for a way to avoid the labor battalion. They were in the same situation as I was so I told them what I had done. With no other plan of action, four of them decided to try it as well. Eventually we were all classified as suffering from mental illness and our hospital reports were forwarded to the army.

At this point we still needed a little army identification book. Everyone had to have one, whether they served in the army or not. The only way to receive this was to have the diagnosis of the private hospital substantiated by a military hospital. The closest such military facility was located in Tizes Orsegi. Dr. Keranyi agreed, for a price, to help me and others obtain the necessary papers for the military hospital.

In the meantime, we found someone who had connections with the military as well. To make a long story short, Dr. Keranyi told us it would be a good idea to obtain another report saying that we also had some other kind of medical problem. I took some aspirin before going to see a Dr. Yavor Paal. I complained of heart problems, and he gave me an EKG. He then wrote a report stating I had heart trouble. His fee was 100 *pengos* and he offered to help others needing exemption papers. Now I had two ways to obtain exemptions.

Knowing there were many young men who needed such exemptions, I became very busy directing people to Dr. Keranyi or Dr. Paal. Later he told me that aspirins don't always work and that I should go to a Jewish doctor, Dr. Lang on Kiraly Gaz who would give certain injections that would be helpful. He even wrote down what kind of injection should be given. I went as instructed and told him the truth–exactly what we needed and why we were there. He responded just as candidly remarking, "Okay. For money, everything can be bought." Now we were really set for action. In addition to all of the others who we assisted, there were many *rabbonim* who came for help who couldn't afford to pay, so I made sure that those who were paying would cover their expenses as well. In this way many *Yiddishe mentschen* escaped the dreaded *Munka Tabor*.

Longing for Home

I hadn't seen my parents since I left for Budapest before Rosh Hashanah in the fall of 1941, and now it was the end of October, 1942. I was very busy preparing people to obtain their exemptions, but I desperately needed to see my parents. I planned to leave on a Thursday night to join them for Shabbos. Since I was considered a mental patient I needed a

I was very busy preparing people to obtain their exemptions, but I desperately needed to see my parents.

Munkacser Jews saying the Tashlich prayer at the Lataritza Bridge.

chaperone to accompany me. My brother was still with me, so he was enlisted to be my chaperone. We made all the necessary reservations, including arranging sleeping quarters on the train, so that we would arrive refreshed for the visit. As we boarded the train and showed the conductor our tickets, a Hungarian army general in civilian clothing boarded along with us. He did not have a ticket, and the conductor was not allowing him entry. With this he asserted, "I don't care if those Jews do have tickets, I am a general in the Hungarian Army and I am going to use their space." Not to be outdone, the conductor shot back, "I'm sorry, Jew or non-Jew, whoever has a proper ticket will occupy that space!" The general immediately smacked the conductor in the face and a fight broke out between the two of them. This fracas went on for several minutes until the police arrived to restore order. No lover of Jews, the police sided with the general and ordered the conductor to remove us from the train. Too Late! The train had already begun to depart and now all of us were on the train: my brother and I, the general, the conductor and the police. The police requested everyone's identification and took down all of the information, remarking that they would check to see if we are draft dodgers at the next station. I commented to my brother that this is not a good situation for us to be in. His response was the obvious one, "And what should we do?!!" I told him that just before we reach Hatvan (a large city that was the next stop) I would pull the emergency brake cord and he should run and tell the conductor that I had suffered a seizure. This is exactly what we did. In the resulting confusion we jumped off the train and made our escape. We began walking to the station. Unfortunately, the police also left the train and were waiting on the platform for a train back to Budapest.

I decided that my only avenue of escape was to act like a meshuganeh, a crazy person.

At this point we were in very deep and serious trouble. I decided that my only avenue of escape was to act like a *meshuganeh*, a crazy person. I approached the policemen and told them that the gold buttons they wore on their uniforms were stolen from me. One of them asked me how I knew this and I responded that I am a prophet and I know this supernaturally. I told him that not all of the buttons are mine and that I can identify the ones that do belong to me. One of the officers remarked to the other that I was a lunatic. Then he asked my brother where we were headed. My brother responded that we were going to Ujhely, to the mental institution located there so that I could be close to my parents. The police told my brother that I'm a dangerous person and should not travel on public transportation. I told my brother to ask them to get us an ambulance to take us to Ujhely, which they did. As we approached the institution I started screaming that I was going to hit the driver, and beat him up. My brother quickly paid, urging him to leave us off immediately, saying we would walk the rest of the way because I was getting dangerous and he could not guarantee the driver's safety. The driver was only too happy to comply. My father, who was supposed to meet us at the train station in Munkacs would not know what had happened. We didn't want our parents to worry, so we immediately went to the post office in Ujhely to telephone the Munkacser Rebbe's office to notify our parents that we were all right and would continue home by taxi from Ujhely. We spent a wonderful Shabbos together with the family and then returned to Budapest on Sunday morning by special train.

Invasion

We remained in Budapest until just before *Pesach* in March, 1943, when we heard that the Germans had invaded Hungary. We were very uneasy about what would happen next. In truth, that is a very great understatement, but when you're in the middle of difficulties Hashem gives you the strength to continue–the desire to live and hope for the best is very strong. Without this it would have been impossible to survive. My parents and brothers were still in Munkacs. I decided that it would be best to go home and try to save the family–perhaps I could bring everyone safely to Budapest. I just knew I had to do something for them. My parents did not agree to any of my plans. They felt the *Ribbono shel Olam* was everywhere, and thus they would be safe wherever they were if Hashem chooses so. The occupation took place very quickly. By Pesach we already had to wear the yellow Jewish star with *Jude* written or stitched on to it. It was a very sad Pesach, but over *yom tov* the Nazis left us alone.

When Pesach ended the police came and told me I had to report for the

When you're in the middle of difficulties Hashem gives you the strength to continue.

Hungarian Jews awaiting deportation at the railway station

Munka Tabor. All of those who I had helped evade conscription were also caught. We were taken to a central waiting area to board a military truck to Kashaw. I positioned myself in the back of the truck and at an auspicious moment jumped down and escaped. I immediately ran home. When I told my father what happened he quoted the following *pasuk* from *Tehillim*, "*...where can you run from before Hashem...?*" I responded that our only chance at this point was to get to Budapest somehow. "Over there I know what is going on, over here I don't know yet," I told him.

The Munkacs Ghetto

A week to ten days later the Jews were forced into a ghetto area that the Nazis had prepared in Munkacs. The ghetto was five or six square blocks, approximately 20% of the original size of the community. Most of the Jews from the surrounding towns were brought to the brick yard where railroad tracks, once used to bring supplies to the brick yard, were now being used to send Jews to Auschwitz. Afterwards, the Jews from the ghetto were taken to the rail yard to be sent to Auschwitz. This meant that these wicked animals knew what they were going to do with us. The plan had been made and now it was unfolding. I remember the Shabbos before we went into the ghetto. I was hiding in the attic of a neighbor's house that faced the *Beis Hamedrash*. Shabbos morning I saw the Nazis bringing the members of the Munkacs *Beis Din* into the *Beis Hamedrash*. They also brought in the Zidtchover Rebbe, Reb Moishele, and the Okliver Rov and other Torah personalities. Before long I heard crying and wailing coming from the building. Later I found out that the Germans had savagely beaten them and mocked them while they were forced to translate *pesukim* from *Tanach* that the Nazis felt degraded the gentiles. Before long I saw them brought out on stretchers. They were beaten bloody and limp and taken to the Munkacser Rebbe's house which later was turned into a hospital.

The ghetto was five or six square blocks, approximately 20% of the original size of the community.

Before that Shabbos, the *Beis Din* had gathered to convene a *Din Torah* with the *Ribbono shel Olam* that salvation should come to *Klal Yisrael*. My father was appointed the representative for *Klal Yisrael*. My father asked me if I would like to witness what was going to take place. No one was allowed to enter except the participants, but my father planned to hide me under a bed that was in the corner of the room, if I wanted. This way I could hear the proceedings. I remained very still while listening to the *Beis Din* present their case. "*Ribbono shel Olam*," they asked, "why is *Klal Yisrael* suffering so? *Ribbono shel Olam*, is there any better people than Your people? *Ribbono shel Olam*, You chose us as Your own, please save us and do not allow us to be destroyed entirely." After that the judges concluded the case in favor of *Klal Yisrael*. One of the judges, saw my foot extending from under the bed, but he said nothing about it. The men were afraid to convene in the building of the *Beis Din* because of the Nazis, so this *Din Torah* was held in *Dayan*, Rabbi Meir Wolfe's house. I was afraid that the Gestapo would find out, but they didn't.

In the ghetto we stayed in my grandmother's house which was next door to the Munkacser Rebbe's house. The Rebbe's house was converted into a makeshift hospital and my father asked me to go and help because there were great numbers of old and ill people who needed care. There were not enough beds, so people were placed on the floor. My father wanted me to help in any way I could: to help feed the infirm, bring water and tea to those with fever, bathe the men and boys–whatever I could to be of assistance. The sentiment was fine, but, in truth, there was very little we could really do. Many of the ill died of hunger and thirst. Though the Nazis were in charge, it was the Hungarian gendarmerie who did not allow us bury our dead in the cemetery. The Rebbe's house had a very large garden and they wanted us to bury them in the garden. Some of the Jews tried to hide among the gentiles and were shot when they were found. Their bodies were also brought to us for burial in the garden. After a while the garden was completely full.

Then the Hungarians decided that they wanted all of the bodies exhumed from the garden and taken to the Jewish cemetery. They provided us with three big wagons for transport. I cannot tell you how unbearable this job was, it is simply beyond description. There must have been a few hundred bodies that we had to transport. Back and forth we went... trip after trip. We opened up several communal graves in the cemetery and buried most of the bodies together. I saw an aspect of the Divine Will involved in this. These people had lived together most of their lives and then they died together. Now they were buried together and would rise together at *Tichiyas Hameisim*. I guess this is symbolic of the eternal character of the Jewish community.

Jews in the ghetto were eventually taken to the brick factory on the outskirts of the town. There was access to the brick yard by train, so the deportations took place from there–one train load after another. My family lived in the ghetto for two weeks before being taken to the factory. I continued working with the sick who remained in the "hospital" in the Rebbe's house. My parents and grandparents were waiting for me to come to the brick yard, but I didn't have the heart to leave the ill alone. Many of the Rebbe's neighbors who had flour, baked bread for those who were ill. Even when we had almost nothing to eat people willingly gave away their food.

The Jews in the hospital were the last group taken to the brick yard and, thus, to Auschwitz. There was only myself and one other Jew to transport the sick, whom we had to carry to the wagons that would take them to the brick yard. We were beaten by the gendarmerie because we weren't moving the people fast enough. To this day I don't know if they didn't want the general community to see what was taking place or they just wanted to clear the Jews out of the city as fast as possible–probably both. It took one full day to complete the transport of the sick. It was unforgettable and unforgivable. That evening, I joined my family in the brick yard. Next morning was the second day of *Sivan*, the *yahrtzeit* of the Minchas Elozer. We remained at the factory for only one night and then we were loaded into the cattle cars and taken to Auschwitz.

It took one full day to complete the transport of the sick. It was unforgettable and unforgivable.

Auschwitz

It was unbearably hot on the train. People were thirsty–there were infants, babies, toddlers, children, adults, grandparents and great-grandparents–and there was nothing to drink. *Remember each person had a name, a history, needs and wants...there were no faceless, nameless Jews on the transports. Six million Jews means six million individuals, just like the person now sitting next to you in class or in your home.* I can still hear the

"Work Makes You Free"

The children were crying because they were hungry... If this didn't split open the heavens I don't know what will.

whistle of the train. We made room for the elderly and the mothers of small children to sit on the floor, but there really wasn't any room. The rest of us stood on our feet for two days. We leaned on one another. The odor was unbearable–the air was heavy and hot. The children were crying. It was not to be believed.

We wanted to *daven* with a *minyan*, which was also a problem since there was no washroom. Everyone had to go where they were sitting or standing, but we wanted to *daven*. We took some clothes and covered up the waste. I remember that my father had a little whiskey with him on the train. To lift our spirits he gave everyone a little *l'chaim* from the flask of whiskey he had with him. He tried to reassure us that we would be okay because today is the Minchas Elozer's *yahrtzeit*. True, we were leaving the city, but we would be coming back, he said. We had *bitachon*–everyone believed that Hashem *Yisborach* will help. We traveled for two days without being given food or water. Whoever had something shared it with everyone else, but it was only crumbs that we had to share. The children were crying because they were hungry and thirsty and their mothers were crying because their children were suffering. If this didn't split open the heavens I don't know what will.

Even after everything we went through our *bitachon* was very great. My father took along *seforim* because we were under the impression we were going to a work camp. In fact, each time the trains returned to continue the deportations, the conductors and guards always brought back cards from those previously deported assuring those in the ghetto that they were doing fine and there was no reason to worry. They said that those who can't work don't have to. Some can sit and learn and the little children will have their own nursery. People read these cards and believed

them, my father was among those who believed. We thought we were going to work camps and would return home as soon as the War is over, then everything will be fine. The men repeated *Divrei Torah* while we traveled. We were optimistic that we would return home.

Finally, we approached Auschwitz. The train pulled in at ten o'clock in the morning. The Gestapo came to the cars with dogs to chase us out. What did I think at that moment? We didn't know what to think. However, a death factory was the last thing on our minds–even though there was a pervasive smell of burning flesh. In truth, we felt like baked flesh ourselves, but we could not know what to make of what was going on around us.

I try to disassociate myself from all of those sensory impressions, otherwise I could not exist. The smells, physical sensations of heat and cold, the sights–I could never live with such constant associations. I've been back to Eastern Europe several times, but told my children and grandchildren that I could not go to see Auschwitz with them. I explained to them that this would break me.

Crematoria Ovens

Electric barbed wire fence

Only another survivor can truly understand this reality. My granddaughter, Rachel, asked me for the names of my relatives who perished in the camp so that she could pray for their souls when she went. I told her that there were too many names to give, close to 100 of my relatives perished there. She took the names of my parents and grandparents. At one of the fields by the crematorium she wrote the names on a piece of paper, stuck the top of a stick through the paper and then embedded the stick into the ground. This was their *matzaivah*, their memorial.

The smells, physical sensations of heat and cold, the sights–I could never live with such constant associations.

In any event, some Polish Jews, who were already in the camp for awhile, came to caution us. They shouted that every young woman with a child should give the child (or children) to their mother or another older person. They should not hold the children's hands or the hand of older people. It was important that they walk *alone* and *straight*. We told them that there were Jews who died on the way, but they just told us to keep on walking. So we went. My father was walking with his *seforim* in his hands. I asked him to put them down and to walk standing straight. He said, "I will. However, my *seforim* I won't leave here because wherever I go there will be people who

Arrival in Auschwitz and Selektion

Neither of my brothers looked old enough to be sent to the right. My brother Dovid and I were sent to the right. At that point we were separated forever in this world. Two of my uncles and their children were sent to the right as well. My two grandmothers and most of their grandchildren and great-grandchildren were also sent to the left.

As my parents walked away I thought, "Oh! My father is going with the other older Jews to sit and learn." I didn't know what really took place until later when a *kapo*, a Polish *Yid*, came into our barracks. He saw we were writing on the postcards the Germans gave us to send to those we left behind. He shouted at us, "Are you crazy?! Are you completely crazy...filling out those cards?" Then he pointed to the smoke rising from the area of the crematoria and said, "There...there are your parents. will want to sit and learn." He was sure he was going to be able to learn. Now he's learning in the *Yeshiva shel Maalah*. My father was only 51 then, but he looked older. We were told that the line on the left would be comprised of the elderly and young mothers and children who would soon be settled. The line on the right was for those who would go to work. They did this so that there would not be a revolt. Their little ruse worked, because everyone stayed calm, more or less.

He was sure he was going to be able to learn. Now he's learning in the Yeshiva shel Maalah.

As we walked down the platform we approached Mengele, *yimach sh'mo*, standing there with his little baton, something like a riding crop. My family and I were all together. He motioned my mother, father and two brothers, Meir Leib, 15 and Shlomo Eliezer, 14, to the left.

Gas chamber and Crematorium III, Auschwitz

Do you see that smoke? That is your parents!" He was yelling at us. His anger was amazing. He continued, "For three years you were eating chocolate and cakes while here we were suffering. Well, now you know what we went through." I thought that we cannot be upset with him because his *tzores*, his pain, was howling from his heart. He had already lost his faith, because he laughed at us when we *davened*. We felt a great surge of pity for him, but at that moment we were still very confused and trying desperately to assess our present situation. I still didn't believe my parents were gone, and certainly not that they had been incinerated. Even after I was liberated if I saw someone driving by who looked like my father I didn't understand why he didn't stop when he saw me. This confused me. "Why didn't he stop," I wondered. It bothered me very much. I never gave up hope of finding him.

I had hoped to find my other two brothers, Yumi and Lali, who were sent to Auschwitz before us, but they were no longer in the camp. They had been sent to another labor camp. We didn't know where they went but we knew they had been here and left. It wasn't until after the War that we found out what happened to them.

After going to the right side we were immediately taken for a haircut, a shower and camp clothing, which was nothing more than striped pajamas and wooden clogs for shoes. The numbers sewn onto the side of my pants and the chest area of my shirt was 37037. Then we sat around until we were assigned to one of the blocks. By evening time we had not been given anything to eat for that entire day. Now we had not eaten for almost three full days.

Cloth made from Jewish hair

The next morning we had to assemble in the *appelplatz*. The *appelplatz* was a large open area where roll call was taken twice each day. We stood there for hours at a time, no matter what the weather. Men would faint...just drop from weakness and exhaustion. If the Germans noticed they would shoot them, so we helped each other by holding up those who were fainting. While standing in line we would be counted over and over again. The most important thing to the Germans was that they know where every Jew was...that every Jew was accounted for. This time we stood there for close to four hours while they read out an endless list of announcements to us. When the German officer would say, "*Mitzin oif!*" we had to take off our caps. Once our caps were off they would begin counting. Again, we were given no food. There were men fainting all over the *appelplatz*, but we still did not receive any food. By late afternoon we went to the barracks and the barracks head, the *stubenelster* (also a prisoner), told us that everybody should go to their...I don't know what to call it...it wasn't a bed. It was a two or three tiered bunk of wood planks that we were assigned to. We were so crowded that we all had to sleep in the same position, and if one of us wanted to turn we all had to turn in unison. By that time, everybody was exhausted and we fell into a much needed sleep.

The most important thing to the Germans was that they know where every Jew was... that every Jew was accounted for.

This was our fourth day without food. It's almost like a side note that we didn't

A Jewish child dying of starvation on a ghetto sidewalk

receive any food, but that's only because so many insufferable events were taking place around us that food seems to have been a secondary issue. Try not eating for four days and you'll see that food is far from a secondary issue. However, compared to the total picture of horrors taking place, food did seem somewhat secondary in importance. Understand that we were thrust into a world that had no precedent. The foulness of the Nazi mind is indescribable. The words of the *Tochacha (Devarim, Parashas Ki Savo 28:15-68)* were our reality. We lived with the following words: *And among those nations you will have no repose, there will be no place to rest the sole of your foot; there Hashem will give you a quivering heart, yearning of the eyes (for salvation), and suffering of soul. Your life will hang suspended, and you live in fear night and day, and your life will not be secure. In the morning you will express, "Who can give us back last night!" And in the evening you will proclaim, "Who can give us back the morning!" because of the dread of your heart that you will fear and the sights that your eyes will behold. (Devarim 28:65-67)*

Try not eating for four days and you'll see that food is far from a secondary issue.

The next day was Shavuos. Again we were assembled in the *appelplatz* where we *davened*. There was a young man in the group who remembered *Akdomos Milim* by heart. Everybody said *Akdomos* together. This was very, very inspiring. In between, however–and to this day I don't know what exactly happened–the announcement was made that something was stolen. The Gestapo came and told us that if the one who did it

Jewish inmates at the "appel" (roll call)

does not step forward ten Jews would be shot. There was a rabbi in the group, Rabbi Rubin, who volunteered. I'm sure he didn't do it, but he stepped forward to protect the other Jews. He was taken away by the Gestapo and we never saw him again. This was Auschwitz. Some people became true *tzadikim* during this period. Rabbi Rubin was one.

That afternoon we finally received some soup and everyone was pushing to be first. We were all starving. The *stubenelster* said, "Wait a minute, you guys. Hold it! You see the fire coming from those chimneys? That's your father and mother. That fire is destroying them right now. They are being burned in the crematoriums. Now behave because you might wind up there." This was the second time we heard this, but we didn't believe. We could not believe it. No! At that point though there were some men who ran to the electric wires that surrounded the camp and committed suicide by electrocuting themselves.

Later in the barracks the *stubenelster* tried to get those who didn't know about the postcard hoax to write postcards. Someone remarked that our families went up in smoke through the great chimneys of the crematoria and the Nazis are asking us to write postcards to them?! Now you can understand why some of the men didn't feel that they could go on living.

By now it had become evening and we organized a *minyan* for *Maariv*. While *davening* a German came into the barracks, saw us praying and started beating us. He screamed at us, "*Farfluchte Yuden! Farfluchte Yuden!* Cursed Jews! Cursed Jews! You still don't know where you are?" We all went back to our bunks. We never finished *Maariv*...we never finished the *davening*.

Photo credit : Aaron Spiegel

Munkacs Ghetto

The next morning was the second day of Shavuos. We were cautioned not to *daven*. Everyone *davened* quietly during the roll call, but not with a *minyan*. It was announced that we were being sent to another camp and that everyone should prepare to go shortly. However, we did not leave so fast, and I think we spent the entire day in the *appelplatz*. When we did leave Auschwitz we were sent to Buchenwald.

Some people became true tzadikim during this period. Rabbi Rubin was one.

Buchenwald

Upon arrival at Buchenwald we were assigned to a barracks. We had no food the entire day until we received some soup that evening, but it didn't agree with me and I got diarrhea...the whole night I was sick. In the morning when we had to go to the *appelplatz* I decided that since I'm sick I'll stay in bed, so

We worked under the supervision of a German SS man who made us sing while walking to work each morning.

I remained in my bunk. This decision had its consequences. During the roll call the count was taken and it was discovered that someone was missing. The Gestapo began a search and I was found in my bunk. I told them I was sick. "Sick," one of them said, "now you are really going to be sick!" They beat me mercilessly. I was taken out to the *appelplatz* on a stretcher.

After dismissal from the *appelplatz* one of the Jews informed me that "...here you are not sick, they don't need sick people here...". Some of my bunkmates washed the blood off me, and since there was no other assembly that day I remained lying in the bunk. The next morning the men made sure that I went to the *appelplatz*.

The Barracks

At that point we were still not assigned to any work, so after we were dismissed we went back to the barracks. However, during the entire roll call the men behind and beside me helped me to remain standing on my feet. This went on for an entire week. Each day they helped me stand so that I wouldn't be shot. It was difficult for me to drink, so the men helped me sip water so that I wouldn't dehydrate. They also shared their bread with me. They put it on top of the little bunk stove to toast it. They kept me alive...thank G-d I survived. By the time we went to the next camp, I had more-or-less recovered. We only stayed in Buchenwald for one week, but it was long enough for me.

On to Germany

We went from there to the coal mining town of Gelena Zeis located in Germany. The Brobeck factory, where the Nazis pressed oil out from coal, was located there. I was assigned with 12-15 other youths (14-15 years of age) to the *shise-commando*, the outhouse cleaning crew. They needed a *fuhrerarbeiter*, a group head, and since I was still weak, they appointed me to the position. We had a truck pulled by a horse with a large tank on it. We dipped a bucket into the pits of the outhouses and then dumped the sewage into the holding tank on the truck. We worked under the supervision of a German SS man who made us sing while walking to work each morning. This was his sadistic idea of fun and he did it to add to our misery. We cleaned the perimeter of the camp and the outhouses by the factory, and the kitchen where food was cooked for the civilians. The kitchen was located 1/4 of a mile away from the factory. This last assignment was very important and helpful, not just for us, but for people in the camp as well. You see, I made a deal with some of the local farmers who brought produce to the kitchen. In exchange for the waste that we gave them for fertilizer (instead of being dumped), they gave us potatoes and carrots in return. We brought the produce back to the camp to share with whoever we could. We tied the bottom of our pant legs, stuffing them full with the carrots and potatoes. We stuffed our shirts as well. This went on until we were caught and warned that we would be severely punished if we continued to do this since it was against regulations to bring anything into the concentration camp. We were warned, but they did not beat us the first time.

Typical Concentration Camp gallows

As I mentioned before, we cleaned the civilian kitchen. One day I asked one of the men working in the kitchen if there was anything to eat. He told me he is not allowed to give me any food, however, he showed me where they throw out the leftovers. He begged me not to tell anyone that he spoke with me, remarking that he didn't need trouble because of us. We started visiting this area of the yard on a daily basis by arranging our cleaning route to go past there. We took what ever we could. One day there were no leftovers, but we found another barrel with hot food. This food had been prepared for the Gestapo. We didn't know that their food was also prepared in this kitchen and not in the camp kitchen. Oh, my! You don't know what we felt at that moment. It was just terrific. We couldn't spend much time hanging around there, so we just took a little figuring we would come back later. We didn't see the Gestapo officer who was watching us. He was guarding the food until it was picked up and brought to the camp. He asked us, "Do you know what you did just now? That is our supper." Then he started beating me. I was the *fuhrerarbeiter* so he started with me first. I fainted. He revived me and began hitting me again. He broke three of my ribs. To this day those ribs are crooked. When he finished beating me he said that I would be hung that night. After that we finished our work for the day. As they brought us back to camp I accepted that I would be hung that night. I recited whatever I remembered from the *Viduy* prayer. I said the *Shema* and then Chapter 23 from *Tehillim*. Upon returning to the camp we reassembled in the *appelplatz* and then went back to the barracks. Some of the men came to give me words of encouragement, but, thank G-d, it wasn't

I made a deal with local farmers... In exchange for the waste we gave them for fertilizer they gave us potatoes and carrots.

necessary in the end because no one ever came. Maybe he forgot. I don't know why, but I know I had *siyata d'Shemaya*. The next day I went back to work and the Gestapo agent never mentioned anything about it.

We were able to obtain food from the German women who did the bookkeeping for the factory and cleaned the officers' quarters. They had a special hall where they worked and ate, and we cleaned their toilets as well. They used to get sandwiches to eat, and many of them couldn't finish so they would give us whatever remained. Again, we shared our booty with the men in the camp. The Gestapo agent who watched over us would go into the room to speak with the women, he had a sister or relative there. He left us to clean the toilets, there were six of them in a row. When we finished cleaning we would wait for the Gestapo officer to return. We didn't mind, in the meantime we were inside where it was warm, and we could relax for a while. One day someone reported us. The *stormfuhrer*, the head of the Gestapo, came to see what was going on. He asked us where our supervisor is and we replied that we didn't know. In truth, we did know, but we didn't want to say. The *stormfuhrer* went outside to seek the officer, but suddenly came back and began beating me. Somebody must have told him that I knew where the officer was. Then he went and brought the officer back to our group, whereupon he began beating me–but not hard. He was only acting for the benefit of the *stormfuhrer* who, convinced that the real culprit had been punished, finally left. The Gestapo officer intimated that I had saved his life. I told him that I could have been hung for being implicated in whatever the *stormfuhrer* thought was going on. He reassured me that nothing would happen to me and that he pretended to beat me so that I would not be punished later in the camp. This is just a small example of how precariously we lived in the camps. In one second, for no overt reason, you could be beaten, maimed, killed...it's absurd to try to fathom the depth of their corrupt and sadistic minds. In any case, this sanitation job continued until the middle of March. This was a blessing because during the winter we were able to work indoors and stay out of the cold. This took place during the late fall and early part of the winter in 1944.

In one second, for no overt reason, you could be beaten, maimed, killed... it's absurd to try to fathom the depth of their corrupt and sadistic minds.

One day our Gestapo officer said, "I want to talk to you. Tomorrow Mengele or some other Nazi is coming to conduct a *Selektion*. Anyone who cannot work is going to be told that they will be going on a vacation to a warmer climate where they will rest and heal and then be brought back to work. Do not believe him. All those who come forward are going to be taken to the crematorium." I went back to the camp and began passing around the word of what was to take place. The officer who told me this was 40 to 45 years old. I never saw him smile, and aside from the time he beat me when I took the Gestapo food, he never talked to me or bothered me. People were laughing at me. "Do you really think the Gestapo are going to tell you what they are going to do?", they asked. One of them told me he will listen to what they are going to say. Some of the younger kids wanted to go with the older people and I warned them not to get ideas about faking being sick or something like that. I warned them that they are playing around with their lives. Two uncles and cousins from my mother's side were with me in the camp. I told my uncles to try their hardest to pass the *Selektion* and show that they are strong and can really produce good work. They laughed at me. The next day I saw my uncles being taken away on the trucks. I didn't even say goodbye ... I didn't know what to say. I begged them, I really begged them not to listen. They went on a vacation from which they never returned.

The March

In the middle of March it was announced that we were leaving the camp immediately. Our whole group boarded flatbed, open train cars. We traveled all night without receiving any food or water. Around noontime Allied planes began bombing the train. The train came to an abrupt halt and we all jumped off. We were starved. Since the train stopped just outside the station of a small town we all began running into the town to get something to eat. However, most of the people refused to give us anything at all. I went to a farm house and asked for something, but was refused. The woman slammed the door in my face and didn't even let me finish my sentence. As I was leaving I saw that there were plates of cooked potatoes placed inside the chicken coop for the chickens to eat. I figured they didn't need it as much as we did, so I took all the potatoes and ran back to join up with the others. I distributed my treasure with my brother and some of the others. At this point there was an alarm sounded and an announcement was made that anyone not returning to the train immediately will be shot. Unfortunately, many of the men were shot for not returning quickly enough. Our group was ordered to leave, only now we had to walk because the train had been destroyed. It was raining. It was a rainy spring day...very cold...and all we had on was our camp pajamas.

No train, no food–only the damp cold rain. Anyone who sat down, couldn't walk or complained he couldn't walk was shot on the spot. We walked for six or seven hours straight, after not having any food for a day and a half. At that time I was five feet and ten inches tall and I only weighed 75 pounds. That evening we stopped at a farm. Everyone laid down on the grass. The Gestapo saw we were pulling out the grass and eating it. They shouted at us, "The grass is for the cattle, not for you Jews. Anyone caught eating grass will be shot." Some people risked their lives because they didn't care anymore. I knew the guards couldn't see too well, it was

We walked for six or seven hours straight, after not having any food for a day and a half.

Jews being transported in open train cars in the snow. Many died of exposure and starvation.

SS men shooting Jews in front of open graves

night, so I also ate the grass. In the morning we started walking again and by the afternoon a truck came with some bread. Everyone received one slice of bread. One slice, that was all, and it was the first time we had eaten in the last few days. We started walking again and we continued on until evening. That night we slept in a park. There was no grass, but we were tired from walking so we just laid down to sleep. By this time half of the group had been shot dead by the guards. The next morning, the third day of our march, we entered Czechoslovakia. We were being taken to the Theresienstadt concentration camp. In one of the towns we passed through on the way, the Czechs who saw our terrible appearance became hysterical. Many of them began throwing all kinds of food for us from their windows. The Gestapo started shooting towards the windows, screaming that they will be killed if they continue to give food to the Jews. It was unbelievable how good those people were to us. They didn't care if the Nazis were shooting at them, they just kept on throwing food. Frustrated, the guards told us that we would be shot if we picked up any food. Unfortunately, if there was a piece of bread, a hundred people jumped at it. The guards enjoyed shooting the Jews who were struggling to get to the piece of bread. One guard threw a grenade and killed a whole group at one time. After this heinous massacre we stopped picking up anymore food. We were afraid to touch it for fear of our lives.

We slept that night–on the ground in the cold rain. Very few of us survived the march.

Theresienstadt

When we arrived at Theresienstadt it was raining, damp and cold. There were no barracks available for us. We were left outside in the rain. This is where we slept that night–on the ground in the cold rain. Very few of us survived the march. Of the 4,000 some men who began the transfer, only about 400 survived. It seems that they were told that 4,000 prisoners were coming, but they didn't even have space for 400 initially. At this point I got a cold and I then developed pleurisy. I was taken into the attic of one of the buildings to rest. There were no doctors, there was nothing, I was just left lying in the attic. There were many men in the attic who had flec typhus. So on top of pleurisy I also developed flec typhus. Flec typhus causes a rash to break out over the entire body, accompanied by fevers of 105 degrees and higher. People died by the dozens from this. I must have been out of it because I don't remember when we were freed by the Russians. One day I woke up (May 8th, but I didn't know the exact date, I was so disoriented) and I realized that we are free because I heard Russian songs being sung in the camp. I inquired about my brother's whereabouts. I found out that when the camp was liberated most of the men, having not eaten for many days, ran into the town where organized food distribution was taking place. However, the food was too rich for their shriveled digestive systems, and many suffered from diarrhea because they could not digest the food and they died like flies. This happened in many of the camps. The liberators thought they were doing a good deed by sharing their food, not knowing it would be as lethal to us as poison. My brother was one of those who died. After all we went through together during the War, how tragic that we were separated at liberation.

I was taken to a hospital in Theresienstadt and began receiving a series of injections. I was given bread for each meal, but I didn't eat it because I was used to saving my food, not knowing when I would need it in the future. This was a conditioned response. It was so difficult to believe when you were told that you will get more to eat for lunch and supper! Eventually, I accumulated so much bread that some of the staff came in one day and told me that I would have to get rid of my stockpile. They began taking it away and I started a fight. I wanted the bread!

Slowly I got better. I was asked if I wanted to remain in the camp for a longer period of time. I was told that they needed guards to watch over the Gestapo members they had caught who were awaiting their punishment. I was given a revolver for this job. No one ever taught me what to do with it, but they gave it to me anyway. Wherever we were we always had some food with us. Now it was the turn of the Gestapo to feel what hunger was like. They began begging for food. I am ashamed to say it, but I gave them some of my food. This went on until after *Tishah B'Av*, at which point I said I would like to go home already. I was given a pair of shoes and told I could go. I still only had my concentration camp pajamas to wear. (Thinking back now, it seems strange that no one gave me a regular, normal suit to wear.) I started walking until I reached a small town. I don't even remember the name of the town. I learned that I could catch a train there for Pressburg. Before leaving I saw a Hungarian gendarmerie in his uniform. For whatever reason, he had cut off the decorative buttons from the jacket. I told him I have no clothes and he should give me his uniform. He responded that he had no other clothing, but I said it didn't matter and that he must give me his clothes, and he did. At this point these great murderers of children and babies were very afraid of what would happen to them. At the train station there was soup being given out for the soldiers and also for the Jews who came from the camps. I told the people that I didn't have a dish–one of the famous tin dishes that the inmates were given in the camps. However, I had a shoe box, so they gave me my food in a shoe box! I was told that if I go to the Jewish Community Council located in the town I would be given 400 *kronen*. I didn't realize of how little value this was, but I went and got the money and then returned to the station. One of the people there was very nice to me. He gave me a plate made out of stainless steel and I went back and got a little more soup. It's important to realize that you considered yourself well off if you had a tin bowl with some soup in it. Just the minimal amount of food each day was considered a luxury. I boarded the overnight train to Budapest.

It's important to realize that you considered yourself well off if you had a tin bowl with some soup in it.

Return to Budpest

We arrived in Budapest at 6:00 am. I inquired if they distributed soup at the station. They did, however, we were too early as they didn't begin operation until later in the day. I was told that there was a bus available to take us to a DP Camp where we could get breakfast and receive assistance with future travel plans. This was very good news. After a half hour of travel we arrived at the camp. There were many, many Jewish children there, as well as adults who had come from various concentration and labor camps. At 8:00 am they announced breakfast was being served. Since it was on a first come-first serve basis, everyone went running to get in line. Breakfast was a slice of bread and a cup of tea, if you had a bowl to put it in (which I now had). This was just great! I asked if the tea came with sugar and was told, "Yes, it's a sweet tea." This was really a great deal! I got onto line. Suddenly, someone starts grabbing me out of line. In the concentration camps if someone tried to break into the line because they thought there wouldn't be enough, you took your bowl and hit him over the head. I was about to pick up my bowl and give the person what he deserved when I take a quick look at the intruder and it turned out to be my own brother, Yumi! After the initial shock wore off, he explained to me that he heard from others who preceded me that I was on my way from Theresienstadt to Munkacs and that I would be passing through Budapest. Initially he had been in Auschwitz, but was sent with a work brigade to clean up the rubble left after the fall of the Warsaw Ghetto, and the destruction caused by the Allied bombing raids. He had been liberated while in Warsaw, and then came back to find me. He told me he had already returned to Munkacs and we should begin our return trip now. I emphatically refused to leave–I wanted my sweet tea. This was my mindset and preoccupation after so much deprivation. "Come", he said, "I'll buy you breakfast. I have clothes for you. We're all ready to go." I refused. I wanted to have tea with sugar. He saw that I was adamant, so he waited.

I wanted my sweet tea. This was my mindset and preoccupation after so much deprivation.

After the tea, he took me to the rooming house we had stayed in before the War. I got a haircut and glasses. This kept us busy all day. The next morning we left for Munkacs.

Munkacs and The Future

It was between Rosh Hashanah and Yom Kippur. My brother had a beautiful apartment in Munkacs. I enjoyed taking showers again. Someone had opened a kosher restaurant so we had a reliable place to eat. On Yom Kippur we *davened* in the big *shul* that was run by the *Kehillah*. The *Rov* was Reb Shaye Gold

Mr. Ostreicher and granddaughter of the Minchas Elozer in front of the Rebbe's house that is now used as quarters for the NKVD, the Soviet Secret Police.

Mr. Ostreicher's grandson saying Tehillim at the grave of Mr. Ostreicher's grandfather, in the new Munkacs Cemetery.

What is there to say about such a time...written pages can't contain the endless stream of emotions that we all experienced.

(a cousin to the past and present Satmar Rebbes). He gave a *drashah* on *Kol Nidre* night. It was the first Yom Kippur of our *new world*. We fasted, cried,prayed and cried some more. What is there to say about such a time...written pages can't contain the endless stream of emotions that we all experienced. That is all I can tell you. After the fast we went to the restaurant to eat. We started talking about what happened to us since we were last home. Each of us related his particular story. You cannot imagine the scene as we recounted our years of travail, pain, loss and liberation. It is a very special group that we survivors belong to...very special. At that time approximately 120-150 survivors had returned to Munkacs. We stayed in Munkacs till *Chol Hamoed* Succos because I came down with pleurisy. Fortunately, there was a Dr. Schreiber there who started me on a series of injections.

On the second day of Succos the Russians began closing their borders with the West. Now we had to solve the problem of escaping from Munkacs. My brother was acquainted with a few Russians and devised the following plan. The Russians locked us inside the wardrobe closets that were in our apartment. They pretended to be moving furniture for Russian military officers relocating further to the West. In this way we passed through the border out of Russia and into the part of Hungary

Mrs. Ostreicher saying Tehillim at her grandfather's grave in Kiraly-Helmec. He was a Dayan in Hungary.

Mrs. Ostreicher's Family - (back row l-r) Chaya Nechama (Mrs. Ostreicher), Mrs. Ostreicher's mother, Rivka, Mrs. Ostreicher's father, Moshe Yosef Weinstein, (middle row) Chava Bina (Agi), Chaim, Dov and (front) Blima Raizel (Vera)

that was still free. *Boruch* Hashem, the plan went off without a hitch.

We stopped in Ujhely (oo-hey) where the Russians let us out of the closets. They received their gallon of vodka and were on their way. We stayed in Ujhely in an apartment we rented for a few days. I again came down with pleurisy and was hospitalized for ten days. Fortunately, someone opened a kosher restaurant in a small house, so my brother and the other returning Jews had somewhere to eat. Slowly I began to get better, though I was very weak and it was difficult to walk. At this juncture I decided we would go to Kiraly-Helmec (Czechoslovakia) where we had an uncle and cousins. During the War I hid there and also spent many Shabbosos before receiving my official discharge papers from the army.

It's amazing after five years of savage destruction, life–more or less–proceeded in a normal fashion.

We arrived in Kiraly-Helmec and were received with open arms by my surviving uncle and cousins. My uncle lost his wife, two children and all of his grandchildren in the War. It was wonderful to be with family and feel at home again. It was at this time that I met my wife. The *Rov* of the town was our *shadchon*. My wife had been in Auschitwz. At one point the women were lined up in front of a gigantic pit that was to be used for their mass grave. One-by-one they were shot dead, falling into the pit behind them. My wife's turn was next when an aid to the officer in charge came running up to stop the executions because the Russians were fast approaching the camp. This is how she survived. Her grandfather was a *dayan* in Helmec. She was from a prominent family in the town. We were married in Helmec and began building our home there. As time went by we were back to doing business as usual. We dealt in importing American cigarettes, barrels of 96 proof whiskey and other commodities to Hungary and Slovakia. It's amazing to think that after five years of savage destruction, life–more or less–proceeded in a normal fashion. We made a very good living from our business and had no thoughts about leaving Czechoslovakia that fast.

Rabbi Eliezer Silver from Cincinnati came to Eastern Europe after the War

Pushke boxes still remaining in the wall of the Shul in Kiraly-Helmec.

to help the survivors start to rebuild their lives. At one point he came to Czechoslovakia and I had a meeting with him concerning my ability to smuggle Jews across the border from Hungary. I pretended to own land on the border between Hungary and Czechoslovakia. By doing this I received a little passport allowing me to cross the border at will. This is how I imported my whiskey and other goods into Czechoslovakia to sell. Over time I got to know all of the border guards and developed a relationship with them.

Rabbi Eliezer Silver

One Friday I was asked to smuggle the Vishnitzer Rebbe, his brother, the Sered Rov, their families and some Yeshiva *bochurim* across the border. I went to speak with the Rebbe, who gave me a big *shalom aleichem* and reminded me that when he once visited Munkacs for a Shabbos, he stayed at our house.

I remember his *zemiros* from that Shabbos. They were heavenly. He sang like an angel.

The Rebbe was heading to Kashau for Shabbos, but I implored him to come to Helmec and spend Shabbos with us. I promised to send a wire to Kashau and tell the *chassidim* to come. Eventually, the Rebbe acquiesced. When I went back to tell my wife, she broke down in tears. How would she prepare so many chickens and other dishes for so many people? I ran around the town and enlisted the help of what turned out to be a small army of people who all began preparing.

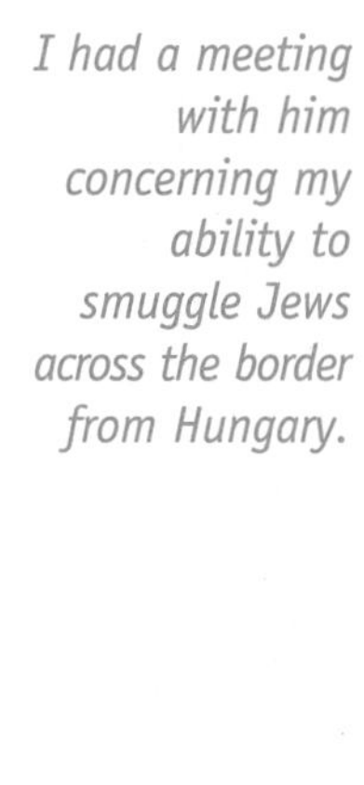

I had a meeting with him concerning my ability to smuggle Jews across the border from Hungary.

Exterior and interior photgraphs of the shul in Kiraly-Helmec

We made a chanukas habayis *that morning because we had completed restoring the* shul*. The Germans had not destroyed the building.*

I brought the *shochet* to the Rebbe so that he could supervise the *shechitah*. We were busy plucking feathers, *kashering* chickens and stuffing straw mattress sacks for the visitors from Kashau to sleep on. I rented a large catering hall in a bar across from my house. I also purchased three barrels of beer so that the owner would not have a loss of income since we would be taking over his tavern for Shabbos. The man asked a tremendous amount for this, but where else would there be enough room? In the end no one slept too much that night as the Rebbe held a very long *tish* that was beautiful to behold. The next morning we *davened* in the *shul*. We made a *chanukas habayis* that morning because we had completed restoring the *shul*. The Germans had not destroyed the building, but all the Torah scrolls were gone along with everything else that was inside. The Sered Rov gave a *drashah* asking what blessing does a person make when he builds a new house. There wasn't a dry eye in the whole *shul*. He told how so many *shuls* were destroyed on *Kristalnacht*, and yet here we were rededicating our *shul*. Little did he know that very soon there would be no Jews left in Helmec to use it. They would all emigrate.

Hungarian passport picture of Mr. and Mrs. Ostreicher with their daughter, Agi.

Eventually, the Communists began to actively take over political control of Hungary. We realized that there is no longer a place for us here. We notified my wife's family–her grandmother and her aunts and uncles–informing them of our intentions to go to America. Her father, mother and five sisters were killed in the camps, otherwise, everyone from her mother's side survived. It didn't take long before we received our certificates to leave Czechoslovakia.

To America

In the fall of 1947, we went to the American Consulate with our papers and were approved for immigration, however, there were still some loose ends. We needed a particular red stamp issued by the Communist government to allow us to leave. It took a little while, but we secured the red stamp. Our first daughter Agi was born when this whole process began, so it took just a bit longer to arrange everything for her. Finally, we were ready to leave for America.

Before boarding the ship at a French port, we stopped in Paris for a few days to visit my uncle. We departed just before Pesach. The Serdohelyer Rov and a whole group of *heimeshe mentshen*, some of whom we knew well, were also on ship with us. The *Rov* asked me to speak with the captain to make arrangements for our *yom tov davening* and for the *Pesach Sedorim*. The Captain obliged by giving us a large ballroom, matzos and raisins for wine. The *Rov* had his own matzoh and wine. We *kashered* an area of the kitchen to cook eggs, and that's what we had for the *seder*. We may not have had much to eat, but the *sedorim* were beautiful, and we had many, many *minyonim davening* with gratitude that Europe was left behind.

We crossed the sea, our own personal *Kriyas Yam Suf*, and arrived safely in the United States, the blessed country, on the second day of *yom tov*. We were told to disembark immediately, and no amount of pleading could get us a reprieve until evening. We spent the rest of the day in a building on the dock. We had already *davened Shacharis* on the boat in the morning. We retrieved our belongings after that evening.

Life In America

After arriving in America I tried several businesses to see how I could make a living to support my family. First I worked as a tie presser, then in the butcher business with my brother, and finally I enrolled in a Hebrew Teacher Training program at Yeshiva University. After two unsatisfactory placements in small towns, I was hired as Youth Leader and Day School principal in Peoria, Illinois. When we arrived, there were only eight Orthodox children in the Day School, and as in many small towns outside of New York, the resistance to a Torah true curriculum was very strong. However, I have the satisfaction of knowing that when we left Peoria 15 years later, there were over 100 Orthodox children in the Day School. In addition, a local youth outreach and activity program that I initiated (arranging Shabbatons and conventions in New York for Jewish children from the Midwest and western states, Nebraska, Montana, etc.), developed

We crossed the sea, our own personal Kriyas Yam Suf, and arrived safely in the United States.

Annual Convention of the Orthodox Union, 1957. Mr. Ostreicher is receiving the NCSY Founders Award. (l-r) Rabbi Pinchas Stopler, National Director of NCSY (National Conference of Synagogue Youth), Mr. Ostreicher, President of NCSY (1957), Rabbi Chaim Wasserman (Assistant National Director of NCSY)

Mr. Ostreicher in front of the Munkacs Yeshiva he built in memory of his father.

into what is now known as NCSY, the National Conference of Synagogue Youth of the Orthodox Union.

We even wrote and produced local television and radio programs about the *yomim tovim* that were broadcast to the community. These were very popular. For a period of time I was the Hillel Director at Bradley University where I initiated a *kashrus* and a Torah study program, the first such program introduced in a major college in the Midwest. After returning to New York and going into business I was able to turn my attention to expanding and strengthening Munkacs *Chassidus* in America and *Eretz Yisrael*. I know that this is something that brings my parents great pleasure in the *Olam HaEmes*. I see myself and my wife like so many other survivors who came to America to rebuild a Torah way of life. To us this was not only a source of comfort, but a mandate from those who perished. I thank Hashem for His constant help in fulfilling this mandate.

The present Munkacser Rebbe

After the War, Mr. Ostreicher came to America where he dedicated himself to bringing the beauty of Torah life to Jewish children in what was, essentially, a spiritually barren America. He received a Hebrew Teacher's License from the teacher training program at Yeshiva University and, speaking English with a heavy Hungarian accent, settled in Peoria. Illinois. Peoria boasted a total of eight Shabbos observant families in the early fifties. Culture and life in the American Midwest was as foreign to the Ostreichers as the moon, yet Mr. Ostreicher used every communication media possible to bring the light of Torah to the Jews of Peoria: building a day school, bringing families into *Yiddishkeit* and launching a program of supervised religious and social activities, including conventions, that was to become known as NCSY– The National Conference of Synagogue Youth. How does a Munkacser *chassid*, barely speaking English, transform an acculturated, Midwestern Jewish community into a town of Torah and *mitzvah* observance? While speaking together on the phone one afternoon, I asked Mr. Ostreicher what incident, what memory, thought or emotion motivated him to accomplish so much in the face of so many obstacles and after so much personal loss and heartbreak. The following dialogue ensued.

Y.K.: Mr. Ostreicher, after all that you experienced – the loss and suffering – where did you find the strength and conviction to accomplish so much? Not only did you remain Torah observant and unquestioning – a remarkable feat in itself – but you became an ambassador for the Torah by bringing *Yiddishkeit* to others, and building and supporting Torah institutions and programs for the past half century.

Mr. Ostreicher: Hashem was very good to me. He sustained me and protected me through the most unimaginable experiences, and for this I love Him and thank Him.

Y.K.: What you just expressed is beautiful, poignant and true, but you did not really answer my question. What was it, what incident or moment, defined your life's mission? Few people accomplish what you have. What was the singular moment that defined your life for the last fifty years?

Mr. Ostreicher: (Silence...prolonged silence.)

Y.K.: Mr Ostreicher....can you tell me?

Mr. Ostreicher: (Again, prolonged silence.)

Y.K.: Please.

Mr. Ostreicher: [*Very slowly*] As you know, after we were liberated from the camps, I returned to Munkacs for Rosh Hashanah. As in previous years, though no longer with my family, I went to the Lataritza River that flowed near my house to say *Tashlich*. As I stood by the river I was stunned to see only a dry river bed – the water was gone – the river had completely dried up. It was so strange. I remember being confused by the onrush of so many different emotions and memories that I could no longer suppress. [*A short pause*] Then it occurred to me that the situation was not strange at all. Why was there no river, because there were no Jews to say *Tashlich*. I pictured how the men and boys – very few years ago – stood on one side of the river bank saying *Tashlich*, while the women and girls did the same on the other side. Only now both sides of the river were empty – completely empty. There were no children. There were no longer any Jewish children alive in Munkacs.

RUSCOVA: REMEMBERING LIFE IN THE CARPATHIAN MOUNTAINS

The Reminiscences of Mr. Chaim Eliezer (Lou) Feig

"I was born in Ruscova, Romania in 1926. Ruscova is a quaint and primitive little town with one street running through it. The whole town is only about three kilometers long. Most of the Jews lived on the main street, while the gentiles lived further back toward the hills. Ruscova is located at the foot of the Carpathian mountains to the east, and near the border with Czechoslovakia and Galicia (Southern Poland) to the north. It is located in the area of Romania called Translyvania.

Ruscova...is only about three kilometers long. Most of the Jews lived on the main street, while the gentiles lived further back toward the hills.

Actually, there were three small towns close together descending from the hills, at the foot of the Carpathian mountains. Ruscova was located in the valley at the bottom of these hills near the northern border of Romania where the train station was located in a town called Leordina, 1.5 miles away. The train ran west to Budapest (the capital of Hungary) and northeast around the Carpathians.

Both sets of my great grandparents were born in Ruscova. Going back 200 years you'll find that my great-grandfather, after whom I am named, was born in Ruscova, but his father came from Galicia in Poland. From both sides of the family I am the fourth generation in Ruscova. Originally, everyone came from Galicia.

My immediate family consisted of eight children, so there were ten of us altogether. Our house had three rooms. In the kitchen we had a table that pulled out at night and turned into a bed. If I remember correctly, three of the boys slept in that one bed. Three of my four sisters slept in the bedroom, the fourth slept with my mother and the last boy with my father. We lived together with my grandparents in one yard. Our house was in the back of the yard and my maternal grandparents lived in a house in the front of the yard. We appreciated family, being together was one of our greatest joys.

When I was a child we didn't have toys like children today. We played with buttons, walnuts and simple things like that. My childhood was so nice, and so sweet, and so good–but don't think that I'm saying this just because youth always seems better. It really was a very sweet time.

There was a well for water about 100 yards from the house. I have memories of *shlepping* the water and it was very difficult. In wintertime the well was frozen and it was very hard to draw water. You had to break through the ice before you could get the pail down to the water.

The street in Ruscova was paved with gravel. We smashed rocks into small pieces and covered the road with this gravel. Otherwise, when the snow melted in the spring and ran down from the mountains the mud would be so thick that it would be impossible to pass through with a wagon. There was no electricity and certainly no cars in Ruscova. If you needed to go somewhere you went by train or hired a wagoner to take you. The County Seat in Viseul-de-sus was about 10 miles away, and Sighet, the home of the famous Rebbe and Sigheter Yeshiva, was about 25 miles due west of Ruscova near the Hungarian border. Sighet was located in the area of Transylvania that went back and forth between Hungarian and Romanian rule. In 1921 this eastern part of Translyvania was taken from Hungary and given to Romania. In 1940 Hitler ordered Romania to give it back to Hungary. Because the area changed hands a number of times we would say that the *baalei battim* in Transylvania changed every Monday and Thursday.

Because the area changed hands a number of times we would say that the baalei battim in Transylvania changed every Monday and Thursday.

The only telephone in Ruscova was located in the post office. If you wanted to call someone, first you sent a telegraph to the post office in the city or town where they resided. The post office would then notify them to be present to receive a call at the determined time, and the person would go and wait until the call came through. You did the same thing if you were calling Ruscova from Budapest or elsewhere.

Mr. Feig as a bochur

Romanian Farm

We counted 320 talaisim *in Ruscova. That's the way we counted families...Life in Ruscova was hard...There were no modern conveniences.*

We counted 320 *talaisim* in Ruscova. That's the way we counted families. So there were approximately 320 Jewish families in the town, with about 3,000 gentiles living there as well. Remember, however, that we only counted the *talaisim*; each Jewish family consisted of at least six or seven people. I know that when the Germans deported us to the ghetto there were about 2,360 *nefashos* that were deported. Before the War I guess there were about 2,500 Jews living in Ruscova.

Life in Ruscova was hard. In the winter it was so cold that we could actually walk on *top* of the snow. That's how crisp and hard the snow became. In the spring it was very muddy from all of the water that ran off from the snow in the mountains. There were no modern conveniences: no running water, no steam heat, no inside plumbing and no electricity. Most of the Jews worked in trades and crafts. They worked as blacksmiths, shoemakers and tailors, etc. Very few were merchants. In fact, in a museum in Tel Aviv I found a picture of a wagoner who I recognized from Ruscova standing in the shop of the village blacksmith waiting to get his horse shod.

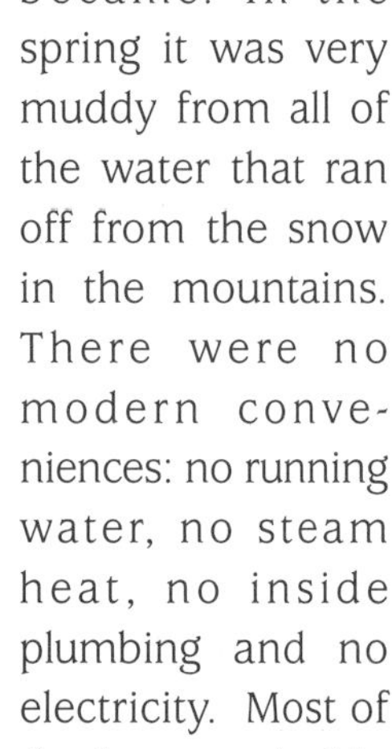

The gentiles in the hills supplied the Jews with wood and some other products. However, each Jewish family had a cow or two to supply at least some of their milk. Most Jews had horses, but only the poorer Jews made their living, their *parnosah*, as wagoners. The Jews owned the fields and the gentiles worked the land for them in return for a certain percentage of the crops-- they were sharecroppers.

Most of the Jewish families had a plot of land on which they planted produce that was essential for their food supply. Potatoes, carrots, corn, wheat, parsley and turnips were grown in addition to other crops. Potatoes, carrots and other such foods that would keep were stored in the cellars for the winter. This was an important part of our diet.

In the fall we brought in from the fields all of the produce remaining from the summer. This was a very big job, especially harvesting the corn.

Well in Chernowitz, Bukovinia

During the week we ate bread made from cornmeal, not wheat. We let the kernels harden on the cob, then we would shuck the cob and remove the kernels, taking them to the mill to be ground into flour. That was our daily bread. I would say about 75 percent of the people in Ruscova didn't make a *motzie*, a blessing over bread, from Shabbos to Shabbos. *Challos* we made from wheat. My mother would get up at 4:00 in the morning *erev* Shabbos to begin making the *challah*. I remember waking up and seeing her kneading the dough.

Often we made *kiddush* over *challah* on Shabbos because there wasn't any wine. Some people bought raisins and soaked them in water for three or four days before Shabbos to make raisin wine. Pesach-time many people had to pawn some of their personal possessions in order to have money to buy wine and *matzoh*. There were two or three places in town where we baked our *matzos*.

Shepherds in a village near Vrchni-Apsa.

Looking back, I would call Ruscova a Baal Shem Tov type town. It was a *chassidishe shtetl* tucked into the foot of the Carpathians. The town was about 150 years old when I was a child. It was founded by Jews who came there from Poland and Galicia. I said before that the life was hard, and besides the *tzsoros* that Jews traditionally faced throughout the centuries in Europe, we also faced real hunger much of the time. You have to picture the scene at breakfast tables in Ruscova with mothers telling their children not to eat too much, that they can only have one slice of bread. I'll never forget that.

Do you know what kind of meat we ate? What *you* throw away, what *you* wouldn't touch, that's what we got from the butcher. You had to be a privileged character to get good portions from the butcher.

Friday night we had fish that was caught by some of the local people who went through the town selling their catch. Then we had soup and some type of meat or chicken. There were times when we didn't have meat at all and my mother would improvise. In winter we had potatoes, dry parsley and carrots, but in summer we had more because we had fresh vegetables growing in our garden. Shabbos morning we had *cholent* and *kugel*. It was kept warm in our oven. In some towns everyone put their *cholent* pot in the bakery oven, but we didn't. We wrapped up the pot and put it in the oven before Shabbos while the coals were still hot and the *cholent* stayed hot, not just warm, until the next morning. Although we usually had enough firewood to keep the house warm during the winter, not everyone did.

I would need several days to tell you about the *frumkeit* in Ruscova.

Besides the tzsoros *that Jews traditionally faced...we also faced real hunger much of the time.*

Jews and peasants in a village in the Carpathian Mountains, 1921

First thing in the morning we ran to the *mikveh*— every day. Those who didn't go to the *mikveh* right away were up saying *Tehillim*. The men could hardly wait to go to shul. There were many *minyanim* each morning. The last *minyan* was at about 10:00 am. After the *minyan* the men would gather together to talk. Politics, particularly the state of affairs between nations and how this affected the Jews, was always a topic of conversation. In Ruscova we didn't live with the security that we have here in America.

Politics, particularly the state of affairs between nations and how this affected the Jews, was always a topic of conversation.

At six years of age I got up at 6:00 in the morning to go to *cheder*. I went to *cheder* before I went to public school. After *cheder* I came home, ate breakfast and then went to public school which ended at 12:30 pm. Then I came home for lunch and went back to *cheder* until 6:00 pm.

The public school was just one big room and the teachers were brought in from Budapest. The Romanian government brought in the teachers, mostly from within Romania itself. Since this area once belonged to Hungary, the government wanted teachers who would inculcate us with Romanian nationalistic ideals. The mayor of Ruscova was appointed by the government as well, to ensure that he was of Romanian lineage. Attendance in public school was compulsory, everyone had to go, but about 95% of the students were Jewish. The non-Jewish children didn't attend the school. They were brought up to take care of their cattle and help on the family farm

Matzeivah of Rabbi Avroham Yehoshua Freund, one of the great Romanian rabbis before World War II. The Satmar Rov and the Klausenberger Rov would consult with him on matters of Torah law.

Shul of the Baal Shem Tov in Pe'atria Niamez, in the Maramaros region of Romania

or in the home, and they didn't come down from the towns further up in the hills to attend school. As I mentioned, most of the Jews lived in Ruscova, so we had to attend school.

There were no street lights. In the winter, when the days were very short, we carried lanterns with us when we walked so that we could see where we were going. We also had to be careful because of the *shekutzim*, the gentile bullies (that's what we called them) who would attack us and pull our *payos*.

I can still remember the way the morning felt in Ruscova. My father would wake me so that I would be on time. I had to awaken very early from the age of five-years-old. To get up at such an early hour, in the winter in the Carpathians was a real *nisayon*, a real test. The house was freezing, there was no heat. We had a pot-belly stove that my father lit each morning before he woke us so that the house would be a little warm when we got up. One time, I remember, my father couldn't afford the wood, so we had to manage without heat.

One winter, when I was older, my father rented a room for my older brother and me in a lady's house that was closer to where we learned so that we wouldn't have to walk so far each morning in the cold. Our house was only about a kilometer away, but in the winter when it is well below zero it was dangerous to walk that far. Then we had to get up even earlier each morning, around 4:30 am, because learning started at 5:00. Our room was right near the *mikveh*, and the Ruscover Rov lived behind the *mikveh*, so if we weren't up on time he would come by on his way to the *mikveh* and knock on the window to get us out of bed. We got up, washed and said our *brachos* quickly because the boy whom we called our *Chazar Bochur*, our review partner, came to our room to learn with us. We had to be at the table and ready to learn at 5:00 am.

One of the few recreational activities we had was when people got together in the morning to go to the post office to see if they had received a letter from their children who had moved away or were studying in a yeshiva in another town. The family was of supreme importance in Ruscova.

I began attending public school when I was six, but before that, when I was five, I began studying the *Alef-Beis* and *dikduk* in a class with a rebbe. In fact, I was considered some kind of a genius because at age 3 when my father made *kiddush* I made *kiddush* with him. I clearly remember him picking me up onto a chair, and giving me a little *kos*, a little cup with a handle. I said "*Yom Hashishi*" together with him.

It is impossible to describe what Shabbos *meant to us, or what a Friday night was like.*

It is impossible to describe what Shabbos meant to us, or what a Friday night was like. Impossible. I cannot. There are no words for me to describe what it was like in the house, especially

Present day shepherd near Shatz, Romania

in the later years, when the boys would come home from yeshiva for Shabbos and we would all be together. To be home and together was so special, the most wonderful thing in the world. You went out in the street and it smelled of Shabbos. From every home you heard *zemiros* being sung. There was no richer person in the world than the simple *ba'al hagolah* who came home on Friday afternoon after toiling all week long. He quickly changed into his Shabbos clothes, and if there was time he ran off to the *mikveh*. He put on his *bekisheh* and *streimel*, while his wife wore her white Shabbos *tichel* (head covering). Royalty! The simple Jew became royalty on Shabbos. I sit here and go back in time in my mind and review what happened to us. I can tell you one thing, if there wouldn't have been a Hitler, I wouldn't have a house now with seven bedrooms and with so many baths. For what? Who needs it? Does it replace the beauty of those three rooms and our family's closeness and the holiness of our way of life? Never.

To be home and together was so special, the most wonderful thing in the world. You went out in the street and it smelled of Shabbos.

The Sigheter Yeshiva

I attended the Sigheter Yeshiva from 1938 until 1941. Each year the yeshiva received a $10,000 grant from the Feuerstein family in Boston. At that time $10,000 was the entire Yeshiva budget. The yeshiva provided the *bochurim* with vocational training as well. Three hours a day the *bochurim* worked on a knitting machine that was set up in one of the halls. *Bochurim* with long *payos* would spin cloth from the machine. Another interesting thing they did was to announce at the beginning of the *zeman* (semester) that whoever knew 40 *blatt Gemora* by heart, with *Tosafos* and some other commentaries by the 7th of Adar, when the *Chevra Shas* made their *siyum*, would receive $100. Many times we didn't have enough firewood in the yeshiva, so we learned our *Gemora* in bed under the covers in order to earn the $100, which I once received.

While I was in yeshiva my father lost a leg, and this caused a very great financial burden on the family. One winter I badly needed a winter coat because all I had was a jacket. My father gave me 1,000 *lei* (Romanian dollars) to buy a coat for myself, but I sent the money back home because I knew how difficult things were at home and told him that someone gave me a coat. In the

Vocational training: a weaving class in Sighet Yeshiva, 1930's

meantime I had nothing, so I wrapped myself with paper for insulation. I also ran back and forth to attend *shiurim*, this helped me to stay warm. My mother was suspicious that I didn't really have a coat, but she didn't know for sure. I stayed in Sighet from when I was 12 until I was 15.

Rabbi Yitzchak Isaac Weiss זצ"ל
The Spinka Rebbe

On to Budapest

In 1942, at age 15, I went to Budapest. Budapest is one of the most elegant cities in Europe. At night, it's like Paris. You can't compare Cleveland to Budapest. I don't know of another gentile city that is more beautiful than Budapest. I left home a young, inexperienced child. I was homesick, all I could think of was to be home with my family. Hitler had given Transylvania back to Hungary and we were no longer allowed to go to Budapest unless we had a permit, which I did not possess. I had long *payos* at the time, and my mother was very afraid they would be cut off if I didn't comb them up and place them over the top of my head so that my hat would cover them. I stayed with my aunt and uncle (from my mother's side) and then I did not feel so alone. After about six weeks I started to attend a public school to learn a trade. In the afternoon I attended an Ashkenazic yeshiva called the *Chevra Shas*.

I began to make connections with people in the city, supplying them with butter and cheese that my sisters made in Ruscova. In return I was paid either with money or clothes and supplies that we could no longer get. We couldn't buy items wholesale anymore because Jews needed a

I went to Budapest... I began to make connections supplying them with butter and cheese that my sisters made in Ruscova.

Ohel of the Spinka Rebbe

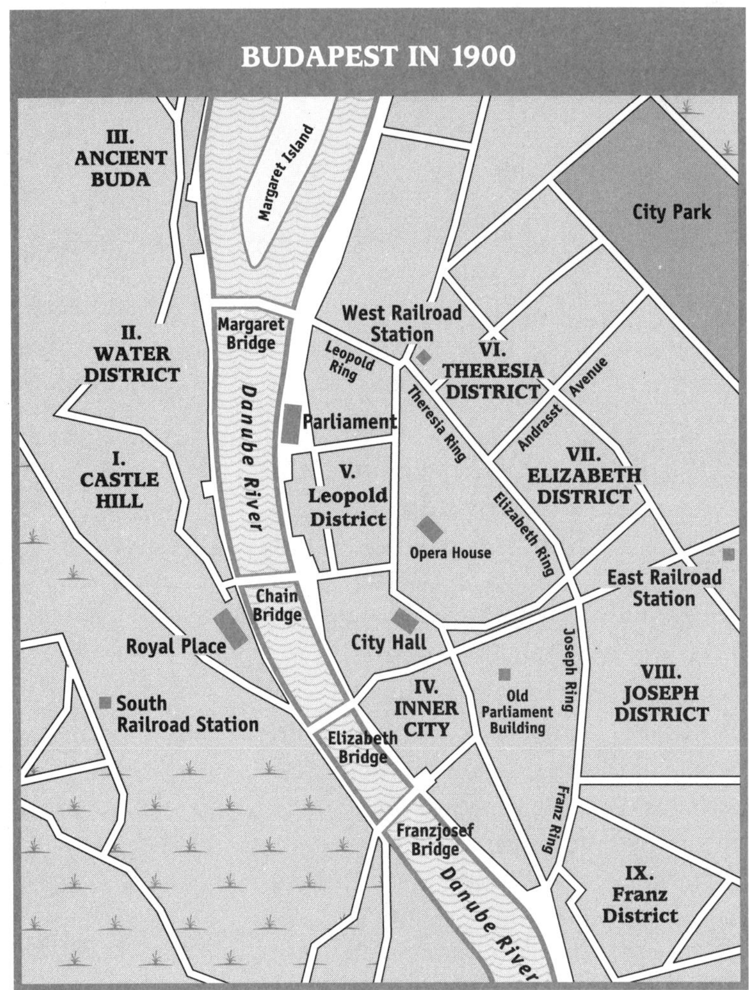

special permit to purchase such merchandise, and since the War was on it was almost impossible to find what we required to satisfy the basic needs of our household. I was once caught at the railroad station smuggling these supplies out of Budapest and was taken to a police station. The police captain interrogated me, but he was kind and didn't punish me. "What are you doing here?", he asked. "You must have a permit to live in Budapest, and you have no such permit allowing you to stay. Why don't you cut off your *payos*," he continued. He told me I could still remain a good Jew without *payos* and that if I cut them off he would give me a permit to reside in the city. I was crying inside, having to go through such an ordeal, and I felt so far away from my parents. I didn't want to do anything that would displease them, because I had such a sense of devotion and love for them. I had no choice, however, for if I didn't obey who knows what he would have done to me. In any case, he took me to a barber shop so that I could have a say in how my *payos* were cut. At least he gave me that option. Afterwards I had a more or less normal haircut. For five months I let my hair grow, so when I returned home my parents wouldn't be upset—because I went home with *payos*.

My parents sent me about 100 pounds of butter a week. I would sell it to manufacturers and to individuals. Since it was war time it was very hard to obtain fat, so people were very interested in purchasing the butter which was in short supply.[32] There were many people who would only eat *Cholov Yisrael* (milk products produced by Jews), so that

Budapest in 1900: in the foreground the scaffolding of the Elizabeth Bridge, under construction

32. The reader is referred to the interview with Mr. Yosef Friedenson in **The World That Was: Poland.**

was an additional reason why I had no trouble selling the butter.

My parents wrapped the butter in paper and packed it in boxes for shipping after keeping it in ice cold well water for awhile. The butter arrived in Budapest from Ruscova in 10 hours by express train. Sometimes, when it was hot, it started to melt and the paper became very greasy from the fat. I re-hardened it by putting it in a tub filled with ice water. No one had refrigerators then, not even in Budapest, though most of the apartments had running water, toilets and electricity. I had my steady customers and I would deliver the butter to them every week. My aunt helped me cut and package the butter for distribution.

By the time I was 16, I was doing big business with my butter or cheese. I had money for myself and I made enough money for the rest of the family as well. After my father's accident in 1940, the financial situation in the house was very bad. I couldn't think of my sisters going to work, G-d forbid. Now I made money for the whole family, and it was good money. After my *payos* grew back I started going home every week on Thursday night. If you took the express train and travelled all night you arrived in Ruscova at 10:00 in the morning. Budapest was 600 kilometers away and it was a hard trip, but I did it so that I could be with my family for Shabbos. Sunday evening when I went back to Budapest my heart ached. This is what a Shabbos at home meant to me. I remained in Budapest until 1944. I kept up my learning and business the entire time. I would buy things on the black market and send them home by train with friends. Now that Ruscova had been given back to Hungary, the Hungarian government brought in government workers who were Hungarian nationals. My parents sent the food supplies to me through the post office in Ruscova, and even though the postmaster was Hungarian my parents were friendly with him and he let the packages go through (of course,

The Parliament

Budapest was 600 kilometers away and it was a hard trip, but I did it so that I could be with my family for Shabbos.

Interior of the Budapest apartment of the former Prime Minister Kalman Tisza

a little bribe every now and then helped). In Budapest they didn't ask any questions when you sent a package. You just had to write down what the contents were and they let it go. If I had been caught I could have gotten into trouble, but, thank G-d, I was only caught that one time.

DEPORTATION FROM THE BUDAPEST SUBURBS

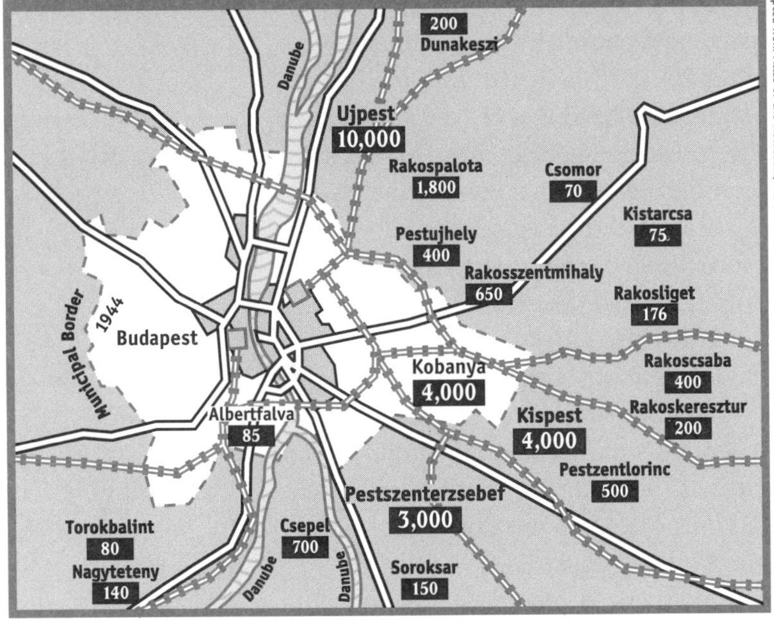

200
Dunakeszi
Danube
Ujpest
10,000
Rakospalota
1,800
Csomor
70
Kistarcsa
75
Pestujhely
400
Rakosszentmihaly
650
Rakosliget
176
Municipal Border 1944
Budapest
Kobanya
4,000
Rakoscsaba
400
Rakoskeresztur
200
Albertfalva
85
Kispest
4,000
Pestszentlorinc
500
Pestszenterzsebet
3,000
Torokbalint
80
Csepel
700
Nagyteteny
140
Soroksar
150

Map text : Adapted from Atlas of the Holocaust, Martin Gilbert

The Germans Invade Hungary

As soon as the Germans entered the city I couldn't stay, because I wouldn't think of being separated from my family.

When the Germans entered Hungary I was in Budapest. If I had stayed there I might have escaped the whole experience in Auschwitz. They entered Budapest itself on Shushan Purim, 1944.

The Ruscover Rov was in Budapest then, and I was together with him in the ghetto. He begged me not to go to back to Ruscova. As soon as the Germans entered the city we had to put on the Star of David armbands. I couldn't stay, however, because I wouldn't think of being separated from my family. He begged me not to go because I wouldn't be able to help them, and he insisted that I should save myself. Despite everything I took off my star and caught a train back to Ruscova. Everyone who looked at me knew I was scared, it was as if they knew I was Jewish. When I arrived home both of my parents cried. I asked why, and, not wanting to hurt me, they gently told me that I should not have come home. My father told me there was nothing I could do to help, and that their one consolation had been that at least one of us would survive. They were very sad for me, themselves, for everyone. It was a very difficult time.

We knew what was going on with Hitler since 1933, and certainly since *Kristallnacht* in 1938. Yes, we knew what was happening, and I wish, I don't know if I really wish, but I wonder if I had stayed in Budapest whether I would have been sent to the camps. Who knows? This is something that one is not smart enough to answer. In any case, I was young and returned home and was very happy that I did so at the time.

When I first came back to Ruscova we had no trouble from the Germans. It was before Pesach so we continued our Pesach preparations. What does preparing for Pesach mean? Cleaning! As soon as Purim was over we started preparing for Pesach. We had hardwood floors, and I remember my mother cleaning the cracks in the floorboards to make sure no *chometz* remained there.

The Germans Enter Ruscova

At one point, before the Germans entered the town, my father ordered my older brother and me to run away to the mountains and hide, which we did. We hid with a gentile family, but we came back for the *Seder* because we didn't want to be away from the family. I guess he had a premonition that something was going to happen. Sure enough, on the morning of *erev* Pesach, two German officers arrived on motorcycle to join the two Hungarian gendarmes who were stationed in Ruscova. I remember that my father was called to City Hall. He was given orders that he had so many hours to prepare a list of every Jewish household and the names of the Jews who lived there, from the newborn infant to the person who was dying. Everyone had to be registered. Father came home and told me that I had to prepare the list. I went from house to house and compiled the whole list. Two years earlier, in 1942, about 100 or so young men from the ages of 21 to 45 were taken away to forced labor brigades by the Hungarians. This means that they were sent to the front to build and repair the bridges and railroads for the German and Hungarian armies.

Towards evening the German army started marching into the town, but before they arrived a regular German army man went to all the Jewish houses to find rooms for the soldiers to stay. They took away our bedrooms, and a German soldier or officer was placed in every Jewish home. We were by the border and in order to be prepared in case the Russians pushed south from Galicia, Poland—which was already under their control—the Germans were reinforcing the front. At least this is what we hoped their presence meant. That *erev* Pesach cannot be described, the crying and the worry—some people already gave up. There were a few men, however, who dared to go to the *mikveh* despite what was happening. In one of the *shuls* where 200 to 250 men usually *davened*, maybe 20 people went to *daven Maariv* that first night of Pesach.

At one point, before the Germans entered the town, my father ordered my older brother and me to run away to the mountains and hide, which we did.

Budapest: round-up of Jewish women, autumn, 1944

In general, many young people left Ruscova to help earn a living for their families, but most returned home for Pesach. This year they came home only to walk into the trap set by the Germans. Nobody knew what was going to happen or what they would do to us. We had wooden shutters on our house, and to give us a sense of security we closed them. It was a terrifying time and we were afraid to go out. The men tied up their beards with scarves or something else so that they would be concealed. That *L'eil Shmurim*, the night when we are watched over by Heaven, we were very afraid, and all the doors were closed and locked. We were naive, thinking that a locked door was going to help us. We never locked the doors in the past because there was no reason to do so.

That L'eil Shmurim, *the night when we are watched over by Heaven, we were very afraid, and all the doors were closed and locked.*

During the *Seder* some people had German soldiers in their homes. We didn't. The next morning some of us dared to go outside, and we found that nothing was happening. In fact, some of the Germans came out and said good morning to us. My grandfather was so naive that he didn't realize what was taking place. He grew up under King Franz Josef who imposed a rule of law and order upon his country. Who would think that people would be thrown out of their houses, and taken away on trains? He didn't understand. However, in the end almost the whole Pesach was calm and uneventful, with the Germans acting cordial and relaxed, there was no violence or cruelty. By the second day the *shuls* were full again.

Deportation

The last day of Pesach, an SS Gestapo officer came to town and went from house to house with the Hungarian officers informing us that in two hours we would have to leave our homes, and that we were only allowed to take with us 40 pounds of personal belongings per person. This was a terrible situation, because even a low ranking officer in the Gestapo was more powerful than a general in the regular army. Everybody was afraid of them because they were Hitler's elite forces. We didn't have to leave that day, but the next day, Thursday, they took us to one of the big *shuls* under armed guard. It was interesting to see that many of the guards were older, some even in their fifties. The Germans had lost a lot of men by 1944, and now they drafted older men to serve, men who

The Emperor-King Franz Josef I and the Empress-Queen Elizabeth drive away from West Station, 1897.

were exempt at the beginning of the War. They were called the *Volksstrum,* something like the National Guard.

We were told that anyone leaving the *shul* without permission would be shot. This is how the Holocaust, the *Churban*, started for the Jews of Ruscova. We were packed into the *shul* and lived on whatever we brought with us. People slept wherever they could rest their head, on the benches or on the floor. It was dark in every house, the town was deserted. We were kept in the *shul* for 3 or 4 days. There was an outhouse behind the *shul*, but you could only use it if the guards allowed. Of course, one of them had his gun trained on you the whole time.

All of the *shuls* and the two big synagogues were full with people.

Round-up of Jews from small villages in Hungary for deportation to Poland.

After several days in the *shul*, we were taken one night by wagon to the ghetto in Felsoviso, the County Seat.[33] All that could be heard were the wagons groaning and wheels turning. The elderly were on wagons, while the younger people and the children walked alongside. The Hungarian guards kept watch over us the entire night.

The Ghetto

An entire part of the city was allocated for the ghetto. We were put together with three other families in a house that barely had room for a single family. We remained in the ghetto for about a month. People are strong and adaptable, for even in those crowded conditions we managed and got used to it. Whoever brought food had food. There were some gentiles who started a black market in the ghetto, so we could pay or barter for what we needed. People held on to their gold, jewelry and money when they left Ruscova, since we didn't know where we were going at first. We ate whatever we could get. Those who had firewood cooked. I can't tell you that we had enough to gain weight, but we didn't have to diet. Shabbos was Shabbos, we tried to keep things the way they had been in Ruscova. We *davened* with a *minyan*, sang *zemiros* and tried to carry on normally. People accepted things the way they were. There was a tremendous sense of *emunah* (belief) that things would change and get better.

The Jews in the town of Sharmash were killed by the Germans and placed in a mass grave. Afterwards, they were buried in separate graves. Those who were identified had their name placed on their grave. This is one such grave.

People are strong and adaptable, for even in those crowded conditions we managed

33. The County Seat was called *Viseul-de-Sus* in Romania, and *Felsoviso* in Hungarian.

As we read in the *Chumash*, ..."Is the hand of *Hashem* limited..?"[34] This was the great *emunah* that the people held on to until the last moment. We weren't skeptical, never once did I hear people complaining that Hashem would not rescue us. Never! It was in the beginning of May, right after Pesach, that we were sent to the ghetto, and some time around *Rosh Chodesh Sivan* the first train transports to Auschwitz began.

We could hear the Russians' guns from the ghetto. It seemed like liberation was right around the corner. In fact, on Pesach we heard the guns from across the Polish border in Galicia. They will be here any moment, we thought, but it seemed that the Russians didn't want to push forward until we were taken away. Some believe this very strongly. They could have taken our town and liberated us. But they gave the Germans enough time to deport us, and then after we were gone they took control of the area. Who wants Jews? Nobody wanted us.

This was the great emunah that the people held on to... never once did I hear people complaining that Hashem would not rescue us. Never!

Anyway, the population of the ghetto was approximately 10,000 *neshamos*, and we were divided into four transports. The Germans had a problem getting enough train cars to deport us. They didn't have cars available because the trains were being used to bring troops and supplies to the battlefronts. The Germans weren't so interested in the Hungarian Jews anymore, but the Hungarian government paid for every *Yiddishe neshamah* that they took away. The Hungarians delivered the Jews all the way to Auschwitz, to Dr. Mengele,

A peasant couple from Bukovina, 1910

34. Bamidbar 11:23

unloaded us and went back and brought another transport. They paid 500 Hungarian dollars for each *neshamah* that was taken away. They paid the Germans to kill us.

Transport to Auschwitz

My family was in the second transport. There were about 71 people in

Hungary: Jews awaiting deportation at the railway station.

Jewish youth from Bukovina, 1903

the cattle car. It was wired shut and had just one little window that was also barred. There was no place to lay down, you couldn't sit, all you could do was lean against the wall or the person next to you. In every car they placed a pail with water and, you'll excuse me, a pail for the human waste. That was for everybody, men, women and children. I don't know if anyone can understand what it means to go through something like this. If somebody had to use the pail, he had to go in front of everyone. Even when you don't eat, you still need to evacuate your body waste. They took us on Shabbos. Believe me, I don't even remember whether we had anything to eat or not during those three days. They loaded us onto the train on Shabbos afternoon and we arrived in Auschwitz on Tuesday, on *gimel* Sivan, the third of Sivan.

Right now I am laboring to try and remember what took place. I remember that we went up through Slovakia to Crakow, and from Crakow into Auschwitz. We didn't actually go into Crakow itself, but we skirted the city on the way to Auschwitz, which was an hour away. At one point the train stopped in a forest and the guards opened the doors. There was no town nearby. My father told my brothers and me to try to run away. He told us that we were not going to a good place. "Try, boys," he said, but no one moved. Besides the fact that it was a very dangerous thing to do, we didn't want to part from each other. I also felt that I might be able to help my parents wherever we were going.

My family was in the second transport. There were about 71 people in the cattle car. It was wired shut.

My father said that the guards would give us postcards and tell us to write to the people left behind, telling them that when the war is over we will be able to return home. He said not to believe anything they told us. Very few people wrote and gave the cards back to the

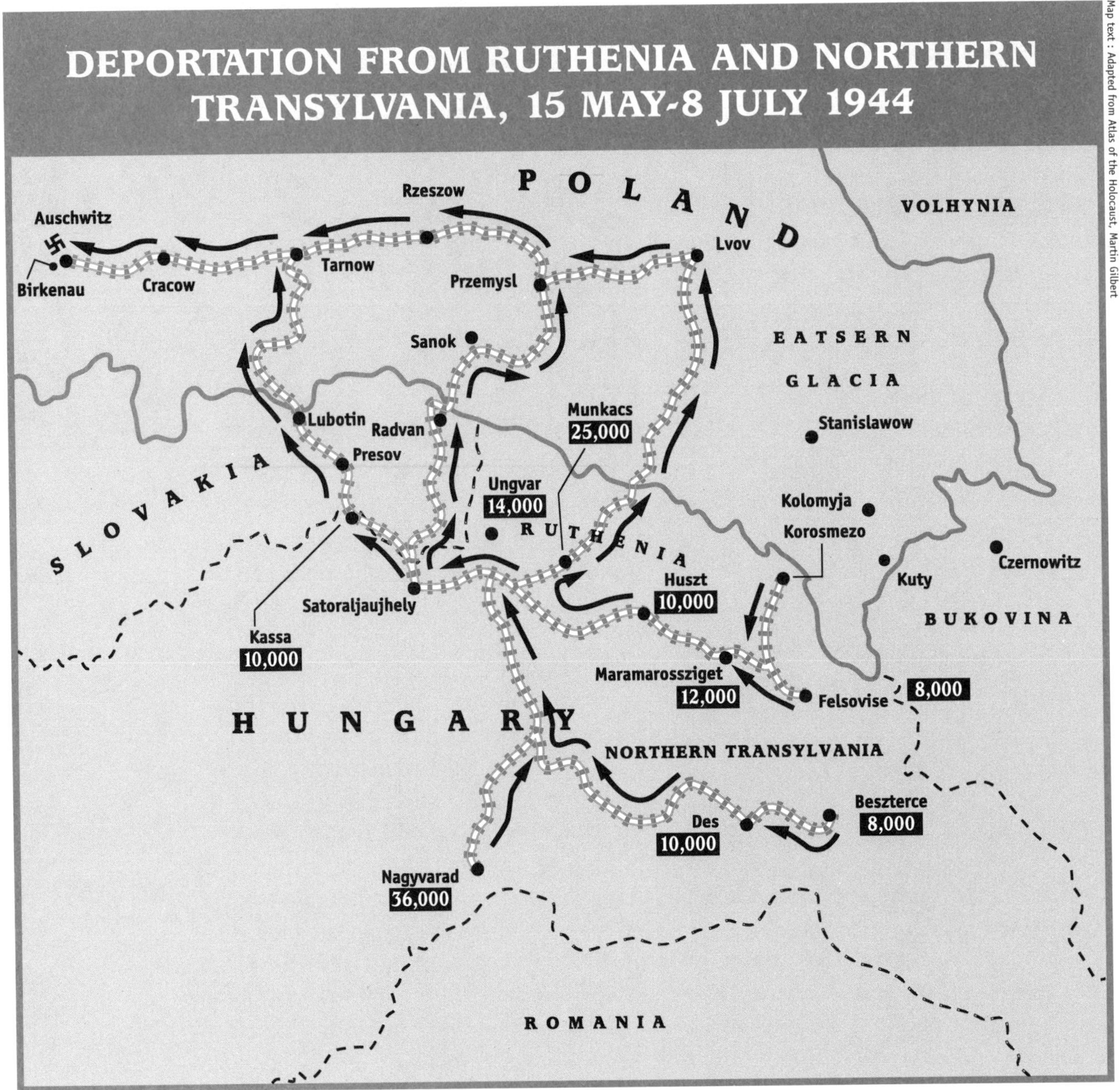

Map text : Adapted from Atlas of the Holocaust, Martin Gilbert

Hungarian militiamen who escorted the train to Auschwitz.

We arrived at the death camp in the evening. Over the gate leading into the camp there is a wrought iron sign that says *Arbeit Macht Frei*, which means *labor makes free*. Try to picture what it was like when we arrived after being packed into cattle cars, under inhuman conditions, for three days. Suddenly the doors opened up and we were routed out of the cars by Germans with their dogs. As we descended from the train there were brilliant spotlights with reflectors magnifying the light shining down upon us. It had been dark in the cars, and now we were disoriented by the blinding light and confusion that reigned upon the platform. The Gestapo men were yelling and ordering us on loudspeakers to leave everything in the car. "Don't take anything with you! Just disembark and get out of the cars!", they screamed. Can you imagine what

We arrived at the death camp in the evening. Over the gate leading into the camp there is a wrought iron sign that says ***Arbeit Macht Frei.***

Photo credit : Capt. S.M. Kasnett

Dog Compound in Dachau Concentration Camp

it was like for the Jewish mothers with their little children? It was unbelievable.

There were prisoners who were trained to meet the cars and facilitate the disembarkation of the Jews—*Kapos*. They were fed a little bit better for this job, but in the end they were also killed. They were Poles, Slovaks, Czecks...from all over. Some were Jewish as well. They became very hardened from all that they saw, so when they came up to the trains they roughly threw people out from the cars. "Leave here, leave everything here! Get out!", they would shout.

I remember there was a young woman with a baby, maybe 11 or 12 months old. The inmate helping her told her to give the baby to one of the older women. In Yiddish he told her to give the baby to one of the old ladies because she didn't need it anymore. He said, "I'm giving the child to this old lady so that you can survive." This is what he told her. If she would have the baby in her arms at the *selektion*, they would have gone to the crematoria together.

Aerial view of Auschwitz-Birkenau

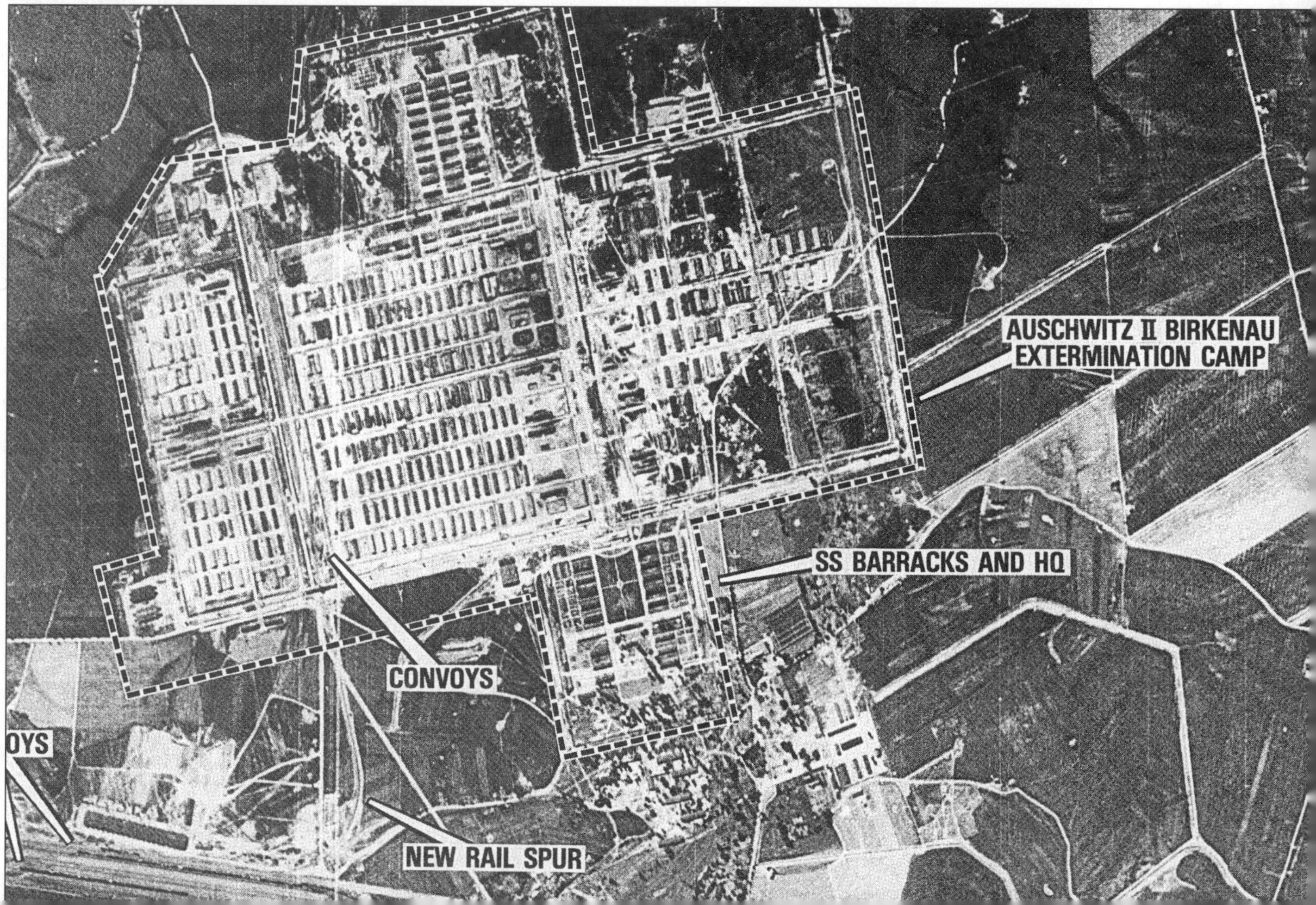

A train arriving at the loading platform in Auschwitz-Birkenau. Jews are still locked inside the sealed cars.

He gave the baby to an old lady who would go to the gas chamber anyway. Now, at least, the mother would survive. Last winter in Florida I met up with her. We were at a Holocaust gathering for the survivors from the Maramaros region of the Carpathians held in February at the Fountainbleu Hotel in Miami. I was looking around and there she was, just standing there. Finally my wife asked her, "Who are you, where are you from and on which transport were you?" She related the story to us exactly as I remembered it. She said that she doesn't know if she should thank the man who took away the baby, allowing her to survive, or curse him till this day. I want you to understand from this incident that tragedies were happening around us every minute.

Although we were in two separate groups we could still see each other. My father was sent to the left... and my mother... went after him.

In any case, once out of the train we were lined up on the platform—the oldest in front, five in a row, men on one side of the platform and women on the other. A German officer came up front whistling a tune, dressed in his Gestapo boots, with his riding crop in his hand. My father and the four boys were on one side and my mother and the four girls were on the other. Although we were in two separate groups we could still see each other. My father was sent to the left, to the gas chamber and my mother, seeing that he was sent left, went after him. She didn't know where he was going, but she wasn't going to be separated from him. My mother was only 49. At one point they announced that anyone who couldn't walk would be transported by van— enclosed vans. Of course, anyone who entered the van never came out again, they were gassed to death in the back of the vans.

My younger brother, who was not yet a bar mitzvah, saw my father and mother go toward the vans, and ran after them. We watched as my grandfather, my aunt with her three little children, and another aunt with her seven children disappeared into the vans. To this day I continue to reproach myself that I did not say goodbye to my mother. I should have said goodbye to her and my father.

Disembarking from the train in Auschwitz-Birkenau

Of course, I didn't know then what I know now.

The remaining Jews who had been sent to the right were then taken to an area something like a swimming pool. First they cut off our hair and made us undress. Next they gave us some kind of disinfectant or soap and made us go into the water which was heavy with disinfectant. When we emerged from the pool we were given striped uniforms and wooden sandals. Then we were marched into a barracks. The head of the barracks was an inmate, supposedly a German gypsy. We reached the barracks in time for the *Zeilappel*, where we stood in the open while they counted us for hours—a daily ritual. There were approximately 1,000 people in each barracks. The barracks was lined with bunks three tiers high, one on top of the other, with eight inmates to a bunk. We slept on the bare boards. If someone wanted to turn on his side during the night, he couldn't unless everyone moved with him.

I have a particular story to tell about my shoes. I saved my shoes, I didn't give them up when we were forced to strip. I carried my shoes into the pool and put them on again when I came out. My barracks was divided into sections, and I was in the sixth section. The head of the barracks had a little office with a bed. Soldiers were rewarded based on the number of people they killed—the more prisoners they eliminated the better the position they received. They also were fed as long as they did what the Germans wanted them to do. The head of our barracks had killed many, many people with his whip and his bat. In the heel of my shoe I had hidden several hundred dollars. I told my brothers that I was going to the barracks head to get us something to eat. They told me that the man is a murderer and that he would kill me and under no circumstance should I go to him. Both of them started to cry, begging me not to go. But I didn't care, I wouldn't listen to them. I took the money and knocked on his door. Speaking to him in German I said, "I have $300, could you give me a piece of bread, we are very hungry." He looked at me, and replied in German, "*Junge*, child, you're not afraid to come to give this to me?" Then he said, "I could take the money and kill you anyway." I replied, "If that is what you want to do then there is nothing I can do to stop you." He looked at me for a second without doing anything, so I told him that I have four sisters who were deported with me (they were placed in Birkenau, another camp in the Auschwitz

The barracks was lined with bunks three tiers high, with eight inmates to a bunk.

Dachau, 1938, Jews and non-Jews alike were forced to stand for many hours.

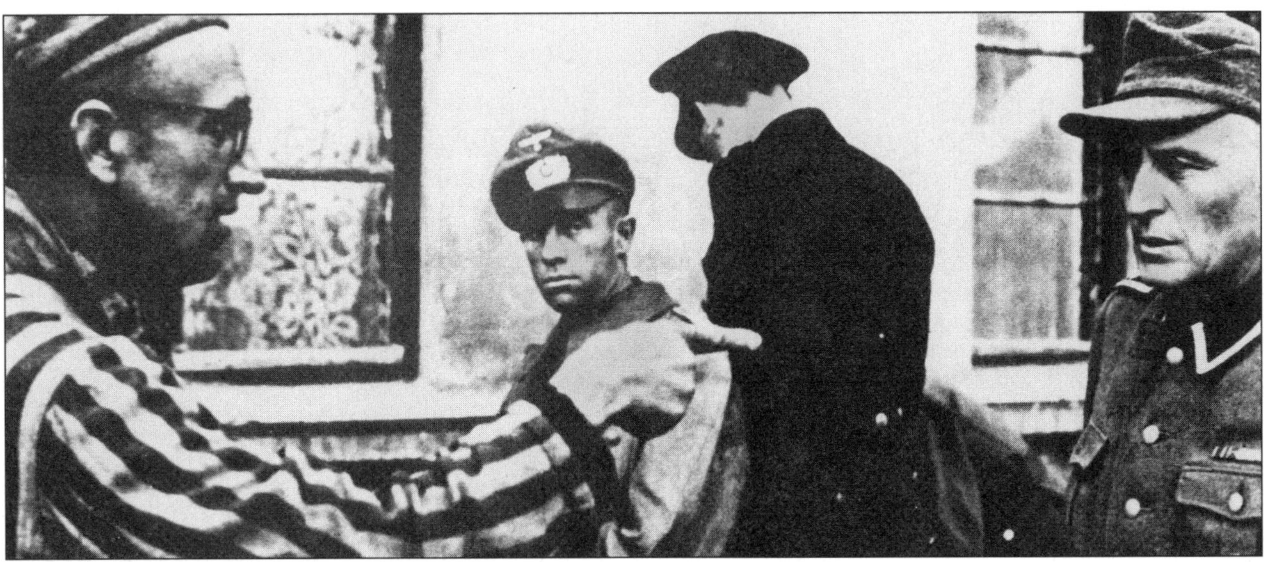

A liberated prisoner points an accusing finger toward a Nazi guard

Each morning we had to get up at 5:00, and we remained at the appelplatz until noon...my two brothers and I tried to remain together.

complex). He asked me who else I came with, and I replied that I had come with my parents. "They are gone," he said. I told him that my younger brother went with my parents when we arrived. "He's gone," he spit out the words. "How about your sisters?", he inquired. I replied that they were in Block 14. I again asked him if I could have something to eat. Amazingly, he gave me a black bread, a tube of margarine and a dish of molasses. I returned to my bunk. You have no idea how the whole bunk was in shock. "He let you go??? He gave you this???", they said over and over again. We split the bread, molasses and margarine with the entire bunk, all 24 men.

Each morning we had to get up at 5:00, and we remained at the *appelplatz* until noon. When we came out to be lined up my two brothers and I tried to hold on to each other, so that we should remain together. The head of the barracks came looking for me the next morning, and when he found me he told me to follow him. I thought this was the end. The previous evening when I spoke with him he had asked me to write the names of my sisters on a piece of paper. He now told me that he had found my sisters and tomorrow he'll take me to see them. You have to understand that something like this never happened before.

The next morning at 10:00 he took me to my sisters' block on the condition that I follow the instructions of their Block Elder. She was a Jewish woman from Slovakia, and she told me that she didn't want a revolution in the barracks, so I was not allowed to enter. She would bring my sisters out one by one. She turned to go into the barracks and I followed her. Seeing this she turned and slapped me on both sides of my face. I looked right and left, but I couldn't recognize anyone because the women had no hair, no scarves, only a little dress with a long stripe painted on the back. I didn't recognize my own sisters. They were brought out for one minute...for one minute. I will never forget those moments, never. They came out and I saw them and then the head of my barracks took out four handkerchiefs for me to give to them to cover their heads. He was a murderer...a German gypsy. The first evening we arrived he must have killed...who knows how many people, yet I had dared to go to him. He, this murderer, now gave me scarves for my sisters. Can you understand this? Until this day I can only believe that it was a miracle. Just as it was decreed who should perish, so was it decreed who should survive, and we survived through miracles. After I gave my sisters the scarves I was taken back to my barracks.

The joy of liberation

Revolt

The next day we again rose at 5:00 in the morning and were sent to the *appelplatz* to be counted. They came and counted us and kept us outside for hours, five, six, seven hours straight. Afterwards we were returned to the barracks. It was hard, very hard. I remember the first day of *Shavuos* we were standing waiting to be counted during *Zeilappel* and some people fainted, they just couldn't stand any longer. In order not to lose them, others would hold them up and thus kept them alive. That *Shavuos* as we stood at attention there was a *Rov* among us from a town in Hungary. We were standing under the burning sun, thirsty, and with no rest for what seemed like forever. Apparently they were trying to completely break us down at that time both spiritually

Prisoners at roll-call

Just as it was decreed who should perish, so was it decreed who should survive, and we survived through miracles.

Ruins of the entrance to the undressing room of a gas chamber

and physically. The Germans were particularly cruel during the Jewish holidays and Shabbos. So this *Rov* decided to fight back. He started to sing *Hallel*. The people looked at him wondering what he thought he was doing, but he just kept singing *Hallel*. Soon everyone became electrified, and joined him, the words started to come from one mouth and then another. When we came to *Ana Hashem Hoshea Na* (Please Hashem us, save now...) you heard voices from all over continuing the refrain. *Unbelieveable*! If you didn't see it happening you missed an open demonstration that it is impossible to break the *emunah* of a *Yid*. Impossible!

If you didn't see it happening you missed an open demonstration that it is impossible to break the emunah *of a* Yid.

It can't be done, no way, and the world and the Nazis didn't understand this fact. These were men who had just lost their families and now they were lost and alone. Who did they know and what did they have left from what used to be their life? Picture it—to be stripped of everything. Yet the men remained there singing. I'll never forget it—that moment when he started singing *Hallel* will always be with me.

Buchenwald & Separation

The day before we were transferred from Auschwitz to Buchenwald, my barracks head said that he would take me to say goodbye to my sisters. He took me to them as he promised. I stayed outside while my sisters came out and we said goodbye. I didn't hear from them and I didn't know anything about them until after we were liberated and I found them barely alive in another camp. We were only in Auschwitz for a short period of time. Life in Auschwitz I cannot describe for you, and I won't try to describe it for you. It was a death camp, that's all it was.

My brothers and I arrived in Buchenwald. On the way to Buchenwald from Auschwitz there were no SS guards watching us, only the regular *Wehrmacht* (army troops) and *Luftwaffen*, soldiers from the German Air Force. Apparently there were not enough SS available anymore. Hitler was sending them to the front to discourage the German soldiers from surrendering to the enemy. He wanted the German troops to fight to the death, and the SS were sent to the front to police the troops. Anyone surrendering was killed by the SS. When we arrived in Buchenwald we were broken spiritually and physically, completely broken. After being beaten and seeing so many dead; and being near the crematoria

SS men in the Belzec death camp

in Birkenau, smelling the flesh of human beings night and day, we were broken.

We were together in Buchenwald for only about three weeks when my younger brother and I were chosen to go to a different camp where approximately 1,000 men were needed to rebuild a munitions plant that had been bombed by the Allies. The factory was near the town of Zeitz (southwest of Leipzig). It was famous for the production of precision photographic glass. We were chosen to help with the rebuilding, while our older brother remained in Buchenwald. I didn't sleep for weeks after that. So many people died the first two months because they couldn't do the work, the result of having practically no food and only a little water. I can't think about it and never spoke about it—it was an experience I never wanted to talk about...it was something unbelievable. After living a normal life again I think back, and wonder was it all possible? Could that really have happened? Can human beings really be so cruel? Was it possible?

In this factory the Germans extracted benzene from coal to manufacture fuel for their planes. The plant had many different sections and altogether it was roughly 8 square kilometers in size—a gigantic complex. We arrived there in the spring of 1944. All of our supplies and food came from Buchenwald. We were instructed to build the labor camp adjacent to the munitions plant so that the Allies would be wary of bombing it lest they accidentally bomb the barracks where we lived.

Every morning we were awakened at about 4:00, and stood at assembly for *Zeilappel*. We were counted until 7:00. After being counted we were marched to the factory. The SS officer in charge of the morning count was called the Report Officer, since he reported to the higher ups about us. He was a *Volksduetch*, a German by lineage, but born and raised in Hungary. One morning in the *appelplatz* the Report Officer announced that they needed someone to paint signs on the barracks and in other places throughout the camp. If any one was a sign painter, a *Kuntzmahler* in German, he should step forward. I didn't have the strength to go on much longer, so I volunteered and said I was a sign painter. He took me out of line and told me that I would remain in camp from now on, I would no longer go to work rebuilding the factory.

I was given paint and brushes and told what to do. He called me *Junge*, meaning young one, because I was young. I guess this was a sign of feelings on his part. He also gave me

After living a normal life again I think back, and wonder was it all possible? Can human beings really be so cruel?

extra food or a second piece of bread. I would shine his shoes and do little things like that for him during the day, and then I would go back to my painting. The extra bread was very well received because I was so thin. This was half of a *geulah*, half a redemption for me. We usually received a half pound loaf of bread each day, sometimes it was a pound loaf. We also were given coffee, or something called coffee that was artificially sweetened. Everyone ran to get it in any case.

A job had been secured for him in the kitchen. This was like being told that you won the lottery...

I did a good job painting. I always had good handwriting, so painting signs wasn't too difficult. After about a week I asked the Report Officer if my brother could also be given work in the camp so that he would no longer have to go to the factory. He said he would think about it. Later he told me to tell my brother (who was 15 at the time) that he should stay in the *appelplatz* the next morning because a job had been secured for him in the kitchen. This was like being told that you won the lottery...it was unbelievable. He worked in the kitchen for a few months, from July until November. We still slept in the camp, but we were very fortunate to have been given such positions. My brother smuggled food out of the kitchen for some of the rabbis, a doctor and a pharmacist who were with us in the barracks. Incidentally, this pharmacist was in the ghetto with us and in our cattle car when we were deported to Auschwitz. He died recently, but he told us that he feels we saved his life with the extra rations that my brother was able to give him.

When the Allied planes flew overhead to bomb the factory the sirens would sound, warning us that the bombing was imminent. Before the bombs were released the Allies would drop leaflets into the camp. They knew exactly where the camp was. They also knew everything taking place in the rebuilding of the factory because the leaflets would

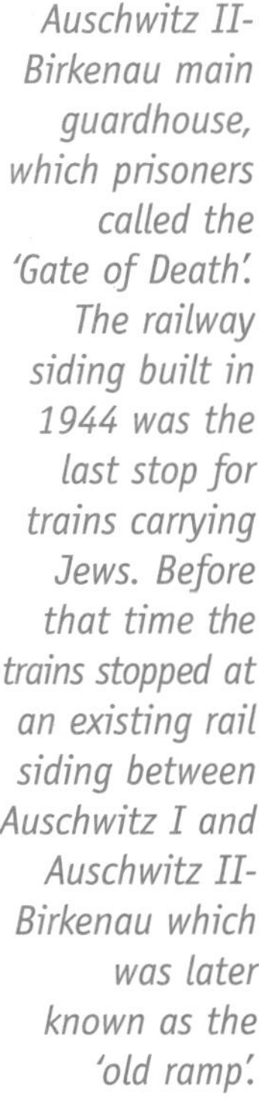

Auschwitz II-Birkenau main guardhouse, which prisoners called the 'Gate of Death'. The railway siding built in 1944 was the last stop for trains carrying Jews. Before that time the trains stopped at an existing rail siding between Auschwitz I and Auschwitz II-Birkenau which was later known as the 'old ramp'.

describe which parts of the factory were rebuilt and beginning production, and then they would bomb that part of the factory.[35]

If they did this, they also could have destroyed the crematoria in Auschwitz, or the train tracks leading to the concentration camps. If they knew which part of a factory was again functioning, they knew about the concentration camps as well, but they didn't do anything about it. I don't think the Allies really wanted to save us. However, this is for another discussion.

When the Allies bombed during the night they would drop markers defining the boundaries of the camp so that certain areas would not be bombed. If the bombing came during the day, the Germans produced an artificial fog or smoke to camouflage the factory. Many people died during these bombings from the shrapnel of the German anti-aircraft guns. My brother and I made up that we would meet in a certain place during the bombings, so that whatever happened to one of us would happen to the other—we didn't want to be separated.

On the 14th of Kislev, November 30th of 1944, at around noontime, the sirens sounded, so we ran to our designated spot and threw ourselves onto the ground. It wasn't even because of the explosions that we hit the ground; the shock waves *after* the explosion were so great that if you were standing you would be thrown violently through the air. On the ground we were somewhat protected. We laid down next to each other as usual, and listened to the sound of the bombs as they exploded—they made a terrible sound. One of them hit very close to us. After the bombing was over and the all-clear siren sounded I called out my brother's name, Dovid Hirsch, but he was quiet and didn't answer. I looked over at him and realized that he was dead, he had been killed. I can't even describe to you what I went through after that. We were eight children and now two were dead and the rest were captive. I asked the Hungarian SS man not to put my brother in the crematoria, but he said he couldn't do this. The next day he told me that Dovid Hirsch was buried in a mass grave since there weren't enough bodies to be sent to the crematoria. I wish I could go back today and find his grave, but this is not practical.

Shoes collected from their victims at Majdanek concentration camp

My brother and I made up that we would meet in a certain place during the bombings, we didn't want to be separated.

Now I was all alone, not knowing if my sisters were surviving in Auschwitz, or my brother in Buchenwald. "And Yaakov remained alone...," this is what you could say about me. It's amazing that even with everything we went

35. For example, "Department 48 is back in production—we will return to bomb it tonight—stay away!"

through, the drive to remain alive was so strong. I always felt that I would survive Hitler. No matter where I was I had this intuitive sense that I would survive and be freed. *Baruch Hashem*, I'm sitting here talking to you today.

The Train

I remained in this camp during the winter of 1944-45, mostly painting indoors. On April 8th, 1945 the Americans liberated Buchenwald. As the Americans came closer to our camp we were put on a train and sent to the Theresienstadt concentration camp in Eastern Europe. On the way to Theresienstadt, which is located in Czechoslovakia, as we were going over the top of a mountain our train was bombed by the Allies. Everyone was panic-stricken. On both sides of the train tracks were forests, and many of us ran away from the train to seek protection in the trees. The people who were killed were in the open car next to the engine. I was in the third car from the engine where only one person was killed.

No matter where I was I had this intuitive sense that I would survive and be freed. Baruch Hashem, I'm sitting here talking to you today.

Many had become so hardened from their experiences during the War that they just stripped the blankets from the dead, leaving them laying on the ground. We were so undernourished that many of us suffered swelling of the feet and legs. We lived with the daily threat of not passing the constant selections. We were accustomed to suffering–because we were always suffering it became part of our consciousness. I remember there was a 17-year-old boy who was killed in front of his father. Try to picture this, the father didn't cry or behave the way you would expect when confronted with the murder of his son. Instead, he went through his son's pockets to see if there was an extra piece of bread; that's how great was the will to survive. Today his son was killed, maybe tomorrow he would be taken away and killed. This is how hardened we were. Our very humanity had been stripped away from us. Everyone was fighting for life, fighting to survive.

The train engine was destroyed and we couldn't move. A Dr. Weiss and his son, who were from Klausenberg, ran away from the train with me. Since it was close to the liberation, there were not enough soldiers or guards to watch the train, so they drafted men 50 and 60-years-old to perform this job. We pleaded with them to leave us. We argued that the Allied front was moving closer, so why did they want to take us back to Theresienstadt, but they wouldn't listen. They kept us in jail overnight, and brought us back to the train the next morning, but they didn't shoot us or kill us. It was our *mazal*, our good fortune.

I can't begin to tell you about the *mazal* that we had. Many times I've asked myself and suffered sleepless nights, perspiring, wondering why I survived. This I've only told to my family. Why was I spared? What for? Had I been killed I would have been one of the *neshamos hakadoshim*, one of the holy martyred souls. I almost reproach myself that I survived. There were six boys from Ruscova who were together with me in *cheder* and yeshiva. We were together during the war, and after the war they went to Palestine, they didn't want to come to America. When I go to *Eretz Yisrael* I visit their graves. They made it through the war in Europe, but were killed fighting in the wars in Israel. I look down and read their names on their gravestones and wonder why am I alive. Sometimes I feel guilty and wonder, why am I here?

Special tracks from Westerbork, Holland to Theresienstadt

In any case, there was an incident on the train I want to tell you about. There were two brothers from Ruscova who were in the munitions camp with me. We were given a towel in this camp every Monday. These two brothers would wrap the towel around their hands to make a blessing over their bread if no water could be found to wash their hands. As we were sitting around after the bombing, one of these brothers saw that there was some water on the train. So he ran to the water to clean his face and wash his hands before eating. There was a murderous guard, Schmidt, who shouted, "Halt, *shtay dort*!" "Stop! Stay there!" Then he took out his gun and shot the boy dead. Just like that.

The next day we were marched on foot with guards all around us. We were being marched to Theresienstadt. Three kilometers from Theresienstadt there was another camp called Litmaritz. First we were taken to Litmaritz. A few days later they sent German prisoners, real prisoners who were taken out of jail, to guard us and march us into Theresienstadt. There were still around 30,000 Jews in Theresienstadt. Theresienstadt was a model camp, the Germans would bring the International Red Cross workers into this camp to show everyone how well the inmates were treated. There was even printed Jewish money in Theresienstadt signed by a Dr. Edelstien from Vienna, with a picture of Moses on one side. Of course, the money was totally worthless.

Theresienstadt and Liberation

We arrived in Theresienstadt in the middle of April, 1945. We were stripped, our hair was cut and we were disinfected. Then we were sent to a barracks. We had to go through a *selektion* every 4 to 6 weeks. Those selected were sent to death in Auschwitz. On the morning of May 5, 1945, we got up and saw red crosses all over the fences. The Germans were gone and Czech militiamen, placed there by the Red Cross, were guarding the camp. On May 10, the camp was liberated by the Russians.

Theresienstadt was a model camp, the Germans would bring the International Red Cross workers to show everyone how well the inmates were treated.

As the SS was withdrawing and fleeing from the battlefront further to the east, they randomly shot into the camp as they went by, but no one was hurt. There were some SS in the camp trying to escape with their stolen money

Can you imagine— to survive the War and then be killed by food after liberation?

and jewels in an armored car. The inmates attacked the car and the money was destroyed—all we thought about was finding food.

When the Russians arrived at the camp with their tanks, one of the commanders of the tank battalion was a Jewish Russian solider. He pulled me up to the tank and gave me some vodka to drink. I went back to the camp and became sick. I fell asleep and woke up that night on a bench at the far side of the camp. When I woke up I was crying, "Where am I... where am I?" Eventually, I made it back to my barracks. The Russian soldiers had gone, but we were safe.

After the liberation about 2,000 people died from diarrhea caused by the food they were given by the Russians. The food could not be tolerated by their starved bodies and it killed them. Can you imagine—to survive the War and then be killed by food after liberation? The Americans were more careful, they put the camps under quarantine and fed the people light foods, very slowly, until their bodies gradually became tolerant of richer, fattier foods. At first they would feed them a little bit of water and matzoh, things like this. People who ate too much died. They were buried in Theresienstadt in individual graves. When I went back to the camp in 1987,

Wobbelin: an American soldier checking a prisoner who had died on the road after liberation.

I saw the graves of some of the people I knew there who died in such a manner.

Reunion and Ruscova

After liberation I smuggled myself out of Theresienstadt,[36] and went to the Red Cross center in Prague. The Czechs were very nice to me. They housed me in a hotel and gave me some clothes—I was still wearing my striped uniform. Every morning I got up and went to the railroad station to check the transports as they came into the station, particularly the women's transports. One afternoon I was standing on the platform when about 40 girls came off a train. I asked one of the girls which town she was from, and she replied that she was from Chust, which is not far from Ruscova. I told her I had an uncle there, and she replied that this man had four nieces in the camp she had just left. When I asked for their names she told me the names of my sisters: Chaitsu, Eidel, Hudia and Raizel.

I passed out right there on the platform. I woke up that night in the first aid room in the railroad station, but I didn't go back to my room in the hotel. I took a train to the area where my sisters' camp was, and when I arrived I asked for directions to the camp which was located in a forest. In front of the camp there was a guard house with a chaplain inside, a Brooklyn boy. He told me to stay where I was while he went to prepare my sisters for their meeting with me. He didn't want them to faint or die from shock. But I couldn't stay still so I followed him to the fence around their barracks and one of my sisters saw me. She started screaming for my other sisters to come, she was yelling

"Women after Liberation"

that I had survived. She called out, "Come! Chaim Eliezer is here. He is alive and he is here!" I spent a few days there, and the commander of the camp gave me permission to take 54 girls back home again to Ruscova and other towns in the area. It was right after the War and everything was in such chaos. However, we made our way back to Prague and then to Vienna. There were thousands and thousands of refugees trying to go back home, and very few trains. I went up to the conductor of a Russian military train from Vienna that was going to Romania to see if I could get the girls on his train. It turned out that he was Jewish, and he arranged for us to be taken on board. He placed some of us in his car, and the rest in the car next to his. Except for his car, the other cars were open because this was a cargo train, not a passenger train. He also supplied us with our food. We traveled three full days to reach Arad, Romania, and then the train continued on to Bucharest, but at this point we

Every morning I went to the railroad station to check the transports, particularly the women's transports.

36. Theresienstadt was under quarantine, and thus the necessity to escape secretly.

Children after Liberation

had to go east, back to Transylvania. The conductor gave me a whistle in case the Russians on the train started up with the girls. One time I actually had to use it. When he heard the whistle blow, the conductor, *natschalnik* in Russian, came running to the girls' car, grabbed one of the Russian men and threw him from the moving train.

I reopened my father's business and saw to it that my sisters were married... after a few years I had to close the store because of the Communists.

I hoped to find my older brother when we got back to Ruscova, but he wasn't there, and I had no clue as to where he was. Our house was destroyed. The Germans had kept horses in the house! The gentile neighbors had stolen everything from the house. While looking through the house I went into the attic where I found the hair from my *upshearin*, my first haircut at three years of age. My mother had put it in a brown bag and placed it behind one of the rafters. I tried to reestablish my home. About 60 or 70 young people came back with some of the adults. Since my father had been the *Rosh Hakahol*, the village elder as it were, they elected me to the same position. So I followed in my father's footsteps. My brother became ill after the liberation and didn't come to Ruscova until July. Thank G-d, we have been together in Cleveland ever since coming to America.

I reopened my father's business and saw to it that my sisters were married. But after a few years I had to close the store because of the pressure from the Communists. This was in 1948. I closed the shutters one evening and that night I left Ruscova for Satmar. One of my sisters left with a group from Bucharest to travel on one of the boats that smuggled Jews into Palestine, but it was intercepted by the British and she spent six months in Cyprus.

I smuggled myself from Satmar (Romania) into Budapest, Hungary, and from there I went to Austria. I had some money, and wherever I went people helped me. This is how we tried to reestablish our lives. Two sisters and their husbands went to Italy, one went to Satmar where she had three children, and the fourth went to Palestine. In Austria there was a DP camp that was full of single men. We had a yeshiva there, with a cook. I was there until February of 1952. Then I went to an American DP camp, but I left there and went to a British camp near Hamburg, Germany, where I worked as an interpreter.

America

Finally I came to America. I don't know who sponsored me, but I came through the American Joint Distribution Committee. I was sent to Cleveland. One sister and my brother were also in Cleveland. My brother was working as a brick layer (he eventually became a successful builder), and I tried this work as well, but I wasn't strong enough. After three days I needed a hernia operation. Then I secured a job working in a shoe store, but left after about nine months to start my own business.

The buyer in the shoe store was a real anti-Semite. There were a few of us working there, and we spoke Yiddish to each other. He couldn't stand this and told us to speak English. I told him, "Thank G-d I am in America and I can speak any language that I want. But you are too dumb to learn another language and are jealous of us." One time he remarked that it was a shame that Hitler left so many of us alive. Hearing that, I took a high heeled woman's shoe, climbed up on the little stool that we used to fit customers for their shoes and hit him on the head with the point of the heel. He started to bleed. I ran into the manager's office and this fellow came running after me. The manager asked me what I did, and I told him to ask the man what he had said to me. When the manager heard what he said he threw him out of the store, saying that he wouldn't have anyone like this working in his business. However, I couldn't stay there much longer because of this incident and the fact that I had become unpopular with the non-Jewish workers. I left and started my own sewing machine business, but eventually I ended up owning a furniture store. I was married in 1956 and I've been in Cleveland ever since.

I live between two worlds. I am very much in the present, having established my business and my long time involvement with the Hebrew Academy of Cleveland. On the other hand, my soul, my heart, hasn't left Ruscova—as you have read. That is the way it is with us, the survivors. We live in two worlds. We witnessed the destruction of one, but, *Baruch Hashem*, we survived to participate in the rebuilding of another. Now we look forward to one final change—the coming of *Moshiach*, speedily, in our days. Amen.

I live between two worlds. I am very much in the present... my soul, my heart, hasn't left Ruscova... That is the way it is with us, the survivors.

SIGHET: REMEMBRANCE OF LIFE IN HUNGARY

An Interview With Mrs. Gizella Weisshaus

> *Before the outbreak of World War II, there were approximately 13,000-15,000 adult Jews living in Sighet making it a good sized city.*

"My name is Gizella Weisshaus, in Yiddish I am called Gittel. I was born in 1929 in the town of Sighet which was part of Romania at that time. The word *sighet* means island in Hungarian, and the town of Sighet is surrounded by three rivers. It is situated at the northwestern tip of the Carpathian Mountains. In Sighet we enjoyed very pleasant weather, and had exceptionally good drinking water, something that was not true everywhere in the Carpathian Mountains area. In Satmar, for instance, not all of the water was suitable for drinking and cooking. We had very cold winters with lots of snow, and there were many poor who didn't have wood to heat their homes. Three houses away from ours lived several poor Jewish families in rented apartments who suffered without heat most of the winter. A family of eight to ten people lived in one or two rooms. It was very crowded and very cold, but they had no choice. This made me sad, because it was very different from how we lived. Originally, we had four rooms, a kitchen and a sun room, but we rented out one of the rooms. I saw how many other families lived, and their poverty was very great. Before the outbreak of World War II, there were approximately 13,000-15,000 adult Jews living in Sighet making it a good sized city. Elie Weisel is also from Sighet, and I know that he said that over 30,000 children from Sighet perished during the War. Each family had many children, but I am only counting the parents.

I am the oldest of seven. I had three younger brothers and three sisters—all of whom were killed by the Germans. My brother Tovia Leib had his Bar Mitzvah just before the War began, so he was 13-years-old. Then came Moshe Aryeh (11), Mordechai (8), Kreindel (6),Rochel (3) and Lifsha who wasn't even a year old when she was killed. I was "lucky," because when we went to Auschwitz I was sent to the right side by Mengele, *yemach sh'mo*, although my mother begged him that I should go to the left with her and my aunt. He wouldn't let

Mrs. Weisshaus (standing) with her parents and (from left) her sister Kreindel and brothers Moshe Aryeh, Mordechai and Tovia Leib. This picture was taken in Sighet, in 1938, when Mrs. Weisshaus was 9-years-old. Except for her, the family perished in the Holocaust.

her take me and pushed me back to the right...that was the last time I saw her. It seems there was a reason that I should survive and keep the family going.

My mother's family lived in Sighet for seven generations. The *Kuntras Hasfakos*, written by Rabbi Yudele Kahn, began this chain of generations. Reb Yudele was a *kohain* and had a *yichus* brief, a genealogy document, that showed he was a descendant of thirty-eight consecutive generations of *kohanim*. My great, great-grandfather, Reb Yosef Leib Kahn, was a son-in-law of the Karlsburger Rov, known as the *Mareh Yechezkel*. His daughter, Chantza, was my great-grandmother. They had a son-in-law, Isacher Leib Halpert, who was my great-grandfather. His son, Yechezkel Halpert, was my grandfather. He helped raise the present Sigheter Rov, Rabbi Moshe Teitelbaum, when he was orphaned at 12 years of age. His parents died young, within months of each other. My grandfather lived across the street from the Rov and felt a responsibility to raise the children after their parents died. My grandfather had four children, two girls (my mother was one) and two boys. He was a Rabbi in Sighet,

Mrs. Weisshaus' maternal grandparents, Rabbi Yechezkel and Rochel Leah (Ostreicher) Halpert. Taken in Sighet before WWII

Mrs. Weisshaus at 8-years-old. Taken in Sighet.

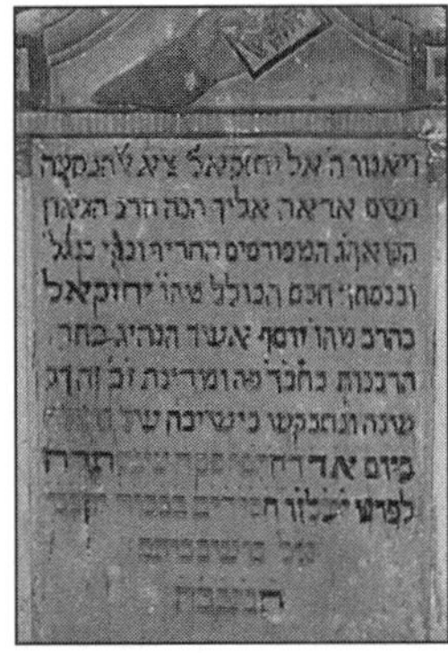

Matzaivah of the Mareh Yechezkel

The Shul of the Mareh Yechezkel

Handwashing basin in the Shul of the Mareh Yechezkel

Matzaivah of the Kuntras Hasfakos. The hands represent the Priestly Blessing.

and many of the *bochurim* came to learn with him and be tested. He always had special treats for them. Peanuts and bananas were rare in Sighet, they had to be grown in warmer climates, but my grandfather always had special fruits and treats for the *bochurim*. This is how I remember him.

I am from a very *chassidic* background. I wore my hair in long braids and dressed in black stockings as a girl. My father, Reb Yosef Stern, was from Satmar and my mother, Sarah, was born in Sighet. When my parents were married, my father came to live in Sighet. My paternal grandfather, Rabbi Elimelech Zev Stern, was also from Satmar. He was a *mashgiach* for the previous Satmar Rov, Rabbi Yoel Teitelbaum, *zt"l*, and he was very close with the Rebbe's family.

I lived at the end of one of two main thoroughfares in Sighet. On one side of this walkway was the large *shul* that belonged to the *Kehillah* (not necessarily *chassidic*). On the other side of this walkway were the offices of the president and other officers of the *Kehillah*. At the beginning of the walkway was the Sigheter Rebbe's house and *shul*. We lived at

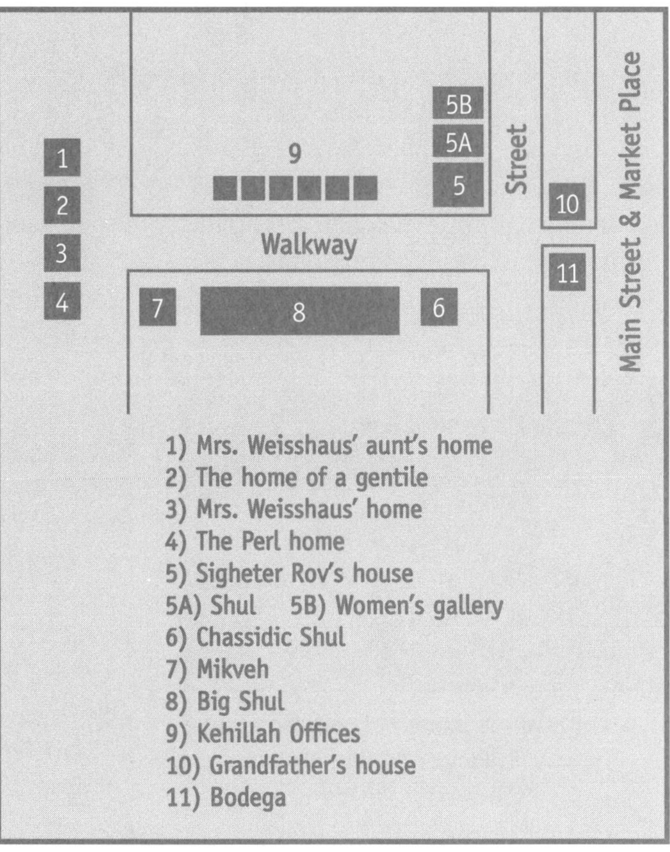

Main Synagogue in Sighet

the end of this corridor, and behind us were fields and the Jewish cemetery.

Twice a year the Satmar *Rov*, Rabbi Yoel Teitelbaum, *zt"l*, came to Sighet for the *yahrtzeit* of his father and grandfather. Once in a while he came for the *yahrtzeit* of other family members, but for these two *yahrtzeits* he came every year. The Rebbe, his father and his paternal grandfather were all born in Sighet.

He stayed next-door to us when he came. The Perl family lived there, and they vacated the house for the Rebbe to use. The Perls had a daughter, Etti, who was my age and we were very close, so she stayed with us on these occasions. Sometimes he was escorted by his son-in-law and sometimes by other *rabbonim*, but whoever it was they always stayed with us. We had four bedrooms, so there was plenty of room for guests. It was very exciting when the Rebbe came.

One *yahrtzeit* was during the winter months and on one of those visits the Rebbe didn't arrive until several hours after the expected time. People had been waiting for him at the house, but he didn't come. Usually he traveled by train and at the station he hired a horse and buggy to take him to the Perl's house, but this time (two years before the War) he came by car. It was snowing that day and the trip took a long time. Anyway, the *mikveh*, located on the side of the walkway, was under renovation at that time. It was heated by big wood burning furnaces and repair work was being done on this heating system. To facilitate this, a large hole was dug in the thoroughfare in front of the *mikveh*. At one point the men went to the end of the thoroughfare to *daven Minchah* in the Sigheter Rov's *shul*. After they left, the Satmar Rov suddenly arrived in his car, but no one was there to greet him except Etti and me. We went running down the lane to the *shul* to tell the men that the *Rov* had arrived. The hole, meanwhile, had been covered up by the snow.

Twice a year the Satmar Rov, Rabbi Yoel Teitelbaum, zt"l, came to Sighet for the yahrtzeit of his father and grandfather.

Matzaivah of the Kedushas Yom Tov (Rabbi Teitelbaum's father)

Matzaivah of the Yitav Lev (Rabbi Teitelbaum's grandfather)

When the men came running up the walkway to greet the Rebbe, many of them fell into the hole. Etti and I were standing nearby and we were laughing and laughing. No one was hurt, thank G-d, so we were all able to enjoy this funny sight and the excitement of the Rebbe's visit in general. We also used to host the Rachover Rov[37] and other *Rabbonim* from that area of Transylvania. The Rebbe's son-in-law survived the War, but he and his wife never had children. After she passed away, he remarried and raised a family.

Photo credit : Torah Personalities

Rabbi Yekusiel Yehuda Halberstam זצ"ל
The Klausenberger Rebbe in his youth

I was also close with Hannah, one of the daughters of the previous Klausenberger Rebbe, Rabbi Yekusiel Yehuda Halberstam, *zt"l*, as well as with the present Sigheter Rebbe's sister, who was also named Hannah (she lived in Los Angeles after the War and only recently passed away). When she was younger, the Sigheter Hannah had to be careful with what she ate because she had a delicate stomach. One time when the Klausenberger Rov's Hannnah was in town visiting the Sigheter Hannah the cook offered her roasted peanuts, but she couldn't eat them because they were too difficult for her to digest. This meant that the other Hannah and I had all of the peanuts for ourselves. We had such a good time eating them together. I truly had a happy childhood...nothing was missing. I had my family, and my extended family and friends. We were very well known in Siget.

I truly had a happy childhood... nothing was missing. I had my family, and my extended family and friends.

My maternal grandfather, Reb Yechezkel Halpert, was involved in learning Torah all day, so it was my grandmother who took care of the income. First, she baked fancy cakes that were sold in the stores. After that she sold coal and wood. Additionally, she and one of my uncles had a matzah bakery. I remember how my father brought our *matzos* home–a man balanced a basket on his head that was full of *matzos* covered with a sheet and delivered them to our house. A few years before the War the community decided that the *matzos* should be packaged properly, so they began wrapping them in brown paper that was tightly closed with string. Before this, however, they were brought home in a basket. I used to help bake the *matzos*. My grandmother hired about 15 women (mostly from the outlying areas) who were very poor and needed money for their families. Some of them slept by her, or she found other space for them to sleep, so that they could save as much money as possible. It was a big operation, just like in the hand *matzos* bakeries in Williamsburg today. She had a *mashgiach* overseeing the entire process. He was constantly checking all of the utensils and monitoring how efficiently everyone

37. The reader is referred to the interview with Mr. Eliezer Feig.

was working. It was a very big operation, but it ran smoothly.

My mother had two brothers, Pinchus and Shlomo. Pinchus eventually moved to Israel where he and his family survived the War. Shlomo, had a physical disability that somewhat limited what he could do. Eventually he married a seamstress who was brought to Sighet to sew a dress for a *kallah* (my mother). Someone proposed the *shidduch* between the two of them, and they married. Shlomo didn't work on a regular basis, he learned and worked from time to time. His wife, however, continued working as a seamstress. She was successful and eventually operated a large seamstress shop, employing 12 other women. They never had children. It is very sad, because when she finally became pregnant after 12 years of marriage, they were taken to Auschwitz. She died pregnant.

My father did not come from a wealthy family, but he worked hard and Hashem blessed his efforts for he became quite wealthy. He dealt in foreign currency. It is because of his success in his currency dealing that I am now the main plaintiff petitioning the Swiss banks to return the Jewish monies in their possession. My father had deposited some of his money in Swiss banks before the War and I have filed a class action suit on behalf of myself and many of the survivors for our monies to be returned. I appeared before Senator Alfonse Damato's Senate Banking Committee that is holding government hearings on the operating procedures, past and present, of the Swiss banks. I also flew to Switzerland to speak before a government committee regarding the disposition of these monies. In this respect, I am somewhat famous because my picture at these hearings has appeared in newspapers around the world. Anyway, the situation has not yet been resolved, but I mentioned it here since we are speaking about my father.

My father was 3 1/2 years younger than my mother. Their *shadchan* was a distant relative from Sighet. My maternal grandmother only had two daughters. My mother was ten years younger than her sister who had married many years before her, so in the intervening time my grandmother was able to accumulate a large dowry for her youngest daughter. My grandmother owned a small restaurant, a *bodega* in Romanian. The restaurant was a block away from the Sigheter Rov's house and close to the main street. She sold cold cuts, cookies, hot prepared foods–it was a small deli restaurant. Sighet was a major town, so many people from the surrounding areas came to Sighet to conduct business. The deli was a place for them to eat, refresh themselves and even transact business.

Sighet was a major town, so many people from the surrounding areas came to Sighet to conduct business.

My father learned full time after he married my mother, but I'm not sure where he learned. Both my father and my grandfather were Munkacser *chassidim*.[38] My father went to Munkacs to learn before he married, but it was not for him for whatever reason. He used to say it was because he missed his mother's cooking! So he returned to Satmar and learned in the yeshiva there until he moved to Sighet after the *chasunah*.

My grandmother placed the dowry in a bank account under both of my parents' names. My father was always asking her permission to take out the money to invest in a business, but she would not allow this. My grandfather

38. The reader is referred to the interview with Mr. Hershel Ostreicher.

was a very important Torah personality in Sighet. He never involved himself in business because he was learning all of the time. My grandmother managed the financial affairs of the household (as I mentioned), so my father's suggestion was foreign to her. My father had the right to take the money out, because it belonged to him now, but he had very great respect for his mother-in-law, and since she was the one who placed the money in the bank, he wouldn't withdraw it without her permission, and *this* she wouldn't allow. Certainly my mother would never do this either without her mother's permission. They asked a few times, but grandmother always refused. One day my father overheard some businessmen in the restaurant saying that the bank where the money was deposited was going to go bankrupt. Initially, my father didn't know what to do, but finally he hit upon the following plan. He payed a policeman to go to my mother and tell her there was an emergency and she should go to the bank immediately. Father reasoned that since she would not take out the money as he had requested on previous occasions, now he needed to create an atmosphere of great urgency that would prompt Mother to act right away. When she arrived he explained to her that the bank was going to close and that they must take out their money. He begged her to withdraw the money. Finally, she acquiesced. Sure enough, a few weeks later the bank closed. When my father explained to my grandmother that fortunately the dowry money had been safely withdrawn, she became very upset. Why? you may ask. It probably bothered her that my father, an inexperienced yeshiva *yungerman*, managed to save the money, while she who was an experienced businesswoman did not. In reality, she was proud and happy that he acted as he did. After this he started his foreign currency business and worked with the businessmen he met at the restaurant. Little by little, he became very wealthy.

My father traveled extensively because of his business... but my mother always had yidden staying with us or eating with us.

My father traveled extensively because of his business and was often not at home, but my mother always had *yidden* staying with us or eating with us. She was a generous and hospitable woman. *Bochurim* from the yeshiva would eat each day by another *baal habayis*–this was called *teg essen*. Every day we had yeshiva boys eating the main meal with us (which was lunch time in Europe). My husband also ate this way when he was a *bochur* learning in Satmar. We had relatives traveling to, or through Sighet on business, so they stayed with us as well. There was a woman in town who was a regular guest for one meal a day. Also there were two sisters, whose mother passed away and their father remarried, one of them came each day. They were not happy with their stepmother, so they moved to a small village outside of Sighet and they found out about my mother. Then there was a divorcee with a child who came to eat with us every Friday night. In addition, a distant relative came to eat with us every Shabbos for the afternoon *seudah*. My mother always said that she preferred when the boys ate with us because they would look into a *sefer* until the meal was ready, whereas the women would just stand around waiting. This is what those days were like. It was easier for us to extend this hospitality because we could afford a live-in maid, and every Thursday and Friday we had someone coming in to scrub the floors.

I remember that one time while my father was finishing a money transaction one of the men involved lost a gold coin. I carefully looked through the restaurant

Жупа — Župa: Maramaros
Городъ — Mesto:

Метрическое свидѣтельство о рожденіи. — Rodný list.

Текущій номеръ / Bežné číslo	Время записи (день, мѣсяцъ, годъ) / Doba zápisu (deň, mesiac, rok)	День, мѣсяцъ, годъ рожденія / Deň narodenia (deň, mesiac, rok)	Имя, полъ, вѣроисповѣданіе дитяти / Meno dieťaťa, pohlavie, náboženstvo	Родителей — Rodičov: имя и фамилія, званіе (занятіе) и мѣстожительство / meno a priezvisko, zamestnanie (postavenie) a bydlisko	вѣроисповѣданіе / náboženstvo	возрастъ / vek	Мѣсто рожденія, если рожденіе произошло не въ мѣстожительствѣ матери / Miesto narodenia, keď matka neporodila v svojom bydlisku	Примѣчанія передъ подписью. Подписи. / Prípadné poznámky pred podpisom. Podpisy.
28	1897. listopad 8	1.	Pinkász chlop. izr	Halpert Chájfel, Kramař; Ošpreicha Rachella; Maramaros-sziget	izr; izr	27; 25	—	Ošpreicha Hné Agy v. r.; Piller Josef v. r. pod matrikar

Добавочныя записи. Исправленія.
Dodatočné zápisy. Opravy.

Удостовѣряю, что настоящая выпись согласна дословно (по содержанію) съ записью в
Svedčím, že sa tento výťah doslovne (obsažne) srovnáva
метрической книгѣ рожденныхъ Vylok метрическаго округа.
s matrikou narodených matrikárskeho obvodu.

Vylok дня / dňa 9. března 1922

Hegedüs
ведущій метр. книги. — matrikár.

Zaplaceno 3 kor.

Vzadné č. 11. (vz. č. 15 m. ú.)
Типографія Школьной Помощи, Ужгородъ.

Czechoslovakian Birth Certificate for Pinchus Halpert

At that time the women gave birth to their children at home, assisted by midwives.

and found the coin. As a result, I became very special with the customers there. I was about five-years-old then. Eventually, my grandmother closed the *bodega* and she and my grandfather moved into Pinchus' house which was empty now that he and his family went to Israel. Until then she lived across the street from the restaurant in a small rented apartment. Actually, at that time my parents and I slept in a small room that we rented, but we cooked and ate by my grandmother. My Uncle Pinchus used to make candy and ice cream in his house. This was his *parnasah*. When I went to him for ice cream, he gave me a scoop on a piece of matzah. He also baked matzah, which wasn't expensive, but an ice cream cone was expensive so that he wouldn't give me. My uncle became very influenced by the Mizrachi movement, and in 1935 he moved to Israel. He took his ice cream and candy equipment with him, but he wasn't able to set up a factory there as planned. Eventually, he took a job as a bookkeeper. In 1936, he returned to Sighet to bring his family to Israel with him. He was in Israel during the War, and died about 12 years ago.

After my grandparents moved, my father rented a house from a local family. We lived in that house for less than a year. I remember this because one of my brothers was born there and he had his *Bris Milah* there. At that time the women gave birth to their children at home, assisted by midwives. No one went to the hospital to deliver. We used Jewish midwives... everyone used them.

Engagement picture of Pinchus Halpert to Esther Rosenberg (Sighet 1918)

Education

There was a Bais Yaakov school in Sighet, but my father didn't permit me to attend. He was a Munkacser *chassid*, and the Munkacser Rebbe, the Minchas Elozer, was not a supporter of the Bais Yaakov movement. I learned privately. First I had an *Aleph-Beis* teacher for two years. He was an elderly man who taught the *Aleph-Beis* to the *frum* children in Sighet. We used to go to his house. He and his wife were not well and they never had children. He couldn't do any strenuous work, so his job was to teach the *Aleph-Beis*. After this I went to public school for six years. The first three years I was in school Sighet was under Romanian control, but for the last three years this area of Transylvania was returned to Hungary by Hitler, and Sighet came back under Hungarian control.

Bnos Agudath Israel in Sighet, 1934

The goyim let us know that we were Jews, that we were different, but I don't remember any overt anti-Semitic acts against me.

My father always had a private teacher who came to the house to give me religious instruction in Yiddish. When Hitler gave Transylvania back to the Hungarians at the beginning of the War (1939), we didn't encounter any special problems in the public school. The *goyim* let us know that we were Jews, that we were different, but I don't remember any overt anti-Semitic acts committed against me. I didn't attend school on Shabbos. In some places they demanded that the Jewish children attend on Shabbos and other Jewish holidays, but not in Sighet. The gentile children received religious instruction in the public school, but the Jewish children did not attend. In my last two years in school we were forced to help the German War effort. How? We had a knitting class where we knitted socks for the soldiers. In truth, we didn't learn too much those years because, aside from knitting socks, the school received miniature furniture pieces from somewhere and we painted them with a Hungarian motif. The school then sold the furniture and made money from our efforts. We also made doormats from braided corn husks. This took place in 1942-1943, the last two years before our area was affected by the War. I was 13 and 14-years-old then.

The Spiritual Environment

The spiritual environment between the two World Wars was very volatile. Many, many of the young people became attracted to the new parties and ideologies that swept through Eastern Europe after World War I: Socialism, Communism, the Bundists, and the irreligious Zionists. In our house we were strictly Orthodox, but in many houses some of the children abandoned their *Yiddishkeit*. The terrible social upheaval after WWI tore at the fabric of the Orthodox world.[39]

39. The reader is referred to the history section, the interview with Rabbi Yosef Landau and the chapter on Sarah Schenirer in **The World That Was: Poland.**

I went to school with a girl who lived three houses away from me. Allegedly, her father was from an Orthodox family, but her mother was not. They didn't observe Shabbos, but on Rosh Hashanah and Yom Kippur her father went to the large *shul* of the *Kehillah*. He wore a *kittel* on Yom Kippur. Some people, who were poor and could not afford to buy a seat for the *Yomim Noraim*, brought a folding chair to *shul* and they sat in the back or in the hallway. This is what this girl's father did. There was great turmoil in the Jewish community of Eastern Europe at that time and tragically, many, many Jews were lost from *Yiddishkeit*.

Many *Rebbes* and their followers lived in Sighet before the War. The Kretchinever Rebbe, the Barsha Rebbe and his *Chassidim*, Vishnitzer *Chassidim* and Antinerer *Chassidim*, among others. There were many small *shtiblach* from the different *chassidic* sects throughout the town. Sighet had a very rich and diverse Orthodox community.

Mrs. Weisshaus and her mother standing behind the Kallah, Miriam Zalcer, her first cousin. The woman to the left of the bride is Mrs. Weisshaus' aunt (her mother's sister) Chaya Rivka Zalcer.

My aunt and uncle, Chaya Rivka and Michoel Zalcer, had a daughter and four sons. The boys studied in the Sigheter Yeshiva (Uncle Michoel was a son of the Munkacser *Dayan*, Rabbi Meir Wolf Zalcer). Many friends came to my cousins to learn together with them. They were special. My aunt had a big garden in the back of her house. She grew all types of vegetables, and her sons tended the garden for her. We only grew trees in our garden because there was no one to take care of a vegetable garden. Such a garden needs constant upkeep. We grew some tomatoes in the front, but nothing like her garden. My aunt was insistent that the boys learn some type of a trade. They were very smart and well learned in Torah, and she wanted them to be able to earn a

Mrs. Weisshaus (with braids) accompanying wedding guests being taken to the train station by horse and buggy.

These were special boys, but they are also an example of the dedication to Torah that was the very fabric of many families.

living. In the morning the boys weeded the garden and in the afternoon they watered the crops, but the whole time they were working they learned–they were always learning. Many boys came to learn with them as they worked in the garden. No matter what she told them to do, they learned! My aunt took over the baking of cakes and cookies for commercial sale after my grandmother retired. This is how she earned a living. She also sold her baked goods to the soldiers as they passed through town. Even the German soldiers bought from her on their way to the Russian front. The soldiers left us alone, more or less, as they passed through. There were certain incidents, but they were isolated. At one time or another my aunt raised angora rabbits, cultivated bee hives for honey and smoked salamis. I'm telling you all of this about my aunt for two reasons. First, you should know how hard people worked to eke out a living then. Second, you should realize the dedication that my cousins showed for their Torah learning. Even though they had to help earn a *parnasah* for the family, their minds and hearts were detached from concerns with their material needs and were always focused on their learning. These were special boys, but they are also an example of the dedication to Torah that was the very fabric of many families. Unfortunately, no one from my aunt's family survived the War.

Provisions for winter

Shabbos and Yom Tov were always very nice. Friday night my father *davened* at the Sigheter Rov's *shul*, but during the day he went to a small *shul* called Eitz HaChaim, joining many other Munkacser *chassidim*. My father was a happy man, and well-known. He had a very good sense of humor and was quick to make up *grammen*. When he was young and a newcomer to Sighet he made a very good impression on the *Yidden* there. Also, his family had a very good name in Satmar. His grandfather, Tuvia Leib, was very close with the Yetev Lev, they were both from Ujhely, Hungary. My father had a close relationship with the previous Satmar Rebbe, Rabbi Yoel Teitelbaum, *zt"l*.

I'm not sure how it was that my father came into possession of the Sigheter Rebbe's Chanukah *menorah*, but for a period of time that's the *menorah* we used each year. I was a little girl of eight or nine when he gave it back. Then he bought a smaller *menorah*, one that my son uses today. My father hid it before he was taken away by the Germans, and I retrieved it after the War. Some of the poorer people used a potato for their *menorah*. They carved out little wells in the potato and put in oil. Some used a *menorah* made out of tin or another inexpensive metal, but potatoes were very common. Most of the oil was made from walnuts because we had plenty of walnut trees growing in the area. We also grew a lot of sunflowers, so there was plenty of sunflower seed oil. Those who could afford it used chicken fat; for baking there was a shortening made from coconuts.

Purim was a lot of fun. My father was always very happy and kept everyone entertained with his *grammen*. The local gypsies walked through the streets playing their instruments as they went from house to house looking for a tip. It was very festive. Purim meant that winter was slowly ending and that soon Pesach would be here. My father made wine for his personal use and stored the barrels in our basement. One year he and some of his friends ran a long rubber hose from the barrels in our basement to the *shul*, so that they would have a continuous flow of wine for Purim. It was very cute. People dressed up a bit, and it was a happy time. My aunt baked for our guests, so we had everything available for those who came to us.

There was a custom on *Shemini Atzeres* for the *Rosh HaKehillah* to make an official visit to the Sigheter Rov. There would always be a cake that was specially baked by my aunt and decorated by my mother for this occasion. One year they forgot to tell my aunt to bake the cake and since she was busy with *yom tov* herself, time just slipped by. You cannot decorate a cake on *yom tov*, but my aunt was permitted to bake. So what could they do now? They cooked beets in a sugar solution so that they were good and sweet, and then asked a *sh'ailah* if they were allowed to cut the beets into different shapes using cookie cutters. They were told they could do this. Then they took the cut beet pieces and arranged them on the cake in a flower pattern. It was very pretty and very ingenious. My mother could decorate a cake beautifully under normal circumstances and she usually did so for my aunt.

Elul, Rosh Hashanah and Yom Kippur were very solemn. People went to the cemetery, asked forgiveness from each other...you saw that people were earnestly trying to change. It was very sincere, very holy...and not commercial like today.

We had a permanently built *succah* in the backyard and only had to put on the *s'chach* each year. For this we used pine tree branches that gave a wonderful smell to the *succah*. It was quite a sight to see the men walking to *shul* with their *lulavim* and *esrogim*.

Pesach time we had a gentile woman come to wash the clothes. Washing clothes was a very big job. We were wealthy, so we could afford more clothing, and we only washed clothes four times a year in Europe. This was not something you did everyday. You don't know what a washing machine means until you have done all the laundry by hand. No idea! You have to be very thankful for a washing machine, because what we wash in an hour today took two days or longer in Europe. Before Pesach this woman came for two days. Our regular cleaning woman prepared the clothes

You don't know what a washing machine means until you have done all the laundry by hand.

A washerwoman

There was a very deep spiritual life among the Orthodox. Ideological battles were raging around us, but we were very secure in our faith.

first by soaking them in a large kettle the night before. The laundry woman washed the clothes three times. First she wrung out the water they had soaked in all night. Then she used something like lye to wash the clothes twice and then she did a final rinse. After that she placed the clothes in a barrel that had an opening at the bottom. It was very interesting–she packed clothes into this barrel until it was full and then put a piece of cloth on top, covering all of the clothes underneath. On top of this cloth she put ashes from burnt wood. She poured hot water on top of the ashes and this water and ash solution filtered through the clothes and out of the opening at the bottom. The ashes worked as a bleach to whiten and brighten the clothes. It was really very effective.

The next day, even if it was freezing, she had to go to the well and rinse the clothes twice. This was a very hard task. After rinsing the clothes she beat the clothes using a wooden pole with a handle. This was all part of the rinsing process which took another half a day. Finally, she hung out the clothes to dry. Even if the clothes froze, eventually they dried and we brought them in to be ironed. We made red hot coals that heated the iron, which was in the shape of a modern day iron, only it was a solid piece of metal.

We were wealthier than many others, as I told you, so we could afford a laundry woman and more clothes to last between each wash. The poorer people had fewer clothes and had to wash more often. Life was hard. Many families were large, with little to eat, no heat in the winter, living in very cramped quarters. You can't compare how we live today and how a poor Jew lived then. However, there was a very deep spiritual life among the Orthodox. Ideological battles were raging around us, but we were very secure in our faith. Sometimes we painted the rooms of our house *erev Pesach*, but we always had gentiles cleaning the house.

In general, it took a good part of the day to prepare a main meal. In the morning we had bread, and once in a while, we had a hot cereal of some sort. In some families they only had corn bread and corn mush to eat. We also ate this from time to time, but not every day. We had a certain type of cheese that you cannot find today in America. We put it on top of the corn meal. I, personally, liked a type of cheese made from goat's milk. We had a normal length summer, but it was cool because we were near the Carpathians. Once in a while my mother and grandmother went to the mineral baths for which Hungary is well known. There was phosphor in the water and that was considered very healthful.

I had a very happy childhood. We always had people in the house and celebrated many happy occasions there. One time my father made a *chasunah* for someone in the house. We always had plenty to eat until Hitler invaded Poland on September 1, 1939, after which food was rationed.

Leading Up to the War

I was only four-years-old when Hitler, *ym"s*, came to power in 1933. Before the War I had no trouble with our gentile neighbor who had two girls. One of the girls was my age, and when I visited them they were pleasant enough to me. Later, I found out they reported my father to the authorities when the Germans first invaded our area. I returned home after the War to retrieve the valuables that I helped my father hide before he was taken away. These valuables included money, coins, jewelry and the silver-

...lős kiadó: ...eich Jehosua;
...rk. és kiadóhivatal: Tel-Aviv, Stand u. 14;
...lefon: 21740;
...nkszámla: Bank-Hámizráchi, 7250, T.-A., Lilienblum u. 48. ...sta Bankszámla 44190.

מרמרוש-סיגעט
MARAMAROSSZIGET

1961. szeptember — תשרי תשכ״ב KIADJA: „IRGUN MARAMAROSSZIGET B'ISRAEL". II. Évfolyam — 8 szám

...J ÉV ELÉ - לקראת שנת תשכ״ב — אנשי סיגט —

Monthly paper published in Tel Aviv in Hungarian, for the survivors from the Maramaros - Sighet region.

There were always incidents of trouble with the gentiles, but we didn't have any pogroms like the Jews in Poland and Russia.

ware that I use today. I helped him to hide many of these things so I knew exactly where to look for them. There was only one place to take the silverware for safe-keeping after I took it from our hiding place in the attic, and that was to the gentile next-door. I kept everything there for a while and then took it back from them. They informed on my father, but they helped me. After the War Russian soldiers were living in our house. I absolutely couldn't stay there and I certainly didn't trust them! The only one I could turn to was this neighbor.

When I went back to Sighet about twenty-five years ago, I found that the only one remaining from that family was their son. He was very happy to see me. He had taken over the land next to his property that belonged to my aunt and built himself a nice house. He probably found some of the wealth hidden in her house and he helped himself to this as well. That is what the *goyim* were like–you never could trust them. Many Jews were murdered by their gentile neighbors when they returned to their villages and towns after the War to reclaim their property.[40] As I remember, there were always incidents of trouble with the gentiles, but we didn't have any pogroms like the Jews in Poland and Russia experienced. You couldn't trust them, this we always knew. Still, we needed them to work for us. We had one gentile bring us wood in the winter, another one came in on Shabbos to take the candlesticks off of the table, some came to clean the house...many Jews employed gentiles for domestic work. Most of the peasants weren't very educated, and this was a way for them to make a living. They didn't openly say they hated the Jews, this they kept to themselves, but when it came to the deportations almost

A Jewish couple preparing their field

40. The reader is referred to the interview with Mr. Yosef Friedenson in **The World That Was: Poland.**

all of them were against us. Except for a very, very small number of gentiles, none of them tried to help us during the War. There were some who did, I don't want to say there weren't *any*, but only very few helped us. How many Jewish children were taken to Christian orphanages to be raised as Catholics, never to be returned to the Jewish nation? Who knows how many are now married to Catholics throughout Europe, not even knowing they are Jewish?! If so many gentiles saved so many Jews, where were all the Jews after the War?

The only change that affected us when the War broke out on September 1, 1939, was that the Germans took Transylvania away from Romania and gave it back to Hungary. Otherwise, we were not mistreated and no one bothered us. We were free until the end of 1943. It is important for you to understand this fact, that the War–the actual German persecutions–didn't start for us until the end of 1943 and beginning of 1944. It was difficult to get food before then, we also had to black out our windows at night so that there was no light to signal our location to the enemy pilots. Also Jewish men were taken to the horrible Labor Brigades,[41] but the actual ghettoes and deportations did not begin until 1944 in our area. In the Labor Brigades, Jewish men were forced to go before the German and Hungarian troops to build roads and bridges and were often exposed to great danger. No one wanted to go, especially if they had a family. In fact, I saved my father from a labor brigade, from the infamous *Munka Tabor*. I'll tell you how this happened.

The War–the actual German persecutions–didn't start for us until the end of 1943 and beginning of 1944.

Everyone tried to avoid the Labor Brigades, and for large sums of money some people bribed their way out of conscription. My father received his notice by mail to report to the officers for his induction examination into the brigade. The officers met in my school yard where I attended class. In the yard there were many tables and benches and at each table something different was taking place. At one table there were medical examinations, at another they recorded your personal history, etc. I went to see what was taking place and if I could find out some information that would assist me in helping my father. I remember that I was very afraid. I was watching one official who was questioning some of the men and I didn't like the feel of the situation, so I didn't approach him. I remained standing in the yard, but I moved to a less conspicuous place. All of a sudden this officer got up and sent a younger officer to take his place. I walked closer to him and he saw me. He joked, 'Girl, what are you doing here? Do you want to go in the army?' 'No, I don't,' I replied, 'but I need your help with another matter.' I saw that he was listening to me, so I continued. I told him we received this notice that my father should report to the army, but that he is already in the army and we have no idea where he is. He took the conscription notice from my hand and signed-off on it, stating that my father was already in army service and was exempt from any further call-ups. I was beside myself with joy. I returned home in triumph and was the celebrity of the house! This took place in 1942. As a treat for what I did, I was allowed to go and visit my paternal grandparents in Satmar by myself. My family took me to the train and off I went. It was very exciting.

41. The reader is referred to the interview with Mr. Ostreicher for a more complete accounting of the horrors of the *Munka Tabor* or forced Labor Brigade.

I knew what was going on in Poland during the War from a very interesting source. We had an extra room in our house that we rented to the *shamosh* of the big *shul*. He was taken into the *Munka Tabor*, and his wife was left alone with her two small children. She couldn't manage alone and had to move in with her father (her mother was no longer living). Before she left, however, she rented the room to someone else. The room was now used as a meeting place for a small club comprised of some of the young men who lived in Sighet. They had something like a shortwave radio, and were able to receive news broadcasts from outside of Hungary. Sure enough, I could also hear the radio because the room was directly behind my parents' bedroom. Some people managed to get newspapers. One person held the paper and 10 others stood around him reading it over his shoulder. That's the way it was. I knew the War was going on, but I didn't know that the Germans were exterminating the Jews–only that there was fighting. Also, I was young and wanted to be happy and enjoy my life, so I didn't think about the War too much. I knew that the adults were concerned and worried, but I was still a child.

War and Deportation

The Pesach before the War started for us, in the spring of 1944, we had German soldiers stationed in our house. Until this time we didn't really see large numbers of Germans. The Hungarians, the *Gendarmerie*, were not good to us, but we didn't see Germans until the spring of 1944. Interestingly, some of the *Gendarmerie* were young gentiles from Sighet who did not necessarily give the Jews a hard time before the War, but they changed after they put on a uniform. The *Gendarmerie* asked people to gather information on non-Hungarian nationals. They also stopped people on the street and checked their identification papers. This was called *legitimatzia*. Everyone had to carry proper identification papers at all times. During the winter of 1943-44 we did not attend school too much because we already had to wear the yellow star. There were places where we *weren't* welcome, so we were careful to stay away. That *erev Pesach*, my father was cleaning his *seforim* outside the house. While he was busy going through the pages a young German soldier came over and asked him if it was true that in the Jewish books it was written that the Jews had to kill gentiles to use their blood for Pesach. My father told him that no such thing was written anywhere... he tried to explain to him...but, in the end, he didn't want to talk too much with a German soldier. It was dangerous to talk too much during the War.

During the winter of 1943-44 we did not attend school too much because we already had to wear the yellow star.

There was a great shortage of food that Pesach, so the *rabbonim* in Sighet allowed the people to eat *kitniyos* (legumes) that year. My father went to buy a sack of potatoes from a farmer outside of Sighet. I went with him, pushing a baby carriage the whole way. We put the potatoes in the carriage, covered it with blankets, and then went home. It was a long walk, but no one thought that we were pushing a sack of *kartofels* (potatoes) so we were left alone. Also, my father didn't want to offend those who couldn't afford to buy potatoes that year. We had plenty of *matzos*, in fact, for weeks afterwards we still had matzah to eat. The *matzos* were better than what we get here. They were very delicious. During Pesach the Germans left us alone–even though they were living in our houses. However, right after Pesach they told us we would be taken to live in a ghetto. All over Transylvania–in Sighet, in Satmar, in Ruscova–all over, there was an order that the Jews not be taken to the ghettos until after Pesach. I don't know why, but that's what happened. They just left us alone. Then the War really began for us.

The War

We were placed in the Sighet Ghetto–a part of the city was partitioned off as a ghetto. Instead of living in our house with four rooms, we were now placed in an apartment with several other families, each family having only one room. My father wasn't with us because the *Gendarmerie* arrested him together with all of the other wealthy Jews before we were sent to the Ghetto. I did see him one more time. The day before he was to be deported to a labor camp in Germany he bribed some guards to bring him to see us. He came escorted by these guards. He gathered us together around my mother and in a whisper, because the guards were in the room, told us that he has money hidden in the walls of the house and in the Union Bank of Switzerland. He was with us for half an hour and then they took him away. He was away from us the entire six weeks that we were in the Ghetto.

The Ghetto was very crowded and there was a general shortage of food. Our whole family was living in one room. In the next room, a smaller room, were my grandparents. We were worried because we didn't know what was going to happen. We weren't mistreated, we were just cut off from the world. Many of the men were already in the *Munka Tabor*,

Women and children on their way to the gas chamber ...Auschwitz

so it was mainly women, children and older or ill men who were in the Ghetto.

There were four transports from Sighet. We were on the second transport, and I was told that my father was on the fourth transport. We were on the train for three days. There was no water, no sanitary facilities–I'm sure you have read what these transports were like already–they were horrible. The children were crying...there was nowhere to sleep...it was horrible.

A women's barracks in Auschwitz, originally a stable for 52 horses

We arrived in Auschwitz on Friday afternoon and went through the infamous first *selektion* on the platform by the train tracks. Mengele, *ym"s*, sent me to the right and my mother and siblings to the left. I never saw them again. Then we were taken to a big room to shower and have our hair cut off. I was 14½ at the time. I was very tired after the shower and I laid down on the floor and fell asleep. When I awoke there was a woman watching over me. I heard whispering that something strange was going on here...that they were killing our parents. I couldn't believe it. I was too young to realize that such a thing could happen. We spent the night like this. Finally we were given our uniforms and then early on Shabbos morning they took us to our barracks. We thought we were going to go to work, but we never did. I was in Auschwitz for two months. We had the *zeilappel* every morning... everything...just as you have already heard about from others. We smelled the furnaces and then I believed what everyone said. The first day I was given something to eat, but I couldn't eat such food. Besides that, I was really only concerned where my mother and sisters and brothers were.

Everything that happened to us in Auschwitz has a story. We went to the bathroom with guards watching us, we slept on boards with no covers, the *appelplatz*–about everything there is a story. I don't go to any Holocaust exhibits

Public latrines in Auschwitz

There were certain people who didn't abuse their position of power over the inmates... they maintained their humaneness... Many others were savages.

because I lived through it. Nothing can compare to living it. Our *blockeldster*, our *kapo*, was a very religious woman from Poland. She was about 40-years-old and she would stand in the back of the *appelplatz* and *daven*.[42] There were certain people who didn't abuse their position of power over the inmates and she was one of them--they maintained their humaneness. However, there weren't too many. Many of these people were savages. Have you ever seen the faces of some of the SS women who guarded the camps? Try not to look, because they are pure evil...ugly, evil faces. What can I tell you?

After Auschwitz, I was sent to Germany to a place called Gelsenkirchen. We helped to rebuild an oil refinery there that had been bombed by the Allies. We were not treated well. What did I do there? We were 2,000 girls and they had us form a human chain to unload bricks and other building materials, sending them down the line, from one girl to the next, until everything reached the construction area. They didn't molest us. We had a piece of bread with a little marmalade or a very small piece of margarine. There was also a soup that was made from leaves or something. We received this soup once a day. We also got one cup of what they called coffee. Who knows what it really was. They put some drugs into this coffee, but what could we do! We couldn't go and get a drink of water, we had to drink the coffee. There were always German guards

Women selected for slave labor

42. The reader is referred to the section of the interview with Mr. Ostreicher that recounts the emotional confrontation he had with a Polish *Kapo* when he was first taken to his barracks after surviving the initial *selektion* in Auschwitz.

watching over us. After we were there for four months, it was getting close to Rosh Hashanah. Remember, we left the Ghetto in Sighet just before Shavuos and we remained in Auschwitz for two months. Now we were in Germany for four months, so it was *Elul* already.

The Germans made an artificial fog with smoke machines to camouflage the factory so that the Allied bombers would not be able to see it and destroy it again. We were living in tents made of cloth and were escorted back and forth to the factory by German guards and their dogs. The guards walked on each side of us, and in front and back of us, always with their dogs. What did they think a bunch of emaciated girls were going to do to them? They were nothing but evil. Once a girl was found stealing some food and right there, on the spot, the Germans shot her. That's how it was.

Photo credit : Capt. S.M. Kasnett

I.G. Farben Co., Frankfurt, Germany, producer of poison gas used to kill Jews.

Anyway, it was still the summer and was not cold yet, so living in the tents wasn't too bad. One day when we returned to our tents we watched in horror as the sky became literally black with Allied bombers. Soon bombs were falling all over and the factory was completely destroyed again. In the confusion of the bombing, I ran away. Some of the tents were destroyed and about 150 girls from my group perished in the bombing. I have a description of the

What did they think a bunch of emaciated girls were going to do to them? They were nothing but evil.

Photo credit : Capt. S.M. Kasnett

A German ball-bearing plant bombed by the Allies.

We manufactured tank shells in Sommerda. One week I worked a 12 hour night shift and the next week a 12 hour day shift.

bombing raids from an article in a German newspaper that someone sent me. It was written by a woman whose two sisters were killed. One died right away, but the other one languished in a nearby German hospital for a while before finally dying. Interestingly, the woman's sister said that there was a German doctor who tried very hard to save her. Not long ago this lady went back and had a monument erected in memory of the women who died. The Germans threw the bodies into craters that were formed by the bombs. Then they poured gasoline over the bodies and burned them. This took place in a wooded area near the tents. Now, at least, there is a monument in their memory–they shouldn't be forgotten.

After we left Gelsenkirchen we went to another camp called Sommerda. It is located in the Thunngia area of Germany. We lived in wooden barracks far away from the factory. Because it was winter, we received heavier clothing and wooden shoes like the Dutch wear–certainly more than we would have received in a Concentration Camp. We also received something like a small blanket and we slept in bunk beds. It was a cold winter, but very few of the women became sick. They treated us better because they needed our labor. The improved conditions made a very big difference. We manufactured tank shells in Sommerda. One week I worked a 12 hour night shift and the next week I worked a 12 hour day shift. We were in this camp for about five months when the front line of the war with Russia receded further and further west into Germany. The Russians were coming from the east pushing the Germans back toward the west, while the Americans were coming from the west pushing the German front line further east. As they retreated, the Germans marched us further into Germany with them. We could hear the Russian shells coming in, that's how close the fighting was to us.

Photo credit : Capt. S.M. Kasnett

Allied air destruction of Germany

While marching, we were surrounded by German guards. At night we slept in barns. They gave us very little to eat, but we were always hungry so we ate the weeds that were growing from the ground where we slept. I stayed close to a girl from Ungvar, a well known Jewish city in the Carpathians (an area that is

Photo credit : Capt. S.M. Kasnett

A small German village, a roof top view of the main street.

now in Ukraine) who was all alone, like I was. Many of the girls were alone. This girl was a very good thief. She stole food from around the factory where we worked, but she needed someone to watch her treasures when she went to work. She knew that I was a very religious girl, so she trusted me. As a reward, she shared her food with me. Eggs, potatoes, potato peels... We got close, so during the march we stayed together.

Liberation

The Germans locked the doors to the barns before they went to sleep. One morning we heard some noises outside of the barn and began banging on the doors. Soon they were opened and we saw Russian soldiers standing on the other side. We were liberated! This friend of mine knew how to speak Czech, and she also knew the area (we were near the Czech border). So she took me and five other girls (three sisters and two of their cousins) and we went to Bern, which was the closest big city. We stayed in a house in Bern for about seven weeks. We went into a very nice house and just took it over. Russian soldiers were in the city as well, so no one bothered us. We had food, but after I ate I became sick. The girls took me to a hospital, but there were no doctors. I just stayed there and rested. I was fortunate, for many of those who survived the horrors of the War died from the kindness of the soldiers who fed them foods that were too rich for their emaciated digestive systems. Many, many Jews died like this.[43] Thankfully, I recovered in a few days. The girls took me back to the house and we stayed there until we regained our strength. Eventually we went out and explored the city. There were many Russian soldiers and Czech partisans all over the city. My friend was very resourceful, and she was always able to find food and clothing for us.

My friend was very resourceful, and she was always able to find food and clothing for us.

Eventually I collected some of the possessions I had acquired in Bern and I decided to go home. I boarded a train and watched helplessly as a Russian soldier grabbed my valise and walked away with it. I started to go after him when I realized that I would have to leave my other valise unattended. In the suitcase he stole I had some very special things from the ammunition factory. Among the stolen items was a *siddur* I had made there, primarily comprised of the Friday night prayers. I took papers from the factory and glued them together. I took some tape and made a

43. The reader is referred to the interview with Mr. Hershel Ostreicher.

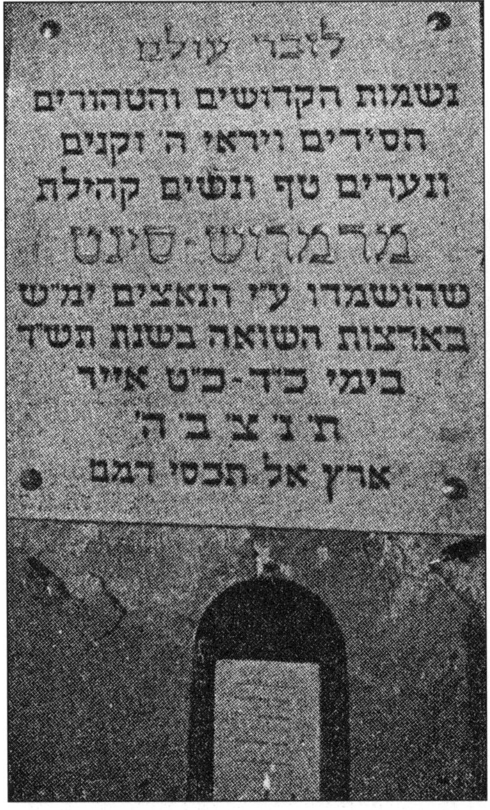

Plaque in memory of the martyred Jews of Sighet killed by the Germans from 24-29 Iyor, 1945.

cover and then I put my prayer book together. I wrote down *L'cha Dodi* and some of the other prayers. It would have been a very nice thing to show to my grandchildren.

When I arrived back in Sighet I found that a group of Jewish girls who had survived the concentration camps were living in the house three houses away from my house. I didn't want to stay alone in my house, so I joined them. Altogether there were five of us. Soon after, Russian soldiers occupied my house. Meanwhile, I still couldn't find the money that my father had hidden in the walls of the house. I did find the silverware right away, as well as two bolts of material that were hidden in the attic wall. The material I was able to sell and earn some money. I helped my father hide these things, so I knew exactly where they were. Although I remembered where he told me the money was, I couldn't find it.

I couldn't believe that I was the only survivor from such a big family... I was sure that someone was going to come back for me.

The first Pesach after I came home someone came to the house and told me that he was a cousin of my father and that I should stay with him for the *yom tov*. I knew his father, his sister, and some of his other relatives, but not him. In any case, I went with him to Tashnad for Pesach. He, his brother and sister survived the War. He survived with his wife and eight children because they were in Romania and, consequently, were not deported. They wanted me to remain with them, but I wouldn't because I thought that some of my relatives will surely come back to Sighet and I wanted to be there waiting for them. I couldn't believe that I was the only survivor from such a big family. Also, I wanted to look for the money. People thought I was crazy–what money!? Even my friends thought that there was something wrong with me because I was looking for this money and I was also sure that someone was going to come back for me.

I finally decided that the money must be in the attic. If everything else was hidden there, then the money must be there also. In truth, I didn't look for the money so carefully at first because I had money from the material that I sold. I knew, however, that for my *chasunah* I would need this money. I had a problem though because there were Russians living in the house. I went up to the attic early each morning using the outside stairway. I took a knife and a spoon with me to cut into the walls and to scrape away the plaster. A few weeks went by and I found nothing. One day I was scraping on a beam and some white powder fell out. The powder was plaster of Paris and the beam was wood. It had to be that my father had filled in the hole he carved in the wooden beam with the plaster, and then he colored it over. Sure enough, I found a few gold coins. These were probably hidden in the last few minutes. Now I knew for sure that I had to keep looking. I kept checking the beams, and I found three more places that contained money and jewelry. In the end, I had dollars, jewelry and gold coins. Only my father's watch still remains in my possession. After this I packed up my belongings and left Siget because I saw that my friends were jealous that I had found this money.

I went to Satmar by train. Upon arriving, I went to a restaurant that I knew about. I told the people in the restaurant that I was looking for a place to stay and that I would pay for my lodgings. I found a family that agreed to give me room and board for one dollar a week. They had relatives staying with them, as well as two yeshiva *bochurim*. The woman realized that it was not appropriate for me to be there. I was 16 already. She found another family for me to stay with, and I stayed with them until I got married. In fact, the *baal habayis*, Avraham Dovid Kepech, arranged my *shidduch*. He saw that there were a few people interested in me because they knew that I had money, and they also knew my family. The Rachover Rov was in Satmar at that time, and he wanted to arrange a match for me with his son. His son had survived the camps, and his father recently brought him home from Germany. He wasn't for me though, and the *Rov* realized this. In the meantime, Avraham Dovid arranged for me to meet my future husband at *Tashlich*. He knew my husband because they had learned together in Satmar. We met again two days later and then we became engaged. I paid Avraham Dovid $75.00 *shadchunus gelt*, and another $75.00 to make a *streimel* for my husband. My husband lived in

I found three places that contained money and jewelry. Only my father's watch still remains in my possession.

Ohel of the Yismach Moshe

Shul in Satmar where
Rabbi Yoel Teitelbaum davened.

Main Synagogue in Satmar

Satmar before the War and had aunts and uncles living there, as well as one grandmother. He learned there with the previous Pupa Rebbe before his Bar Mitzvah, and afterwards for six years in the yeshiva of the Satmar Rebbe, Rabbi Yoel Teitelbaum. My husband jokes with me that because I had money I was able to find such a good *shidduch*. Seriously, we were very happy, and it was nice to be happy again–to begin life over in that sense. I was a young bride and I wanted to be happy. I told my husband-to-be that I had one request at that time, that he *had* to wear a *streimel*. My father wore a *streimel*, but my husband's father didn't. Nonetheless, if he wanted to marry me then he had to wear a *streimel*.

We were very happy, and it was nice to be happy again–to begin life over in that sense.

I had around three thousand dollars and at the time you could live for a month on four dollars, I had a small fortune. My husband had an uncle who survived the War, his mother's brother. He was from Satmar and was a well-known personality in the Satmar *Kehillah*. He didn't wear a *streimel* and he was trying to get me to reverse my decision that my husband must wear one–not everyone wore *streimels* after the War. He asked me to go for a walk so that we could talk and he would have a chance to convince me. I would not listen to him for anything. I told him that this was one of the conditions of the *shidduch* and that's the way it's going to be. In the end it was settled according to my wishes. This uncle was one of the *unterfirers* for my husband. We made

After the chasunah, 1946 in Satmar,
(with the streimel!)

Before the chasunah in Satmar, 1946

that she, her husband and her child survived the War. She used to lend this wedding dress to others. She wanted me to use it as well. The dress was tight on me, and I told her that I wanted to buy my own dress. There was no material available in Satmar, so I had a seamstress order the material for me and make me a dress. I paid $49.00 for that wedding dress, which was a fortune then, but afterwards thirty-three other brides went to their *chupah* wearing that dress. The very next morning after my wedding a *kallah* came to take the dress for her wedding that night. The dress went from one *kallah* to the next. The dress was returned to me after I was smuggled into Hungary, and by then it was a very well worn dress, something that made me very happy.

I paid $49.00 for that wedding dress, which was a fortune then, but afterwards thirty-three other brides went to their chupah wearing that dress.

I also had to make a *shietel* for myself because you couldn't buy one ready-made. I went to Klausenberg for this purpose. Soon after the War there were airplanes shuttling between Satmar and Klausenberg, so I took an airplane ride to Klausenberg. I was wealthy so I could afford it, but it was an experience

a nice *chasunah*, and because I had money I was able to hire a photographer, otherwise I would not have any pictures at all. Who had money for something like that after the War? Pictures were a luxury that were very expensive. In Satmar there was a lady from Romania who had a wedding dress sewn from material that was taken to Israel and held by a lady as she walked around *Kever Rochel*. She had a feeling that this was the reason

Wedding Day (1946 in Satmar) Mr. and Mrs. Weisshaus in center. Seated next to them is Mr. Weisshaus' oldest brother, Shlomo, and his wife. Mr. Weisshaus' younger brother, Yitzchok, standing; the shodchan, Avrohom Dovid Kopecs is playing the violin.

Rabbi Yoel Teitelbaum
The Satmar Rebbe זצ"ל

Rabbi Chaim Meir Hager
The Vishnitzer Rebbe זצ"ל

Rabbi Yekusiel Yehuda Halberstam
The Klausenberger Rebbe זצ"ל

Rabbi Yisrael Spira
The Bluzhover Rebbe זצ"ל

American Jews should realize, that life was hard to almost impossible after the War. People lost their entire families

that I wouldn't wish on anyone. It was a very small plane traveling close over the tops of the mountains. The plane was shaking and vibrating and I was very scared. In Klausenberg my father had a few cousins, and I stayed with them until my *shietel* was finished.

Life was still so unsettled at that time. The War had just ended and almost nothing had returned to normal–how could it!? To return to what we had before the War was impossible, you can't bring back what doesn't exist anymore, but people are brave and they fought very hard to reestablish their lives. This is something that the American Jews should realize, that life was hard to almost impossible after the War. People lost their entire families: men lost their wives and children, women lost their husbands and their children, children lost their parents and their siblings–whole families were wiped out. The only thing we could do was rebuild, and to accomplish this Hashem allowed some very great people to survive to help us rebuild. The Satmar Rebbe had one daughter who died as a young child. He had another daughter, a very beautiful girl, who passed away one year after her marriage. She had a difficult pregnancy and did not survive. Then he went through the War and lost everyone. Yet he came to America and not only rebuilt individual lives and families, but a whole vibrant *chassidus* as well. He was an amazing man, a man whose *emunah*, whose belief in Hashem was unshakeable. He suffered personally, and he suffered all the pain and loss experienced by his *chassidim* and *Klal Yisrael*. Despite everything he remained an ever flowing fountain of pure *emunah* and *bitachon* in Hashem. This was also true of the Klausenberger Rebbe, the Vishnitzer Rebbe, the Pupa Rebbe... they enriched one world that was lost and then through their own personal *bris* of fire with Hashem lived to build another. This is what all of us did...the well known and the unknown...we rebuilt. This is what Hashem wanted from us. The Satmar Rebbe, the Klausenberg Rebbe, the Pupa Rebbe, the Bluzhover Rebbe–they all lost their own families, wives and children, but they encouraged broken men to remarry and raise families. They encouraged grieving women to remarry and rebuild. They took care of orphans–finding them

The Satmar Dynasty

Name	Biographical Information
The *Yismach Moshe* Rabbi Moshe Teitelbaum	Rov in Ujhely, Hungary Born: 1759 Died: 1840
Rabbi Eliezer Nissan Teitelbaum (son of the *Yismach Moshe*)	Rov in Sighet Born: 1785 Died: 1855
The *Yetev Lev* Rabbi Yekusiel Yehuda Teitelbaum (son of Eliezer Nissan Teitelbaum)	Rov in Sighet Born: 1807 Died: 1883
The *Kedushes Yom Tov* Rabbi Chananya Yom Tov Lipa Teitelbaum (son of the *Yetev Lev*)	Rov in Sighet Born: 1835 Died: 1904
The *Etzei Chaim* Rabbi Chaim Hersh Teitelbaum (son of *Kedushes Yom Tov*)	*Av Beis Din* (Head of Rabbinical Court) in Sighet Born: 1879 Died: 1926
The Satmar Rebbe Rabbi Yoel Teitelbaum (son of *Kedushes Yom Tov*)	Rov in Satmar and Williamsburg, New York Born: 1887 Died: 1979
Rabbi Moshe Teitelbaum (son of the *Etzei Chaim*)	Present Satmar Rebbe, Williamsburg, New York Born: 1915 (in Sighet)

room and board, yeshivos to learn in, skills with which to earn a living and then they helped them to marry and build their own families. It was almost impossible to imagine that such a thing would happen, that the *chassidus* of these sects would be rebuilt and prosper, *bli ayin hara*. This is all miracles...we have to realize that this is miraculous. You see how great is the soul of a Jew, that from the midst of destruction *Am Yisrael* can again be rebuilt. Miracles. You see that we are the Eternal People, that we are Hashem's people.

After the *chasunah* we stayed in the house where my husband's uncle lived before the War. It was like a castle. I was exactly 17 years and three weeks old when I got married. We always had help in my parents' house, so I almost never cooked or baked. I saw how it was done, but it wasn't my responsibility–now I had to learn. We started out with four people in the house: the two of us, my husband's younger brother and a maid. Some refugee children from Romania came to Satmar and people were asked to sponsor a child's meals,

You see how great is the soul of a Jew, that from the midst of destruction Am Yisrael can again be rebuilt.

so one of the boys ate with us. We didn't live so close to the center of the city–my husband used to take the boy back to where he stayed on his bike, otherwise I hired a wagon to take him back. I also hired a wagoner when I needed to go shopping. That's how we started out married life. I couldn't cook, but I sought out advise from some of the other wives and eventually I learned. I furnished my house very nicely. I ordered custom-made furniture, carpets...everything. I remember my mother telling me that the things you buy when you are first married are the easiest things to buy, because after you have children it becomes very difficult to spend money on house furnishings. I had money at the time, so I decided to furnish the house and make it very nice and comfortable for us.

In the end, a person has nothing from this world–only the Torah *and* mitzvos *that he fulfills.*

After I became pregnant, I heard some anti-Semitic remarks in the marketplace. I came home and told my husband that I think we should leave Satmar, that I don't want our children to live through what we experienced. I also didn't want us to live under the Communists. We were married in 1946 and this took place in 1947. We hired a guide to smuggle us across the border into Hungary (Satmar was under Romanian control after the War). I sold some of our silverware and took whatever else we could carry. Everything else was left behind. We called one of our relatives and told him to take whatever he wants, but he was single and didn't need anything yet. Later we found out that one of the city officials moved into our apartment. We had to leave in absolute secrecy because it was not legal for us to be smuggled into Hungary. We couldn't sell things and draw a lot of undue attention to ourselves. We just had to leave everything behind. This is one of the lessons of the Holocaust, that, in the end, a person has nothing from this world–only the Torah and *mitzvos* that he fulfills. You leave the world with no other possessions than that. We went to Budapest where my grandfather's brother lived. We rented a small apartment and soon after our first son, Yechezkel Yosef (named for my father and grandfather), was born. We made the *Bris Milah*, it was lovely. My parents would have been so happy.

After our son's birth we left Budapest and went to Prague for a few weeks and then on to Austria. At that time we didn't know where we were going to settle because we had no relatives in America. There was no one to sponsor us. My husband bought visas for $150.00 to go from Budapest to Costa Rica. We didn't even know where Costa Rica was, but we needed to get out of Europe because we couldn't live under the Communists, and we were uncertain what would be with Germany–G-d forbid there should be another Holocaust. To say we were very wary of the political scene in Europe at that time is a gross understatement.

To America

In Prague we were told that people were going to camps for displaced persons, or DP Camps. From Prague we went first to Vienna for a few weeks, and then to a place called Linz. We stayed in a DP camp there for about half a year during which time my husband was asked to join two others and open a restaurant where he would serve as the *mashgiach*. After the camp in Linz was closed we went to another camp in Austria called Welz. There we started to plan to come to America. This meant that we had to sign up for an immigration number. Those who had relatives in America had preference for visas, while we would have to wait. There was a quota system, and only so many foreigners could enter at one time. Our number finally came up and we arrived in New York at the end of 1950. By this time our second son, Akiva, was born and he was six months old when we arrived in America.

We settled in Williamsburg and had four more children: Elimelech Wolfe, Sarah, Hindi and Rivka. My husband learned how to operate a sewing machine. For many years he was a sewing machine operator in a factory and I did some sewing at home to make extra money. We struggled in the beginning, but I was very happy because we were free from the hatred of the *goyim* in Europe. However, I never thought that our children would grow up to live in a world like we have today–it is a different world than we imagined. When we arrived the Jews were a small remnant of the past, and now we have seen a rebirth like no one could believe. I am very grateful for this, *Boruch Hashem*.

When we arrived the Jews were a small remnant of the past, and now we have seen a rebirth like no one could believe.

PORTRAIT OF A HUNGARIAN TORAH PERSONALITY

A Tribute to Rabbi Sender Deutsch, זצ"ל
"The Lion From Brezna"

eb Sender was a quintessential Jew! He embraced the entirety of the Jewish nation, and though a Satmar Chassid and the right-hand-man and confidant of the Satmar Rebbe, Rabbi Yoel Teitelbaum, זצ"ל, Reb Sender crossed all boundaries and was equally respected by the *Litvishe Roshei Yeshivos* as well as the many other *chassidic* Rebbes who make up the Torah world of Orthodox Jewry. Born and raised in Brezna, he was a survivor who lost his family during the Holocaust. Reb Sender came to America committed to help rebuild Torah in this country and, particularly, in the Satmar community. *Ahavas Yisrael*, the very *midah* that epitomized Moshe *Rabbeinu*, is the *midah* that most distinguished Reb Sender. It was through this *midah* that he focused his great intellect and many skills, creating a life of Torah activism on behalf of Jews around the world יהי זכרו ברוך.

Reb Sender was a quintessential Jew! He embraced the entirety of the Jewish nation... Ahavas Yisrael, is the midah that most distinguished Reb Sender.

The following tribute to Rabbi Sender Deutsch זצ"ל *was transcribed from an interview conducted with his son, Yidel Deutsch, Williamsburg, New York, April, 1999.*

My father, ע"ה, was known to the Orthodox Jewish world as an educator, a writer, an author, an orator and, above all, as an intelligent and compassionate *Yid*. He was a global person. He possessed an innate sense of Jewish history, the dynamics of the Jewish community and human nature in general. Reb Sender spoke with authority on a wide variety of topics. Throughout his life he was relentless in his pursuit of truth and knowledge. He was never idle; I never saw him eat without also being engaged in some kind of productive activity. He had the ability to conceive an idea, and then anticipate its development, outcome and impact.

Reb Sender was a linguist by every definition of the word – a man who knew the exact meaning of each word he spoke. Well-known *rabbonim* called him for the most accurate and sensitive explanation of a *posuk*, or to understand why a word or expression is used precisely in this manner and in this specific *posuk* while it is employed in an entirely different way in another *posuk*. These were questions he answered without hesitation.

My father was a highly respected individual, not only in the Satmar community, but in the orthodox world in general. Yet, he was an intensely private family man as well. When we would walk together with him as children, he was a completely different person – intimate, fun and loving. He almost never spoke about any of his communal endeavors at home. We, the family, found out in which activities he was involved by reading about it in a publication, or by hearing about it from a third party. He was a very warm person while in his family environment, very much in contrast to his controlled and cognitive approach to community and business affairs. When I was a child, my father wasn't home as much as I would have liked because of his involvement in the community. He was always engaged in the public forum through his speeches and articles. He was a very dynamic speaker and an excellent writer and editorialist. He used these gifts to articulate the Satmar position on religious, social, economic and governmental issues.

He often went on trips to Europe to assist the orthodox communities there. He was, in fact, a true ambassador for Orthodox Jewry. He always took one of the children or grandchildren on these trips, using the opportunity to show us where the Orthodox communities existed before the War. He took us to see the graves of the *tzaddikim*, the *shuls* and other places of interest in Jewish life. He was interested in everything we were involved in and was very attentive to our needs. We couldn't fool him, he easily perceived if anything was troubling us. Although usually not demonstrative in public, when it came to performing a *mitzvah* it was a different matter entirely. You could actually see how affectionately he embraced the *mitzvah* he was performing or the person he was helping.

Interestingly, hundreds of letters from his correspondence recently came into our possession – expressing and sharing his concern in other's *simchas*, and, unfortunately, in their sorrows. He wrote beautifully and not in a general manner, rather the words and phrases were specific to each person. He was able to address each situation in such a meaningful and poignant way. Many times people came to speak with him and seek his advice and because of their burden, some became loud or abusive. He never took any of this to heart. Calming the person, he did whatever he could to alleviate their immediate pain and difficulties. He would take whatever actions necessary to help. After listening to them he escorted each one as they left the house, encouraging them as they went on their way, reminding them that they are not alone.

He was always engaged in the public forum through his speeches and articles... He was, in fact, a true ambassador for Orthodox Jewry.

Rabbi and Rebbetzin Deutsch with a three week old grandson

A sampling of some of Reb Sender's macrame for the succah

Before a Pesach *seder* or Succos Reb Sender stayed up very late several nights before, preparing for the *yom tov*. It was common to find him up at 3:00 in the morning *erev* Succos weaving beautiful macrame stars and designs from colored paper that he would hang on the walls of the *succah*. He was consumed with each *mitzvah* he performed. Pesach night was always very special because he would explain *Yetzias Mitzrayim* with great clarity and depth. He was so knowledgeable about the history of Egypt during that time period. He had an encyclopedic mind and his breadth of knowledge was comprehensive.

The Satmar Rebe constantly elicited his opinion on a wide range of issues and found him to be an excellent sounding board.

My father was a person who operated in many fields of endeavor, simultaneously, but he didn't confuse the issues at hand. He was careful never to respond to an individual or political personality in a disparaging manner. Even when attacked or criticized directly for a personal or communal position he took on an issue, he never took it to heart. He saw himself as a general of the Satmar community, and considered his work as holy. In this capacity, he felt it his duty to continue his efforts as the Satmar Rebbe directed without personalizing issues or comments. The Satmar Rebbe called upon my father constantly to elicit his opinion on a wide range of issues and found him to be an excellent sounding board. He was an objective person with an extremely strong mind, and this, I feel, was a sign of his inner strength and confidence. When he disagreed with another, he did so in the most respectful manner. Though Satmar has many differences with other *chassidic* groups, he instructed the community that the traditions of each *chassidic* group and Rebbe were to be respected, for each Rebbe is considered a leader in *Klal Yisrael*. When there are differences of opinion regarding highly sensitive and urgent issues only the *issue* should be passionately addressed, and even then always intelligently and with respect for others.

My parents, who are first cousins, were married in Mishkolcs in 1945. My mother, Rochel Malka, תחי' is a true *Eishes Chayil* in every respect. Together they raised 6 children *(bli ayin hara)* with great love and devotion. Over the years my mother served as hostess to many important functions and meetings, several of which took place in our home. In the DP camp in Windsheim, Germany where they lived for three years before coming to America, my father was the motivating force behind the building of the *mikveh*. Additionally, he was very instrumental in helping the survivors arrange the paperwork they needed for their passports and visas. He impressed everyone he worked with and stayed for a longer period of time in the DP camp in Germany to accomplish this. While there, he published a *sefer* for the Klausenberger Rebbe. In the camp my father compiled the lists of those who perished and survived. He even went to the train station on many occasions to intercept survivors and question them – to the best of their knowledge – regarding this information. This was a great *chesed* that he performed for the survivors. My parents finally emigrated to America in 1949.

After arriving in the U.S. we lived on East 4th Street in the Lower East Side where my father established the *Chareidim Shul*. It was a very popular *shul* and on Shabbos *and yom tov*, after *davening*, many of the *chassidim* walked over the Williamsburg Bridge to be with the Satmar Rebbe – sometimes three or four times during the course of the holiday. Then we moved to Williamsburg where my father worked at the Yiddish paper the *Morgen Journal*. After that he went to work for Shulsinger Printing House, working the night shift for 8 years. He had experience in the printing business from his father's printing shop in Brezna. During the day he had other jobs and tried to begin his own business. Meanwhile, when preparing manuscripts for printing for the Rebbes who sought to reprint many of the *seforim* that were lost during the destruction of World War II, he noticed errors in the text and passages that needed clarification. Calling the Rebbes, he pointed out what needed correcting and in this manner he developed a very good reputation. Eventually Reb Sender assumed ownership of the **The Yid**, a weekly Yiddish newspaper, where he served as editor for close to forty years.

Of greater importance, however, was the time he spent with the Satmar Rebbe during the day. My father's family were Sigheter *chassidim* in Europe. After the War, the Rebbe, who was a descendant of the Sigheter dynasty, asked him to remain in close contact and work together with him to rebuild the Satmar community. My father was one of the driving force behind the building of

A young Reb Sender (on right) with the Satmar Rebbe (seated) in 1964

the *mosdos ha'chinuch* and other communal organizations for Satmar. The first Satmar Yeshiva started with 6 boys. From these 6 children there are now over 17,000 boys and girls in Satmar *yeshivos* in New York State (*bli ayin hara*), and from that initial one room school there are now between 25 and 30 major school buildings serving the Satmar community. You can imagine the foresight and effort necessary to guide a community in its growth from a handful of families with 6 children to what the Satmar community is today. Housing, medical care, schools, jobs, *shuls*, teachers, a financial infrastructure, care for the elderly – a whole community had to be rebuilt. Eventually, Satmar began a program called *Rav Tuv* for Russian immigrants. My father was very instrumental in starting this organization and often traveled to Vienna where many Russian Jews went after leaving the Soviet Union on their way to America and Israel.

He became the Rebbe's "Secretary of State and the Interior."... One of his great accomplishments was the restoration of the old cemetery in Ujhely.

Reb Sender at the Upsherin of one of his grandchildren

When the Satmar Rebbe began writing his *seforim*, he asked my father to publish them. Soon he became a constant companion to the Rebbe, and it was at that point that he became the Rebbe's "Secretary of State and the Interior." For many years my father also recorded the Rebbe's Shalosh *Seudos shmussen* which were held very, very late at night. He would *daven Maariv*, make *havdalah* for us and then go to the Rebbe's *Beis Hamedrash* to write the *shmues* as the Rebbe spoke. Later that night, he would bring the transcription to the Rebbe to edit.

One of his great accomplishments was the restoration of the old cemetery in Ujhely (E-hely), Hungary, where the Yismach Moshe is buried. Twenty-five years ago the Hungarians wanted to put a road through the cemetery and the Rebbe asked my father to see what he could do to prevent this. He put tremendous effort into this endeavor. Even when Hungary was a Communist satellite state, and it was difficult to obtain a visa for entry, he plodded on. In the end, after going there many times to meet with various Hungarian officials, and without anyone knowing, he restored the cemetery and paid to have a wall and gates erected using his own funds. In addition, he built a rest area for those who go to say *Tehillim* at the Yismach Moshe's *kever* and a *mikveh* for the thousands who go there on his *yahrzeit*. Only a few weeks ago, the Hungarian government relinquished ownership of the cemetery to the Satmar *Chevrah Kadisha* (Burial Society). Now it belongs to the Satmar *Kehillah* and its preservation is no longer threatened.

Almost four years ago, a meeting of very influential individuals was called in Reb Sender's house. At this meeting the World Council of Orthodox Jewish Communities was established to formulate a plan to have Jewish assets taken by the Germans and hidden in the Swiss banks returned to the Holocaust survivors. These funds would also be used to support *shuls* and *yeshivos* for the European communities that were reestablished in America.

My father never gave voice to his disappointments and the difficulties he faced. He was steadfast – everyday– continuing his activities and pursuing his goals, always focused. Undaunted. He never boasted about his accomplishments, nor took credit for his many great deeds.

What was the driving issue in his life? He desired to accomplish whatever the Rebbe wanted in building the Satmar community. This was his focus and no matter what it took my father wanted it to be done. In return, the Rebbe promised my father his blessings and that he would be successful. His concern was for the growth and stability of the Satmar community in the long run. He made decisions that others did not understand initially, but he never gave up these initiatives. No matter how difficult, he never revealed any emotion except *bitachon*.

The Satmar Rebbe commented about my father many years ago that, "He is the type of *chassid* who respectfully questions my decisions. Other *chassidim* wouldn't speak this way to the Rebbe, but he had the strength of character to speak up on my behalf – even to me! This is why I respect and value his opinion." On another occasion the Rebbe called Reb Sender the *Mishlam*, the one who possesses all good qualities. The Rebbe and my father were extremely close and their relationship was one of complete mutual understanding.

He was steadfast... continuing his activities and pursuing his goals, always focused... His concern was for the growth and stability of the Satmar community.

During his final days, he told us that he knows that we will soon be going through a very difficult time after his passing, but he instructed us to be strong and never give up hope. Although his last few weeks were very difficult, he guided us until the end. The news of his passing brought sorrow to the entire Jewish community. On the 11th of Elul 5758 (September 2,1998), Reb Sender was laid to rest in the Kiryas Yoel Cemetery, right next to the Satmar Rebbe, זצ"ל.

VIGNETTES OF DIVINE PROVIDENCE (Hashgachah Pratis)

Escape to Budapest (Mr. Erno Friedman)

I was with two friends in Budapest in 1944. We had just entered a second floor apartment on Kaziney Street when the secret police broke through the front door. Quietly, but there was no mistaking their intent, we were told to come with them. They led us down the hallway and into an apartment building where another thirty Yidden were standing with suitcases scattered all about. These Jews had assembled in order to be smuggled out of Budapest when the police suddenly raided the apartment just before they could begin their dangerous journey. Now we were being rounded up together with them. I had not yet totally entered the apartment, and was still standing somewhat in the entrance hallway, near the kitchen. My friends were already inside. From a room further back in the apartment we could hear the cries of Jews being brutally beaten.

Mr. Friedman, 8 years-old, mother Rosa Friedman, sister Lily, in 1935

After being hit a number of times, one of the Yidden standing in the large room just off the hallway fainted and fell to the floor. Another person standing by was told to go to the kitchen and bring a pitcher of water to pour on the prostrate form. As the man went into the kitchen, I took the chance of going into the room with him. The worst that could happen is that I would be beaten for doing so, but this was a chance I was willing to risk. As I followed him – unmolested – into the kitchen, I told this man that I was going to try to escape. He understood that he couldn't join me because they were expecting him to return, so he nodded to me to continue with my plan.

Mr. and Mrs. Erno Friedman

The kitchen windows faced the front of the apartment building, toward the main street. I advanced to the windows and opened one of them. I had to act immediately, a second delay could be the difference between freedom and torture, or death. I planned to jump to the street when I noticed that the adjacent apartment, from where we were taken, had a porch that was some distance away. At times like this one does not consciously review the situation at hand, rather, a deeper, more intuitive sense takes over. I climbed onto the window sill, took one big leap and somehow traversed the distance, landing safely in the middle of the porch. Hashem was with me yet again, because when I tried the window in order to enter the apartment it was open! I quickly entered, exited through the main door, raced down the steps we had come up only a short while ago and escaped to the street. As I entered the street I saw a police vehicle speeding toward the apartment. Earlier, while I was captive in the second apartment, I heard one of the police call for a transport wagon for their prisoners and now it had arrived. I was afraid that it was coming for me or perhaps, somehow, I had been discovered . . . the kind of thoughts one has when terrified and urgently seeking cover. Fortunately, I was able to blend in with the pedestrian street traffic and make my escape.

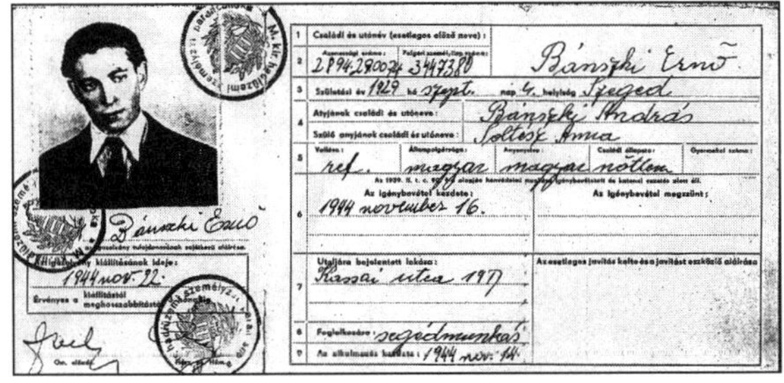

1 Családi és utónév (esetleges előző neve): Bánszki Ernő
2 2894290024 3447380
3 Születési év 1929 hó szept. nap 4. helység Szeged
4 Atyjának családi és utóneve: Bánszki András
Szülő anyjának családi és utóneve: Soltész Anna
5 Vallása: ref. Állampolgársága: magyar Anyanyelve: magyar Családi állapota: nőtlen Gyermekei száma:
6 Az igénybevétel kezdete: 1944 november 16. Az igénybevétel megszűnt:
7 Utoljára bejelentett lakása: Kassai utca 19?
8 Foglalkozása: segédmunkás
9 Az alkalmazás kezdete: 1944 nov. 14.
Bánszki Ernő
kiállításának ideje: 1944 nov. 22.

Forged ghetto I.D. papers showing employment in a defense industry.

I was spared, but sadly my friends were transported to Auschwitz and did not survive. This is only one of many such miracles that Hashem performed for me during the War.

Kedves egy drága jó apukám!
Mi hála Istenek egeszigesek vagyunk
melyet neked is kivánunk a jó Istentől
Kedves apukam csak arra kérlek hogy
nyugodt majd csak meg segit a jó Isten
hogy meg együtt leszünk. Kedves apukám
ha csak tudol írni akor irjal mentül
gyakrabban most már egyebel nem
tok csokolunk 1000 szer az egeszcsalad
tól külön a szerető lanyod Helén
választ

TRANSLATION OF A POST CARD FROM A GIRL IN THE GHETTO TO HER FATHER

My dear and best Father,

We thank G-d that we are healthy and pray that G-d grants you only good, as well. My dear Father, I beg that you should not worry about us, because G-d is good and will help to ensure that we will all be together again. My dear Father, if it is possible for you to write us, then please write often. I will now end my letter with 1,000 kisses to you from everyone in the family.

Your loving daughter,
Helen

This post card was given to me by a 16 year-old girl in the Nyirgyhaza Ghetto. She requested that I mail it to her father (which I was unable to do), who had been taken into forced labor in the infamous *Munka Tabor*, Hungarian Jewish Labor Battalions. He had been sent to the Russian front. Within six or seven days this girl was deported from the ghetto and taken to Auschwitz.

A PARAGON OF MESIRAS NEFESH
Mr. Yaacov Yehoshua Fried

My name is Betzalel (Zoli) Schultz.[1] *I was born to my parents Franya and Bluma, z"l, in Slovakia in the city Benesca-Bitritz, July 21, 1931. In 1944, after the Nazis invaded Slovakia I was sent to Plaszow Concentration Camp in Crakow. I said I was a a watchmaker and was sent to a division of Henkelworke in Berlin to have my skills tested.*

While waiting to be tested, a young Jew approached me. He encouraged me and helped me to pass the test. Thus, I was accepted as a watchmaker. As a boy of thirteen, I didn't really know much about repairing watches and I needed help. The young man introduced himself as Yaacov Yehoshua Fried. He took me under his care and helped me to finish my daily quotas. Whatever poor, meager food we received depended on how much work we produced. Yaacov Fried, who was an expert watchmaker, gave up the extra food he was entitled to by helping me finish my daily quota. This went on for months. He stayed near me and helped me.

Yaacov was not only an expert watchmaker, but was liked very much by everyone. He was even able to influence the Germans and help many prisoners who were to be punished for not working enough or accused of petty sabotage. Yaacov always succeeded in canceling all such punishments.

On April 21, 1945, as the Russian army neared the concentration camps, the Germans gave orders to evacuate the 60,000 inmates from our camp. The hundreds of Jews left among this multitude were divided into columns of prisoners and ordered to march to an unknown destination. We were forced to march between 30-40 kilometers a day. Those who collapsed on the way were shot to death by the Germans. I weakened after two days and did not have the strength to continue. Yaacov,who was in the same column, carried me on his back for the next two weeks, again saving my life.

Chazal *say that whoever saves* **one** *Jewish life it is as if he saved an entire world. Yaacov Fried saved numerous lives as well as his own, how great must be his merit! In his* zechus, *I was able to make* aliyah *after liberation and raise a family. And my family knows very well the amazing story of the one to whom I owe my salvation – Yaacov Fried.*

Yaacov Yehoshua Fried was born in the late spring of 1920 in the *shtetle* Velky-Buchco, near Sighet. His parents, Yosef and Gita, had a total of eleven children, two of whom died when very young. Yaacov's paternal grandfather, Leib Fried, married Rivka Landau, a descendant of Reb Yecheskel Landau, the *Noda B'Yehuda, zt"l.*

In the mid-1930s, the Fried family struggled to support themselves on their small farm. Yosef noticed some produce and some firewood missing occasionally. He decided to hide in the dark with his young but already strong son Yaacov to try and catch the thief. One night, they heard a wagon approaching and readied themselves for action. However, when they recognized the wagon driver as a fellow Jew from their own village, they remained quietly where they were until he departed. Not daring to shame the man, they allowed him his late night forays until they found a more honorable way to help him and his family.

The Fried family was well known for their *tzedakah* and *chesed*, sharing the little they had with friend and stranger alike. Indigent travelers, of whom there were many, would stop at their house, to have their filthy, lice-ridden, clothes washed and receive a warm meal and a bed overnight. One widow and her two children were given free use of a back room with its own kitchen for their living quarters. They helped care for her children. This is but another example of Yosef's concern for others that he instilled in his son Yaacov and his other offspring, so they would have empathy for others and take extreme measures, if necessary, to alleviate their pain. These sterling *midos* were the only inheritance he left his children after going to his death in Auschwitz.

In 1935 at the age of 15, Yaacov won a contest for having learned the entire *Mesechta Kiddushin* with *Rashi* and *Tosefos ba'al peh*, by heart. In his late teens, Yaacov was forced to leave yeshiva and help his struggling parents. He was apprenticed to a watchmaker. As a young man, he became one of many forced conscripts into the extremely anti-Semitic Hungarian military. As part of the Jewish brigade, Yaacov was given tools instead of weapons.

1. This letter is translated from the original Hebrew correspondence

Yaacov Yehoshua Fried after liberation. Triangular stamp of the Concentration Camp is partially visible on top upper left side.

However, he so impressed his sergeant that he pointed him out to his commanders, boasting that when a sledge was put into Fried's hands, sparks flew. On one occasion, while working on railroad tracks Yaacov lifted an iron rail weighing 670 pounds up to his thigh with his bare hands This great physical strength would enable him, as well as many others, to survive the tortures and deprivations of the concentration camp.

In the spring of 1944, the Jewish residents of Velky-Buchco joined so many others in being deported to concentration camps. Yaacov's kallah, Mirel Pollack, ended up in a camp as well. Her parents, Tzvi and Itta, and her two sisters, Chaya and Chanci, were selected for death on arrival in Auschwitz. She and her two brothers, Yoel and Avraham, were sent to the right side which meant life. Mirel, however, saw a small child crying on its way to the left side that was designated for death and she went towards the child. The infamous Dr. Mengele grabbed Mirel by the arm and threw her violently back to the side she was originally sent to. Of Yaacov's family, his parents, oldest brother Mottel, who had a slight limp, and two youngest sisters were selected for death on arrival. Yaacov and his other five siblings – Dori, Aigi, Shaindi, Rudi and Moishy – were spared, to work at brutal labor. They were subject to beatings and humiliation of every sort while being slowly starved.

Yaacov was selected to work as a watchmaker, risking his own welfare and even his life on numerous occasions to save others from punishment and death. On one occasion, an SS corporal began to beat one of the Jews in Yaacov's workplace with the obvious intention of killing him. Yaacov rushed to an SS officer who appreciated this tall, strong Jew's skill, imploring him to stop this murder. The officer obliged and the Jewish victim was spared. This was just one occasion of many where this noble and heroic man intervened to save others.

On the day of liberation after more than two weeks of murderous forced marching with only an occasional handful of grass for food, Yaacov, like so many others, overate. He became very ill, but fortunately survived.

After recovering in a D.P. Camp in Germany, Yaacov heard the unbelievable news that his kallah had also survived the concentration camp and was on her way by train to join him. Their emotional reunion was witnessed by other survivor relatives and friends with tears of joy and pain. The married and lived in Bad Reichenall until after the birth of their daughter, Ita Gita, when they moved to Netanya, Israel.

In 1952, Mirel gave birth to a son, Yosef Tzvi. At the bris, Yaacov was approached by his cousin, Sarah Forkush, and her husband, Yeedel. Married for almost six years, they had not been blessed with children and were now asking Yaacov for a brochah. Yaacov blessed them that they should have twins by this time next year. Almost to the day one year later, Sarah gave birth to twins, a boy whom they named Motti and a girl Shoshy. They had no children after their twins.

By 1955, Yaacov's thriving business had declined drastically due to socialist governmental policies and he was forced to move his family to Bronx, New York, to join some of his survivor siblings. Life was very hard. One morning on his way to shul Yaacov heard a loud explosion. A propane gas truck had exploded. Yaacov aided the stricken driver by smothering his burning clothes with his coat, burning his wrist in the process. This experience intensified his Auschwitz nightmares. He received a monetary settlement as a result of this accident and made a fresh start in business.

Years later, on September 13, 1970 (13 Elul, 5730) Mirel was nifter at home, succumbing to cancer at the age of 48. She was buried in Natanya, the city she and Yaacov had always planned on returning to. Yaacov and his teenaged son moved back there together, leaving behind his, by then, married daughter. Illness caused him to returned to New York years later and he was nifter on Rosh Chodesh Adar, 5758 (February 18,1988). He was laid to rest beside his beloved wife in Natanya.

Wedding picture of Yaakov Yehoshua and Mirel in Germany after Liberation.

GLOSSARY OF TERMS

ahavas Torah– love for the Torah

aliyah– honor of being called to the Torah

Amen– word recited after a blessing to show one's acceptance of the truth of that blessing

Amora– Talmudic Sages who interpreted the words of the Tannaim

amud– lectern, platform

askan/askanim(pl)– communal worker

Av Beis Din– chief judge of the rabbinical court

aveilus– mourning

Avodas Hashem– Service to G-d

b'revach– comfortably

baal habayis/ba'alei battim(pl)– head of a household, working man learning part-time

baal teshuvah– repentant or returnee to religious observance

badchon– jester, merrymaker

bas– daughter

behaimah/behaimos(pl)– livestock

bein hasedorim– time between morning and afternoon study sessions

Beis Din– Jewish court

Beis Hamikdash– the Holy Temple in Jerusalem

Beis Medrash (Beis Hamedrash) / Battei Medrash(pl)– study hall of a yeshiva

bekisheh– black caftan

ben Torah– Torah scholar

bentching– prayer after meals

bentch licht– light [Shabbos/Yom Tov] candles (Yiddish)

bimah– podium upon which the Torah is placed and read in shul

bitachon– trust in G-d

Bnei Torah– people who follow the teachings of the Torah

bochur / bochurim(pl)– unmarried male student

Boruch Hashem– thank G-d

brochah/brochos(pl)– blessings

bubby– grandmother (Yiddish)

chaburah/chaburos(pl)– organized learning groups

chachom/chachomim(pl)– sage

challah– special loaf of bread made for Shabbos and Yom Tov

chametz– leavening; substance forbidden on Pesach

chanukas habayis– dedication of a new house or building

chassid / chassidim(pl)– follower of a Chassidic movement

Chassidei Umos HaOlam– Righteous Gentiles of the World

chassidic– adhering to Chassidism

chasunah– wedding

chatzer– courtyard

chaveirim– friends

chavrusah– learning partner

Chazal– (acronym for **CH**achomeinu **Z**ichronam **L**i'vrocha) the Sages from the time of the Mishnah and Gemora

chazon / chazonim (pl)– leader of the prayer service; cantor

cheder / chadorim (pl)– orthodox elementary school (usually taught in Yiddish)

cherem– excommunication, ban

chesed– kindness

Cheshvan– the eighth Hebrew month

Chevra Shas– a group that learns Gemora

Chevrah Kadisha– burial society

chiddushei Torah– Torah novellae

chilul– descecration

chinuch– education

chizuk– strength

chochmah– wisdom

chodesh– month

Chol Hamoed– intermediate days of Succos and Passover holidays

cholent– a hot dish of meat, beans and potatoes that is served on Shabbos (Yiddish)

choson– groom

Chumash/Chumashim– the Five Books of Moses

chuppah– wedding canopy

churban– destruction

daven– pray (Yiddish)

dayan/dayanim(pl)– judge

derech eretz– good manners, respect

dikduk– Hebrew grammar

Din Torah– judicial case based on Torah law

divrei chizuk– words of encouragement

divrei Torah– Torah lectures (literally, words of Torah)

drashah/drashos (pl)– sermon

Elul– the sixth Hebrew month

emunah– faith in G-d

Eretz Yisrael– the land of Israel

erev– before, eve of... (erev Pesach, erev Shabbos)

erlicher– honest, moral (Yiddish)

esrog/esrogim(pl)– citron fruit (one of the four species used on Succos)

frum– religious (Yiddish)

frum balabatim– religious working men who are heads of households

frumer yid– a religious Jew (Yiddish)

gabbai/gabbaim(pl)– a) Synagogue official b) Shamosh

gadol/gedolim (pl)– great religious leader

Galus– exile, Diaspora

gaon/gaonim (pl)– genius; brilliant Torah schola

gelt– money (Yiddish)

Gemora / Gemoras (pl)– book of the Talmud

geulah– redemption

goyim– gentiles

hagalah– rinsing (esp. for kashering vessels for Pesach)

hakafah– circuit (with Torah scrolls on Simchas Torah)

halachah– Jewish law

Hallel– song of praise composed of the Tehillim written by King David

hanhaleh– administration

Hashem– G-d, the Creator (lit. "the Name")

hashgachah pratis– Divine Providence

hasmadah– diligence, perseverance

Haskalah– Enlightenment movement which disregarded many Torah laws and traditions

hatzalah– rescue

hatzlachah– success

Havdalah– ceremony at the conclusion of Shabbos and Festivals

heimishe– an Orthodox Jew of similar conviction and outlook (Yiddish)

hesped/hespeidim(pl)– eulogy

heter– permit, license

hislahavus– enthusiasm, deep emotion

illuy– prodigy, genius

k'nas– fine

Kaddish– prayer recited by a mourner (or other individual) in honor of the deceased

kallah– bride

kana'ie– zealot

Kaporos– atonement ritual performed before Yom Kippur

kapoteh– long day coat worn by chassidic Jews (Yiddish)

kashruth– laws of keeping kosher

kavonah– thoughtful intent

Kedoshim– martyrs

kedushah– holiness

Kehillah/Kehillos– community/ communities

kever– grave

kiddush– prayer over wine made before eating on Sabbath and holidays

Kiddush Hashem– Sanctification of G-d's Name

kiruv– drawing near

kivitlach– notes with requests given to Chassidic Rebbes to include in their prayers on behalf of the petitioner

Klal Yisrael– the Jewish Nation

Kohain– priest

Kollel– Rabbinical Seminary

korban/korbanos(pl)– sacrifice(s)

lamdon / lamdonim (pl)– accomplished learner

levayah– funeral

limud HaTorah– Torah study

limudei kodesh– religious studies

loshon hara– tale bearing

m'challel Shabbos– profaning the holiness of the Sabbath day

m'chazek– give spiritual and moral strength

Ma'ariv– the evening prayer service

Machzor– special books of prayer for High Holidays and Festivals

maggid / maggidim (pl)– preacher, lecturer

makome Torah– a place of Torah learning (and living)

malshin– slanderer, informer

marktug– market day (Yiddish)

marror– bitter herbs

mashgiach / mashgichim(pl)– 1. spiritual advisor and mentor of a yeshiva 2. supervisor of kosher food production

maskil / maskilim (pl)– follower of the Enlightenment

Matan Torah– time of the receiving of the Torah

matzaivah– memorial monument

matzliach– successful

maven– knowledgeable, expert

mechanech– teacher

mechiras chametz– sale of chametz to a non-Jew before Pesach

mechitzah– partition

mekubal(im)– mystic(s)

melamed / melamdim (pl)– Torah teacher (male)

Melaveh Malkah– meal eaten after Havdalah in honor of the departing Shabbos

menahel– principal

menuchah– rest

mesader kiddushin– person officiating at a marriage

meshorerim– singers

mesiras nefesh– self-sacrifice on behalf of the Torah

Mezuzah/Mezuzos(pl)– small parchments with passages from the Torah, affixed to most doorposts of Jewish houses

midah/midos(pl)– character traits

mikveh / mikvaos (pl)– ritual bath

Minchah– Afternoon Prayer Service

minhag– custom

minyan/minyanim (pl)– quorum of 10 men necessary for conducting a prayer service

mischazeik– to be encouraged

mispallelim– worshippers

Mishnayos– books of the Oral Law

misnagdim(pl)– opponents of the Chassidic movement

mitzvah/mitzvos(pl)– Torah commandment

mizrach vant– the eastern wall of the synagogue (the most prestigious seats)

modreigah– level

Mora D'asra– Rabbi of a shul

moser– informer

Moshiach– the Redeemer, the Messiah

motzei Shabbos– end of Shabbos (Saturday night)

Musaf– Additional Prayer Service recited on Shabbos and Festivals reflecting the added holiness and joy of the day. Commemorates the special communal offerings brought in the days of the Holy Temple.

mussar– study of ethical behavior

nedavah/nedavos(pl)– donation

nefesh/nefashos(pl)– souls

negel vasser– ritual washing of the hands after sleep

neshamah/neshamos(pl)– soul

niftar– the deceased

nifter– die

niggun– tune, melody

nisayon– test

ohel– tent

Olam Hazeh– This World

oneg Shabbos– enjoyment of Shabbos

Oy Vey– exclamation of concern or distress (Yiddish)

parnasah– income, livelihood

pasuk– verse

payos– side-locks (side-burns)

petirah– death, passing away

pikuach nefesh– saving an endangered life

posek/poskim(pl)– Rabbinic authorities who decide Jewish law

psak halachah– final legal ruling

pushke– charity box (Yiddish)

rebbe– religious leader or teacher

rebbetzin– wife of a religious leader or teacher

Ribbono Shel Olam– Master of the Universe

Rosh Chodesh– beginning of the Jewish month

Rosh Hashanah– the Jewish New Year

Rosh HaYeshiva / Roshei Yeshiva (pl)– dean of the yeshiva

Rov / rabbonim (pl)– Rabbi of a congregation and community

ruach– spirit

ruchnius– spirituality

seder / sedorim (pl)– learning session

sefer / seforim (pl)– religious book

seichel– intellect, understanding

seudah– festive meal

Shacharis– Morning Prayer Service

shadchon– matchmaker

sh'ailah/sh'ailos(pl)– questions concerning Jewish law and practice

shalosh seudos– the third Shabbos meal

shamosh– a) Synagogue caretaker
b) Rebbe's assistant or personal secretary

Shas– complete set of Talmud

Shechinah– Divine Presence

shechitah– ritual slaughter

shecht– to slaughter an animal according to Jewish law

sherayim– remainders of a Rebbe's meal, eaten by his chassidim

shidduch– match (for marriage)

shiur / shiurim (pl)– 1. class 2. lesson

shiva– seven day mourning period observed for the death of a close relative

shleimus– completeness, perfection

shliach mitzvah– emissary for a mitzvah

shliach tzibur– person leading the prayer service

shmues / shmussen (pl)– lecture on ethics and proper conduct

shochet / shochtim (pl)– ritual slaughterer

Shomer Shabbos– Sabbath observer

shtetle/shtetlach(pl)– villages (Yiddish)

shtible/shtiblach(pl)– Chassidic shuls (Yiddish)

shul– synagogue

sifrei kedushah– holy books

Sifrei Torah– Torah scrolls

simchah/simchos (pl)– joy, joyous occasion

Siyata D'Shemaya– G-d's help

smichah– rabbinical ordination

streimel– round fur hat worn by chassidic Jews (Yiddish)

Succos– the holiday of Tabernacles

siyum– completion (usually of a Talmudic tractate)

tallis/talleism– prayer shawl

talmid chachom/talmidei chachomim– Torah scholars

talmid / talmidim (pl)– yeshiva student

Talmud– explanation of the Oral Law (*Mishnah*)

talmud Torah– study of Torah

Tanach– books of the Torah, Prophets and Writings

Tanna– Authority quoted in the Mishnah

tefillah/tefillos– prayer(s)

tefillah b'tzibbur– public prayer (with a minyan)

tefillin– phylacteries

teharah– purification

Tehillim– the book of Psalms written by King David

Tishah B'Av– the 9th of Av, a fast day commemorating the destruction of the Beis Hamikdash

tzaddik/tzaddikim(pl)– righteous person

tzadeikes– righteous woman

tzedakah– charity and kindness

tzenuah– modest woman

tzibur– community, congregation

tzidkus– righteousness

tzoros– troubles

ushpizen– Divine Guest (forefather who legendarily "visit" during Succos)

Viduy– confess (recited on Yom Kippur and before death)

yahrtzeit– anniversary of a person's death

yahrtzeit shiur– a Torah lecture given on the anniversary of one's death

yemach sh'mo– may his name be blotted out

yeshiva/yeshivos– schools where Torah is taught

yeshiva gedolah– religious high school

yeshiva k'tanah– religious elementary school

Yeshiva Shel Maalah– Heaven, where the souls of the righteous dwell

yichus– important family lineage

Yid / Yidden (pl)– Yiddish word for a Jew

yirah– fear, usually associated with fear of Heaven

yiras Shomayim– fear of Heaven (G-d)

Yomim Noraim– Days of Awe

Yom Kippur– Day of Atonement

yom tov– religious holiday

z"l-zichrono l'vrachah– May his memory be a blessing

z'man tevillah– time of ritual immersion in a mikveh

z'man– A specific amount of time; a school session

zechus– merit, privilege

zemiros– Sabbath songs

zocheh– to merit

BIBLIOGRAPHY

Encyclopedia Judaica, Keter Publishing, Jerusalem, Israel, 1976

Fuchs, Abraham, **The Unheeded Cry**, Mesorah Publications, Brooklyn, New York, 1986.

Gilbert, Martin, **The Atlas Of The Holocaust**, William Morrow, New York, New York, 1988

Hoyt, Edwin P., **Hitler's War**, McGraw-Hill Publishing Company, New York, 1988

Kasnett, Yitzchak, **The World That Was: Lithuania**, Hebrew Academy of Cleveland, Cleveland, Ohio, 1996

Kasnett, Yitzchak, **The World That Was: Poland**, Hebrew Academy of Cleveland, Cleveland, Ohio, 1997

Kranzler, David, **Thy Brother's Blood: The Orthodox Jewish Response During the HOLOCAUST**, Mesorah Publications, New York, 1987

Levin, Nora, **The Holocaust**, Crowell Publishers, New York, 1968

The Encyclopedia of the Holocaust, Macmillian Publishers, New York, 1990

Rakeffet-Rothkoff, Aaron, **The Silver Era,** Feldheim, New York, 1988

The Stone Edition: **The Chumash**, Mesorah Publications, Brooklyn, New York, 1993

Note: For a comprehensive listing of additional books and related materials, **please see page 272**

The Student Guide to THE WORLD THAT WAS: HUNGARY/ROMANIA

Questions, Topics for Research and Discussion, Activities and Map Exercises

by Rabbi Yitzchak Kasnett, M.S.

Student Exercises

Questions for—
THE HISTORY OF JEWISH LIFE IN HUNGARY

Note to teacher and student: both Thy Brother's Blood by David Kranzler and The Unheeded Cry by Abraham Fuchs are invaluable resources for additional information to answer many of these questions. The student is referred to the Bibliography for complete information on these volumes.

1. What is "polemic" literature?
2. What form did anti-Semitism take in the 1890s in Hungary? What parallels can you draw to German anti-Semitism as it developed in the 1930s?
3. What is a "canard" and how was it used against the Jews of Hungary (and elsewhere) during WWI?
4. In what three distinct territorial divisions were the Jews of Hungary recognized?
5. Write a short biographical report on the *Chasam Sofer* and his influence on Hungarian Jewry.
6. When was the General Jewish Congress convened?

Group Exercise–

7. Pick one of the *chassidic* groups of Hungary and write a short report on the history of that sect. This exercise can be completed in small working groups.

Class Discussion–

8. When was the number of Jews in institutions of higher learning restricted to 5%? Hold a class discussion concerning this everyday fact of life that Jews faced throughout their exile in Europe: the restriction on Jews from owning property, starting or entering into a business, which days business could be conducted, special residence taxes, etc. This is not (thank G-d) part of the American-exile experience today, so it is not part of our consciousness. However, it will be very beneficial to discuss this issue within the class regarding the number of Jews who can live in a certain area, hold certain jobs, the numbers of schools that can be opened, restrictions on owning property, etc. (See questions 9, 10 and 16).
9. When was the "First Jewish Law" enacted? Who was included and what regulations did the bill contain?
10. What was the "Second Jewish Law"? What did it contain and what resulted from its enactment?
11. How did the Jews respond to the First and Second Jewish Laws?

Class Project–

12. Do you think the response of "greater emphasis on their patriotic attachment to Hungary" is a mistaken response? What historical precedents

can you bring to support your contention? In small working groups prepare your answers in well formulated and documented essays. This exercise will require very mature thinking and thorough discussion.

13. What was the state of Jewish demographics after WWI?
14. How many Jews lived in Hungary in 1930?
15. Fill in the following chart:

DATE	TERRITORY ANNEXED	NUMBER OF JEWS
11/2/38		
3/15/39		
8/30/40		
4/41		
Population of Hungary in 1/41	**Total Number of Jews in 1/41**	**Percent Jews Constitute of Total Budapest Population**

16. When was the "Third Jewish Law" passed? What were its effects?
17. What took place in the autumn of 1941? January, 1942?
18. When were the Jewish labor battalions organized? What was the eventual outcome?
19. What took place on March 10, 1942? What were the positive and negative outcomes of this event?
20. Explain the political posturing behind Kallay's pledge of resettlement in April, 1942.
21. In April of 1943, what was the German response to Kallay's initiatives against the Jews?
22. What political moves did Kallay make at the end of 1943?
23. Create a chart reviewing Kallay's actions during the War in trying to maintain a balance between satisfying the German demand for action against the Jews while simultaneously attempting to maintain the lives of the Jews (even while persecuting them) in order to steer Hungary in a positive position to make peace with the Allies if possible. Use the headings supplied below, adding as many rows as you need.

PRO-GERMAN ACTIONS AGAINST THE JEWS	ACTIONS TAKEN AGAINST DEPORTATIONS OF THE JEWS

Student Exercises

24. When did the Germans occupy Hungary? What promoted this action and what was it called?
25. Prior to German occupation, how many Hungarian Jews had been killed? What per cent of the population was this?
26. Make a chart filling in the following information (using the column headings below) from March 13, 1944 until July 9, 1944. Add as many rows as you need for your chart.

DATE	GERMAN ACTION AGAINST THE JEWS OF HUNGARY	NUMBER OF JEWS INVOLVED IN THESE ACTIONS (WHEN NOTED)

27. Create a chart filling in the requested information.

AREA	NUMBER OF GHETTOS	NUMBER OF JEWS IN THE GHETTOS
TOTAL		

28. Who was Aron Marton? Why is he unique and why is this a resounding condemnation of the Hungarian people in general?
29. In what ways did some Jews escape deportation? In general, in which area did they reside?
30. Who is the "Haman" who administered Auschwitz?
31. Write a short report about the Kastner Transport. Refer to The **Unheeded Cry** and **Thy Brother's Blood** as main sources for this report.
32. Write a short report on the Kastner-Brand-Eichmann negotiations. Again, refer to **The Unheeded Cry** and **Thy Brother's Blood** .
33. What does "*entjudung*", mean?
34. What took place on October 15, 1944?
35. What did Eichmann do before leaving Hungary on August 24th? When did he return?
36. Create and complete the following chart adding rows as necessary.

BUDAPEST JEWS FROM JUNE 15, 1944 UNTIL BEGINNING OF OCTOBER, 1944		
Date	**Actions Taken by Germans/Hungarians** (list names of individuals or institutions involved)	**Facts and Figures of What Transpired**

37. What plans were implemented against the Jews after October15th? What was the outcome?
38. When did the Russians reach Budapest? When did they occupy the city?
39. What happened to many of the Jews in the labor battalions at the end of the War?

Class Exercise–

40. 98,000 of the capital city's Jews lost their lives during the fascist Arrow-Cross party rule and reign of terror. Take a reference atlas (or other such reference book) and list the cities and towns in America with populations of 98,000 or less. Divide the alphabetical listing of the cities among several working groups of students with each group responsible for listing the cities with names starting with those letters of the alphabet. How many cities and towns were listed and, thus, could have been completely wiped off the face of America? Does the number 98,000 mean more to you now? Discuss this exercise in class.
41. What rescue and protection efforts were attempted on behalf of Budapest's Jews?
42. How many Jews (and those considered Jews) survived the War? How many perished? What per cent of the over all population are those who perished?
43. How did anti-Semitism remain active after the War?

Student Exercises

Questions for— THE HISTORY OF JEWISH LIFE IN ROMANIA

1. When did Jews originally settle in Romania?
2. Why was Walachia important to the Jews in ancient times?
3. What took place in 1648-1649? Prepare a short report on this bitter time. The book, **The Year of the Sword**, by Avner Gold, published by CIS Publications in Lakewood, New Jersey, is a historical fiction of that period of time and is well worth reading. Some material may be too disturbing and upsetting to read. Please have your teacher or parent review the material first.

Class Project–

4. What charters were enacted to attract Jews from Poland? When did this take place and what were additional reasons for attracting Jews from other countries? How is this part of the cycle of European anti-Semitism that existed for over a thousand years? Please explain the steps in this cycle: a) From a political/economic perspective, and b) From a spiritual perspective. Both of these perspectives should be discussed in class before beginning your essay.
5. What took place in 1579?
6. Why is Jassy a place of infamy for the Jewish people?
7. What laws were enacted in 1640? By whom?
8. What was the first "modern day" trouble for the Jews of Romania?
9. What is a "protectorate"?
10. From 1835 in Moldavia and Walachia (and in Romania in general), what was the attitude towards the Jews?
11. The "Pale of Settlement" is a well known expression of the Jewish experience in Russia. What does it mean, how did it start and what purpose did it serve?
12. What is the *Chacham Bashi*? When did this position begin and what purpose did it serve?
13. What problems did the office of *Chacham Bashi* encounter and, eventually, why was it abolished?
14. What is a "guild" and what purpose did it serve?
15. What was the internal structure of Romanian Jewry like in the early 1800s?
16. Who was involved in the Crimean War, why was it fought and how was it concluded with the Peace Treaty of Paris? How did this affect the Jews?
17. What was the Jewish population of Romania in 1859?
18. What does the word "suffrage" mean and how many Jews were naturalized in 1864?

Student Exercises

19. What took place in 1866 and how did it affect the Jews of Romania?
20. Who is Ion Bratianu and what actions did he take against the Jews? How did the Romanian government respond?
21. How did Romania respond to the demands for Jewish civil rights at the Congress of Berlin in 1878? Who convened this congress, what was its purpose and the eventual outcome of its goal for the Jews of Romania?
22. What took place in 1893?
23. What was the National Democratic party and who founded it? See if you can find any biographical material on these two men.
24. Complete the following table and explain the politics behind the statistics:

% of Jews living in cities:________	**% of total urban population:________**
% of Jews living in villages:________	**% of total rural population:________**

25. Complete the following table:

1899: % OF JEWISH POPULATION IN VARIOUS TOWNS IN MOLDAVIA	
Falaticeni	
Dorohoi	
Botosani	
Jassy	
Gertsa	
Mihaileni	
Harlu	
Panciu	

26. Jews comprised only 20% of all artisans, in which six crafts did they constitute the clear majority?

CRAFT	PERCENT OF JEWS

Student Exercises

27. In what industry did Jews own more than half of the industrial firms?
28. Complete the following table:

ROMANIA: DISTRIBUTION OF JEWS BY OCCUPATION	
Agriculture	
Industry and Crafts	
Trade and Banking	
Liberal Professions	
Various Other	

29. What was the political and social situation for the Jews of the following provinces annexed to Romania after the fall of the Austria-Hungarian Empire?
    a. Bessarabia
    b. Transylvania
    c. Bukovina
    In small working groups, write a short report of the history of the Jews in one of these provinces.
30. What affected the occupational structure of the Jews in the 1930s? Explain how this was a repetition of the cycle of persecution that occurred in each country. Through research and your own projections, what is the effect of such a situation on the population regarding both the short and long term effects?
31. Romanian Jews mostly immigrated from which two countries?
32. What effect did the German penetration into the Romanian economy have on the Jews? (See question 30.)
33. In the summer of 1940, how was Romania reduced in size territorially?
34. Why did Romania become a satellite of Nazi Germany in June of 1940? What resulted from this in August of that year?
35. What took place on September 6, 1940 and what resulted from this over the next five months?
36. When did the Iron Guard revolt against Antonescu, what took place during the revolt and why did Hitler support Antonescu?
37. What was the political aftermath of this revolt and its subsequent effects?
38. When did the massacre of the Jews of Jassy take place? Write a short report on the events leading up to the destruction that took place.
39. From July 3 until September 1, 1941 what was the disposition of the Jews of Bukovina, Bessarabia and Dorohoi?
40. After September 1, what measures were taken against the Jews?
41. What happened to the Jews sent to Transnistria?

42. What was the *Bukarester Tageblatt*? What purpose did it serve?
43. What happened to the deportation plans of July 22, 1942?
44. Why were the Romanians willing to allow Jews to be deported to Transnistria and then to emigrate to Palestine?
45. From 1942 to August 1944 how many Jews escaped Romania? How did they escape and what two tragedies occurred?
46. What financial pressures were brought against the Jews at the beginning of 1943?
47. How were they Jews of Transnistria saved from slaughter by the retreating Germans?
48. Who is Ira Hirschmann and what role did he play?
49. What took place on August 23, 1944?
50. What per cent of the Jewish population of Romania survived the Holocaust?
51. What demographic effect did the War have on the Jewish population of Romania?
52. After having read the Romanian History section and answered many of these questions, what is your emotional reaction to the Jewish experience in Romania? What is your opinion of the Romanians?

Student Exercises

Questions for Interview with Rabbi Weiss—SURVIVAL IN BUDAPEST

Class Assignment: questions 1-4 are interrelated and should be studied and answered together.

1. In one sense, why did Hitler feel compelled to wage World War II?
2. On what day did World War I begin?
3. Write a brief summary of the events that led to WW II.
4. There is an excellent overview explaining *Tishah B'Av* in the book on *Megillas Eichah*, published by Mesorah Publication. It will be very beneficial to review that essay in answering this question from the perspective of a member of *Am Yisrael*. In order to understand the social and political forces that shaped Hitler's thinking, refer to **Hitler's War**, by Edwin P. Hoyt, published by McGraw-Hill, 1988. Explain how the spiritual causes of the Holocaust created the overt social and political causes. This question should be thoroughly discussed in class before beginning your essay. Additionally, any information that you can provide concerning the beginning of WWII and its inherent relationship to how WWI ended will be helpful. When possible, copy this material or summarize it for hand-outs for the members of the class.
4. What did the Skoloya Rebbe pray for after WWI ended? How does this relate to question 3?
5. Write a brief summary of Rabbi Weiss' comparison of the Holocaust and our present exile to the exile in *Mitzrayim*.
6. Where was Rabbi Weiss born?
7. When was Czechoslovakia created?
8. What is the Sudentenland?
9. How did recent political events in Czechoslovakia differ from those in Yugoslavia with the collapse of the Soviet Union?
10. How many children from Czechoslovakia are thought to have survived WW II? How do you interpret this phenomenon in light of the answer to question 9?
11. How old was Rabbi Weiss in 1939?
12. Who was the first president of Czechoslovakia?
13. What does it mean that the Czech part of the country where Rabbi Weiss lived was called the "little America of Europe"?
14. What was the mental and emotional disposition of the Weiss family when the War began?
15. What is a Communist? A Fascist? Explain the differing ideologies and how they would conflict.

16. What kindness did the *Yid* in the Gestapo office do for Mr. Weiss? What happened because of his actions? Do you think he knew that this could be the result, yet he acted anyway? Explain.
17. What incident occurred when Mrs. Weiss was in the headquarters? Could you have acted in a similar manner?
18. What does Rabbi Weiss mean when he says "Just like that, like a robot, he reverted to his Nazi Persona?"
19. What is "*siyata d'Shemaya*?"
20. What incidents of salvation took place on the train to Hungary, and what was so astonishing given the horrid circumstances?
21. Where did the Weiss family go in Hungary and why did Mr. Weiss leave the family?
22. What does the word *me'sheberach* mean, and how is it used by Rabbi Weiss? What was the outcome of the incident? Why was it possible for "*Zaidy* to take out his cane and gave me a spanking worse than the one I received from the *rebbe*"? Could such an incident happen today? Explain, keeping in mind Rabbi Weiss' statement at the end of that paragraph that so much more was accomplished in learning in Europe than in America during the course of one year.
23. Why was there no such thing as a parent disagreeing with a *rebbe*?
24. Why did the Weiss family have to "quietly disappear"? What kind of feelings do you think they experienced? Write 10 adjectives that describe that feeling (or feelings).
25. What was Mr. Weiss really doing in Budapest and why could he not tell his wife?

Class Discussion and Exercise

26. Why are most things in life relative? Discuss this question in class and answer it using at least three poignant and powerful examples from this interview. In addition, explain why such an understanding can be of the greatest benefit in life. Finally, for students in the higher grades, why is understanding relative meaning not just rationalizing? Explain in a well thought-out essay, after first discussing this question in class. Be sure to provide examples and illustrations from your own life experiences.
27. How did the Hungarians lure the Jews into enslavement as Pharaoh did? List the steps taken.
28. How old was Rabbi Weiss when he had to wear the yellow star, and what did he do about it? Why was this advantageous, though dangerous?
29. Why does Rabbi Weiss feel that his family was saved during the War?

Student Project

30. Move your family into one half of one room for a few days (if possible) and record your emotional, physical and mental reaction to this exercise.

Student Exercises

31. Though Rabbi Weiss states that a mentally unstable woman screamed at the wounded Germans and placed them in danger – which, of course, was not helpful – what would you like to say to a few of those heartless murderers of Jewish babies and young children? Write an essay to the German nation expressing your emotions. The more artistic students can create an art work (any art medium) to express their feelings. You may divide into small groups to compose this essay.
32. Explain why it was an inane accusation that the Jews were signaling to the American bomber pilots.
33. Imagine you are in the bomb shelter reciting the *Shema* as the bombs are falling. Record your thoughts and emotions as that time in the form of a diary entry.
34. What does it tell you that even the non-religious recited *Shema* with such devotion? Explain.
35. What does it mean to act "unilaterally"?
36. Write a short report on the governmental figures who ruled Hungary during WW II.
37. What did Mrs Weiss do when the Germans entered the bomb shelter? On what other occasion did something like this occur?
38. How does Rabbi Weiss describe the German army? What does "incarnate" mean?
39. Why was Mr. Weiss stationed in an army compound? What did this mean?

Class Project

40. Imagine standing in a room seeing your parents (or other relatives) crying as they parted, knowing that they may never see each other again. Write 10 words that express your emotions or draw a picture depicting this scene. Be sure that the picture expresses the emotions of the separation, so use colors that effectively convey the emotions present at that time. You can use any artistic medium you wish.

Class Discussion

41. Imagine risking your life to eat a potato. Don't do anything, don't write anything, just sit and think about this for a few minutes and then discuss it with the other members of the class.
42. Compose a story that the man in the pot belly stove might have related about this hair raising episode.
43. What is your response to the offer of the Church? How did the Jews of Budapest respond? What example of this do you have in *Tanach*?
44. What did the *shicker* say and how did people respond to him? How did Mrs. Weiss respond? How would you have responded? Describe an incident when you were doubtful as to the veracity of what someone was telling you and why you decided to believe this person or not.

Student Exercises

45. Did you ever think that spare shoe soles would be important to take when running for your life? What would you have listed as important? What do you learn from this? Explain.

46. What mental subterfuge did the Germans inflict against the Jews?

Classroom Discussion and Research Project

47. There is a perception that the Jews "went like sheep to the slaughter." Do you think this is a canard, a lie and shameful protest by gentiles to cover their guilt, or do you think that there is truth to this statement? What statement by Rabbi Weiss is the critical element to consider regarding this question? Discuss this question in class, review some of the sources in the Reading List, consider the overall situation of the Jews under German control and, in small working groups, present your opinion to the class in a well organized and persuasive presentation. When possible, bring source material to substantiate your contention.

48. Why is it sometimes safest to hide in the "lion's den"? What happened in this interview to that effect and why is it termed "lion's den"?

49. If you have ever been to a bungalow colony or a camp, you know that (usually) there is only a small crawl space underneath the building and that it is usually overgrown with weeds and other things that creep on and in the earth. Imagine what it would be like to have to hide there for a long period of time and express your thoughts to the class.

50. Do you think anyone really knew what to do to be saved during the Holocaust? Think about how people were saved and refer to some of the sources in the Reading List. Write a statement that presents your conviction and position regarding how the survivors, in fact, survived.

51. Fill in the following table using adjectives, adverbs and anecdotes describing and contrasting how life has proceeded for you and for Rabbi Weiss. Add on as many rows as you need.

RABBI WEISS: "This is how lives proceed, with one decree of annihilation after another."	YOU: "This is how life proceeds..."

Student Exercises

52. Rabbi Weiss comments that one ". . . always had to be careful, very careful." Explain how living like this affects one emotionally, physically and mentally.

Research Project

53. Who was Raoul Wallenburg and what did he do for the Jews of Budapest? There are many sources available to you to use in your research to answer this question.

54. Did the Germans honor their agreements with the Swedish government? Explain.

55. In the form of a diary entry, put yourself in Rabbi Weiss' place and record your thoughts and feelings when he went to receive the Swedish protection papers. Think for a while about the position he was in before writing your entry.

56. Have you ever been given any tickets to "*Gan Eden*"? What do you think is your ticket to *Gan Eden* and what do you think *Gan Eden* really is?

57. How does fear motivate someone? Describe the various thoughts that you think Rabbi Weiss may have had racing through his head as he escaped from the *rugginturs*.

Multi-media / Art Project

58. In any artistic medium, express what his block looked like to Rabbi Weiss as he returned home to see that the Germans had ripped up the street and surrounded the buildings. For those students who are not artistic, perhaps you can supply the lighting and background sounds that would appropriately reflect the mood of that scene.

59. List 10 words that describe Rabbi Weiss' psychological-emotional state as he stood knocking at the door surrounded by Germans.

Classroom Discussion

60. Discuss the impact of the following statement by Rabbi Weiss: "I later found out that my parents greatly despaired, thinking they would never see me again, and that I would never get the message they left with the doctor and thus find them! When I arrived at the new building the joy of our reunion was beyond description. To be reunited was overwhelming." Did you or one of your siblings ever get separated from the family during an outing, etc.? Use this as the emotional jump-off point for this discussion.

61. What is a good reason never to eat the fish from the Danube River? In what other river did a similar situation take place.

Class Activity

62. Using some type of identity document, a calligraphy pen and any other supplies necessary, attempt to forge the document by copying it very carefully. See if you can employ the potato as the Jews in Budapest did. While this may be somewhat of an enjoyable activity, imagine that your life may well depend on how well forged these papers really are.

Student Exercises

63. Define the expression ". . . subtle – almost imperceptible – dictates of Divine *Hashgachah*."
64. Define the words "clandestine" and "duplicitous."
65. How was the Polish underground repaid for their treachery against the Jews of the ghetto?
66. What took place on August 23, 1939, and what was the importance of this event?
67. What did Hitler try to learn from Napoleon?
68. What tactical error did Hitler make in his invasion of Russia?
69. This question has two parts:
    a. Describe the emotion in the room the morning Mr. Weiss decided that he would remain with the family.
    b. What emotion or thought did you experience after reading about the finality of Mr. Weiss' decision and Rabbi Weiss' statement, "That was it, we would all share the same fate, and if we perished, we would perish together"? Explain.
70. What is "systematic humiliation" and what is it calculated to achieve?
71. What were the four levels of the Hungarian war machine that was so effectively used in fighting hapless Jews, but didn't fare too well against their Russian enemy carrying guns?
72. What strategy did Mrs. Weiss devise to rescue her husband in the park? List at least two moral lessons that can be learned from this episode.
73. Make a list of what one must do and think of in order to infiltrate the Hungarian Nazis as that guard did.
74. After reading that 80 people in a small apartment was considered *Gan Eden*, how will you view being in a crowded situation in the future?
75. What is your response to Mr. Weiss' efforts to bring a stove into their room in the apartment?
76. What do you learn from Rabbi Weiss' comment that "Every such little improvement in our living condition was a *ye'shuah gedolah*, a great salvation, for us. This was a real luxury: a stove for cooking"? Explain.
77. Can you imagine a young child sifting though piles of dead bodies looking for a relative?
    Explain.
78. The cellar or the upper floor? Which would you have chosen: to be killed (possibly, maybe even likely) by a bomb or a bullet? Explain.
79. What is conditioned behavior?
    List several examples of this from our interview.
80. Cite an example where something seemingly very unfortunate turned out to be a blessing, literally a real life saver.

Student Exercises

Class Project

81. When one does not have proper nutrition, what are the progressive symptoms of malnutrition? Ask a doctor, nurse or nutritionist to explain this to you. Additionally, you can write to the local Department of Health for information on this topic.

To be considered . . .

82. The next time someone in your house asks you to go to the store (or do some other errand) and you don't want to because it may be a little hard, or you may be a bit lazy, remember Rabbi Weiss' trip to the local pharmacy and maybe it will make it easier for you to – thankfully – be able to perform the errand safely and without worry.
83. On what date was the Weiss family liberated from the Budapest Ghetto?
84. Why did Mrs. Weiss want to speak in Russian with the Russian soldiers? Why did Mr. Weiss instruct her otherwise? What incident took place and who was right?
85. What occurred in Budapest directly after the Russians liberated the city? What teaching does Rabbi Weiss quote regarding this situation? Research the commentaries to this teaching and explain why it is so important. What other such teachings/instructions support and augment this teaching from this same source?
86. How did the Weisses make *Pesach* in the spring of 1945? Comparing this to how you prepare for *Pesach*, what lesson(s) can be drawn from the comparison?
87. As you are approaching the tunnel pressing yourself into the roof of the train car, what are your thoughts? Record them as a diary entry after having arrived home safely that evening. Be sure to use vivid and descriptive words that convey the drama of the situation as experienced by Rabbi Weiss' parents.
88. What frightening incident took place during the train trip from Hungary to Prague? After describing what happened, record your reaction to this pitiful predicament. As in question 87, be sure to use vivid and descriptive words that convey the emotional intensity of the situation.

Small Group Research Project

89. The two serendipitous discoveries of survivors that Rabbi Weiss mentions are only two examples of such meetings. Research some of the books in the bibliography, and from other sources as well (including speaking with survivors and their relatives when possible and appropriate) and see if you can record other such meetings.
90. In one short paragraph, Rabbi Weiss defines the true heroism of the Jewish people during the War. Comment on his statement and research other such *acts of heroism* in the sources listed in the bibliography and from other sources as well.

Questions for Interview with Mr. Ostreicher— REMEMBERING MUNKACS

1. Why was Munkacs known as an "*Ir v'aim b'Yisrael*"?
2. Could the incident with the shopkeeper on *erev* Shabbos take place today? Explain why or why not.
3. How many *Battei Medrash* were there in Munkacs?
4. Besides the Munkacs *chassidus*, what other *chassidic* sects were represented in the city?
5. What is a *kanai*?
6. How did the experience of the Jews of Czechoslovakia differ from that of the Jews in Poland?
7. What type of action did the Czech tax collection officials employ to obtain their revenues? Could this happen in America? What protections do Americans enjoy from such practices? Did the Czech actions foster overtones of anti-Semitism?
8. What dialogue ensued between the Minchas Elozer and Dr. Edward Benes?

Research Project: Designing a research project using variables when a direct answer is not apparent:

9. Did the Czechoslovakian's lazy attitude toward religion mean that they persecuted the Jews less than the more religious gentiles of Poland, Hungary and Romania? There may not be any readily available statement answering this question, so, as a class, define the variables or factors to research that will help you in compiling the facts necessary to formulate your answer.
10. What role did the Mr. Ostreicher's father fulfill for the Minchas Elozer? What political office did he seek?
11. What are some of the more important communities that made up the Carpathian-Russian area?

Small Discussion Group Exercise

12. Mr. Ostreicher says that, "In general, for the Jews of Eastern Europe it was far from simple living in such a precarious situation with such neighbors." What is your response to this statement? Consider the ramifications of this statement, or discuss it in small groups, before committing your thoughts to paper.
13. Who was Reb Yosef Zorach, and what were his accomplishments?
14. Eat a piece of bread and a little piece of onion (or green pepper, etc.) for dinner for a few nights one week. Then write an essay entitled "How Far – or Close – We are to The World That Was . . ." Submit these essays to The Living Memorial at the address found on the back of the volume, care of Rabbi A. Leibel Scheinbaum.

Student Exercises

15. Record your response to the quote, "My mother told me that no one will ever look into my stomach to see what's there, but people will always see how I present myself. My mother is concerned that I should always look neat and presentable."

16. Why is the wrought iron inscription on Reb Yosef Zorach's porch important?

Class Project

17. Write to the organization, *Asra Kadisha*, 203 Penn Street, Brooklyn, NY 11211, (914)783-9626, concerning efforts that have been extended to save and restore Jewish cemeteries throughout Eastern Europe. Additionally, you can contact Agudath Israel of America at 84 William Street, New York, New York 10038, for information regarding this issue. Compile the information into a bulletin-board display with maps showing the location of cemeteries that have been restored, those yet to be restored and reports highlighting the progress, success and difficulties encountered in these various initiatives. Finally, Mr. Reuven Dessler, who is responsible for the restoration of the Jewish cemetery in Kelm, Radin and Volozhin can be contacted at the address for The Living Memorial on the back of this volume.

Class Project

18. What is the organizational structure and history of your yeshiva? Investigate these issues and write a short history of the yeshiva or Day School, including pictures and, if possible, an interview or two – perhaps it will be used in the next dinner journal or other such publication. Be sure to record all of the personalities and efforts expended to bring the idea of the yeshiva from idea to fruition.

19. What valuable lesson about Torah did Mr. Ostreicher learn in Slotfino?

20. What cities are located in the Oberland area of Hungary, and which are located in the Unterland area?

21. What 10 adjectives would you choose to describe Mr. Ostreicher's feelings about the Munkacs of his youth? Make a list and then compare your word choices with the others in the class to see which words are chosen most frequently. Obviously, you must do the first part of this exercise completely independent from everyone else in the class.

22. Why was it *impossible* to speak with the Minchas Elozer the day after Rosh Hashanah? Who would you choose for such a purpose?

23. Locate Trieste, Italy on a map. Where in Italy is it located, and what large cities are located nearby?

24. Based on Mr. Ostreicher's description of the Minchas Elozer's behavior during the Succos holiday, what 10 words would you use to describe his personality?

25. How much is the *kronen* worth in today's financial market?

Student Exercises

26. Mr. Ostreicher remarks that the spirit of Chanukah in Eastern Europe was much different from that in America today, and that giving gifts has everything to do with America and nothing to do with Chanukah – "Our enjoyment was more spiritual in nature." Explain his comments in detail, and why you agree or disagree with his observation.
27. Explain the terms *kopelia* and *meshorerim*.
28. Explain the connection the Minchas Elozer made between Purim and Yom HaKippurim?
29. What does the word *spielers* mean?
30. Before *Pesach*, what functions did the *mikveh* provide to the community?
31. What does the expression *Yekki* mean.
32. What activities took place *Shavuos* night in Munkacs?
33. Do you find the same level of exuberance and endurance during your *yomim tovim* that was exhibited in Munkacs? Explain.
34. When did the Hungarians enter Munkacs, and what measures did they take to begin their oppression of the Jews?
35. What is the weight of a *deca*?
36. Why did Mr. Ostreicher's family lose their lease on the *mikvaos*?
37. How old was Mr. Ostreicher when he left for Budapest? Who went with him?
38. Where did Mr. Ostreicher stay when he first arrived in Budapest? What surprise did he find there?
39. Where did Mr. Ostreicher go initially to begin investigating a prospective business? What business did he get involved in and how did he do in this endeavor?
40. What do the words *flokon* and *korton* mean?
41. Using an atlas, or other reference source, calculate how far it is from Budapest to Munkacs in miles and kilometers.
42. What was the second business that Mr. Ostreicher engaged in while in Budapest?
43. What is a *napshis*? A *razia*?
44. Where were the Polish nationals sent after being caught by the *Gendarmerie*? What happened to them?
45. When was Rabbi Rabinowitz arrested by the *Gendarmerie* and what happened to him?
46. Describe the *Yomim Noraim* in Munkacs in 1941. Imagine the scene in the city beyond what is conveyed in the actual words of the interview in order to create a description that truly conveys the condition of the Jews in Munkacs at that time.
47. What took place by the grave of the Darkei Teshuvah? On what date did this happen?

48. When did Rabbi Rabinowitz leave for the relative safety of Budapest and what did he get involved with there?
49. What did the men do to try to avoid military service?
50. Why did the Germans ask for Hungarian soldiers and how many were sent to the front?
51. What took place on January 2, 1942?
52. What unusual events took place in Budapest after January 2, 1942?
53. When did Rabbi Rabinowitz escape from Budapest, where did he go and what did he take along with him? What happened to his *rebbetzin*?
54. Who was Nicolas Horthy and what happened to him?
55. Who succeeded Horthy and what implications did this have for the Jews?
56. When did the Germans occupy Hungary?
57. When did Eichmann come to Hungary?
58. Fill in the following table:

PLACE OF DEPORTATION	NUMBER OF JEWS DEPORTED
Carpatho-Russia	
Hungary proper	
TOTAL	
DATES AND NUMBER OF DAYS DEPORTATIONS LASTED	
NUMBER OF JEWS KILLED DURING THIS TIME PERIOD	NUMBER KILLED
Every Week	
Every Day	
Every Hour	
Every Minute	

59. Describe the situation of the Jews in the Hungarian Army in 1941 and what eventually happened to them and those in the infamous *Munka Tabor*.
60. Why didn't the Munkacser Jews believe the reports of the Polish Jews regarding the Germans?
61. Recount the story of the *moser* and his partner Getzel and your response to it.
62. What dealings did Mr. Ostreicher have with a *moser*, when did the incident take place, what was the consequence and where did Mr. Ostreicher go immediately afterwards?

63. Compose an essay expressing your perception of just how difficult everyday life was – emotionally, financially and spiritually – for the Jews of Hungary during the year of 1942.
64. Describe the plan Mr. Ostreicher devised to save himself, and many others, from being inducted into the *Munka Tabor*. Additionally, record your own thoughts regarding his actions and the qualities of character that support one taking such action. Finally, make a list of the thoughts and details that he must have entertained in order to successfully accomplish such an endeavor.
65. What took place on the train from Budapest to Munkacs that Thursday afternoon? How was the situation resolved? Could you have thought so quickly or acted so realistically, and, after everything that took place, could you still have enjoyed the Shabbos as much in the end? Explain.
66. Write an essay explaining how you would have held up under the constant pressures and situations of danger that seemed to confront one at every turn. What statement does Mr. Ostreicher make that explains the secret to one's survival under such circumstances? (Refer to questions 63 to 65.)
67. Until when did Mr. Ostreicher remain in Budapest?
68. How did Mr. Ostreicher's parents respond to his plans to return to Munkacs?
69. What did Mr. Ostreicher's father say when his son had escaped from the truck transporting him to the *Munka Tabor*? Explain the meaning behind this expression.
70. How large was the Munkacs Ghetto? What percent was it of the original size of the community? Could you and your family fit into that percentage of your present living space? Fill in the following table to complete this exercise.

Current Living Space in Square Feet	50% of Current Living Space in Square Feet	25% of Current Living Space in Square Feet	10% of Current Living Space in Square Feet	2% of Current Living Space in Square Feet

71. Describe the scene in Rabbi Meir Wolfe's house as Mr. Ostreicher saw it from underneath the bed. You may do so in words, or in an artist's depiction of the scene using any art medium that you desire.
72. Where did the Ostreichers stay in the Ghetto?
73. What did Mr. Ostreicher do while in the Ghetto? Did it help?
74. Where were the dead originally buried in the Ghetto? Why?
75. Why were the bodies exhumed and transported to the Jewish cemetery? What aspect of Divine Will did Mr. Ostreicher see in this seemingly inexplicable decision of the Hungarians?
76. Where did Mr. Ostreicher remain after his parents were taken to the factory for deportation? Why?

Class Project

77. In some manner, render the number 6,000,000 in individual and distinct terms. Use any manner of expression to accomplish this: written, artistic, miniature model representation, mural, etc.
78. How did Mr. Ostreicher's father, Reb Mencahcem, attempt to lift the spirits of those in the cattle car?
79. Describe the "cycle of anguish" that existed inside the transport cars.
80. What did the Hungarians operating the trains do to trick the Jews on the transports? Did their scheme work? Explain.
81. What psychological mechanism does Mr. Ostreicher employ to deal with the environmental impressions that trigger memories of the War?
82. Explain why our Matriarch Rachel's simple *matzaivah* is so poignantly appropriate.
83. Those who survived the War with their faith in Hashem unblemished belong to a unique and special group. What qualities of soul must have been present to have enabled them to become part of this hallowed fellowship?
84. What did the Polish Jews tell the people as they left the transports? What was Reb Menachem Ostreicher's response to his son's instructions?
85. What ruse did the Germans employ to maintain order after the transports arrived?
86. From Mr. Ostreicher's family, who was sent to the left and who to the right?
87. Where did Mr. Ostreicher think his father was going? Who told him the truth and where and how did this take place? Why was the man so angry and what was Mr. Ostreicher's response?
88. What did Mr. Ostreicher hope to discover after the War?
89. What happened to Yumi and Lali?
90. What was Mr. Ostreicher's number?
91. By the afternoon on *Yom Kippur*, after not having eaten for 16 or 17 hours, how do you feel? How do you think you would feel after not eating for 67 hours?
92. Mr. Ostreicher commented that "The most important thing to the Germans was that they knew where every Jew was...that every Jew was accounted for." What lesson was being taught to us through these German murderers?
93. How do you feel after not having any food for 90 hours? (Refer to question 91.)
94. Explain why food became a "secondary" issue.
95. What two events took place during the *appel* the first day of Shavuos?
96. Explain, in detail, what the statement, "Some people became very, very great during the War" means.
97. The Talmud tells of two brothers who sacrificed themselves to save their community. Find that account in the appropriate tractate and present it to the class.

98. In the form of a diary entry, enter the comments and reflections that Rabbi Rubin might have written explaining his decision during the *appel* on Shavuos.

99. Against what backdrop did Mr. Ostreicher's barracks receive their food for the first time in over four days.

Class Project

100. In any artistic medium, recreate the scene of the men in Mr. Ostreicher's barracks being dispersed while trying to *daven Maariv*. Use colors or model figures that convey the terror and sadness of the scene. A wall mural (drawn or a collage) for display in the hallway with the accompanying text is one idea.

101. What does the expression "*farfluchte Yuden*" mean?

102. How did you spend the second day of the last Shavuos? How did Mr. Ostreicher spend the second day in Auschwitz? Write three good lessons you can derive from this comparison that will help you to deal more positively with difficult or inconvenient or aggravating situations in the future.

103. What was Mr. Ostreicher's introduction to Buchenwald and what acts of kindness did the men in his barracks show him?

104. Locate the town in Germany where Mr. Ostreicher was sent after Buchenwald. In which part of Germany is it located and what other cities are nearby?

105. What job was Mr. Ostreicher assigned to in the new camp? What was the SS man's sadistic idea of fun?

106. What deal did Mr. Ostreicher make with the local farmers and who benefitted from these transactions?

107. What discovery did Mr. Ostreicher make one day about where the leftovers were thrown away? What happened there and what was threatened for later? How did Mr. Ostreicher respond? How would you have responded in such a situation? Record your thoughts in the form of a diary entry as those last few hours tick by.

108. Did a sandwich ever represent a grave and potential danger to you? Explain why or why not from the viewpoint of Mr. Ostreicher's situation in the bookkeeper's office and in light of his statement, "This is how precariously we lived in the camps . . . it's impossible to fathom their corrupt and sadistic minds."

109. How does the situation when the Gestapo officer warned Mr. Ostreicher not to be fooled by Mengele into believing that they would be taking a vacation strike you? Explain your reaction to this strange interaction between the two of them in a short essay that examines the possible causes that motivated the Nazi to act in such a manner.

110. What happened during the train ride after the camp was evacuated in March? Where did Mr. Ostreicher find food?

Student Exercises

111. How much did Mr. Ostreicher weigh during the forced march after the train was destroyed? What were the weather conditions at that time and what happened when they rested at the farm?
112. By the time the march had reached the park, how many of the group still remained alive?
113. On which day of the march did the remaining Jews enter Czechoslovakia? Which Concentration Camp were they taken to?
114. How did some of the Czechs respond to Mr. Ostreicher's group as they entered their town, and how did the German guards respond?
115. Record your response to the "heinous massacre." Imagine that these guards were brought before you for trial, how would you address them as you sentence them to receive their final punishment in this world?
116. How many men began the march and how many were still alive when they reached their destination?
117. What happened to Mr. Ostreicher after reaching the Concentration Camp? What happened to his brother, and many others, after the liberation?
118. What happened to Mr. Ostreicher and his bread supply in the hospital? Why did he react as he did?
119. What job did Mr. Ostreicher take for a while in the Concentration Camp? What was he given when leaving the camp and how did he eventually acquire a suit of clothing?

Class Discussion

120. What do you need to consider yourself fortunate? With what did Mr. Ostreicher feel fortunate that day at the train station? Compare the "relative" states of being fortunate and try to come to a decision as to what is really essential for one to feel truly fortunate in this world.
121. Did you ever think of sweet tea as a really great treat!? Explain.
122. Who surprised Mr. Ostreicher while he was waiting in line for his sweet tea? Where had this person been and how did Mr. Ostreicher react to the whole situation? Finally, where did they stay in Budapest?
123. Mr. Ostreicher comments that their Yom Kippur in Munkacs was "...the first Yom Kippur of our new world", a statement made in its most literal sense. How can we also make each Yom Kippur the first Yom Kippur of our new world? Explain how Mr. Ostreicher's statement and perspective can aid us in making this a reality.
124. How does Mr. Ostreicher describe the Yom Kippur of 1945 in Munkacs?
125. What did the Russians begin on the second day of Succos, and what plan did Mr. Ostreicher and his brother devise to respond to this dilemma?
126. Outline the events that took place once Mr. Ostreicher and Yumi reached Kiraly-Helmec?
127. How was Mrs. Ostreicher saved during the War? What is your response to the manner in which she was saved? What do you learn from this act of salvation?

128. Write a short biography of Rabbi Eliezer Silver. Material regarding this exceptional personality can be found in **The Silver Era** and **A Fire In His Soul**. (Refer to Reading List for more information on these two volumes.)
129. Describe the Shabbos that the Vishnitzer Rebbe spent in Kiraly-Helmec.
130. Why did the Ostreichers leave Czechoslovakia? When?
131. When did the Ostreicher's arrive in America and who did they travel with on the ship?
132. Mr. Ostreicher refers to the trip across the Atlantic as "...our own personal *Kriyas Yam Suf*." Did you ever have a *Kriyas Yam Suf*? Explain.
133. After the War, what was the defining moment of Mr. Ostreicher's life?

Questions for Interview with Mr. Feig—RUSCOVA: LIFE IN THE CARPATHIAN MTS.

1. Students artistically inclined should draw a picture of how they envision Ruscova. Any artistic medium is acceptable. This can be a group project.
2. Mr. Feig used the expression, "We appreciated family..." Family should *always* be appreciated, however, explain why the term "appreciated" is particularly appropriate for this time in history.

Group Exercise

3. In groups of four or five, make up a game with formal rules that can be played with walnut shells. Each group should then teach their game to the class. After you have finished, make a list of the skills involved in such an exercise.

Group Exercise

4. How many buckets full of water are needed to fill a bathtub? How much does an average-sized bucket full of water weigh? Carry a bucket of water up and down a flight of stairs (with permission and only if not harmful to your health). After doing this a few times, write a paragraph detailing any new perspectives you may have regarding indoor plumbing.

Group Exercise

5. In view of the previous exercise and the conditions in which our interviewees lived, do we make too much of the more materialistic and superficial aspects of life? Discuss this question in small groups, debate the pros and cons, and come up with a group *Statement of Perspective* to be read to the class.

Student Exercises

Group Exercise

6. There was only one phone is Ruscova and to make a call required days of planning. Before making a call that you really want to make, stand by the phone, note the time and then wait 30 minutes to place the call. Observe and record your response to this experiment. What three lessons did you learn from this and explain how you can benefit from them. Share the results of this experiment with the class.
7. List 7 to 10 ways that ". . . no running water, no (steam) heat, no inside plumbing and no electricity . . ." would generate appreciable changes in the way you live.
8. Place a few carrots and potatoes in dirt in a cool and dark place in the cellar or basement. Let them remain there for several months and then prepare them for eating (check to see that they did not rot). Fill in the following chart:

Compared by:	Fresh Carrots & Potatoes	Stored Carrots & Potatoes
Smell		
Color		
Taste		
Texture		

9. Bread was home baked in Ruscova. When you are hungry for a piece of bread (or muffin) gather together the necessary ingredients, prepare the dough (or batter) and bake it. Explain why this is a helpful exercise for good character development.
10. When you are hungry, take two slices of bread and then, after eating the first, put the second slice back. Record your response in the following table:

Mental Response/Reaction	Physical Response/Reaction	Emotional Response/Reaction

Mental Response/Reaction	Physical Response/Reaction	Emotional Response/Reaction

11. "In Ruscova we didn't live with the security that we have here in America." What is the intent of this statement and how does it define the history of the Jews in exile?
12. Mr. Feig states that he ". . . would need several days to tell you about the *frumkeit* in Ruscova." Read each part that follows and then answer in one integrated essay.
    a. Do you feel that you could make the same statement about your religious environment and observance? Why or why not?
    b. What additional dimension of meaning is added to this question when considering the aspect of security mentioned in question 11?
    c. Compare and contrast your religious environment with that of Mr. Feig, identifying factors that are alike in the two environments and those that are different. Fill in the following chart to help you visualize these factors, and then include them in your answer.

Factors that are Alike	Factors that Differ

13. Most of the non-Jewish children did not attend the public school. Why?
14. Do you define going to the post office to see if a letter arrived a recreational activity? Why or why not? Explain. Additionally, do you write letters, or just pick up the receiver? What are the advantages to writing a letter over a placing a phone call?
15. What is the definition of royalty? Explain how Mr. Feig uses this word. Know that his usage is laden with meaning. Penetrate the depth of his intent in your answer. Be sure to use richly expressive language to convey your answer.

Student Exercises

16. Would you think of going without a winter coat to help your family? Explain.
17. Americans tend to be consumers. How would you react to being placed on a waiting list for the things you need? Describe how you would respond to such a situation mentally, emotionally and behaviorally.
18. Record your response to Mr. Feig's butter and cheese business.
19. A kilometer equals how many miles? If it is 600 kilometers from Budapest to Ruscova, how many miles does this equal?
20. Describe your feelings and thoughts while taking the Budapest to Ruscova train as Mr. Feig did.
21. Describe the emotions Mr. Feig experienced whenever a package of butter or cheese arrived in Budapest.
22. Should Mr. Feig have listened to the Ruscover Rov and remained in Budapest? Explain the pros and cons of staying and leaving from your perspective and state what you would have done and why. Finally, explain why you agree or disagree with his decision to leave.
23. When did the Germans invade Hungary?
24. How would you have coped on the train ride back to Ruscova feeling that everyone was looking at you, knowing that you were Jewish and trying to hide yourself? Have you ever been in a situation where you felt that people were looking at you for some reason? When and why? Explain.
25. Describe your reaction to the response of Mr. Feig's parents when he arrived home from Budapest. How would you have responded in his place? Were his parents correct? Explain.
26. What three words most describe your response to Mr. Feig's statement, "They were sad for me, themselves, for everyone."
27. How did the German obsession for chronicling the details of destructive actions work for them and against them?

Group Project

28. Create a work of art (in groups and using any art medium – collage, charcoal, watercolor, miniature model, mural) of what *Pesach* was like in Ruscova in 1944. Be careful to reflect the overall atmosphere of the town and the specific mood of the people. You may depict any of the scenes as mentioned in the interview. Use appropriate colors, etc. In this exercise you are painting your words and the colors are the adverbs and adjectives – use them effectively.
29. Describe the conditions in the Felsoviso Ghetto.
30. Prepare a report on life in any of the major ghettos during WWII. The Warsaw Ghetto and the Lodz Ghetto are only two of many such ghettos. (Refer to Reading List in this volume for appropriate sources).
31. Create an artistic rendition of what life was like in a ghetto from a child's perspective.
32. Write a diary entry describing your day in one of the ghettos as you perceive what life must have been like in such a place.

Class Discussion

33. "We could hear the Russian guns from the ghetto." If you had been in the ghetto, how would you feel knowing that liberation was close at hand, only to realize that it was not to be? Why was it that when the battlefront was collapsing on all sides – the Russians from the east and the Allies from the west and south – the Germans and Hungarians concentrated so much of their war effort on the destruction of the Jews?

Research Question

34. Document the attitude of the Czarist governments and, in turn, the Communist government towards the Jews.

35. Draw or build a model of one of the cattle cars used to take the Jews to the Concentration Camps. An extremely accurate and detailed description of this horrible experience can be found in the book **Beyond the Tracks** by Ruth Mermelstein, published by the Orthodox Union and distributed by Mesorah Publications, 1999 pages 61-71.

36. Why didn't Mr. Feig try to escape to the forest when his transport to Auschwitz stopped for a brief period of time?

37. What deception did the Hungarians employ to perpetuate the idea that the transports were not dangerous? Did it work?

38. What is a *Kapo*?

39. You have probably seen a picture of the infamous unloading platform by the train station in Auschwitz. List 10 words expressing your emotions and thoughts when looking at that platform.

Individual or Group Exercise

40. Create a dramatic rendition of the scene at the unloading platform in Auschwitz when the transports arrived. Use any medium as stated in previous exercises.

41. In detail, describe your reaction to the story of the young woman and her baby upon her arrival at Auschwitz.

42. "I want you to understand from this incident that tragedies were happening around us every minute." Reread this part of the interview several times. Then reflect on this quote for several minutes. The next time some frustration, irritation or inconvenience occurs, see if recalling this quote helps you to resolve the situation more easily and with a clearer perspective regarding one's priorities in life.

43. Write a poem expressing the anguish that separation caused to so many Jewish families as they reached that spot in front of the evil German officer in his Gestapo boots and skull and cross-bones insignia, when he pointed his riding crop left and right, sending Jews to death or starvation and torture.

44. What can you learn from the goodbye Mr. Feig never said to his mother and father? Explain.

Student Exercises

45. The following exercises are important for gaining a greater appreciation for the deprivation suffered in the concentration and labor camps (With parental permission only):
    a. Sleep on the floor, preferably without a carpet, and without a pillow. Do not use the blanket as a pillow. Try not to be too warm.
    b. Sleep with as many siblings as possible cramped into one bed (make sure the bed frame can hold the combined weight). Do this for a few nights – only one blanket for everyone and no pillows.
    c. Imagine yourself standing outside in the winter, clad only in pajamas. Think about this as you walk down the street, shivering, on a cold winter's day bundled up in your coat, scarf and gloves!

46. Describe your reaction to the impact of the drama expressed in the picture of the prisoner pointing at one of the two defeated German guards. Describe the emotions expressed by each face and create the probable dialogue that transpired during that encounter.

47. Mr. Feig writes that he stood in the *appelplatz* for many hours each day. Describe how you feel after standing in line for only one-half hour:
    a. In a pleasant environment?
    b. In the heat of summer?
    c. In the cold of winter?

    What do you learn from each of these situations individually, and from the exercise as a whole, that you can apply to daily life to improve your outlook, attitude and behavior?

48. How many calories will a person receive from 1/24th of an average sized loaf of bread? How thick will this piece be? With a parent's permission, eat only one such slice at each meal for a week, even though the rest of the meal is as usual.

49. "You have to understand that something like this never happened before." Explain why his quote is such an understatement of the fact.

50. Record your reaction to the juxtaposition of the two pictures on page 177 (women liberated and men at *appel*) After writing your response complete the following table with words that describe each picture:

"THE JOY OF LIBERATION"	"PRISONERS AT ROLL CALL"

51. How did the Germans use Jewish holidays as weapons of psychological and emotional warfare? Use this interview and research other sources from the Reading List to document your response.
52. How did the Rov "fight" back? Why was this response a decisive weapon (see question 51) and what eternal lesson is there in his response? Craft your answer in a well delineated essay.
53. What sensation did you experience as you read about the *Hallel* recited in the *appelplatz*?
54. In order to transcend their lives in *the world that was* and their experiences during the Holocaust to live their present "normal" lives, what do you think a survivor must do to live in a new environment and build a new life? In small groups, research the answer using sources from the Reading List. Additionally, speak with several survivors and pose this question to them. Perhaps one or two would come to the class to speak and be interviewed. As they are getting older, the survivors are speaking out more and more in public forums. Be sure to prepare your questions beforehand so that you will be well prepared when the interview begins, but don't be afraid to ask earnest questions spontaneously during the interview.
55. Did you ever consider half a slice of bread as a personal *geulah*? What things do you consider your personal *geulah*? What lesson do you learn regarding this concept from this particular perspective?
56. Did you ever think of kitchen chores as "winning the lottery"? Next time you are asked to do some kitchen chore, consider it from Mr. Feig's perspective when he was in the labor camp. What other everyday situations can you reconsider in this manner? List them below:

Student Exercises

EVERYDAY CHORES for RECONSIDERATION (including present attitude)	NEW PERSPECTIVE & ATTITUDE

57. The Allies lack of response to the overt slaughter of the Jews of Europe is very disturbing and something that is not openly discussed even today. Present a short synopsis of this situation to the class, including any meetings with government officials and conferences that were held during the war years to awaken Allied sympathy to this situation. The books: **A Fire In His Soul, The Unheeded Cry** and **Thy Brother's Blood** listed in the Bibliography are excellent source material for this question.
58. In the form of a diary entry, write what you think Mr. Feig would have written on the day his brother was killed by the bomb blast.
59. "I always felt that I would survive Hitler. No matter where I was I had this intuitive sense that I would survive and be freed." How does this quote appertain to Mr. Feig's previous statement, "Just as it was decreed who should perish, so was it decreed who should survive..."? Explain the connection between the two quotes.
60. Explain what, "Many had become so hardened from their war experiences. . ." and "Our very humanity had been stripped away from us" mean in terms of the actual transformation of the human personality.
61. Many survivors express feeling guilty that they lived through the tortures of the war while many, if not all, in their families perished. The expression, "Sometimes I feel guilty and wonder why I am here", is an expression from the soul of many survivors. In the form of a letter to "a survivor", answer this question to the best of your ability. You can write to a woman or a man, but know that the content will vary for each. You may prepare this letter in small groups, discussing the various issues involved before writing. Present your letter to the class.
62. Write a eulogy for the *bochur* who was murdered by the German guard for going to get water to wash his hands.
63. On what day was Theresienstadt liberated?
64. Why were so many camp inmates killed by the food that was given to them by the Allies after liberation? What went wrong and what should have been done?
65. What is a quarantine and what purpose does it serve?

66. Mr. Feig suddenly found out that his sisters were alive. Many others discovered that relatives survived in an equally shocking way. Try to find out about some of these reunions from the source material listed in the Reading List and by asking survivors or their families when possible. Write an essay describing these events.
67. What did Mr. Feig do after finding out where his sisters were located? Trace his route on a copy of one of the maps in the Student Study Guide.
68. Explain how you would feel finding the hair from the *upshearin* as Mr. Feig did.
69. Trace Mr. Feig's movements from the time he left Ruscova in 1948.

Questions for Interview with Mrs. Weisshaus—SIGHET: REMEMBRANCE OF LIFE IN HUNGARY

1. What does it mean that Sighet was part of Romania "at that time"?
2. What does Sighet mean in Hungarian and why is the name significant?
3. How many Jews lived in Sighet before WWII?
4. How many children from Sighet are estimated to have perished during the War?

Class Project

5. In question 4 you were asked to give the number of children who were killed at the hands of the Germans and their gentile collaborators. If you read through the interview you should have found the number and answered the question correctly. Fine! Exercise complete. No, not quite yet! A number can be very cold and unfeeling, not always communicating the truth it represents. This is particularly true of larger numbers. In order to correct this, divide the number of students in the class into the number of children who perished. Then, on a scroll to be displayed in the room, or as a memorial to be hung in the classroom or in the hallway, each student should write that many names* to represent the children who were killed. In this way, you will always remember that there was a living child, like yourself, behind each number.

   *(The actual names used and how often an individual name is repeated is not important, just knowing that there was a living Jewish child like you, your brothers, sisters and your classmates who were among those murdered is memorial enough.)
6. List Mrs. Weisshaus' siblings and their ages before the War began.

Student Exercises

7. How are the reflections and attitudes similar and different for Mr. Ostreicher, Mr. Feig and Mrs. Weisshaus when they were separated from their parents on the unloading platform in Auschwitz? What does this tell you about each of our interviewees?
8. Make a chart of Mrs. Weisshaus' genealogy as mentioned in the interview.
9. Why did the Satmar Rov come to Sighet?
10. Describe the humorous incident that occurred on one of the Satmar Rebbe's visits to Sighet.
11. Following the snow incident and the "peanut" incident (and because of other incidents found throughout the section, "The Spiritual Environment") Mrs. Weisshaus says, "I truly had a happy childhood...nothing was missing." What defines her perspective and definition of "happy"? What is your definition of "happy"? Where do you and Mrs. Weisshaus agree or disagree and how do each of your perspectives and definitions define your environment and *Yiddishkeit*? Explain yourself in a well thought-out essay. You may want to discuss the question in small working groups before beginning to write.
12. Describe the steps involved in making hand baked *matzos*.
13. From Mrs. Weisshaus' perspective, in the form of a diary entry, record your thoughts after hearing about your cousin Shlomo and his wife's death – especially given the particular circumstances.
14. Why is Mrs. Weisshaus involved in the Swiss Bank scandal?
15. Write a brief report concerning the revelation of the Swiss Bank - Nazi conspiracy in confiscating Jewish money during WWII, and subsequently denying that it was deposited in the banks. How was the scandal revealed and what ensued after the information became known to the public?
16. Do you agree (or disagree) with Mrs. Weisshaus' father's plan to retrieve his dowry money from the bank? Explain.
17. Describe your impression of Mrs. Weisshaus' family life in Sighet.
18. What is "*teg essen*"?
19. Where did Mrs. Weisshaus attend school, and what took place during the last two years?
20. How old was Mrs. Weisshaus when WWII broke out?
21. Explain why the "spiritual environment between the two world wars was very volatile." Refer to the interview with Rabbi Landau in **The World That Was: Poland** for a precise analysis of this situation. Additionally, refer to the source material listed in the Reading List.
22. What does "allegedly" mean?
23. Record your impression of Mrs. Weisshaus' remembrance of her aunt, cousins and what life was like then. It is a very accurate and microcosmic viewpoint of life in Transylvania and the Carpathian Mountains.

Student Exercises

24. List five things you can do to make Elul, Rosh Hashanah and Yom Kippur holier "and not commercial like today." You are referred to Mr. Ostreicher's interview as well as the interviews in **The World That Was: Lithuania** for many interesting remembrances of these holy days in the towns and villages of Lita.

25. What is your reaction to the laundry situation as described in the interview? Could you adjust to such a condition? Why or why not? Explain in detail.

Class Exercise

26. Collect an assortment of rags. Wash half according to the procedure delineated in the interview and the other half in a washing machine. Under proper supervision, secure wood ashes and bleach the hand washed rags as per the directions in the interview. After using bleach in the machine wash, compare the two washes. Fill in the following table with the results of this experiment:

WASH VARIABLES	HAND WASHING	MACHINE WASHING
Basic cleaning		
Whiteness		
Smell		
Time to complete		
Number of steps involved		

27. In passing, Mrs. Weisshaus observes that "Life was hard. Many families were large, with little to eat, no heat in the winter, living in very cramped quarters. You can't compare how we live today and how a poor Jew lived then. However, there was a very deep spiritual life among the Orthodox." Additionally, in **The World That Was: Lithuania**, the Telzer Rosh HaYeshiva, Rabbi Yosef Leib Bloch, *zt"l*, taught, " . . .that an increase in materialism inhibits intellectual growth, eventually diminishing one's greatness in Torah and faith." Two statements made by two significantly different personalities from two vastly different environments and, yet, there is a singularly unifying perspective that resonates in each statement. What is that perspective and why can two individuals who are so different perceive and express the same underlying principle of truth? In a formal essay, answer this question in great detail providing supporting material from other sources.

28. How old was Mrs. Weisshaus when Hitler, *yemach sh'mo*, came to power? In what year did this take place?

29. In the section **Leading Up To The War**, Mrs. Weisshaus discusses the relationship between the Jews and their gentile neighbors. This discussion is the content of the first two paragraphs of that section. Record your response to her comments, how it would have affected you, and whether you think something like this could happen in America or only in Europe. Certainly give reasons supporting your opinion and discuss the question in class before committing your thoughts to writing. In particular, respond to the comments at the end of the second paragraph beginning with the sentence, "There were some who did..." (Source material is available, refer to the Reading List.)
30. Until when were the Jews of Hungary (more or less) free from German entrapment? What deprivation did they suffer before that?
31. What is the *Munka Tabor* and what is your response to Mrs. Weisshaus' story about the *Munka Tabor*? What did she receive for her part in the story?
32. How did Mrs. Weisshaus know about what was taking place during the War? What was her response to the news? Do you agree or disagree with her? Explain.
33. When was the German presence finally felt in Transylvania?
34. What is *legitimatzia*?
35. What was life like in Sighet during the winter of 1943-44, what incident took place *erev Pesach* and how did the Jews spend *Pesach* that year? (Refer to Mr. Feig's interview as well.)
36. What are the two reasons they covered the potatoes with blankets? Which is the most important?
37. What took place throughout Transylvania after *Pesach*, 1944?
38. How did Mrs. Weisshaus see her father for the last time and what took place during that meeting?
39. On which transport was Mrs. Weisshaus and her family?
40. How long was Mrs. Weisshaus in Auschwitz? Where did she go next and what did she do there?
41. Each of our interviewees reacts to Auschwitz differently: in tone, emotion and detail. Do you see any significance in this? Explain.
42. How were the Jewish women escorted back and forth to work? What is Mrs. Weisshaus' reaction to this, and how does her comment castigate the Germans for the shameful nation they are.
43. What kindness was performed for the women killed by the bombings? Why is such a memorial important? Explain.
44. Why were the women treated better in Somerda and what kind of slave labor were they forced to do there?
45. Who did Mrs. Weisshaus befriend on the forced march into the interior of Germany? Where was she from and what special talent did she have?

Student Exercises

46. From where was Mrs. Weisshaus liberated by the Russians, and where did she go afterwards?
47. What happened to Mrs. Weisshaus at the train station on the way back to Sighet?
48. Who did Mrs. Weisshaus find when she arrived in Sighet? How did she earn some money?
49. Why didn't Mrs. Weisshaus remain with the family of her father's cousin so that she wouldn't be alone?
50. What did Mrs. Weisshaus have to do to find the money in the attic?
51. Why did Mrs. Weisshaus leave Sighet and where did she go?
52. How did Mrs. Weisshaus meet her husband?
53. Where did Mr. Weisshaus live before the War?
54. Record your immediate response to Mrs. Weisshaus' statement, "Seriously, we were very happy, and it was nice to be happy again – to begin life over in that sense. I was a young bride and I wanted to be happy."
55. What condition did Mrs. Weisshaus set before the *chasunah*? How was this situation resolved?
56. How much did it cost to live for a month at that time? How many years (approximately) could Mrs. Weisshaus live with the money she had in her possession?
57. Why did the woman in Satmar believe she and her family survived the War?
58. Was it only because she was able to share the wedding dress that Mrs. Weisshaus was happy? What is the deeper reason for her happiness?
59. Where did Mrs. Weisshaus go to have a *streimel* made and how did she get there?
60. Write a three page report explaining how *Klal Yisrael* was revived after the devastation of the Holocaust. In addition to using Mrs. Weisshaus' moving explanation as the central theme for your report, use sources from the Reading List for additional information.
61. Write a biography of one of the following *chassidic* leaders:
    the Bluzohver Rebbe
    the Klausenberger Rebbe
    the Pupa Rebbe
    the Satmar Rebbe
    the Vishnitzer Rebbe
62. Where did Mrs. Weisshaus live after her *chasunah*?
63. What happened in 1947 and what were the consequences of that incident? What lesson did Mrs. Weisshaus learn from this?
64. Trace Mrs. Weisshaus' route from 1947 until she arrives in America.
65. When did the Weisshauses arrive in America?
66. What was Mrs. Weisshaus' initial expectation of the immigrants when they first arrived in this country?

Student Exercises

RECOMMENDED READING AND SOURCE MATERIAL

There are many resources not listed here that are available on various aspects of the Holocaust (children, concentration and labor camps, diaries, biographies, historical essays, politics, etc.), including audio-video and interactive classroom materials. **It is strongly recommended that these materials be reviewed by an appropriate school official before being introduced within the classroom**. Many of these resources contain shocking and frightening contents, including pictures of naked and mutilated bodies, that should not be viewed by children. Additionally, many are published by various groups bearing their own perspective of the Holocaust, often in contradiction with a Torah point of view. It is strongly suggested that even the material listed in this Reading List be reviewed for specific age appropriateness before being introduced in the classroom.

CIS PUBLICATIONS

180 Park Ave., Lakewood, New Jersey 08702 — 1-908-905-3000

Holocaust Diaries Collection

Banet, Chana Marcus, **They Called Me Frau Anna**, CIS, Lakewood, 1990

Eilenberg, Anna, **Sisters In The Storm**, CIS, Lakewood, 1992

Friedman, Chaim Shlomo, **Dare To Survive**, CIS, Lakewood, 1992

Gabel, Dina, **Behind The Ice Curtain**, CIS, Lakewood, 1992

Holczler, Moshe, **Late Shadows**, CIS, Lakewood, 1989

Kacenberg, Mala, **Alone in the Forest**, CIS, Lakewood, 1995

Krakowski, Avraham, **Counterfeit Lives**, CIS, Lakewood, 1994

Pomerantz, Yitzchak, **Itzik, Be Strong!**, CIS, Lakewood, 1993

Sanik, Leibel, **Someday We'll Be Free**, CIS, Lakewood, 1194

Werdyger, Duvid, **Songs of Hope**, CIS, Lakewood, 1993

Other Related Publications from CIS

Alfasi, Yitzchak, **Glimpses Of Jewish Warsaw**, CIS, Lakewood, 1992

Alfasi, Yitzchak, **Glimpses Of Jewish Frankfurt**, CIS, Lakewood, 1993

Beilis, Mendel, **Scapegoat On Trial**, CIS, Lakewood, 1992

Chazan, Aaron, **Deep In The Russian Night**, CIS, Lakewood, 1990

Eibeshitz, Y. and A., **Women In The Holocaust**, Volumes 1 & 2, CIS, Lakewood, 1994

Gevirtz, E. and Kranzler, D., **To Save A World**, Volumes 1 & 2, CIS, Lakewood, 1991

Pomerantz, Rachel, **Wings Above The Flames**, CIS, Lakewood, 1992

Pomerantz, Rachel, **The World In Flames**, CIS, Lakewood, 1993

Winston, Rabbi Pinchas, **The Eternal Link**, CIS, Lakewood, 1990

Winston, Rabbi Pinchas, **The Unbroken Chain of Jewish Tradition**, CIS, Lakewood, 1986

FELDHEIM PUBLISHERS

200 Airport Executive Park, Suite 202, Nanuet, New York 10954 — 1-914-356-2282

Allswang, Dr. Benzion, **The Final Resolution**, Feldheim, New York, 1989

Araten, Rochel Sarna, **Michalina: Daughter Of Israel**, Feldheim, New York, 1986

Baumol, Rav Yehoshua, **A Blaze in the Darkening Gloom**, Feldheim, New York, 1994

Benisch, Pearl, **To Vanquish The Dragon**, Feldheim, New York, 1991

Bunim, Amos, **A Fire In His Soul**, Feldheim, New York, 1989

Firer, Benzion, **The Twins**, Feldheim, New York, 1981

Fox, David, **Greatness In Our Midst**, Feldheim, New York, 1955

Glicksman, Devorah, **A Sun And A Shield**, Feldheim, New York, 1996

Granatstein, Yechiel, **One Jew's Power-One Jew's Glory**, Feldheim, New York, 1991

Grossman, Rav Reuven, **The Legacy Of Slabodka**, Feldheim, New York, 1989

Grossman, Rav Reuven, **The Rosh Yeshiva**, Feldheim, New York, 1988

Kahn, Betzalel, **Citadel Of Splendor**, Feldheim, New York, 1995

Klein, R.L., **The Scent Of Snowflowers**, Feldheim, New York, 1989

Lamet, Rosalie, **City Of Diamonds**, Feldheim, New York, 1996

Leitner, Yecheskel, **Operation: Torah Rescue**: Feldheim, New York, 1987

Rakeffet-Rothkoff, Aaron, **The Silver Era**, Feldheim, New York, 1988

Schleimer, Sarah M., **Far From The Place We Called Home**, Feldheim, New York, 1994

Schiff, Rabbi Elyakim and G., **The Five Gates**, Feldheim, New York, 1994

Shain, Ruchoma, **All For The Boss**, Feldheim, New York, 1984

Shapiro, Chaim, **Go, My Son**, Feldheim, New York, 1989

Sinason, Jacob H., **Saba Marches On**, Feldheim, New York, 1993

Sonnenfeld, S.Z., **Voices In The Silence**, Feldheim, New York, 1992

Student Exercises

Unsdorfer, Simcha Bunim, **The Yellow Star**, Feldheim, New York, 1983

Zaitchik, Rabbi Chaim Ephriam, **Sparks Of Mussar**, Feldheim, New York, 1985

MESORAH PUBLICATIONS

4401 Second Avenue, Brooklyn, New York 11232 — 1-718-921-9000

Birnbaum, Meyer, **Lieutenant Birnbaum**, Mesorah Pub., Brooklyn, 1993

Bromberg, Rabbi Y.A., **The Sanzer Rav And His Dynasty**, Mesorah Pub., Brooklyn, 1986

Dansky, Miriam, **Rebbetzin Grunfeld**, Mesorah Pub., Brooklyn, 1994

Finkelman, Shimon, **Reb Chaim Ozer-The Life and Ideal of Rabbi Chaim Ozer Grodzenski of Vilna**, Mesorah Pub., Brooklyn, 1987

Finkelman, Shimon, **The Chazon Ish**, Mesorah Pub., Brooklyn, 1989

Finkelman, Shimon, **Reb Moshe**, Mesorah Pub., Brooklyn, 1986

Friedenson, Joseph, **Dateline: Istanbul**, Mesorah Pub., Brooklyn, 1993

Friedenson, J. and Kranzler, D., **Heroine Of Rescue**, Mesorah Pub., Brooklyn, 1984

Friedman, Peska, **Going Forward**, Mesorah Pub., Brooklyn, 1994

Fuchs, Abraham, **The Unheeded Cry**, Mesorah Pub., Brooklyn, 1984

Gottlieb, N.Z., **In The Shadow Of The Kremlin**, Mesorah Pub., Brooklyn, 1985

Granatstein, Yechiel, **The War Of A Jewish Partisan**, Mesorah Pub., Brooklyn, 1986

Kranzler, David, **Thy Brother's Blood**, Mesorah Pub., Brooklyn, 1987

Mermelstein, Ruth, **Beyond the Tracks**, Mesorah Publications, Brooklyn, 1999.

Pekier, Alter, **From Kletzk to Siberia**, Mesorah Pub., Brooklyn, 1985

Prager, Moshe, **Sparks Of Glory**, Mesorah Pub., Brooklyn, 1985

Rosenblum, Yonason, **The Vilna Gaon**, Mesorah Pub., Brooklyn, 1994

Rosenblum, Yonasan, **They Called Him Mike**, Mesorah Pub., Brooklyn, 1995

Rosenblum, Yonason, **Reb Yaakov**, Mesorah Pub., Brooklyn, 1993

Rubin, Chana Stavsky, **Tomorrow May Be Too Late**, Mesorah Pub, Brooklyn, 1995

Schwartz, Rabbi Y. and Goldstein, Y., **Shoah**, Mesorah Pub., Brooklyn, 1990

Sorasky, Aaron, **Reb Elchonon**, Mesorah Pub., Brooklyn, 1982

Wahrman, Rabbi Shlomo, **Lest We Forget**, Mesorah Pub., Brooklyn, 1991

Wein, Rabbi Berel, **Triumph Of Survival**, Mesorah Pub., Brooklyn, 1990

Wolpin, Rabbi Nisson, **A Path Through The Ashes**, Mesorah Pub., Brooklyn, 1986

Wolpin, Rabbi Nisson, **The Torah Profile**, Mesorah Pub., Brooklyn, 1988

Wolpin, Rabbi Nisson, **The Torah Personality**, Mesorah Pub., Brooklyn, 1980

Wolpin, Rabbi Nisson, **The Torah World**, Mesorah Pub., Brooklyn, 1988

Wolpin, Rabbi Nisson, **Torah Luminaries**, Mesorah Pub., Brooklyn, 1994

Wolpin, Nisson, **Torah Lives**, Mesorah Pub., Brooklyn,

Worch, Renee, **Flight**, Mesorah Pub., Brooklyn, 1988

Worch, Renee, **Survival**, Mesorah Pub., Brooklyn, 1992

Yoshor, Rabbi Moses M., **The Chaftez Chaim, Vol. 1 & 2**, Mesorah Pub., Brooklyn, 1985

Zakon, Miriam Stark, **Silent Revolution**, Mesorah Pub., Brooklyn, 1988

AGUDATH ISRAEL OF AMERICA

84 William Street, New York, New York 10038 — 1-718-921-9000

Ashes to Renewal, 1997

CHINUCH PUBLICATIONS

Lakewood, New Jersey

Surasky, Aharon, **Giants of Jewry**, Chinuch Pub., Lakewood, 1982

THOMAS Y. CROWELL CO.

New York, New York

Levin, Nora, **The Holocaust**, 1986

RABBI ELCHONON HERTZMAN

61 Harrison Ave, Apt. 5-D, Brooklyn, New York 11211

Hertzman, Rabbi Elchonon, **The Mashgiach**, Jerusalem, 1981

HOLT, RINEHART AND WINSTON

383 Madison Ave., New York, New York 10017

Dawidowicz, Lucy S., **The War Against The Jews: 1933-1945**, 1975

JUDAICA PRESS

123 Ditmas Ave., Brooklyn, New York 11218 — 1-718-972-6200

Oshry, Rabbi Ephraim, **Responsa From The Holocaust**, Judaica ,Brooklyn, 1983

Oshry, Rabbi Ephraim, **The Annihilation of Lithuanian Jewry**, Judaica, Brooklyn, 1996

KETER PUBLISHING HOUSE

Jerusalem, Israel

Encyclopedia Judaica, 1978

Student Exercises

MACMILLIAN PUBLISHERS

1633 Broadway, New York, New York — 212-654-8500

Encyclopedia of the Holocaust, 1990

McGRAW-HILL PUBLISHING COMPANY

1221 Avenue of the Americas, New York, New York — 212-512-2000

Hoyt, Edwin P., **Hitler's War**, 1988

WILLIAM MORROW AND COMPANY

New York, New York 10019 — 1-800-843-9389

Gilbert, Martin, **The Atlas of the Holocaust**, William Morrow, New York, NY, 1988

VINTAGE BOOKS

New York, New York — 1-800-733-3000

Eliach, Yaffa, **Hasidic Tales of the Holocaust**, Vintage Books, New York, 1988

INTERACTIVE CLASSROOM MATERIALS

JACKDAW PUBLICATIONS — A Division of Golden Owl Publishing

P.O. Box 503, Amawalk, New York 10501 — 1-800-789-0022 or 1-914-962-6911

The Holocaust (an interactive classroom materials kit)